Contributions to Economics

For further volumes:
http://www.springer.com/series/1262

Lars Weber

Demographic Change and Economic Growth

Simulations on Growth Models

Physica-Verlag

Dr. Lars Weber
FOM Hochschule für Oekonomie
& Management gGmbH
Hochschulstudienzentrum Leipzig
Käthe-Kollwitz-Straße 60
04109 Leipzig
Germany
lars.weber@fom.de

Dissertation, Brandenburgische Technische Universität Cottbus, 2009, submitted under the title "Aging and Shrinking Societies and the Consequences for Economic Growth – Simulations on a Semi-Endogenous Growth Model with System Dynamics"

ISSN 1431-1933
ISBN 978-3-7908-2589-3 e-ISBN 978-3-7908-2590-9
DOI 10.1007/978-3-7908-2590-9
Springer Heidelberg Dordrecht London New York

Library of Congress Control Number: 2010925229

Cover design: WMXDesign GmbH, Heidelberg

Printed on acid-free paper

Physica-Verlag is a brand of Springer-Verlag Berlin Heidelberg
Springer-Verlag is a part of Springer Science+Business Media (www.springer.com)

To Doreen, who made it happen
and to Nele Aurelia, the joy of my life.

Foreword

The general conditions for long-term economic development in Germany have recognizably changed. The population is aging and shrinking. This means that essential areas of economic systems, such as productivity and growth, and especially for German social security systems, need to become accustom to the basic changes in the structured data. The country could be moving into troubled times. If the productivity increase falls short, then increasing limits will be placed on the latitude of real wages. And the financial basis for social security systems will begin to waver, especially for the pay-as-you-go system.

Lars Weber's work directly examines this field of tension. The author shows a conclusive and rich analysis, which measures the obtained results in respect to the attenuation of negative demographic change effects.

The work presented by Lars Weber is marked by three features.

First, the work is of eminent importance for practical economic policies. Hereafter, all short-term stabilization efforts for economic policies should ask a central question, which measures the potential long-term growth damages and can be moderated as a result of demographic rejections.

Second, the author uses clean, demanding and appropriate theoretical argumentation as the basis for his work. Constructing an analysis from the demographic determinants and its economical effects, along with the replication of economic growth theories, Lars Weber develops a self-constructed large-scale demographic growth model, which is absolutely new in this form.

And third, the author selected system dynamics as his methodological analysis instrument, which due to its highly intellectual claims can often prove difficult. However when it is used properly, one can more accurately represent challenging, interdependent and complex problems, and thus can present mutual dependences of pertinent economic sizes quite excellently.

On the basis of his developed demographic growth model, the author discusses three possible scenarios. The result is that Scenario 1 (family orientation) is more fitted to a long-term strategy, which can be supported temporarily by reinforced education efforts (Scenario 2). For the short-term only a reinforced immigration (Scenario 3) helps.

I have followed this work with curious attention and critical sympathy as it pursued and I am happy that this research project was completed successfully by the author in the Chair for Macroeconomics on the Brandenburg University of Technology in Cottbus. Thanks are also due to the federal state of Brandenburg and the university, both of which, despite financial difficulties, were able to attain funds to secure a successful project within the Chair.

I wish this book, from which a willing politician or also a theoretically interested economist can profit, a warm reception.

Professor Dr. Wolfgang Cezanne
Berlin, December 2009

Acknowledgments

The goal of this book is to enlighten the reader about the connections between the much-discussed demographic change and growth theories from a theoretical point of view, and to present a broad and comprehensive perspective on the different aspects. In addition, the gap between theoretical work and practical situations is bridged through numerous tested simulations and scenarios. The work was accepted in September 2009 as a doctoral thesis in the Faculty of Mechanical, Electrical, and Industrial Engineering at the Brandenburg University of Technology, Cottbus. The entire work was written from the perspective of a system dynamics specialist. One can say that the last 6 years have been dedicated to a re-study of economics. Through this, I have won new outlooks for the application of System Dynamics, found explanations for old questions and embarked upon a completely new understanding of the economic world. Many a time, I had the feeling that previously a veil had covered my economic eyeglasses, which was lifted through the new ideas of System Thinking and System Dynamics – a clear view was suddenly possible.

Although every doctorial candidate writes independently, primarily in the lonely and late hours of the night, such a large work would not be possible without the support of professional and personal comrades.

My doctorial advisor Professor Dr. Wolfgang Cezanne was my mentor, model, and exchange partner. The freedom he granted me to dive deeper and deeper into the field of economics and System Dynamics made this work possible. Without his endorsement, my repeated research at the University of Bergen, Norway, and at the Worcester Polytechnic Institute, USA, would not have been possible. I also thank Professor Dr. Klaus Serfling for his work as a secondary evaluator and Professor Dr. Christiane Hipp for her activity as the committee's chairwoman. Both contributed crucially to the fast and smooth completion of the review process.

My research brought me into contact with many interesting people, who shared with me the interest in System Dynamics. I feel honored to have met founder Professor Jay Forrester personally and hope that this work serves as a building block for a new and improved economic perspective. I also need to emphasize the fruitful co-operation with Professor Michael Radzicki and Professor David Wheat. Both were influential role models.

I also thank the entire Chair of Macroeconomics on the BTU Cottbus, which, over the last 6 years, has become my scientific home. I look back happily on the extremely helpful co-operation and pleasant work environment. Margret Pötzsch, as the good soul of the Chair, particularly assisted me in the last phase of this work, especially relieving me of all the small administrative tasks the Chair requires. My dear colleague Claudia Lubk was always open to a scientific exchange and became a good friend. Dr. Isabelle Jänchen provided answers to many small questions about economics. I am very much looking forward to future collaborations. I thank Steffen Jenkel, who supported both the literature search and the production of diagrams for this work.

For the correction of linguistic errors, I thank Kate Pierce-McManamon very cordially. Her fast and supportive completion of this book was crucial to its accelerated execution.

A long friendship connects me to Matthias Kaiser. I first met him as an open and interested student in my courses and later he became an appreciated colleague of the department. Today I am honored to call him a valuable friend. I will always be grateful to him for his technical and personal support.

To my beloved girlfriend Dr. Doreen Schwarz I owe a great deal of thanks – without her, this work would simply have never been finished. Her untiring moral support, love, and faith in us moved this book forward. Especially during the most difficult phases of this work, she provided an outlet for other problems and unwavering strength. It is comforting to know that there is a person at my side who has so much in common and accompanies me through so many ups and downs. In this year of completion, our daughter Nele Aurelia healthily entered the world, making our lives complete.

Surely it is not always easy for one's family to accept the importance of a scientific exile and for their patience during this time I thank them from the heart, especially my mother Heidrun Weber and my brother Sven Weber. Unfortunately, it was not possible for my father Hans-Joachim Weber and my grandfather Professor Dr. Dr. h. c. Manfred Bachmann to see the completion of this educational step. Their contribution to this work, however, is larger than they would have anticipated. This book is also dedicated to them.

I hope that the reader will encounter exciting views of new aspects in demography and economics, which will inspire them to explore further considerations. I appreciate feedback at any time (info@simthemis.com).

Lars Weber
Cottbus, December 2009

Contents

List of Figures

Chapter 1
Introduction

The greatest constant of modern times is change. Accelerating changes in technology, population, and economic activity are transforming our world, from the prosaic – the effect of information technology on the way we use the telephone – to the profound – the effect of greenhouse gases on the global climate. [...] All challenge traditional institutions, practices, and beliefs."
(Sterman, 1994, p. 291)

1.1 Problem Statement

Phrases such as "demographic change", "fertility decline" and "aging society" are commonplace terminology in most industrialized countries. Western Europe, especially, is facing a mounting challenge: How to solve unknown problems of an aging and shrinking society? In fact, Japan is facing this problem as well and much earlier than Western Europe, but the time-lag is not long enough to observe the tide of events in Japan and to adopt Japan's best practices.

Demographers have addressed this problem continually; and since the late 1970s the literature on this issue has grown exponentially. However, as psychologists argue – humans are 'present orientated' and refuse long-term thinking – challenges are neglected as long as there are no signs of change. John M. Keynes addressed this very accurately (Keynes, 1936, p. 14):

> An era of increasing population tends to promote optimism, since demand will in general tend to exceed. [...] But in an era of declining population the opposite is true. [...] Thus a pessimistic atmosphere may issue; and although at long last pessimism may tend to correct itself through its effect on supply the first result to prosperity of a change-over from an increasing to a declining population may be very disastrous.

One can easily understand that knowing is not enough when policy-makers refuse to act with foresight. Since the turn of the millennium more and more industrialized countries, especially in Western Europe, started to feel the first

L. Weber, *Demographic Change and Economic Growth*, Contributions to Economics,
DOI 10.1007/978-3-7908-2590-9_1, © Springer-Verlag Berlin Heidelberg 2010

offshoots of demographic change. Increasing attention to this topic brought about a change in the scientific literature. Today, numerous books and papers shed light on economic issues of the demographic change. Most of these books are either very descriptive – naming simply facts and figures (Birg, 2000; Hamm, Seitz, & Werding, 2008; Schumpeter, 1996c; Kaufmann, 2005) – or are extremely theoretical (Auerbach & Herrmann, 2002; Leim, 2008).

Additionally, it is remarkable that published economic growth theories, which attempt to understand long-term economic development, do not focus explicitly on population structure and change. Instead, very often it is simply assumed that the population grows exponentially. While this might be true for the world as a whole, it only works in most countries if the country in question exhibits positive population growth rates. A small amount of literature highlights the combined growth theory and population development (Gruescu, 2006; Howitt, 1999; Kremer, 1993). Examples of this will be presented in Chap. 3. However, there is a research gap between very precise demographic models from population scientist and rather simple models from economists.

Before outlining the aims and content of this work, the next subchapter will briefly connect the major fields of the author's interests and provide the interconnections within this topic.

1.2 Connection of Systems Dynamics, Economics and Demographics

Jay Forrester used the term "system" for grouped parts that operate together towards a common purpose (Forrester, 1968, p. 1). More specifically, the system is a set of interrelated objects, has a *system purpose* and consists of *system elements*. Furthermore, a *system structure* determines the *system identity*, which is lost if the system is destroyed (indivisibility). The characteristic constellation of the elements and the determined function are essential (Bossel, 1994, p. 22).

Founded on the definition of a system, John D. Sterman derived that the characteristics of dynamic complexity, as systems, are (Sterman, 2004, p. 22):

- *Dynamic*: Everything changes. Even what might appear to be unchanging varies over extended periods of time.
- *Tightly coupled*: The system elements interact strongly.
- *Governed by feedback*: Actions feed back on themselves. Decisions cause changes and trigger others to act.
- *Nonlinear*: Effects are rarely proportional to their case. Local acting can have effects on distant system elements.
- *Path-depended*: History matters as many actions are irreversible. Often doing and undoing have dramatically different time constants.
- *Self-organizing*: The dynamic of a system arises from its internal structure.

- *Adaptive*: Rules and Capabilities change over time. Evolving over time leads to selection and proliferation.
- *Counterintuitive*: Cause and effects are distending in time and space so that one tends to look for causes next to the event.
- *Policy resistant*: Complex systems overwhelms the ability to understand them. The result is often a failing or worsening of the situation.
- *Characterized by trade-offs*: Time delays feedback different responses in the short- and long-term. Often a worse-before-better behavior occurs.

From these characteristics one can easily conclude that social and economic systems are complex and dynamic systems. Time delays, nonlinearities, feedback structures, all lead to policy resistant and counterintuitive behavior. These characteristics are not totally new. Already in the 1930 is Joseph A. Schumpeter wrote about dynamic approaches which are often neglected:

> But 'static' analysis is not only unable to predict the consequences of discontinuous changes in the traditional way of doing things; it can neither explain the occurrence of such productive revolutions nor the phenomena which accompany them. It can only investigate the new equilibrium position after the changes have occurred. It is just this occurrence of the "revolutionary" change that is our problem, the problem of economic development in a very narrow and formal sense. The reason why we so state the problem and turn aside from traditional theory lies not so much in the fact that economic changes, [...] but more in their fruitfulness. (Schumpeter, 1996, pp. 185–186)
>
> Demographic problems within economic systems stress the importance of time delays, in particular. At first glance it seems that there is no real demographic change, because industrialized countries face continual population changes. This has been true for the last 500 years and will be true in the future – this is not a new phenomenon. The term "demographic change" addresses, more correctly, the challenge of – in relation to demographic time periods – *a sudden aging and shrinking process.*

But if one can subsume economics and demographics as disciplines that deal with complex systems, one has to question, which would be the appropriate method to analyze and understand these systems in order to derive policies for the future actions. Today's challenges will not be solved with "one-way logic models" (Scheidges, 2009). The Noble Prize awarded to Joseph Stiglitz (Fricke, 2009) and Fredmund Malik (Malik, 2009) argued that, in contrast to extremely specialized models, a totally new approach is needed, particularly in respect to the "systemic view".

Forrester – the founder of the field of system dynamics – saw reasons for the plight of economics and the inappropriate use of methods as the result of a long path-dependent tradition in economics. He argued (Forrester, 1979, pp. 81–82):

- The *tradition of equilibrium analysis* has diverted the attention from the stocks accumulation and their incorporation, as they serve as a system memory of the past. The stocks govern action to create the future.
- The *traditional perception of deductive logic* as proper scientific method has caused a misfit between theory and real-world structures.
- The *tradition of individual personal research* has kept the economic profession fragmented. The emphasis on personal academic research has split the economic system instead of focusing on systems approaches.

- A *traditional insistence on theory* occurred by limiting tools of algebra and two-dimensional diagrams. Simplicity kept the economic field from understanding the complexity of economic life.
- *Traditional theory has focused on optimization* of behavior of individuals. This obscures the nature of real life, where incomplete information, uncertainty and lack of understanding of the consequences of decisions dominate.
- The *tradition of short-term prediction* has obscured the more feasible objective of using models to discover policies and to change economic behavior.
- The *tradition of separating search for model structure from search for parameters* has hampered the chance to observe both directly from real life. This separation has resulted from the two-stage development in economics. First comes the theory and second follows the econometric parameter selection as an own process.
- The *tradition of validating models by statistical analysis* neglects identification of feedback loop structures. Such structures often reveal ambiguous and misleading results in statistical analysis. A more demanding form would be to generate a broad range of behavior patterns that can be compared with actual behavior.
- The *tradition of focusing on solvable mathematical equations* has often restricted models to linear form. This excluded nonlinear relationships with their important economic behavior.

Why is a modern approach to economics so important? When one takes a closer look at the current discussions regarding demographic change, one discovers the need for a deeper understanding of complex systems with time delays, non-linearity and feedbacks especially for policy-makers. Over time the importance of economic interdependencies will increase. The challenge is to enhance the ability to understand causalities and to give policy-makers more confidence regarding long-term control.

One way to approach economic problems in a complex and dynamic environment might be the ability to think in systems ("systems thinking"). A good outline for the dimensions of systems thinking was created by Günther Ossimitz (Ossimitz, 2000, p. 52). He distinguished four dimensions:

(1) *Thinking in Models*: Knowledge base that one can only understand models as an simplified reality, specific factors are stressed and others are forgotten.
(2) *Thinking in Loops*: thinking in cause and effect chains and their interrelations as well as thinking in loops.
(3) *Dynamic Thinking*: Consideration of time changes, non-linearity and evaluation of stocks and flows.
(4) *Steering systems*: Ability to control and steer systems.

System dynamics is a technique to approach causal and simulation modeling, within systems thinking (Moffat, 1992, p. 7). More formally, the methodology of system dynamics can be defined as:

> A rigorous method for problem identification, system description, qualitative modeling and analysis of change in complex systems; which facilitates and can lead to quantitative modeling and dynamic analysis for the design of system structure and control (Wolstenholme, 1985, p. 1052).

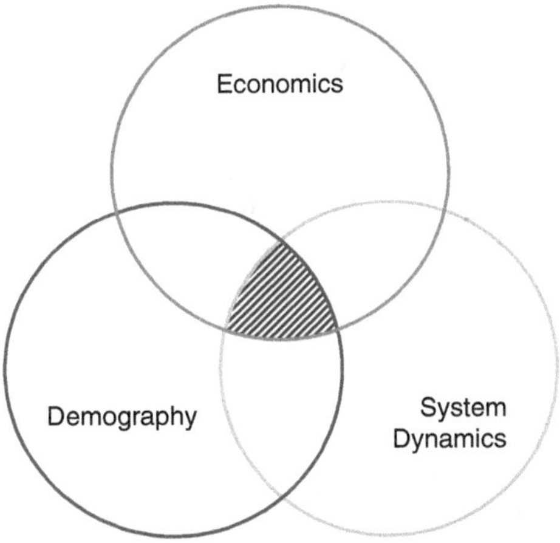

Fig. 1.1 Overlapping research fields
Source: own figure

System dynamics emphasizes the connection and interactions among various elements of a system. This methodology applies inputs from several traditional sciences, thus system dynamics holistically processes explanations of a problem from different theoretical perspectives (Moffat, 1992, p. 10). The system dynamic approach is based on the cybernetics thread, decision theory, experimental computer simulation and mental problem solving techniques (Rothengatter & Schaffer, 2006, p. 184). Barry Richmond commented that the consequent continuation of systems thinking will occur with the help of computer technology. Thus, system dynamics is a part of systems thinking (Richmond, 1994, p. 3).

Figure 1.1 shows the overlapping scientific fields. The lower right circle represents the adopted simulation method. The adopted method deals with problems from the fields of economics and demographics. The overlap of these three scientific fields shows the focus of this work. For example, Khalid Saeed stressed that growth models should deal with limiting factors and soft variables. System dynamics modeling can implement these limiting variables in formal models and, therefore, helps to understand the structure of these classical growth theories better (Saeed, 2008).

Narrowing the work-specific topic leads to the next subchapter where the aims of this study are presented.

1.3 Aims of the Study

The long-term behavior of economic growth variables such as production, capital, and capital investment follows, in most cases, a standard exponential form. Economic growth models, starting with Robert Solow's in 1956, try to explain the structure behind this behavior (Solow, 1956). The developing growth theory extends the core idea of an accelerating capital investment by adding new modules on to existing theories. Since Solow's growth publication, sectors on labor, technology or intermediate goods have been modified or added to the very basic model of neoclassical growth. One of the latest models in the neoclassical growth family was presented by Charles Jones (Jones, 1995a). It stressed the importance of population growth for sustaining an increase of economic welfare. Jones' model also corrected the empirical flaw of Romer's endogenous growth model (Romer, 1990) between the total productivity growth and the number of researchers in R&D (Verspagen, 2007, pp. 506–507). According to the Romer-model both variables must highly correlate, but in reality, the total factor productivity stayed constant over the past, whereas the number of R&D workers rose.

Paul M. Romer argued that "technological advance comes from things that people do" (Romer, 1994, p. 12). Concluding this, it is very important to refocus attention in growth models on people and the population as a whole, for a deeper understanding of growth. As mentioned earlier, there have been only a few attempts in scientific research which combine the latest theoretical growth models with an augmented and detailed population sector. Alexia Fürnkranz-Prskawetz emphasized that the "link between demographic structure and economic growth is very innovative and deserves to be considered in future research" (Fürnkranz-Prskawetz & Alexia, 2002, p. 179). Figure 1.2 illustrates how several sectors further differentiate the exponential growth pattern. The work in hand contributes to this scientific stream by implementing a new population sector, on which all other sectors depend. In order to fit with empirical observations, the sector is added to the semi-endogenous model from Jones, as it fits with the empirical observations. One can see how the previous works from Solow, Romer and Jones are interconnected. This work presented here is directly based on Jones' model.

This work brings two scientific fields together by applying theoretical demographic aspects from different fields – not only economics – to an extended system dynamics model. This will help policy-makers to understand the consequences of aging and shrinking more accurately. It is not intended to add country-

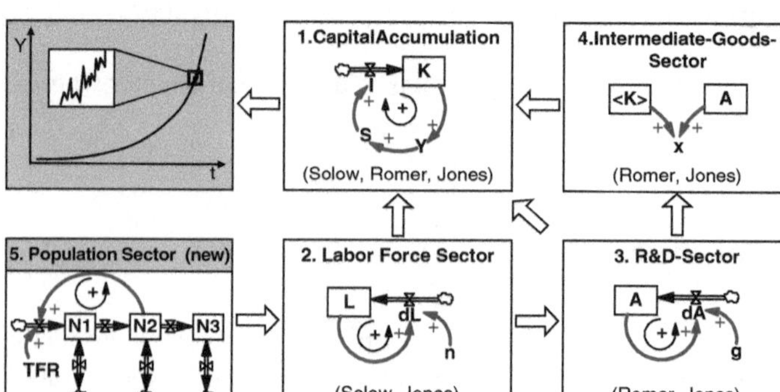

Fig. 1.2 Core idea of the presented work
Source: own figure

specific graphs and figures for different scenarios. In fact, the reader will rarely find any concrete facts as to one specific country. This work approaches demographic challenges from a very theoretical perspective, and brings cause and effect together holistically – while being economically orientated. After analyzing this in detail, most of the outcomes are integrated into a complex semi-endogenous growth model. With this application policy-makers and scientists can test various scenarios of future developments and reduce failure costs for decisions in practice.

This work consists of three parts. First, it focuses on research and comes to terms with the scientific past regarding growth theories and demographic theories. Second, the focus shifts to the construction of the extended semi-endogenous growth model, which allows applying theoretical aspects in practice. And third, the adoption of a new growth model with realistic policy scenarios is brought to center stage. Although the last part is conceptual, the model is easily transferable to country-specific models based on particular empirical data.

The central research question for this work is:

What behavior generates a semi-endogenous growth model with a detailed population sector for the case of an aging and shrinking economy?

Following this question the aims of this work are summarized as follows:

1. This work provides an overview of theoretical aspects of demographic change.
2. This work provides an overview of neoclassical growth models and their behavior in the case of demographic change.
3. This work presents a new semi-endogenous growth model with explicit formulation of population.
4. This work shows the economic consequences of an aging and shrinking society on the basis of this new semi-endogenous growth model.
5. This work shows several policy scenarios to overcome the economic effects of the demographic change.

Additionally, this work seeks to provide all theories in a consistent visual form, with an emphasis on the characteristics of complex dynamic systems. Thus, different theories for a comprehensive overview about growth and demographic theories are unified.

1.4 Outline of the Study

For a better understanding, the following subchapter outlines the structure of this study. Figure 1.3 visualizes the sequences of the subchapter.

Chapter 2 presents demographic determinants and their economic impact. The aim of this chapter is twofold. First, the *effects on population* and their important demographic factors, such as fertility, mortality, migration and population structure, are analyzed with regard to their influencing factors. Second, the *economic effects* of a change in those demographic factors are reviewed. The emphasis here is

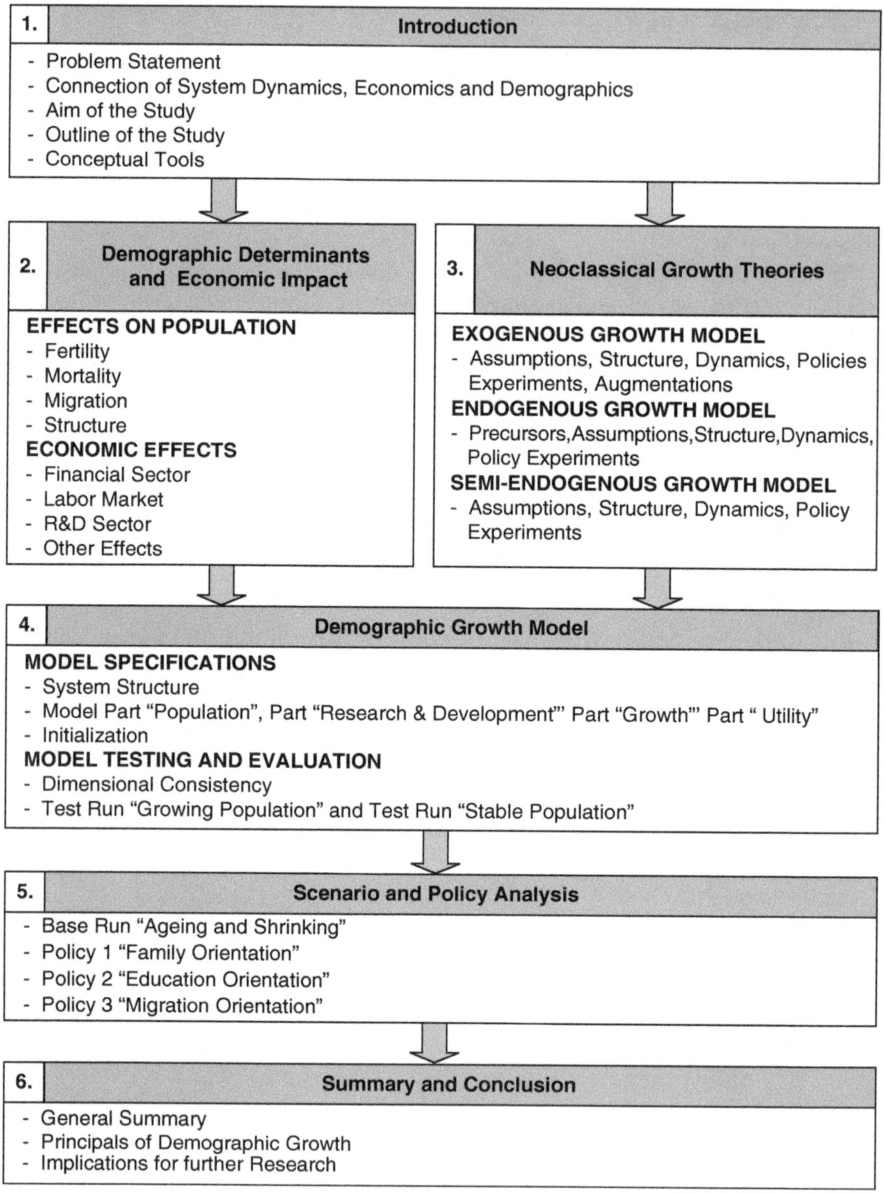

Fig. 1.3 Outline of the presented work
Source: own figure

on the financial sector, the labor market, and the R&D sector. For every demographic factor and every economic effect, the possible future behavior is outlined. A detailed list of the investigated theories appears in Fig. 1.3. In doing this, the chapter follows a stringent theory-based structure rather than a case orientated description of country development.

Chapter 3 is devoted to the neoclassical growth theory. This chapter focuses on the foundation of the self-constructed semi-endogenous growth model. Therefore, it presents main models, namely the *Solow-model*, the *Romer-model* and the *Jones-model*, which all follow the same analysis. Every subchapter starts with the particular assumptions, continues with the model structure to the dynamics of the model and finishes with important policy experiments. Additionally, important precursors or augmentations are reviewed. The focus for every model is on the demographic aspects.

Chapter 4 explains the new and self-constructed *demographic growth model*. After a short introduction about the research method and its implications, the model is presented in greater detail. General explanations about the model and the model boundary are part of the subchapter "*Model Structure*". Following the introduction, the model is reviewed in steps, beginning with the part "Population". This new contribution is important to understanding the later simulated behavior. The parts "Research & Development", "Growth" and "Utility" follow. Whereas the part "Utility" is newly presented research, the other two parts follow Jones' semi-endogenous growth model. But the "Growth" section is significantly extended in support of the population sector's model structure. The second subchapter "*Model Testing and Evaluation*" in Chap. 4 initializes the demographic growth model and evaluates the correctness of the model structure through test runs for both growing and stable populations.

Chapter 5 culminates the precursor work of this thesis with several simulations. The *base run* presents the model behavior for any typical demographic aging and shrinking process. Key variables of the outcome are explained. In addition, three policies to overcome the negative behavior are tested. First, the "*Family Orientation*" scenario assumes a stabilizing of the total fertility rate at the replacement level. The second scenario "*Education Orientation*" tests the influence of a raise in education towards more high skilled labor. The third and last scenario "*Migration Orientation*" focuses on the impact of immigration for the economic system.

Chapter 6 summarizes the results and connects the major aims of this work. In addition, future research questions are outlined and explained. Also possible next steps are briefly presented.

1.5 Conceptual Tools

System dynamics is a form of causal modeling (Moffat, 1992, p. 12). This work follows a stringent scope of standardized representation for all models. Therefore, it is necessary to introduce the reader into the major symbolic of System Dynamics.

1.5.1 Causal Links

Every system dynamics model consists of stocks, flows, auxiliaries and constants (Kleinewefers & Jans, 1983, p. 22). Causal connections can be founded on either empirical research or formal deductions (Strohhecker & Fischer, 2008, p. 74). Causal links serve the information flow and are linked by arrows. Figure 1.4 shows two examples at the top.

Each causal link has an assigned polarity, indicating how the dependent variable changes in relation to the cause. A positive (+) link indicates "same direction", which means if the cause A increases than the effect B increases, but also if A declines, than B declines. A negative (–) link means "opposite direction": an increase in C causes D to decline and vice versa (Sterman, 2004, p. 139).

Link polarities describe the structure of the model. They do not indicate the behavior of the variables. This becomes evident if one assumes multi-causal links (as in Fig. 1.4) (Strohhecker & Fischer, 2008, p. 79). The two lower examples show possible splits – an input split and an output split (Kleinewefers & Jans, 1983, p. 33). The resulting net-behavior of G depends on the mathematical equation. Thus, if can also occur that a variable (i.e. G) increases, but with a shrinking growth rate.

If two variables can be connected either positively or negatively, the link should be separated into two unambiguous, multiple pathways, with at least one more item in between (Sterman, 2004, pp. 146–147).

To summarize, the very correct phrase for a positive link would be (adopted from Sterman, 2004, p. 141):

If A *increases*, B *increases above* what it would have been and vice versa.

And for a negative link follows:

If C *increases*, D *decreases below* what it would otherwise have been and vice versa.

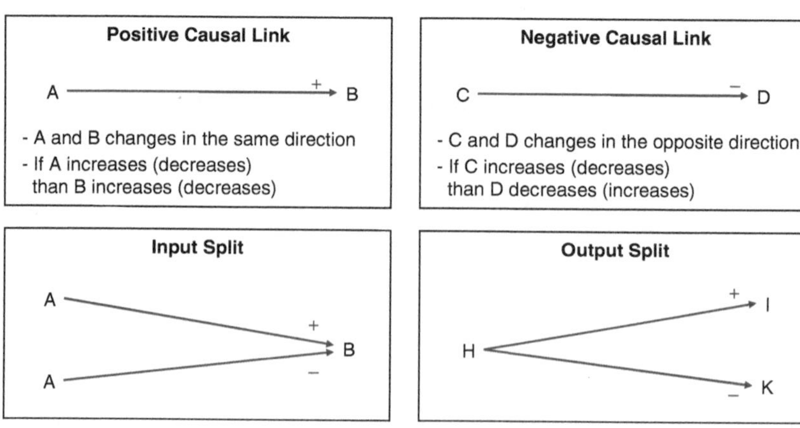

Fig. 1.4 Causal links
Source: own figure

1.5.2 Stocks and Flows

Stocks are altered by their inflows and outflows. Usually a stock is represented as a rectangle. Inflows have pipes (or arrows) pointing into a stock. Outflows have pipes (or arrows) directing out of a stock. Valves control both flow types. The clouds represent the openness of the model and characterize the sources respectively. Thus, they indicate the model boundary. Clouds have an infinite capacity and never constrain the flows (Sterman, 2004, p. 192). Figure 1.5 gives an example of a stock and flow structure.

Since stocks are critical for system behavior, they have the following major characteristics for the dynamics (Mass, 1980, pp. 98–110; Sterman, 2004, pp. 195–196):

- *Stocks stand for the system state*, because every rate and auxiliary can be calculated from them.
- *Stocks link rates of flows*, as an outflow can also be an inflow for another stock. This creates cascades (aging chains).
- *Stocks provide systems with inertia and memory*, as they accumulate past events and can only change trough inflow and outflow.
- *Stocks are sources of delays* which can induce overshoot and oscillation, as material in process (flows) lags for at least one period in time in a stock.
- *Stocks can induce opposing short and long-term effects* if they are cascaded.
- *Stocks decouple rates of flows*, as they absorb or amplify differences between inflows and outflows.
- *Stocks underlie multiple modes of economic behavior*, as adjustment times of stocks can differ
- *Stocks can propagate long-term economic changes.*
- *Stocks can measure the determinantes of economic welfare.*

A stock is measured at a certain point in time and a flow is measured over a period of time (Kleinewefers & Jans, 1983, p. 25). Stocks are usually a quantity measured in units, whereas the connected flow must be measured in units per time period since they change the stock over a certain time (Sterman, 2004, p. 198).

1.5.3 Auxiliaries and Constants

The set of mathematical equations for the model requires only stocks, flows and the exogenous constants. Often auxiliaries are introduced to ease understanding and

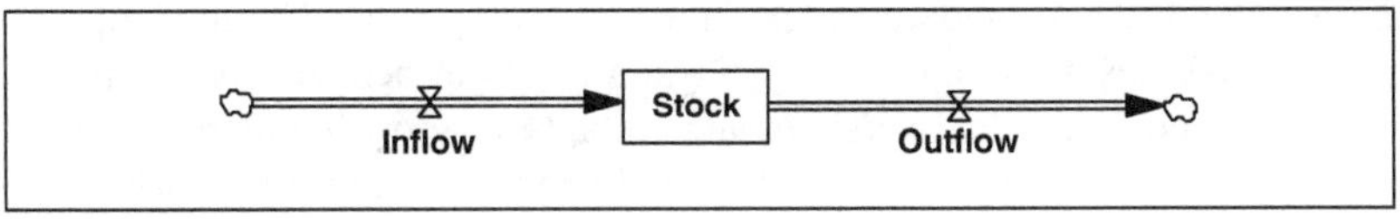

Fig. 1.5 Stock and flow
Source: own figure

provide greater model clarity. These variables ideally represent ideas of the modeler. Transposing the mathematical equations can always eliminate auxiliaries (Sterman, 2004, pp. 202–203).

Constants do not change during the simulation period and they are outside the modeling focus. Whereas a causal link never goes into a constant, an auxiliary always has an information inflow. In both types, information can be linked to other flows or auxiliaries. Note that a stock can only change through its flow and not through a direct link of an auxiliary or constant.

1.5.4 Feedback Loops

Feedback loops are one of the central structures which generate change in models. Interacting variables within the feedback loops create the behavior of the system (Moffat, 1992, p. 14).

A feedback loop is derived from a causal link chain of at least two variables that eventually returns to the beginning. Every loop has a designated polarity, created by the link polarities of all included causal connections. There are two possible loop polarities: positive (reinforcing) and negative (balancing).

John Sterman suggested tracing every link polarity of the loop. The total polarity then comes from the sign of the open loop gain (SGN), a term from the control theory. A more applicatory rule is to count the number of negative loops. If the number is even, the loop is reinforcing (positive). If it is uneven, the loop is balancing (negative) (Sterman, 2004, pp. 144–146; Bossel, 1994, pp. 57–59).

Reinforcing (positive) loops accelerate the variable values. Often, but not always, this leads to a destabilization (Bossel, 1994, p. 59). One simple structure is a standard exponential growth pattern. The stock depends only on its own growth rate. This basic structure is part of many processes (Bossel, 1994, p. 113) also in economic growth models. Figure 1.6 shows this simple stock flow pattern and its behavior.

Balancing (negative) loops signify that an initial disturbance is reversed after passing through the loop. Often, but not always this has a dampening effect on the variables (Bossel, 1994, p. 59). Like the exponential growth pattern, the standard pattern for balancing is an exponential decay. Often this is also referred to as goal-seeking behavior because it reaches a final stable value, which can, but not must, be zero. Figure 1.7 presents the equivalent structure and behavior.

There are additional standard patterns for reinforcing and balancing loops. If one merges the schemes and implements delays, a different behavior is possible, as is oscillation, sigmoid growth, overshoot and collapse or growth with overshoot. One can find a good introduction to modeling and analysis of the different patterns of loop structures in Diana Fisher (Fisher, 2001, Fisher, 2005) and John Sterman (Sterman, 2004).

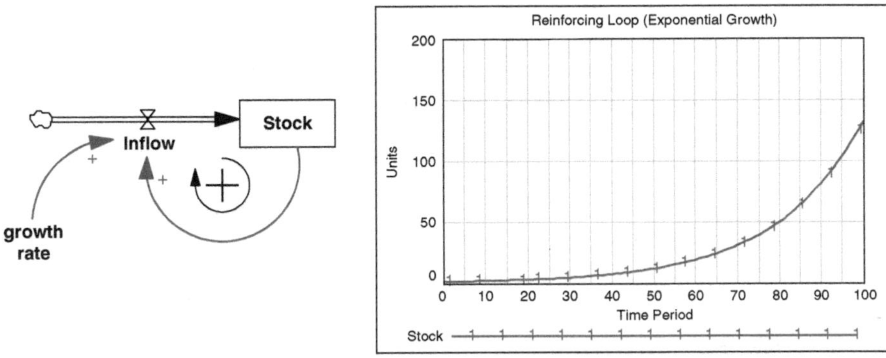

Fig. 1.6 Reinforcing loop
Source: own figure

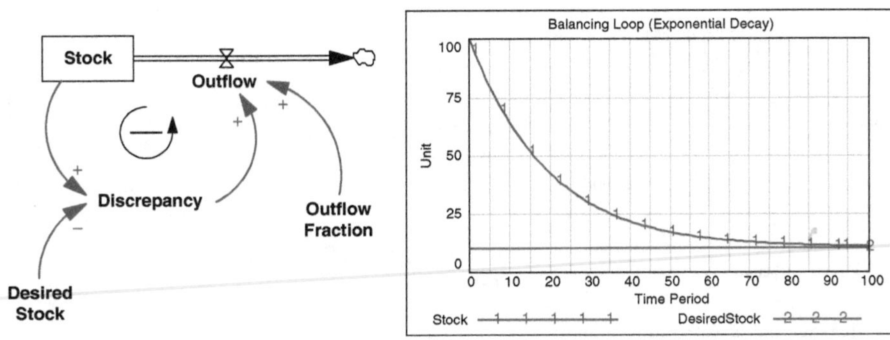

Fig. 1.7 Balancing loop
Source: own figure

1.5.5 Delays

Delays evolve from stocks and are pervasive. A delay is created, if the output lags behind the input. Delays can be distinguished in material or information delays. There are also pipeline delays, but as they refer to more discrete events, they are not outlined here. Delays in causal-loop-diagrams are usually depicted by a double crossed line (see Sect. 1.5.6).

Material delays can be either first or higher order delays. As in stocks a rectangular distribution of units is assumed, the probability that any particular unit is the next to flow out of the stock is the same for all units in that stock (Sterman, 2004, p. 416). An example of a first order delay is shown in Fig. 1.8. On the left, one can see the structure of the delay; on the right, the connected behavior of the stock and the outflow is visualized. At time t=20 the inflow rises. One can see – it takes time for the outflow to equal the inflow.

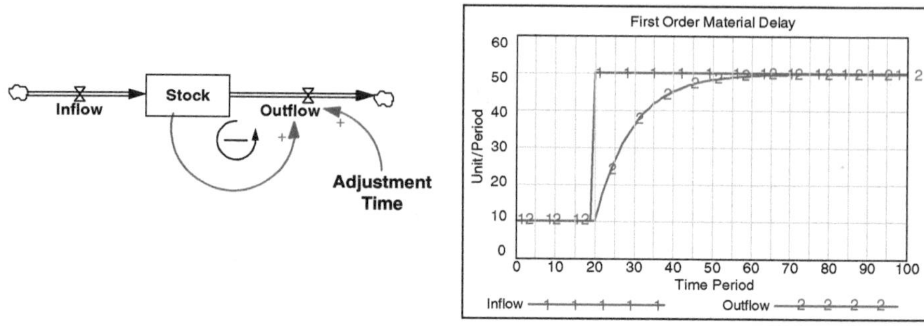

Fig. 1.8 First order material delay
Source: own figure

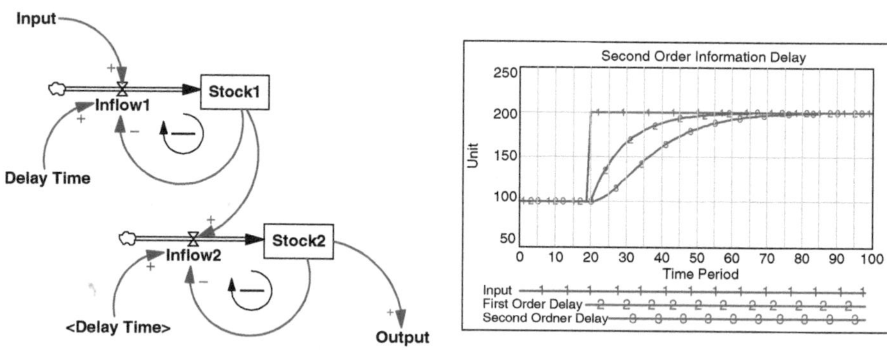

Fig. 1.9 Second order information delay
Source: own figure

Grouping several stocks together can create higher order delays. A fifth order delay would therefore consist of five first order delays. The higher the order of the delay, the smaller is the variance of the output (Milling, 2008, p. 225; Sterman, 2004, p. 420).

Information delays build another group of delays. They are important, since many systems channels exist with information feedback. The major difference to material delays is that information delays smooth the input value, whereas material delays also decrease the amplitude (Sterman, 2004, p. 430).

Figure 1.9 shows, for example, a second order information delay. The difference to a second order material delay is only that the information of the stock1 is connected to the inflow of stock2. A material delay would connect the out- and inflow to a cascade, thus the material would flow to the second stock and not only the information.

1.5.6 Causal-Loop-Diagram and Stock-Flow-Diagram

There are two different ways of illustrating the model structure – causal-loop-diagrams (CLD) and stock-flow-diagrams (SFD). Each possibility has its unique advantages and disadvantages.

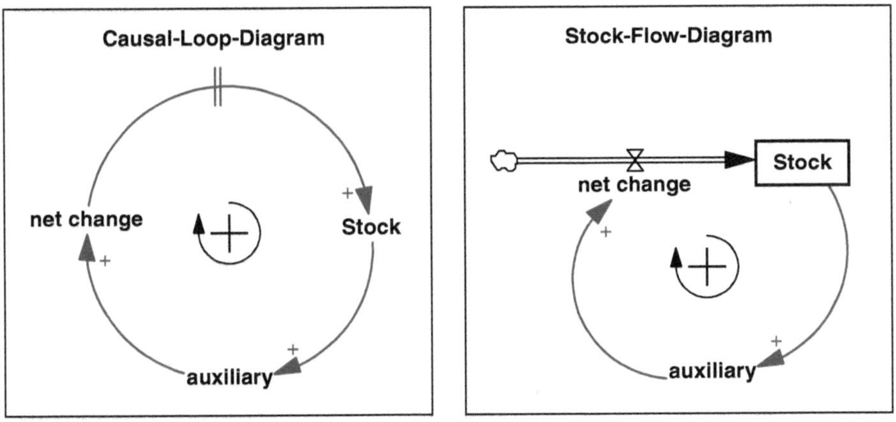

Fig. 1.10 Comparison of causal-loop and stock-flow-diagram
Source: own figure

Causal-loop-diagrams are the most important tool in representing the feedback structure and are therefore commonly used. They are excellent for (Sterman, 2004, p. 137):

- Quickly capturing hypothesis and the cause of dynamics
- Eliciting and understanding mental models
- Communicating the important feedback loops, which are probably important for the problem

Casual-loop-diagrams are a simpler form of systems illustration, than a stock-flow-diagram. Although they are often easier to understand, these diagrams have some weaknesses. First, they do not distinguish between stocks and flows. And second, some loops are only loosely formulated (Sterman, 2004, pp. 167–168).

Figure 1.10 shows, for example, the difference between a causal-loop-diagram (left) and a stock-flow-diagram (right).

With these introductory remarks, one can now proceed to the first theoretical chapter about demographic effects and their economic consequences.

Chapter 2
Demographic Determinants and Economic Impact

To this very day [...] the connection between population development and economic growth is one of the (unsolved) main questions in economics.

(Rürup, 2000, p. 8, translated into English)

2.1 Introduction

This chapter investigates the effects of the demographic change on economic factors. This simple cause and effect link is split into two separate foci (see Fig. 2.1):

1. Determinants of demographic factors
2. Economic effects of demographic factors

First, the population determinants – factors that change the population – will be analyzed in Part I. These factors include fertility, mortality, immigration and emigration, as well as, the population structure itself, which one can see in Fig. 2.2. This is necessary for the testing scenarios on economic growth in Chap. 4 Thus, in order to determine 'real-life' policies, this chapter shows how and where possible connections between the different elements exist. For example, this chapter explains a causal connection between income per capita and fertility rates. After debating the determinants of demographic factors, one can endogenize fertility, mortality and migration.

Once the determinants of demographic factors are discussed, the effects of these factors on economic parameters will be analyzed. Important effects and those that can be displayed later in the model are examined in the second part of this chapter (Part II in Fig. 2.1). In addition, a short subsection presents important economic effects of the demographic change, which are not considered in the new, self-developed demographic growth model, such as consumption patterns, pension schemes and infrastructure. When all of the economic effects are combined, one can determine the total effect of demographic change on economic growth. In addition to income Y the income per capita or the total utility are both good indicators to evaluate social welfare.

L. Weber, *Demographic Change and Economic Growth*, Contributions to Economics, 17
DOI 10.1007/978-3-7908-2590-9_2,

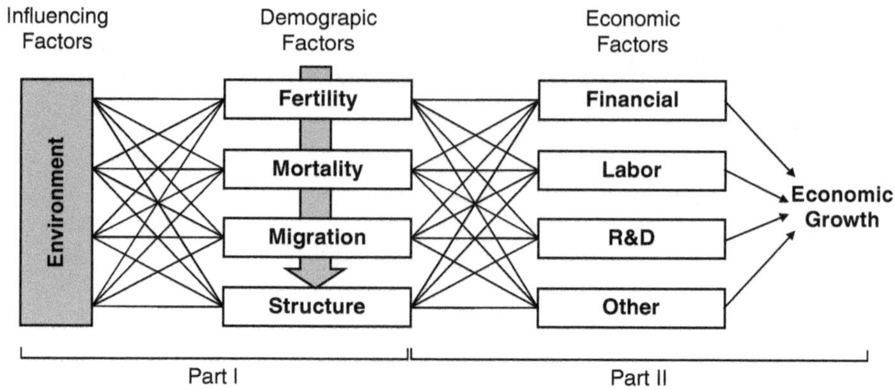

Fig. 2.1 Overview of Chap 2
Source: own figure

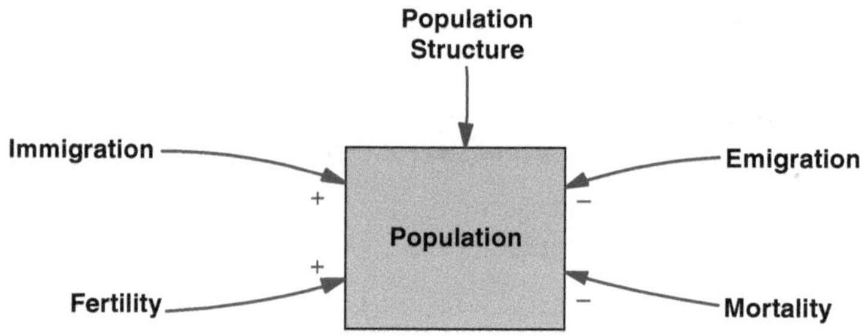

Fig. 2.2 Population determinants
Source: own figure

2.2 Effects on Population

This chapter investigates the demographic effects on a theoretical level. It is not intended to present country specific examples or to introduce the historic development of important key indicators. Nevertheless, it is sometimes necessary to visualize empiric data to show the connection between theoretical implications and real observations. They serve in this case as an example for standard patterns.

To describe a population more accurately, one can distinguish measurements for stocks and flows. Stocks are determined by degrees of a certain point in time, whereas degrees of flows are focused on a period of time. Reproductive measurement follows flows (Mueller, 2000, p. 2).

2.2.1 Fertility

2.2.1.1 Definition

There are several ways to measure and define fertility. First, one must distinguish between fecundity and fertility. **Fecundity** constitutes the biological ability to have children, whereas **fertility** is the case-by-case physical realization of fecundity (Mueller, 2000, p. 61).

Fertility is not only a special event for the future parents, but also provides feedback to the number of children itself. If, for example, the child dies, the probability for the couple to have further children again rises. Additional factors in future fertility decisions include the number of existing children and the mother's age. Fertility also fluctuates depending on economic and political conditions (Mueller, 2000, p. 62).

Besides the very simple way to count the number of births, the **crude birth rate** (CBR) is expressed:

$$CBR = \frac{number\ of\ live\ births\ in\ a\ year}{mid - year\ population} = \frac{B}{P} \tag{2.1}$$

The advantage of the crude birth rate is the easily identified variation of the population's fertility changes. However, it completely ignores the concept of risk. Because the births are related to the total population instead of the women's childbearing age, crude birth rates are not completely comparable over time, as they neglect age structures (Rowland, 2003, p. 236).

The likelihood of having a child varies by the age of the women. One could calculate **age-specific fertility rates** (ASFR) by calculating the number of births of all women assigning a specific age to the total number of women in this age-cohort with (Rowland, 2003, p. 236):

$$ASFR_x = f_x = \frac{number\ of\ births\ in\ a\ year\ to\ women\ in\ a\ age\ group\ x\ to\ x + n}{mid - year\ population\ of\ women\ in\ aged\ group\ x\ to\ x + n} \tag{2.2}$$

This ratio is often related to a group of 5-year cohorts, although detailed research may require single year statistics. Figure 2.3 presents an example of age-specific fertility rates for Germany in 2006. The age-specific fertility rate varies over time as the age of young potential mothers may also change over time (see Sect. 2.2.1.4). It is also important to state, that this ratio may differ from country to country. Depending on the differences, research must adopt this essential key figure within their models and simulations.

To provide regular assessments of the current situation synthetic cohorts are required. If the rates remain constant for a prolonged period of time, then the synthetic cohort will correspond to the real cohort. Synthetic cohorts are compiled by using information from various cohorts over time (Rowland, 2003, p. 239). One

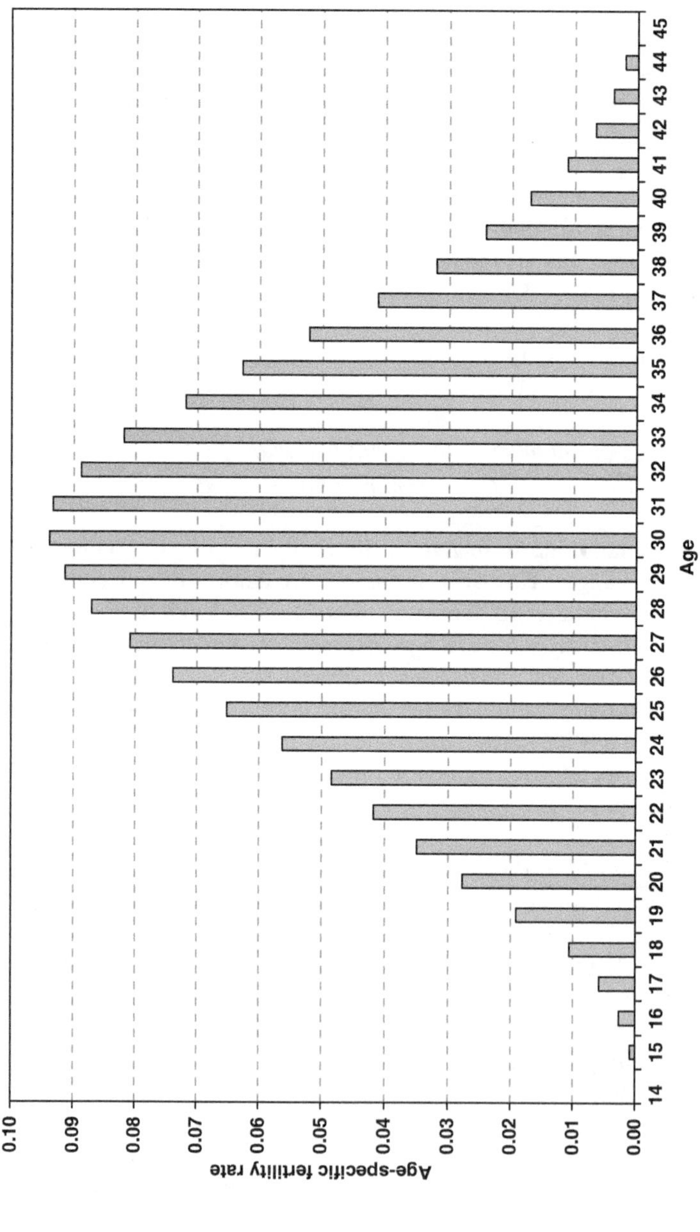

Fig. 2.3 Age-specific fertility rate of Germany 2006
Source: own calculations, data: Federal Statistical Office, 2008, p. 51.

well-known measure is the **total fertility rate** (TFR). The total fertility rate is derived from the age specific fertility rate and acts as the measurement for a cumulated fertility rate for a fictive age cohort (Mueller, 2000, pp. 66–67). Whereas, the crude birth rate measures the number of births per population based on exact numbers, the TFR is a theoretic value. One can write the formula:

$$TFR = \sum_{x=15}^{49} ASFR_x = \sum_{x=15}^{49} f_x \tag{2.3}$$

To assume constant rates over time is unsound; however the total fertility rate provides a precise indication of the fertility level in any given year. One can also estimate whether the fertility level is above or below the current replacement level (Rowland, 2003, p. 241).

The exact value for the TFR, while maintaining a constant population size (replacement level fertility), depends on both the probability of having a girl instead of a boy, and the total mortality of women from their birth until the end of their childbearing age. Industrialized countries have the boy to girl ratio 0.5 and a low mortality rate within the relevant age group, thus, maintaining a TFR close to 2.1. One can see that a high TFR above the replacement level does not automatically imply that a population grows, due to other factors such as migration.

The Fig. 2.4 presents a chart showing how TFR develops over time in Great Britain – subdivided for Scotland, England and Wales. It also indicates the replacement level fertility at 2.1. From the mid 1960s until the mid 1970s the TFR dropped

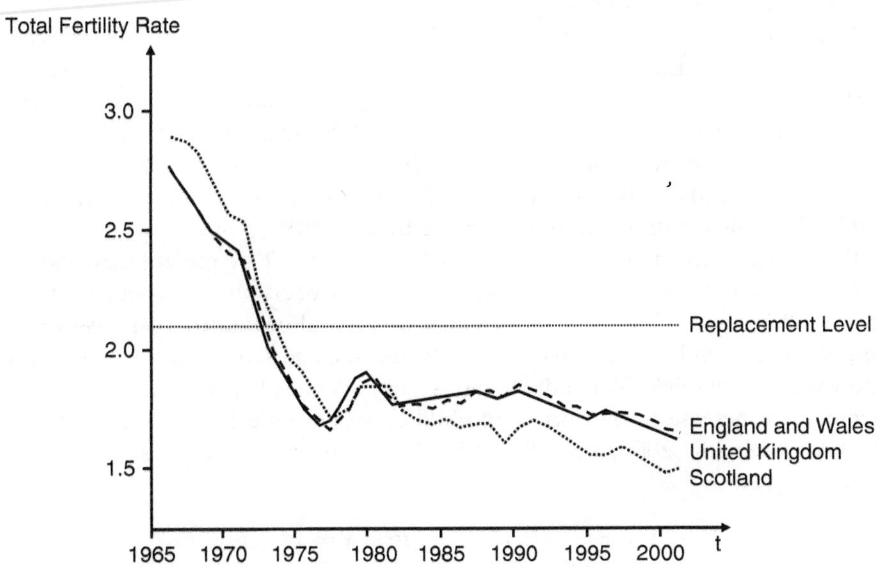

Fig. 2.4 Total fertility rate of Scotland, England, Wales
Source: Chamberlain & Smallwood, 2004

significantly below the replacement level. One can also see that it has continued at this weak level until today.

The **average age of maternity** (AAM, Total) is another key indicator; showing the point in life a woman decides to have children. It describes the velocity of population change (Mueller, 2000, pp. 62–63). If the average age increases, then it will take longer to renew the population. From the graph, one can see that if there is a shift in the point of time in which a woman decides to have a baby, then the births will decline as long as the AAM increases (tempo effect). Figure 2.5 provides a good overview, in which the average age for maternity is shown for all Canadian women. In addition, the graph also indicates the average age of mothers for their first-borns (1st order). For almost all industrialized countries the pattern is comparable. One reason behind the upward trend is later explained in Sect. 2.2.1.4.

2.2.1.2 Economic Theory of Fertility Choice (Barro/Becker 1988, 1989)

In the late 1980s, economists started looking more closely at microeconomic determinants for family fertility, with the purpose of implementing this decision process into their models. They adopted traditional household and consumer theories for their basic analytical model. The optimization theory helps to explain family size decisions. Robert Barro and Gary Becker were among the first who presented an economic view on fertility decisions (Becker & Barro, 1988, Barro & Becker, 1989). To explain the entire model in detail would go beyond the scope of this work, however the Barro–Becker article is the foundation of other economic works presented in the following section.

In a nutshell, the core idea of this theory **links the parents and children through altruism**, thereby optimizing a family choice on fertility (Barro & Becker, 1989, p. 481). Barro and Becker neglected life cycle considerations and assumed a two-generation model – childhood and adulthood. Women give birth at the beginning of the adulthood, without taking marriage or spacing of childbearing into account. The utility of the parents depends on their consumption, the number of children and the children's utility (Barro & Becker, 1989, p. 482).

Regarding utility maximizing households – for a set of preferences under a budget constraint – one must consider the fertility decision as a special kind of consumption good. Thus, fertility becomes a **rational economic response to the household demand**, relative to other goods. Income and substitution effects apply. The expected number of children varies and is dependent on the households' income. An increase in the 'price' of children would reflect a decline in fertility (Todaro & Smith, 2006, pp. 282–283). The mathematical expression for this relationship is:

$$C_d = f(Y, P_c, P_x, t_x) \; with \quad x = 1, ..., n \tag{2.4}$$

C_d is the demand of surviving children as a function of household income Y, net price of children P_c (anticipated costs and benefit of children), price of all other

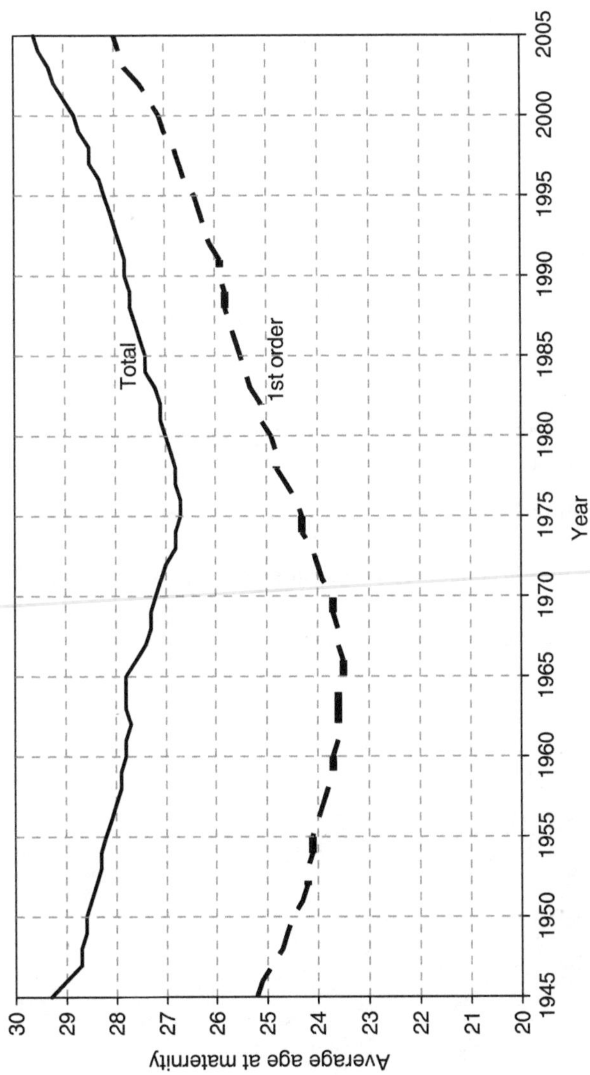

Fig. 2.5 Average age of maternity in Canada
Source: own figure according to Milan & Martel, 2008, p. 20

goods P_x and the preference for the other goods t_x. Following classical conditions, the derivatives behave as follows:

1. $\partial C_d/\partial Y > 0$: Increasing **household income** leads to greater demand for children.
2. $\partial C_d/\partial P_c < 0$: Demand for children is negatively connected with the net **price of children**.
3. $\partial C_d/\partial P_x > 0$: An increase in **all other prices** leads to an increase of children demand.
4. $\partial C_d/\partial t_x < 0$: The greater the **preference for alternative goods** the fewer the children demand (Todaro & Smith, 2006, p. 283).

An increasing household income gives way to more supported children and thereby an increase in fertility (income effect). However, this also leads to better schooling and higher wage rates (opportunity costs), which all together increases child-raising costs (substitution effect). The substitution effect can exceed the income effect, especially if the potential parents are highly skilled (Dickmann & Seyda, 2004, pp. 39–40). The cost of children can be affected by several variables (Braun, 2000, pp. 328–329):

1. The direct financial expenditures for education
2. The childrens' work for the household (discharging the family budget)
3. And the opportunity costs for child care

Figure 2.6 shows a simplified diagram of this theory. It follows a standard two-goods model, marking the difference on the x-axis – **number of children desired** – and the **total number of goods** consumed by parents on the y-axis. The indifference curves are named $I_{1,2,3}$ and the satisfaction increases to the upper right. The household income is shown as line a–b. Point e indicates the optimal decision

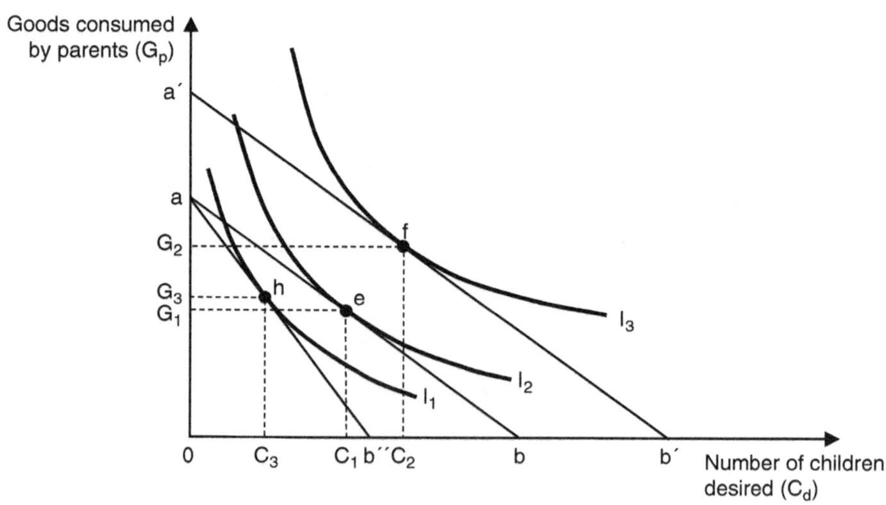

Fig. 2.6 Economic theory of fertility
Source: own figure according to Todaro & Smith, 2006, p. 284

with (C_1;G_1). An increase in the family's income is shown by an upward moving a–b-line. (C_2;G_2) indicates the new set of goods. An increase in the price of children, relative to the other goods, causes the household to substitute commodities for children. The budget line shifts downward to a–b″ with (C_3;G_3) as new set of goods (Todaro & Smith, 2006, p. 285).

Barro and Becker also proved that:

> the steady-state rate of population growth is positively related to the degree of altruism toward children and to the steady-state long-term interest rate, and it is negatively related to the rate of growth between generations in per capita consumption (1989, p. 498).

Furthermore, the model shows that a rise in income increases fertility and that the Harrod-neutral technological progress lowers fertility (Barro & Becker, 1989, p. 498). This model overcomes the Malthusian population system, which has an unfavorable implication of a positive connection between fertility rates and per capita income (Barro & Becker, 1989, p. 499).

The **fertility decline** in most industrialized countries has been explained by the secular decline in child mortality. However, Becker and Barro added a new explanation for occurrence. The authors showed that a permanent decline in the child mortality level does not affect the demand for children within all generations (Becker & Barro, 1988, p. 16). Some decline in fertility has been connected to the increase of social security systems or other social transfers. Becker and Barro discussed these effects, indicating that a growing public transfer to the elderly would reduce the demand for children (1988, p. 17).

2.2.1.3 Easterlin Hypothesis (1961)

The **Easterlin hypothesis** goes back to a series of papers by Richard Easterlin, starting with the American Economic Review article "The American Baby Boom in Historical Perspective" (Easterlin, 1961) and culminating in the epilog of his book "Birth and fortune" (Easterlin, 1990). Easterlin built upon the work of his numerous predecessors. Originally, he suggested that a mechanism was responsible for long swings (Kuznets business cycles phenomena) in US economic growth. He theorized that this was caused by the interactions of aggregated demand, labor market conditions and household growth (Easterlin, 1966, p. 1092). Later on, the theory shifted towards an explanation of changing fertility rates. This subsection examines Easterlin's many papers (Easterlin, 1965, 1966, 1990).

Easterlin connected the long-swing mechanism to secular developments (Easterlin, 1966, p. 1092). In his understanding, recent past changes in economic growth were mainly due to **immigration swings**. However, as the source of labor ceased, cycles were induced through movements in birth rate and labor force participation (Easterlin, 1961, p. 898). Easterlin argued that young adults are the key factor in explaining swings.

Easterlin theorized that a **tradeoff** between children and consumption eventually influences fertility decisions. Additionally, he assumed that the priming of preference through a period of time in the childhood is based on the parent's standard of living and the specific economic conditions (Braun, 2000, pp. 321–322). If the birth cohort is relatively small, compared to their parents' childbearing cohort, than later – after they grow up – there will be lower competition in the labor market. This gives this new generation the chance to negotiate relatively high wages and achieve a high-income level. With increasing **living standards**, the possibility of having children becomes ever more affordable; thereby contributing to a rise in fertility. For their later children, the effect is twofold. First, as parents become accustomed with their high standards of living, children expect ex-ante an equal level for themselves. Secondly, large cohorts do not perform well in the labor market, as their quantity is not scarce for labor market demand. On the labor market they cannot realize a high wage level or sustain their expected living standards. Both effects – low standard of livings and high lifestyle expectations – lead to a negative future perspective. Consequently, the birth rate declines. For the following generation, the economic situation will flip (Braun, 2000, p. 324). Economic growth is typically connected with a rise in aggregated demand, and associated with investments and an increase in aggregated supply. With the investment in capital stock, wages will rise and the unemployment rate will decline (Easterlin, 1965, p. 502).

Easterlin's findings changed and improved continuously, however his core hypothesis, presented in Fig. 2.7, is reflected in a causal-loop-diagram. The characterized business cycles (swings) are represented in the balancing loop (highlighted). The labor market conditions develop over time due to changes in supply

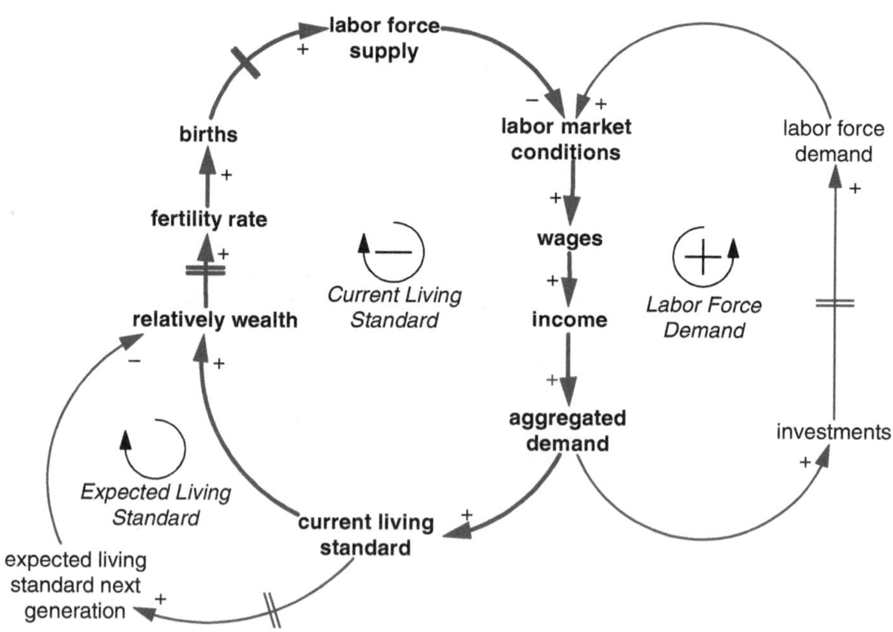

Fig. 2.7 Easterlin hypothesis
Source: own figure

and demand. The labor force supply has a delayed increase if the fertility rate rises. This occurs when the standard of living is above the primed previous standard. Interestingly, this structure creates ups and downs endogenously because of its second order differential equation system. The cycle length is determined by the delays in the system as a whole.

In contrast to Becker and Barro's approach, Easterlin's hypothesis accounts for the **shifting of people's preferences**, and challenges the neoclassical economic model. Easterlin's model presents an advantage in its close proximity to other fields of research, such as sociology or psychology (Macunovich, 1998, p. 54). One can state that Easterlin presented a modern, systemic view on business cycles. By introducing feedback into his concept, one can label Easterlin as a system dynamic specialist. In conclusion, Easterlin predicted the swings in labor demand as the driving initial element for demographic change (Easterlin, 1965, p. 504).

2.2.1.4 Biographic Theory of Fertility (Birg 1991)

Young adults face two fundamental decisions at the beginning of their lives: their commitment to appropriate schooling and their occupational choice. These choices are very often connected to family enrichment. Theoretically, this can be represented as a sequential game with infinite decisions. Herwig Birg's theory builds on these lock-in effects. He made his first attempt towards a **unified theory** on life decisions in his book "Biografische Theorie der demografischen Reproduktion" [biographic theory on demographic reproduction] (Birg, Flöthmann, & Reiter, 1991). Birg combined economical, sociological and psychological explanations in one theoretic approach. The theory outlines how and why fertility declines in industrialized countries (Birg 2004, pp. 66–67).

According to Birg, a resume is a personal **biographic sequence** with single items. Proceeding from one element to the next is referred to as **biographic mobility**. Based on a mathematical model, the number of all permutations of a biographic sequence is the **biographic universe,** and the open possible projection of the biographic universe is known as the **virtual biography**. One can see that specific individual decisions – e.g. children – shrink the virtual biography and increase the space between the biographic universe and virtual biography. The lost options are considered opportunity costs (Huinink, 2000, p. 382).

Birg's theory has three fundamental implications (Leim, 2008, pp. 42–43):

1. The individual bases decisions on his/her past experience and resources.
2. The resume is a multi-dimensional process with interacting elements.
3. The biography is based on a social context and environmental conditions.

A graphical illustration of the biographical theory for fertility is shown in Fig. 2.8. This shows a classical decision tree, highlighting Birg's definition. Note that this is only one tree with a specific order of elements. Originally, Birg considered five biographic elements: schooling, occupation, household, marriage and first child. This creates a 5!=120 permutations (Leim, 2008, p. 44).

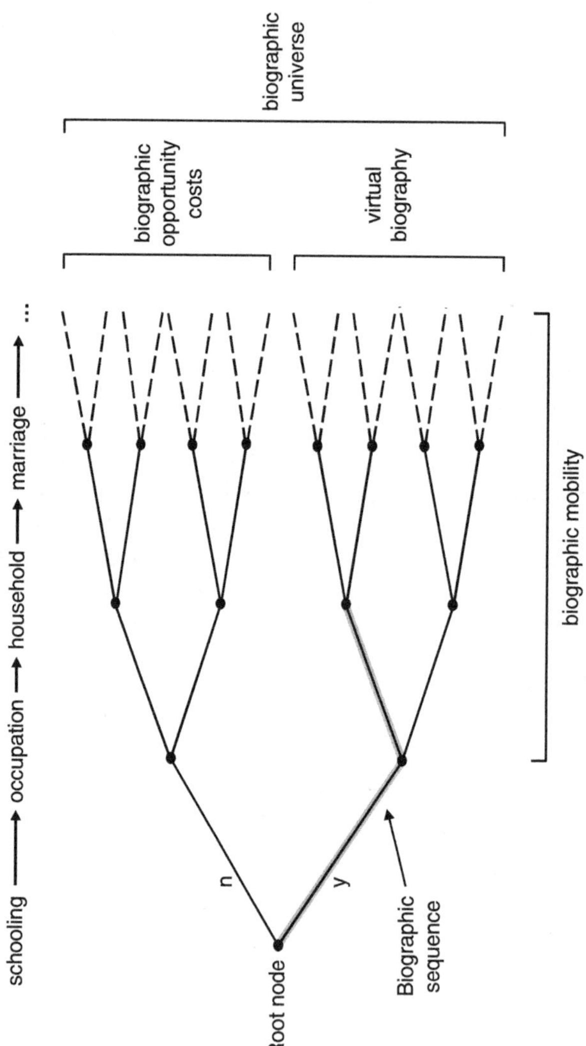

Fig. 2.8 Birg's biographic theory of fertility
Source: own figure

Birg's main thesis explains that under constantly changing social, economical, cultural living conditions, the **risk for irreversible biographic decisions** rises. It is rational to avoid long lasting decisions in order to maintain the freedom of choice (Birg, 2004, p. 66). Given this, it could be rational for both partners to postpone starting a family (Dickmann & Seyda, 2004, p. 41). Occupational flexibility is especially targeted in this regard. The consequence, however, is a decline in fertility rates, as the number of women not having children increases. Birg theorized that the fertility decline is not a question of having only one child instead of two or more, but a question of having children or not having children (Birg, 2004, p. 67).

Birg's rational-choice approach concludes that a pro-children decision conflicts with raising the opportunity cost within biographic sequences. Additionally, it affects the economic spheres (Dickmann & Seyda, 2004, p. 41).

Based on the event of a first child, one can draw several hypotheses (Huinink, 2000, p. 383):

- The larger the biographic universe, the higher will be the opportunity costs.
- The smaller the biographic universe, the higher the biographic mobility.
- The greater the discrepency between the current biographic sequence and the desired one, the lower the mobility.
- If one lowers biographic mobility than the probabilty of having a child increases.
- Biographic opportunity costs increase when occupational choices increase.

From the resume perspective, there are biographical, allocated, compatible challenges to solve. A reliable perception and the ability to reduce uncertainty about future events play an important role. Anticipating priorities and commitment can increase the biographical perspective. In addition, every person tries to increase both their needed resources and the security about future decisions. These resources are necessary to decide compatible challenges, i.e. occupation and family. Opportunity costs will decline if one sets an order to the conflicting compatible challenges (Huinink, 2000, pp. 384–385).

Birg's theory explains the declining fertility rates through **shrinking group sizes**. The attitude pro or against something does not change over time. Just because of lock-in situation through sequential decisions, an increasing number of women in childbearing age fail to think long-term and cannot or will not avoid the trap of a closing biological window.

2.2.1.5 Other Fertility Theories

The strong connection between marriage, sexuality and parenthood was first decoupled by Lujo Brentano (1910). He saw an increase in **economic thinking** regarding children connected with an increase in education and economic wealth. This includes proactive planning. As the altered position of women in the society negatively alters the number of marriages so does the number of children (Brentano, 1910, p. 10). In addition, Brentano examined the case of upper-class fertility decline.

Sociologists often challenged economic approaches and attempted to complement their theories. In 1987 Dirk J. van de Kaa postulated a **Second Demographic Transition** (SDT) for industrialized countries, characterized by new patterns in behavior (Office for Official Publications of the European Communities, 2007, p. 33). Van de Kaa wrote that changes in fertility and family formation are manifested in (2002, p. 10):

- Postponement of births so that the fertility declines substantially below the replacement level
- Increasing mean age of marriage and a fundamental first marriage decline
- Strong increase in divorce and dissolution of unions
- Strong increase in the number of sexual partners
- Persistend raise of extra-marital births
- Shift in contraceptive behaviour

His argument that the fertility declines is mainly caused by women's pursuit of **self-development** and **autonomy**. Additionally, there is an increase in the hedonistic value orientation (Huinink, 2000, p. 371).

The "**Value of Children Theory**" by Lois W. Hoffman and Martin L. Hoffman (1973) compares the costs and benefits of parenthood. The work differentiates various kinds of benefits. Thus, one can distinguish between economical, psychological and socio-cultural components. Based on empirical research they found specific value categories, listed here (Hoffman & Manis, 1979, p. 585):

- Primary group ties and affection
- Stimulation and fun
- Expansion of self
- Adult status and social identity
- Achievement and creativity
- Morality
- Economic utility

In contrast to these benefits there is also a direct fear about the offspring's future, thus parents consider opportunity costs. Whereas economic theories stress the importance of rational decisions, Hoffman and Hoffman's theory attaches value to psychological effects. This leads to a strong decreasing marginal benefit of children with a negative impact on the number of children per household. The emotional benefit fluctuates marginally between countries, but as societies focus on economical thinking, the greater the increase in psychological benefits for children (Huinink, 2000, pp. 374–375). A decline in the fertility rates within industrialized countries must therefore reflect a decline in personal benefits for having children.

2.2.1.6 Trend and Effects on Fertility

The most common indicator to measure fertility is the total fertility rate. The presented theories explain why fertility changes over time. Unfortunately, this does not take the future development of fertility probabilities into consideration. Thus, as the number of women who postpone birth rises, the fertility rate will inevitably go down (tempo effect). But if these women still wish to have the same number of children at an older age, then the fertility rate again rises (quantum effect). The total fertility will decline as long as the process of postponement occurs and increases (Office for Official Publications of the European Communities, 2007, pp. 34–35).

Especially, the biographic theory of fertility shows that the share of infertility may increase. Fertility is likely to stabilize, but on a standard below the replacement level.

The work of Wolfgang Lutz, Vegard Skirbekk and Maria R. Testa (2005, pp. 9–15) adds to Easterlin's hypothesis. As outlined in Fig. 2.9, there are three components that contribute to low fertility:

1. **Population Dynamics**: caused through the negative momentum (LFT1)
2. **Sociological Reasoning**: declining family size in younger cohorts (LFT2)
3. **Economic Rationale**: increasing expectations of young people and income decline; based on Easterlin's hypothesis (LFT3)

The three components create four reinforcing loops seen in Fig. 2.9. The causal-loop-diagram creates cyclical behavior due to the balancing cycling loop with two important delays. These factors, along with the presented theories, can explain future projections in industrialized countries with a cyclical persistently low level of fertility.

2.2.2 *Mortality*

Mortality is one of the most independent variables in demographics, as there is no direct linkage to other demographic and economic variables. Mortality measures are needed to address various aspects of change, such as the following (Rowland, 2003, p. 193):

- The overall mortality can reveal trends over time and within countries.
- Differences between age groups can be used as a key indicator for transition processes.
- Differences between socio-economic groups show the extent of inequality.

2.2.2.1 Definition

One of the best-known indicators is the **crude death rate** (CDR). It measures the number of deaths to the middle aged population and it is, besides the crude birth rate, on important factor which changes population over time. It is expressed (Rowland, 2003, p. 194):

$$CDR = \frac{D}{P} = \frac{number\ of\ deaths\ in\ a\ year}{mid-year\ population} \tag{2.5}$$

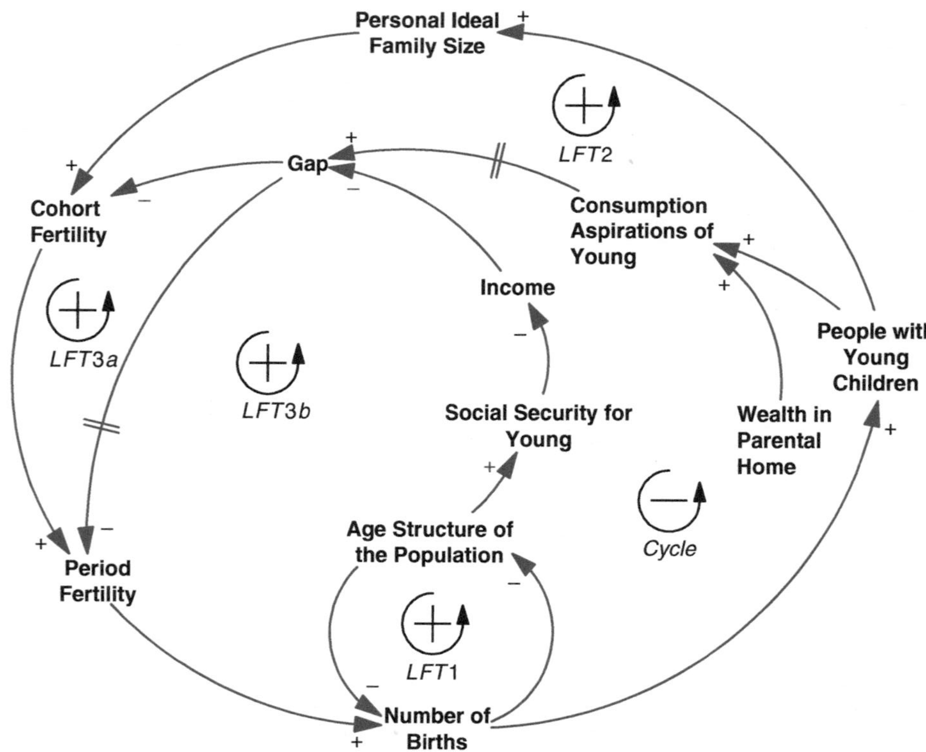

Fig. 2.9 Low fertility trap mechanism
Source: own figure according to Lutz, Skirbekk, & Testa, 2005, p. 11

The crude death rate is used primarily to show long-term trends in mortality. Recently, industrialized countries were able to decrease the overall mortality. In most populations, the **age-specific death rate** (ASDR) follows a U-shape curve. It starts with a relatively high infant mortality rate and declines to its lowest level around the age of 10. After this it rises continuously. Mathematically, the death rate is expressed:

$$\begin{aligned} Age - specific\,death\,rate &= \frac{deaths\,per\,year\,at\,age\,x}{mid - year\,population\,aged\,x} \\ M_x &= \frac{D_x}{P_x} \end{aligned} \tag{2.6}$$

Figure 2.10 represents the 2006 mortality rates in France, sorted by age. It follows the law of mortality proposed by Benjamin Gompertz in 1825. He expressed an exponential increase in death rates. Figure 2.10 is therefore presented in a log-scale. Interestingly, there is a higher mortality between the ages of 15 and 30. This is not a natural, but rather human induced mortality, and primarily caused by motor vehicle accidents (Rowland, 2003, p. 203).

One can easily list additional mortality indicators, such as infant mortality rates or sex specific ratios, but this would go beyond the scope of this work. Nevertheless, one measurement is especially important for countries with low mortality rates, as most industrialized countries are: the **cause-specific death rates** (CSDR). This rate addresses specific health problems. The indicator is age-independent; however, certain illnesses correlate with certain age groups, i.e. degenerative diseases in later life. Further progress in improving survival rates depends on monitoring the causes of death. This also includes identifying social and medical interventions and preventive programs (Rowland, 2003, p. 203). Expressed:

$$\begin{aligned} Cause - specific\,death\,rate &= CSDR \\ &= \frac{deaths\,in\,a\,year\,from\,particular\,cause}{total\,mid - year\,population} \end{aligned} \tag{2.7}$$

Some of the presented key measurements are also part of life tables. These examine:

- Number survived age x
- Probability of dying between age x and age $\times + 1$
- Number of deaths per age
- Average life expectancy

Estimates and projections for various purposes are based on life tables. These life tables are the best-known inventions in demography (Rowland, 2003, p. 266).

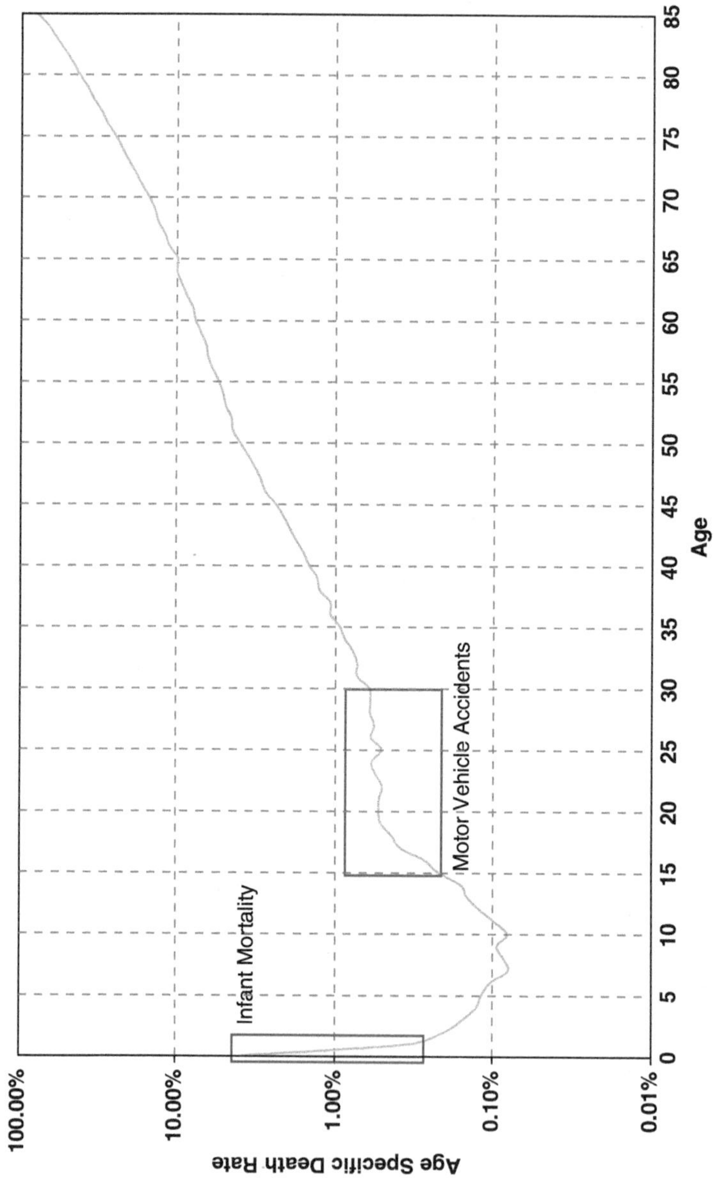

Fig. 2.10 Age-specific death rates
Source: own figure, data: Eurostat

2.2.2.2 Determinants of Mortality

As Amartya Sen wrote, mortality is not in itself an economic phenomenon (1998, p. 3). There is **no economic theory on mortality**. While fertility is based on economic thoughts, mortality seems to be exogenous. Influences that reduce mortality often have distinctly economic causes (Sen, 1998, p. 3).

David Cutler and his colleagues (Cutler, Deaton, & Lleras-Muney, 2006) analyzed the main determinants of mortality. They showed that **nutrition** improves through agricultural yields, which in turn led to greater bacteria resistance. **Public health** improvements are plausible as a factor for mortality decline. This includes macro-components, such as sanitation systems, pasteurizing milk or vaccination programs, but also micro-factors such as changes made by individuals (washing hands, protecting food, healthy lifestyle). **Urbanization** decreases mortality, due to the easier entry of public health systems. **Vaccination** increases the survival rate with a very high impact factor. In addition, vaccination produces positive network effects. **Medical treatments** and development of new therapeutics contribute greatly mortality decline. But this consists of years in good health. **Early life factors** have a positive effect on long-term success. The fetal origins theory supports robust correlations between birth weights and utero-nutrition to mortality rates. It is obvious, however, that early life factors are a proxy for an unknown number of factors. It seems obvious as well that genetic predisposition or parental life style and living environment have an important impact on mortality.

Cutler et al. continued to predict that individuals with lower incomes, lower wealth, lower education levels, or lower social status often die younger than the median group. This is true for many countries and periods. One explanation might be the connection between public access to **medical care** programs. In many cases, this is connected to individual income. But medical healthcare cannot explain everything. Outside of economics, the current dominant theory links poor health to low status and "**psychosocial stress**". Often such persons psychologically assume little control over their own lives. Cumulative distress leads to a rise probability of diseases. Although the exact underlying mechanism is still unclear, it is accepted that **education** leads to mortality decline.

It is also certainly true that personal income is a basic factor for both quality of life and mortality. The **probability of dying** is affected by poverty and economic deprivation (Sen, 1998, p. 5). But as outlined here, it is only one variable.

One can spell that persons with a lower socio-economic status have, on average, a reduced life expectancy, which can explain greater stress levels and lifestyles. Good health correlates with genetic predisposition, lifestyle factors, and a healthy diet, refraining from smoking and excessive alcohol use (Office for Official Publications of the European Communities, 2007, p. 41).

2.2.2.3 Trend and Effects on Mortality

Life expectancy has **changed dramatically** over the past centuries and decades. Thomas Hobbes described the lifestyle of Homo sapiens until the first agricultural revolution in 10,000 B.C. as "nasty, brutish and short" (Hobbes 1998, p. 84). Their life expectancy was about 25 years, which changed little throughout the Roman Empire. Around 1700 the life expectancy of one of the richest nation at this time – England – was only 37 years (Cutler et al., 2006, p. 99). Mortality decline is, therefore, a phenomenon of the modern times, beginning with industrialization and increasing welfare.

The decline in mortality is called **epidemiologic transition** and was first presented in a paper by Abdel Omran (1971, pp. 516–517). He described a three-stage model:

- The **Age of Pestilence and Famine**: life expectancy is low and variable vacillating between 20 and 40 years.
- The **Age of Receding Pandemics**: life expectancy at birth increases steadily to about 50 years.
- The **Age of Degenerate and Man-Made Diseases**: life expectancy raises gradually above 50 years.

As this refers to the past, it is of minor interest to this work. However, in the recent past a fourth stage was added to describe the development in industrialized countries more effectively. Typical for this phase, social and spatial disparities are based on changes in society values. Sometimes this is distinguished by an accelerated and delayed transition (Bähr, 2004, p. 174). The fourth stage – **Age of Delayed Degenerative Diseases** – includes (Rowland, 2003, p. 192):

- Continuing survival, especially in older age groups
- Decline in mortality for certain diseases
- Improved diagnosis and treatment
- Greater role of individual responsiblity
- Rising prevelance of degenerative diseases

The life expectancy for male and female populations differs. Male death rates are generally at least 50% higher than female rates (Keyfitz & Caswell, 2005, p. 71). The effects of the fourth transition stage along with the difference in death rates by sex are illustrated in Fig. 2.11. The figure compares different synthetic generations and their evolution over time. Every generation starts with 100,000 people. One can see that due to the mortality decline, the population is aging and that female mortality rates are lower than that of males.

The trend shows a steady decline in mortality rates (Spiegelman, 1958, p. 32). Sometimes this process is addressed as '**rectangularisation**', due to the increasing U-shape curve. This leads to lower mortality rates for middle aged populations. Thus, most people will die either very young or very old.

The question, therefore, arises: How will late-life mortality develop in the future? Extending life expectancy will present a major impact for economic consequences, i.e. social security system, actuarial calculations or health costs. Figure 2.12 presents the mortality for German males over the last century. The right boundary is of special interest: the late **life mortality rate shows a deceleration**. This does not follow the Gompertz–Makeham-Law, which states that death rates grow exponentially with increasing age (Olshansky & Carnes, 1997, p. 10). It is still in discussion

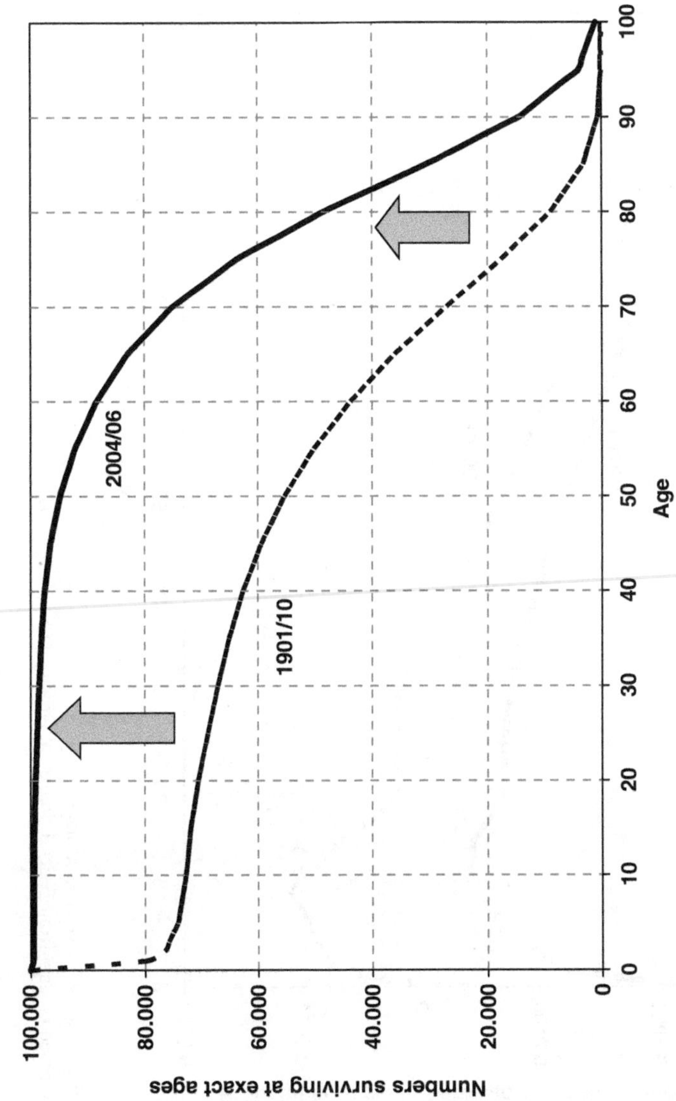

Fig. 2.11 Survivors at exact age
Source: own figure, data: Destatis

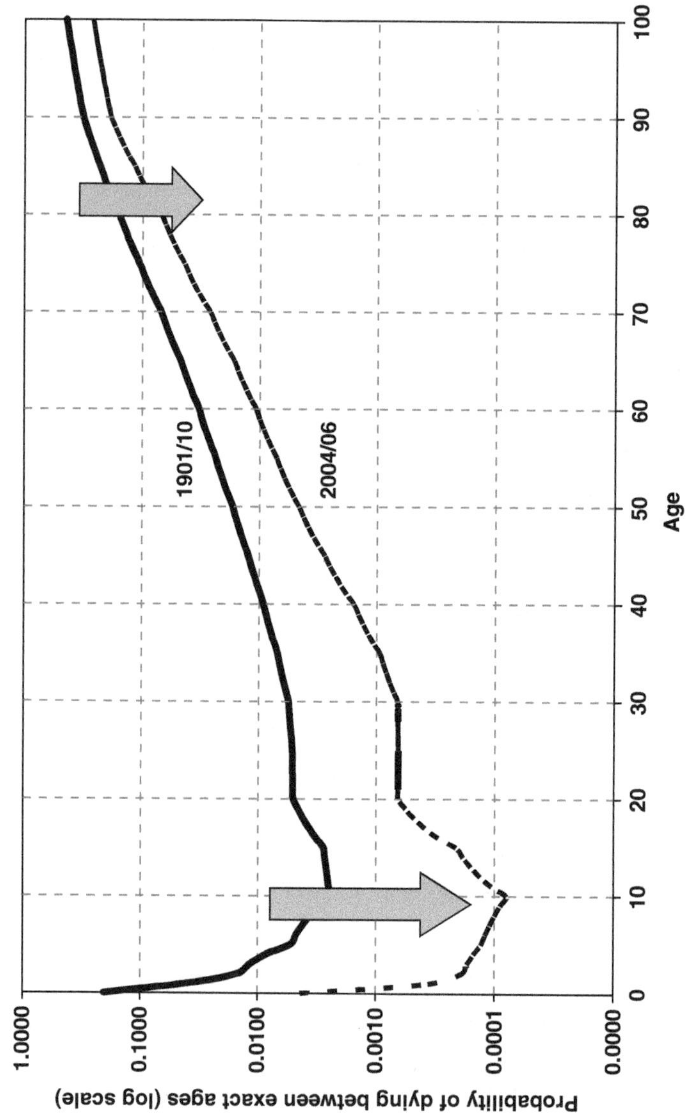

Fig. 2.12 Probability of dying between exact ages
Source: own figure based on data from Federal Statistical Office, 2008

whether there is a limit of life or an extension of life spans throughout the next decades. Empirics predict a decline in late life mortality, as seen in Fig. 2.12 (Office for Official Publications of the European Communities, 2007, p. 40).

2.2.3 Migration

The literature on migration and migration theory is vast and very heterogeneous. As Frank Kalter explained (2000, p. 438) the topic migration is highly interdisciplinary, but every scientific discipline agrees on the prominent impact of migration to a nation. Douglas Massey et al. (Massey, Arango, Hugo, Kouaouci, Pellegrino, & Taylor, 1993) and Gordon DeJong and Robert Gardner (DeJong & Gardner, 1981) presented an extensive overview of migration. Both contributions serve as a good point of departure for further exploration. This subsection concentrates on three different approaches. While the push–pull and the gravity approaches are very macro-economically orientated, the behavioral approach focuses more on the micro-economic level. Macro and micro approaches are so-called traditional views on migration and can still explain migration very precisely. Finally, a new idea of social network and social capital is presented, which is more recent and could explain migration from a sociological perspective.

2.2.3.1 Definition

To correctly define migration one should distinguish it from movement in general. According to Christopher Delbrück and Bernd Raffelhüschen (1993, p. 341) migration is the permanent or semi-permanent change of normal residence for a person, a family, or a household. Depending on the distance of movement, the movement is labeled international, inter-regional, or local migration. Under the term "mobility" the definition of migration is subsumed. Mobility includes circulation, which is defined as daily or weekly commuting. Traditionally, a spatial dimension plays a vital role in analyzing migration. Jürgen Bähr (2004, p. 243) differentiated between domestic and international migration. As the latter, demographic change is based on a macro-economic model, domestic migration is neglected.

Wilbur Zelinsky outlaid his hypothesis of the mobility transition, in which he argued that developing a nation requires changes in general mobility. Zelinsky's five phases are (Zelinsky, 1971, pp. 230–231):

1. **The Premodern Traditional Society**: little residential migration and only limited circulation.
2. **The Early Transitional Society**: massive rural to frontier movements, major outflows of emigrants and significant growth of circulation.
3. **The Late Transitional Society**: further increase in circulation, still strong rural–urban movements and declining emigration.
4. **Advanced Society**: strong urban to urban movement of migrants, significant net immigration of unskilled and semiskilled workers from relatively underdeveloped

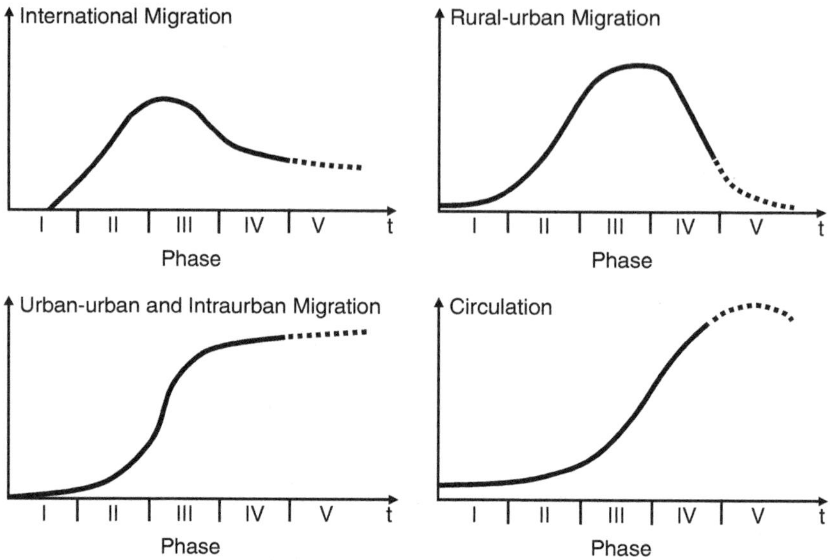

Fig. 2.13 Zelinksy's mobility transition
Source: own figure according to Zelinsky, 1971, p. 233

countries, maybe international migration of professionals, vigorous accelerating circulation.

5. **A Future Super Advanced Society**: almost all domestic migration is interurban and intra-urban, acceleration of circulation, strict political control of movements.

The main idea of Zelinsky's empiric inductive theory connotes a connection between socio-economic development and different mobility patterns. Figure 2.13 presents international migration, rural–urban as well as urban–urban migration, and circulation.

In this hypothesis, several factors, including political factors or specific situations for countries, are not considered. Interdependencies between social, economic and technologic developments are not taken into consideration. Zelinsky's theory is more descriptive and provides no theoretical explanation for the recent changes in migration. With this, the universal transferability is not given (Bähr, 2004, p. 251).

For consistency, some principal migration measures are presented here (Rowland, 2003, p. 397):

$$\begin{aligned} \textit{Rate of net migration} &= \frac{\textit{arrivals} - \textit{departures}}{\textit{population}} \\ \textit{Rate of gross migration} &= \frac{\textit{arrivals} + \textit{departures}}{\textit{population}} \\ \textit{Migration effectiveness ratio} &= \frac{\textit{net migration}}{\textit{gross migration}} \end{aligned} \tag{2.8}$$

Net and gross migrations are easily understandable, where as the effectiveness ratio is more complicated. The migration effectiveness lowers as more people move in and out, known as population redistribution. This ratio provides an overview whether it is a one-way or two-way exchange (Rowland, 2003, p. 400).

The German geographer Ernst G. Ravenstein published two papers both entitled "**Laws of Migration**" (Ravenstein, 1885, pp. 198–199, Ravenstein, 1889, pp. 286–288). He found several so-called "laws", which present rather hypotheses than laws. Ravenstein's main findings could be summarized as follows:

1. Main incentives to move are economic orientated
2. Most of the migration is only short distance
3. Migration often follows in waves
4. The larger the distance of migration the larger the industrial target area
5. The percentage of rural migrants is higher than of urban migrants
6. Most migrants move from rural to urban areas
7. Urban areas grow more through migration than through natural growth
8. Each migration produces a counter migration with opposite direction
9. Women often move short distances
10. Men often moves long distances
11. Families does not migrate as much as singles
12. Migration increases with industrial development and improvement of infrastructure

Ravenstein's ideas continued and built the foundation of later gravity-models, which will be explained in the next section.

2.2.3.2 Macroeconomic Push–Pull and Gravity-Models

Originally, to explain labor migration, the macroeconomic theory of international migration was founded. Migration is caused by the geographic differences in demand and supply of labor. Countries with low capital intensity (K/N) have a low equilibrium market wage, while countries with limited endowments of labor are determined by a high market wage. The resulting differential causes people to migrate from low wage countries to high wage countries. Consequently, it forces the wages to level out until the difference is zero, within a new equilibrium. But the flow of labor in macro-models along skill lines must be clearly recognized and distinct (Massey et al., 1993, p. 433).

This simple and compelling perspective has strongly shaped the intellectual basis for immigration theory. It contains several propositions including (Massey et al., 1993, p. 434):

1. The international migration of workers is caused by wage differences
2. Migration will only occur in the presence of wage differentials
3. Highly skilled workers migrate corresponding to return on human capital and differ from wages of workers

4. Primarily, the labor market induce the flow of labor and other kind of markets do not have an important effect
5. Governments could control migration flows be regulating the labor market

Gravity models borrow the main idea from **Newton's theory on gravity** with two mass points represented by the size of two populations. The distance and other factors construct a force of attraction that represents the migration flow. Stuart Dodd's model is a very good example of this model type (Dodd, 1950). Prior statements go back to George Zipf (1946). The main equation is as follows:

$$I_E = k \cdot T \cdot \frac{I_A \cdot P_A \cdot I_B \cdot P_B}{L} \tag{2.9}$$

The expected interaction I_E depends on a constant k for each type of interaction. T stands for the total time of interacting, L for distance parameter, $I_{A/B}$ for a non-specified per capita activity and finally $P_{A/B}$ for population.

The left model in Fig. 2.14 presents the stock-flow consistent model from Dodd. The two populations are the stocks and the system is a closed system. The migration flow I_E depends on the external factors and the populations. The movement goes only one direction from the less attractive to the higher one. Gravity models belong to the same model family as epidemic models from biology or as the Bass model (Bass, 2004) as an example of diffusion of the word of mouth effect. The right side of Fig. 2.14 shows the evolving behavior of the migration flow and the two populations. Both stocks follow a classic S-shaped curve and indicate the non-linear behavior and the shifting loop dominance. First, the reinforcing loop (indicated by a plus sign) takes over the power as long as the migration reaches its maximum; second, the balancing loop slows down the flow till all people moved from A to B.

Kalter criticized the assumed symmetry in such gravity models. He argued that the paradigm could not explain two flows in different directions; but in reality this happens more frequently than in a single flow. He also mentioned that the static connection between the factors does not explain mechanisms of movement (Kalter, 2000, p. 442).

To overcome this critique, the gravity model can be augmented by push and pull factors. **Push factors**, like high unemployment rates in the home country, increase the migration flow and **pull factors** strengthen the attractiveness. Examples of this are high wage ratios or high employment rates. The central hypothesis of this theory explains that the tendency to migrate increases with the amount on job vacancies, income differences and the number of migrants in the destination country (Haug, 2000, p. 3).

2.2.3.3 Micro-economic Behavioral Models

Adding on to the macro-level migration theory, the micro-economic approach is based on individual choice. Rational actors decide to move because of a personal cost-benefit analysis showing positive returns. International migration

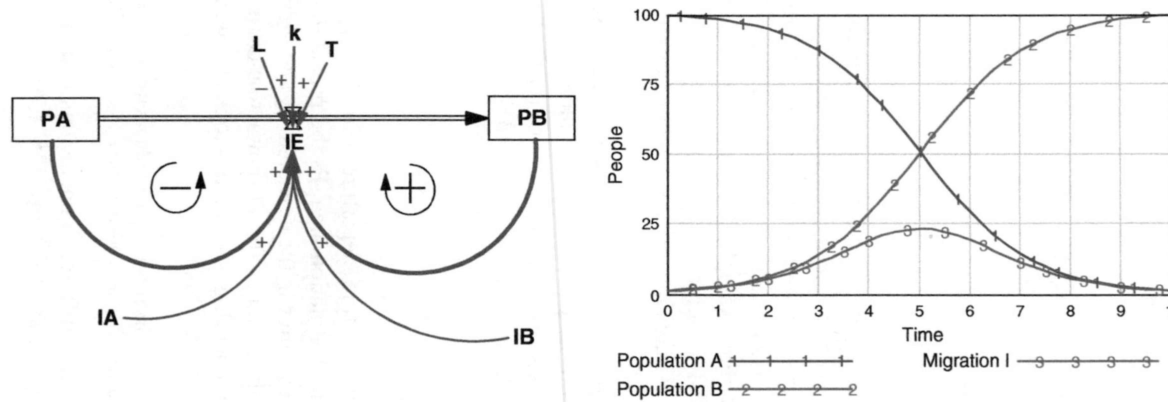

Fig. 2.14 Dodd's gravity model
Source: own figure

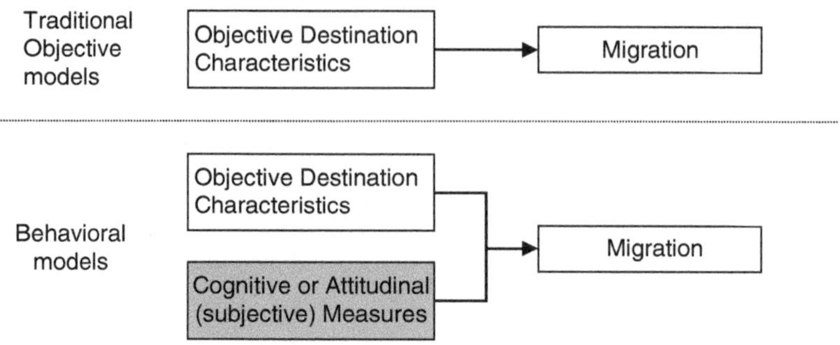

Fig. 2.15 Comparison of macro and micro migration theories
Source: own figure according to Desbarats, 1983, p. 12

thus becomes a theory of investment in human capital. Figure 2.15 shows the difference between the macro- and micro-economic models. In addition to the objective destinations, subjective measures help determine the tendency to migrate. Thus, migration changes with this behavioral approach and sheds a micro-economical view on migration itself. For example, the workers decide to migrate where they can be most productive. But before moving workers must undertake investments, such as, learning a new language, cost of traveling and psychological costs (Massey et al., 1993, p. 434).

The method orientates itself on the **net present value concept** (NPV), by discounting future returns with the probability of obtaining a job and comparing it with the discounted costs. A positive net present value (NPV) forces the worker to move. This is illustrated as (Massey et al., 1993, p. 435):

$$NPV = \int_{0}^{n} [P_1(t) \cdot P_2(t) \cdot Y_d(t) - P_3(t) \cdot Y_o(t)] \cdot e^{-rt} dt - C(0) \tag{2.10}$$

The NPV is calculated just before departure with P_1 as the probability of avoiding deportation from the destination area, P_2 the probability of employment at the destination, Y_d are the earnings in the new area. P_3 and Y_o reflect the income in the home country and finally C stands for all transaction costs.

Larry Sjaastad conducted pioneering work on this topic. He was the first one who argued:

> to treat migration as an investment increasing the productivity of human resources, an investment which has costs and which also renders returns (Sjaastad, 1962, p. 83).

From this framework slightly different conclusions can be compared to the macro-economic focus (Massey et al., 1993, pp. 435–436):

1. Migration stems from different earning and employment rates.
2. Individual characteristics that lower the transaction costs will increase the probability to move.
3. Aggregated migration flows are simple the sum of individual decisions.

4. The size of the differential NPV determines the size of migration.
5. Migration only occurs through differences in the labor market; other markets are not taken into account.
6. Governments control migration mainly through wage policies.

Instead of focusing on individual risks and wage differentials, the new economics of migration orientated itself on households and families. Therefore, a wage differential is not a necessary condition to migrate. Movements occur as a **wish to diversify risks**. An expected gain in income might lead to different effects for households as they could differ on the household income in total. For governments, this perspective unfolds a new policy to control migration flows, via insurance programs. In addition, shaping the income distribution might lead to an increase or decrease in migration if the specific household income (high or low) benefits from subsidies (Massey et al., 1993, pp. 439–440).

A good model, which combines the push–pull theory and microeconomic behavior, goes back to Everett Lee (1966, p. 50). He argued that the decision to migrate depends on:

1. Factors associated to the origin
2. Factors to influence the area of destination
3. Intervening obstacles
4. Personal factors

There are countless influencing factors in the origin and the destination area, as well as obstacles that determine the decision process. But, as Fig. 2.16 shows, certain positive (+), negative (−) or neutral factors (o) push and pull the migration flow. Sonja Haug wrote that the perception of these factors is not relevant in the current state. In addition, she argued that Lee's theory is only a pre-model decision theory, because Lee did not explicitly explain the mechanism of the migration (Haug, 2000, p. 8). But instead Lee derived a hypothesis from his model, which explained migration and counter-migration more accurately. Therefore, Lee's work has had almost the same influence on migration theory as Ravenstein's Law of Migration (Kalter, 2000, p. 453).

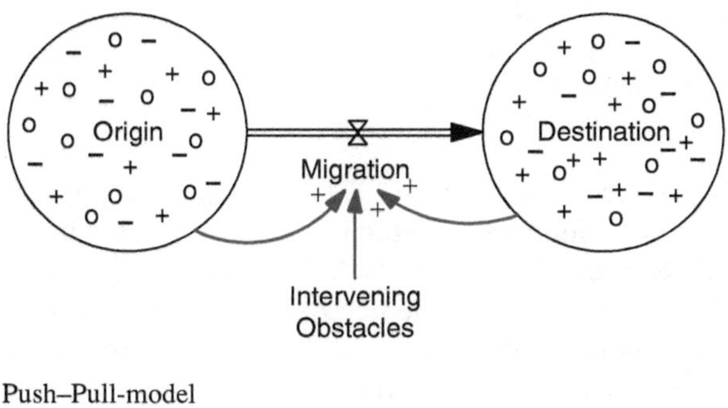

Fig. 2.16 Lee's Push–Pull-model
Source: own figure according to Lee, 1966, p. 50

2.2.3.4 Sociological Considerations

Meso-orientated approaches embellish the migration chains. **Social networking** explains why people tend to move (Haug, 2000, p. 19). Personal relationships between migrants, such as kinship, friendship or shared community in the origin and destination area can increase the probability of moving (Massey, 1990, p. 63). But it is not possible to build up cause and effect chains to explain in detail whether social networks hamper or support migration. Taking this into account, Massey summarized (Massey et al., 1993, pp. 449–450):

1. Migration occurs as long as the network connection is not diffused widely.
2. Sinking costs of migrant networks cover the presence of wage differences in empirics.
3. Once established migration networks deprive of governmental control.

The term **social capital** is closely connected to the term social network. Social capital is the capacity of individuals to make use of resources, such as contacts or information (Haug, 2000, p. 22). It refers to intra- and inter-connections in social networks.

The change of social capital or social networks over time creates **path dependencies** as they connect future events to their own past. The probability of this occurrence depends on the historic path. Myrdal (1957) called this cumulative causation, referring to the fact that each migration act alters the social context and has consequences for additional movements (Massey et al., 1993, p. 451). This could lead to a self-preserving migration effect (Haug, 2000, p. 25).

2.2.3.5 Trend and Effects on Migration

Gordon DeJong and James Fawcett (1981, p. 50) listed the main motives for migration, as:

- Wealth
- Status
- Comfort
- Stimulation
- Autonomy
- Affiliation and
- Morality

Zelinsky's work about mobility (1971) transition implies several **future trends** for certain migration factors, which reflects these main motives. Lawrence Brown and Rickie Sanders (1981, p. 181) deduced from Zelinsky particularly that migration of all social groups will oriented themselves upon job opportunities, in tertiary small and medium enterprises-sectors. Formal communication channels will take on an important role as sources of information and reduce the chain migration. The dominant pattern of migration will be inter- und intra-urban.

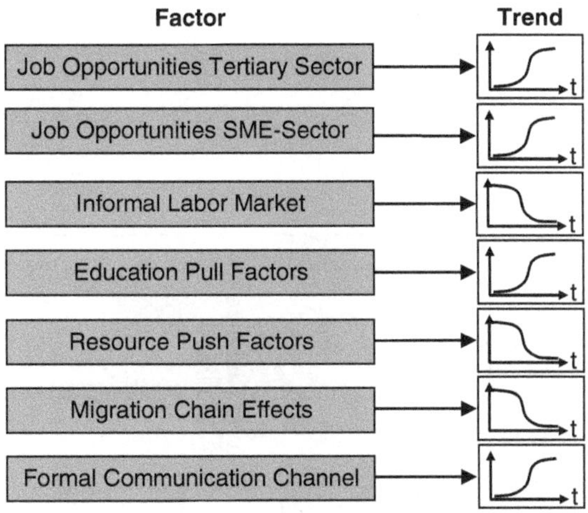

Fig. 2.17 Future trends of mobility pattern
Source: own figure according to Brown & Sanders, 1981, p. 180

Figure 2.17 shows the long-term trend for those factors and illustrates the shifting pattern.

Based on the presented theories one can see that individual motives and the environment influence the migration. In summary, the major movements in migration are presented in Fig. 2.18, containing macro-economic motives, individual motives as well as social motives.

This subsection shows that the economy is one of the major drivers of migration decisions. The Fig. 2.18 shows that economic motives are the key factors for migrating working age population. Hence, this migration flow is very high. If the economic motives ceases then the motives change, e.g. towards family orientation (Harbision, 1981, p. 233).

2.2.4 *Structure*

2.2.4.1 Definition

Population stock is derived from the changes over time from its flows. The stock changes through the flows of births, deaths and migration. The concepts behind the associated flows were previously presented. Population growth is the sum of natural flows and the net migration, seen as (Rowland, 2003, p. 29):

$$\Delta P_t = (B_t - D_t) + M_t \tag{2.11}$$

The population at point t is:

$$P_t = P_0 + \left(\sum_{i=1}^{t} B_i + \sum_{i=1}^{t} D_i \right) + \sum_{i=1}^{t} M_i \tag{2.12}$$

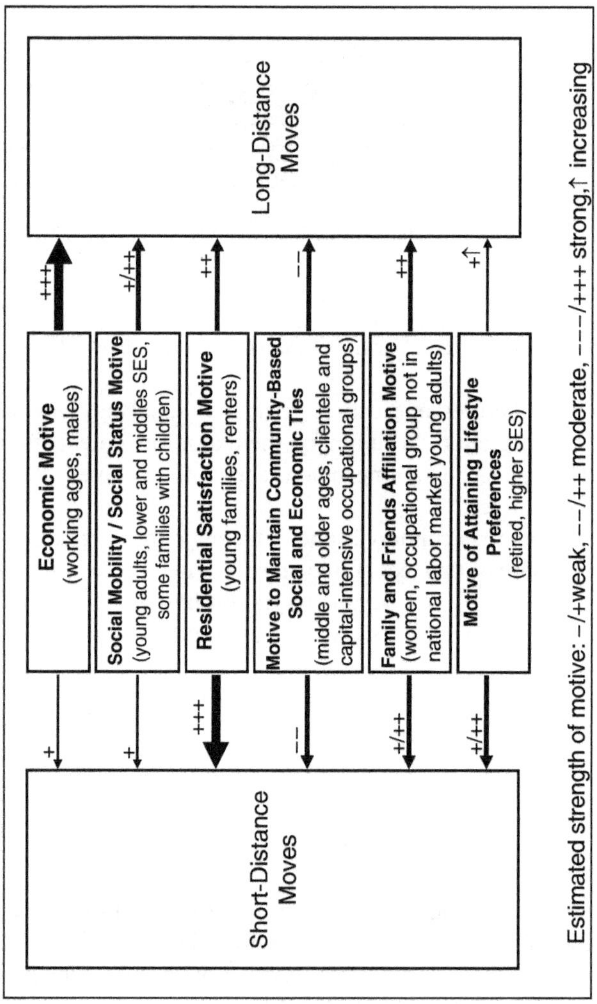

Fig. 2.18 Major Motives of Migration
Source: own figure according to DeJong & Fawcett, 1981, p. 40

Often the population is subdivided further into sex and age groups. All additional projections are always based on the number of women in childbearing age; therefore, it is important to split the population into male and female through a given **sex ratio**:

$$sex\,ratio = \frac{number\ of\ males}{number\ of\ females} \tag{2.13}$$

The sex ratio at birth is estimated 105 boys to 100 girls (about 51% male); however it can differ significantly for later age groups. Very often one assumes, for the sake of clarity, equality.

For economic purposes and further analysis, one can name several important dependency ratios. The denominator can change thereby creating new ratios (Rowland, 2003, pp. 85–86).

The general **dependency ratio** (DR) focuses on the number of children and aged persons in comparison to the working age-group, expressed as:

$$DR = \frac{P_{0-14} + P_{65+}}{P_{15-64}} \tag{2.14}$$

The dependency ratio can be split easily into a **child dependency ratio** (CDR) and an **aged dependency ratio** (ADR). The **economic dependency ratio** (EDR) is closely connected with the activity index and shows how many people depend on one worker. It is defined as:

$$EDR = \frac{total\,population - labor\,force}{labor\,force} \tag{2.15}$$

To compare different economic dependency ratios over time one has to refine the data further. It is worth to note that one can compare the age groups only if there is a causal, economically founded connection (Mueller, 2000, pp. 12–13).

A very interesting, but often unused, indicator stems from Ernst P. Billeter's work (1954). Billeter went one step further with the EDR and divided the population into three groups:

- Pre-productive (**children generation**): age 0–14
- Productive (**parents generation**): age 15–64
- Post-productive (**grandparents generation**): age 65+

The age specification was changed to match the current working situation in industrialized countries. The ratio is defined:

$$J = \frac{P_{0-14} - P_{65+}}{P_{15-64}} \tag{2.16}$$

Billeter measured demographic aging by increasing the post-productive value to the pre-productive value, throughout the parent generation. The nominator becomes negative if the grandparent's generation exceeds the children's generation, as is the case in most industrialized countries. A high negative value characterizes a very aged population. The main advantage of this indicator is the aging index or the share of people aged older 60. In this case, the equation is twofold. First, it includes the whole age spectrum of a population. And second, it is very sensitive to changes in the composition (Luy & Caselli, 2008, p. 10). Billeter's index has a long momentum and spans a connection between the two population extremes. Therefore, it can work as an early indicator for demographic change.

Like the Billeter J, **population momentum** denotes the long-term potential for change in the overall size of a population. Momentum growth was introduced by the famous demographer Nathan Keyfitz (1971). The momentums characterize the potential for growth which is inherent within the population's age structure. The potential to change comes from the age structure. To reveal this, one has to compare the initial population with the stationary population. In a stationary condition, the fertility is at the replacement level, mortality does not change and the net migration equals zero (Rowland, 2003, p. 327). Mathematically, it follows:

$$Momentum = \frac{P_{stationary}}{P_{inital}} \tag{2.17}$$

A declining population results in values between $0<M<1$, whereas a growing population has values greater 1.

2.2.4.2 Population Pyramids

Population pyramids connect age groups and sex differentiation. They are the most important and often visualized figures of age structures und population projections. One can distinguish stable, growing, and shrinking populations. From the shape and the differences between male and female, one can deduct information about the structure and near dynamic transformation of the population (Mueller, 2000, pp. 16–17).

The following Fig. 2.19 is taken from Rowland (2003, p. 99) and is presented here as summary.

One cannot determine use the pyramid's shape to determine if the population is stable, growing or shrinking. However, the shape is influenced by mortality, fertility and migration. Demographic transitions, fertility and mortality are linked, with a certain time lag, to a net change. Under the assumption of non-excessive migration, this creates a very stable pattern. Thus, the pyramid shape is associated with developing countries, whereas bell shapes are connected to maturing industrialized countries. The last one leads later to the shape or an urn, as a symbol for shrinking (dying) societies.

2.2.4.3 Malthusian Growth Model

In 1798, Thomas Malthus was probably the first to present a theoretical relationship between population growth and economic development (Malthus, 1826). His idea

Young	Broad-based, triangular age profiles with high proportions of children and high fertility and high mortality.	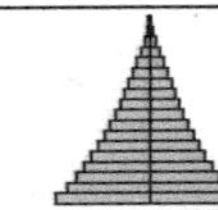
Very Young	Very broad-based, triangular profile with very high proportion of children, associated with large families and declining mortality	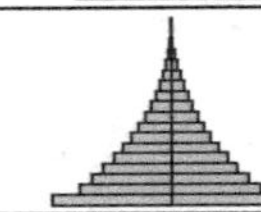
Mature	Transitional between young and old types of profile but still with a relatively high representation of children	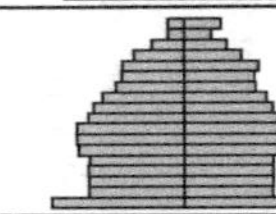
Old	Rectangular age profile with similar numbers in each age group up to those where mortality is high, indicates low birth and death rates	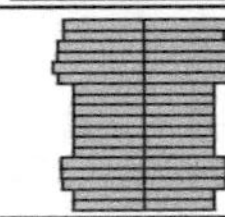
Undercut	Appreciable deficit in the child age groups such as arising from a recent decline in the birth rate	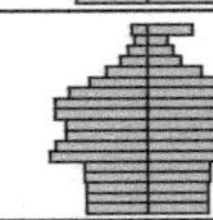
Declining	Numbers and proportions diminish through younger age groups, denoting long-run persistence of low fertility, negative population momentum	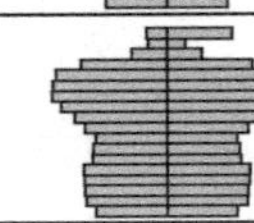
Unimodal	Pronounced peak in one age group or a number of adjacent groups, pattern can arise from inward migration of young adults	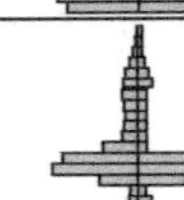

Fig. 2.19 Population pyramids
Source: own figure according to Rowland, 2003, p. 99

of **constraint growth** has endured until today. Malthus' system dynamic perspective led him remarkably close to the explicit feedback structure (Richardson, 1999, p. 66). An extremely famous neo-Malthusian Growth model is WORLD3. The model is presented in the book "The Limits to Growth" by Donella Meadows, a research group led by Jay W. Forrester (Meadows, 1972; Randers, & Meadows, 2004). Forrester published in 1971 a scientific predecessor entitled "World Dynamics" (Forrester, 1971). This World3 model adopts the assumption of constraint growth.

Malthus postulated the tendency for populations to grow geometrically and for fixed factors, such as land, food supplies to grow with an arithmetic rate. Because of the food supply, which cannot grow as fast as the population, the per capita incomes have the tendency to fall, which, in turn, can lead to a stable population. One can only prevent this through moral constraint and by limiting parents' own progeny. Malthus' idea led to the phrase **'low-level equilibrium population trap'**, sometimes also referred to as the **Malthusian population trap** (Todaro & Smith, 2006, p. 278).

Figure 2.20 shows the feedback structure for the Malthusian population trap. Malthus identified three negative loops, which control the reinforcing birth loop. The ability of land to support population growth is regulated by two mechanisms (Richardson, 1999, p. 67):

- Preventive checks: societal responses to control birth
- Positive checks: all things that shorten life

The right section of Fig. 2.20 shows the population development. Without checks, the population would continue to grow exponentially, however the balancing loops gain power over time and lead to a declining net growth rate.

Malthus' idea was criticized for three major reasons (Todaro & Smith, 2006, pp. 280–282):

1. It does not take into account the impact of technological progress.
2. The macro relationship between population growth and income per capita was empirical rejected (Huinink, 2000, p. 343).
3. It is focused on per capita income that would be actually a microeconomic founded household orientated income.

Despite the criticism Malthus received his implicit feedback structure is fundamentally sound (Richardson, 1999, p. 66).

Founded on the Malthusian population trap, the research group under the supervision of Jay W. Forrester at the MIT developed **a model to simulate world changes**. The "Limits to Growth" book for the Club of Rome raised in the 1970s a long ongoing debate about ecological sustained growth and possible limitation factors. The book was published in an extremely interesting time when the traditional economic theory failed to explain 'new' problems like stagflation (Moll, 1991, p. 124). The authors projected, in 12 scenarios, possible patterns of behavior for a large number of variables. Most well-known is the scenario on overshoot and collapse (Meadows et al., 2004, p. xi).

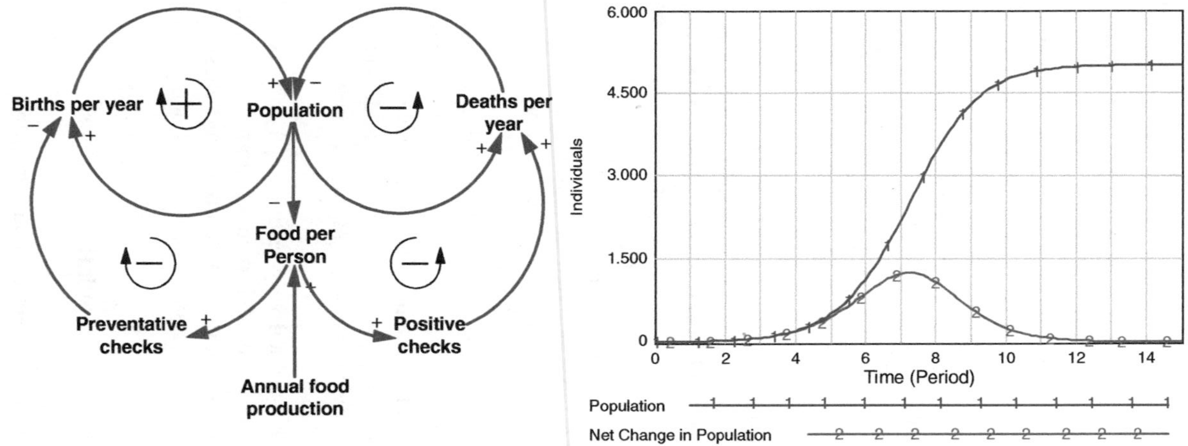

Fig. 2.20 Malthus' theory of population growth
Source: own figure according to Richardson, 1999, p. 68

The main population pattern from demographers is based on Malthus' ideas. Figure 2.21 shows a slightly modified causal-loop-diagram, were some variables are omitted for clarification. The loop structure is similar to Malthus and the idea of mismatch of resources to their extensive usage. Meadows et al. added a variable "service capital" which affects births via a second accelerating loop. The idea on preventive and positive checks can therefore be found the World3 model.

The main criticism for the book was the missing explanation of the depletion of resources. More importantly, the World3-model vastly underestimates the role of technology. To abandon the key factors of economic growth and substitute them with the concept of a comprehensive economy was seen as simply impossible. A free market economy would adjust via a price mechanism at the beginning of resource scarcity. In addition, this would stimulate research in technology and would enable future progress (Moll, 1991, pp. 116–117).

However, the objection made by economists has some serious flaws. Backing the idea of technological progress is the assumption of infinite substitution (Moll, 1991, pp. 117–118). The question of technology's role for growth has to be answered. Contrary to the extremely optimistic view with a never-ending technological progress, a growing community founds their growth models on neo-malthusian ideas. They gain support from the recent discussion on climate change. Nevertheless, there are few additional objections to the model. First of all, it is not presented in an easy-to-read fashion and for many it works as a **black box**. Secondly, and much more dangerous, are scientific arguments to the book. The presented connections are only justified through **logical deduction** without presenting the founding theories first. However, a more detailed description can be found in the World Dynamics book, where especially economists will found macro and micro founded explanations for the model behavior (Forrester, 1971).

The book "The Limits of Growth" has changed the way in which one can look at the world. It presents clearly new questions about nature, growth and industrialization. There are **two essential messages**: On the one hand, one has to look at global problems and their interconnection. On the other hand, one has to start thinking seriously about global environment problems in connection with economic planning (Moll, 1991, p. 121).

The World3 model was outlined very briefly, as it is one of very few examples that embed population structural models in an economic framework. Unfortunately, the model is too simple when looking at demographic questions, and thus cannot work as an enhanced model in economic growth and demography.

2.2.4.4 Trends and Effects on Population Structure

The population structure changes over time and is influenced only by the associate flows of births, deaths and migration. Future development, therefore, depends on trends of fertility, mortality, and migration. The changes will depend on the current structure and they will be more incremental than radical. Indicators with long-term perspectives, such as the momentum or the **Billeter J**, can indicate

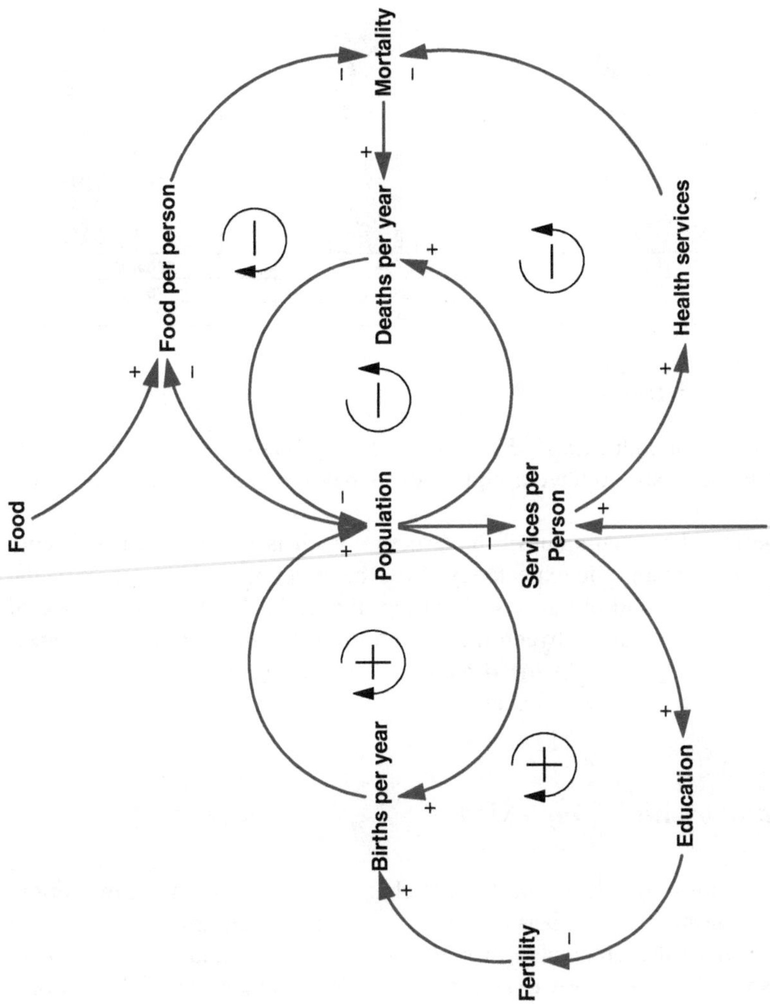

Fig. 2.21 Limits to growth: population sector
Source: own figure according to Meadows et al., 2004, pp. 142–145

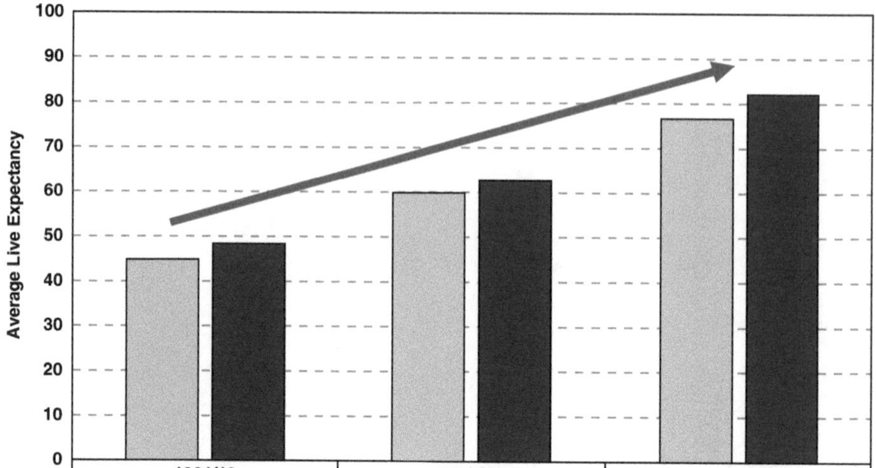

	1901/10	1932/34	2004/06
Men	44.82	59.86	76.64
Women	48.33	62.81	82.08

Fig. 2.22 Increasing life expectancy
Source: own figure, data: Destatis

future directions. For industrialized countries, facing the so-called demographic change it is characteristic to have a high dependency ratios and a strong negative Billeter J.

The only effect that occurs out of the structure itself is aging, as it is evolving over time. With increasing life expectancy rates, the effect of aging increases as the spread between young and old grows over time. Figure 2.22 shows the change of life expectancy in Germany between the beginning of the last century and today. The indicators already point in the direction of further development; the aging process will increase this development.

2.2.5 *Summary and Conclusion*

This chapter examines the determinants that change fertility, mortality, migration, and the population structure. This is important, as later scenarios may change those determinants. This subchapter also provides a theoretical foundation. The main theoretical aspect focuses on few examples of current behavior from industrialized countries to show significant patterns. This differs to other literature, which is devoted to demographic effects.

The theories on fertility are numerous. In addition to the important economic theory from Becker and Barro, the biographic theory of Birg and the Easterlin hypothesis were presented. Figure 2.23 provides a concentrated view on the main factors from those theories and how they individually affect fertility. The above presented indicators are displayed to the right of fertility. The main factors are

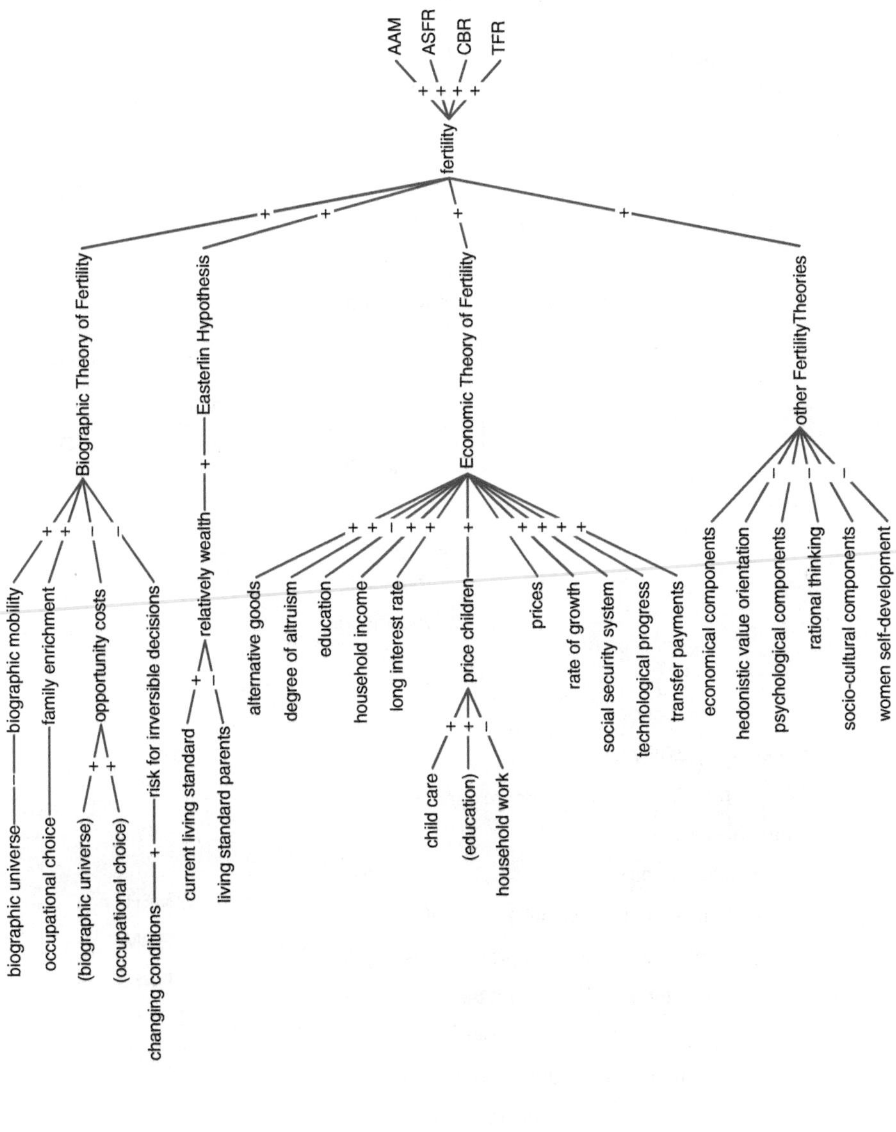

Fig. 2.23 Determinants of fertility
Source: own figure

household income and other economic factors. All components increase the fertility except opportunity costs, risk for irreversible decisions, education or change of women values.

Mortality is a very non-economic population determinant. As Fig. 2.24 shows, mortality is mainly affected by medical health factors. There is also a strong connection between health and economic situations. Often a high personal income can lead to extra individual health effects.

The literature on migration is vast, but unfortunately no theory can consistently explain all of the major motives to move. This is not surprising because there are so many different reasons for people to change their place of residence. Very often

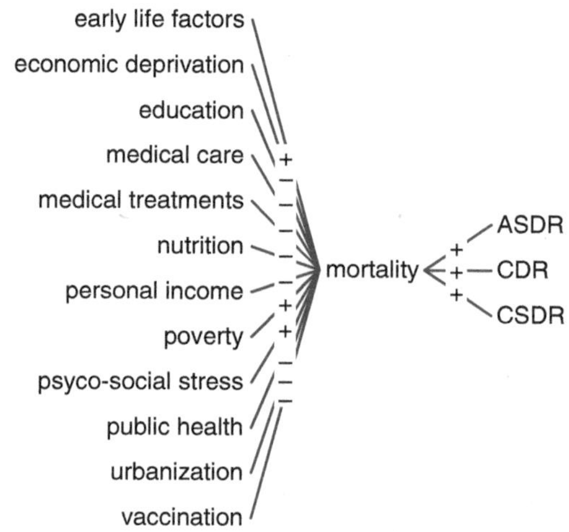

Fig. 2.24 Determinants of mortality
Source: own figure

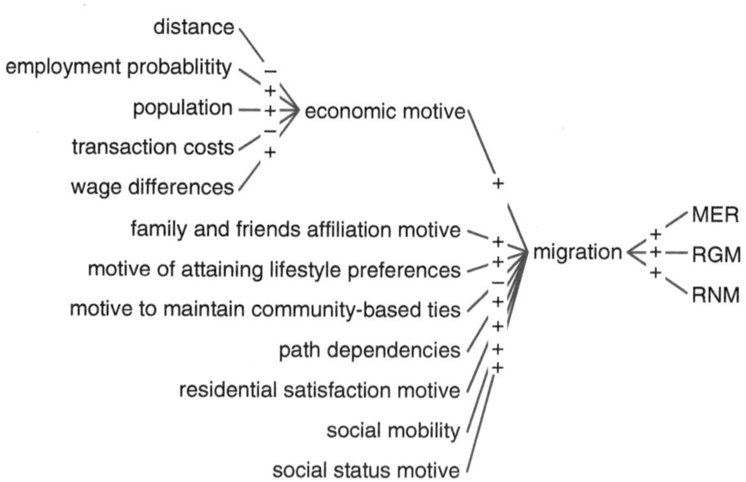

Fig. 2.25 Determinants of migration
Source: own figure

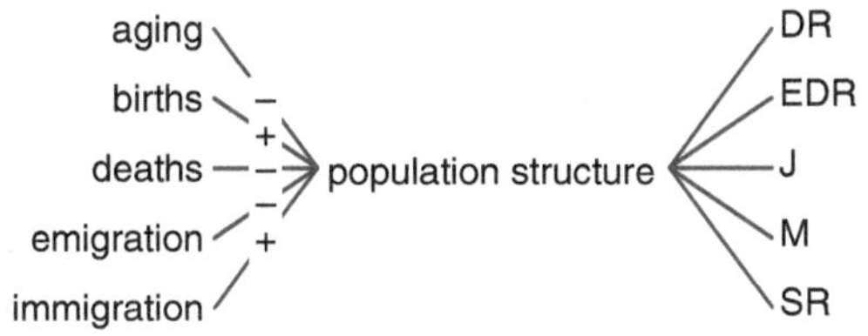

Fig. 2.26 Determinants of population structure
Source: own figure

economic motives foster intentions to move, but one should not underestimate social and cultural motives. Figure 2.25 shows a representative summery of these major motives.

Finally, the population structure itself is investigated and the main determinants are shown in Fig. 2.26. As mentioned, the structure changes either through aging or through their associated flows. The population structure is often used in the literature to present future conditions and for presenting population pyramids and dependency ratios. Aging is special, as seen through the long demographic lags, and the future aging effects are latently within the current structure. Population pyramids are a good way to visualize this.

2.3 Economic Effects

Demographic changes have various effects on the economy. Since a population consists of people and an economy needs people to produce and consume, the number of economic interdependencies are innumerable. Consequently, the effect of an aging and shrinking society changes the intensity of these effects and thereby influences many economic factors. This subchapter outlines important economic impacts, which will be integrated later in the simulation model.

2.3.1 Financial Sector

2.3.1.1 Lifecycle Hypothesis of Consumption

The hypothesis for lifecycle consumption goes back to the Nobel Prize awarded Franco Modigliani for his papers on consumption analysis and lifecycle considerations (Modigliani & Brumberg, 1954; Ando & Modigliani, 1963). The concept of the lifecycle hypothesis implies that **aging may affect saving rates**. While this might be true, it should be considered that numerous other factors can also influence saving patterns throughout a lifetime. Empirical studies looking at both an aging population and income trends can accurately represent rates of uncertainty, liquidity constraints or public saving developments (Mc Morrow & Roeger, 2004, p. 31; Brugiavini, 2002, p. 14).

The success of the lifecycle hypothesis is built on **microeconomic grounding** and a **solid empirical explanation** (Mc Morrow & Roeger, 2004, p. 34). Ralf

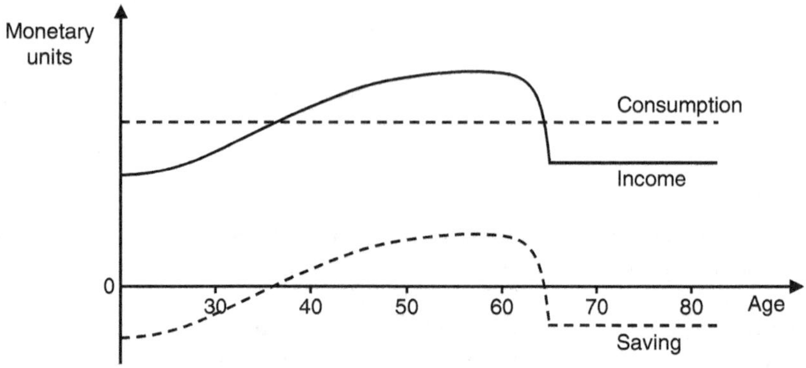

Fig. 2.27 Consumption and saving patterns
Source: own figure according to Börsch-Supan, Coppola, Essig, Eymann, & Schunk, 2008

Rodepeter presented the lifecycle hypothesis and consumption decisions in his book "Consumption and Saving Decision in Lifecycle" (Rodepeter, 2000, pp. 8–9). He explained that economic subjects maximize their utility under the constraint of their assets. Individuals desire to smooth their lifetime consumption and even-out cyclical income fluctuations in order to provide the fundamental effect for savings over their lifespan (Mc Morrow & Roeger, 2004, p. 33). While, income (including transfer payments) increases the individual's current assets, consumption acts as the asset stock's outflow. The development over time is shown in Fig. 2.27. The saving will increase if income increases. Usually, the saving ratios after retirement are assumed to be negative. But empirics show that saving ratios in some countries are positive even after retirement, however, in this case, they are lower than during working age (Matthes & Römer, 2004, p. 315).

Depending on the individual assets, an interest rate is paid as either a credit or a debit rate. Savings are defined as the change in the asset stock between two periods. Thus, the rational acting subjects do not hold any assets beyond their death. One can write (Rodepeter, 2000, pp. 8–9):

$$A_{t+1} = A_t(1 + r) + Y_t - C_t \tag{2.18}$$

Assuming a perfect capital market, with equal debit and credit rates, the discounted consumption equals the income over lifespan and an initial asset value with:

$$\sum_{t=1}^{T} C_t(1 + r_t)^{-t+1} = A_0 + \sum_{t=1}^{T} Y_t(1 + r_t)^{-t+1} \tag{2.19}$$

Usually, the lifecycle model assumes a utility function, which is either a time additive or inter-temporal separable. The total utility adds up to the sum of all discounted period utilities as:

$$U = \sum_{t=1}^{T} u_t(C_t)(1 + \rho)^{-t+1} \tag{2.20}$$

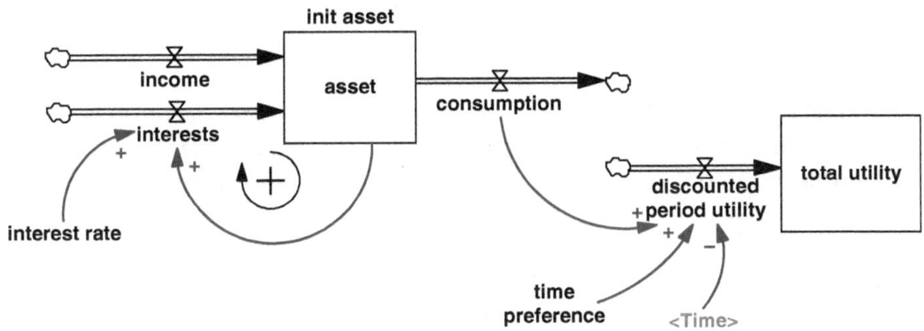

Fig. 2.28 Lifecycle hypothesis
Source: own figure

One can also merge the utility function and the lifecycle hypothesis into a stock-flow-chart as presented in Fig. 2.28. The exogenous variable, which determines the utility function, is income Y which can individually be influenced over time. All other exogenous factors are immutable.

Kieran McMorrow and Werner Roeger analyzed two other concepts of saving patterns over time in 2004 (Mc Morrow & Roeger, 2004, p. 33). One is referred to as the **bequest model**, where it is assumed that the time horizon for optimization is not ones individual life span, but rather a multi-generational timeframe with strong links of the current generation to their descendants. In most cases, this approach focuses on two generations or an infinite period of time. The second theory argues that the main motive to hold savings is future uncertainties, like unpredictable fluctuations or disruptions in income. In this case, the accumulated assets have the function of a **buffer stock**. A buffer stock helps to smooth uncertain income over time. Thus, it is intuitive that the buffer is associated with uncertainties and will decline if income rises.

Besides the plausible idea of a permanent income, the lifecycle hypothesis fails to implement both income uncertainty and the buffer stock savings. The theory assumes highly rational and perfect forward-looking consumers to appropriately compensate for their lifetime consumptions. However, a substantial number of individuals do not have perfect foresight due to (McMorrow & Roeger, 2004, p. 34):

- The uncertainty of future wealth calculations and income flows which make individuals more risk averse
- The use of more simple rules of thumb such as monitoring buffer stocks

Since the lifecycle model can be extended to implement bequest motives, Agar Brugiavini replied to the model critics:

> The lifecycle theory is "flexible enough to allow for numerous generalizations, it is coherent with the literature on labor supply and portfolio choices, and it produces a number of interesting implementations" (Brugiavini, 2002, p. 10).

2.3.1.2 Ricardian Equivalence and Saving Patterns

In addition to population trends and income developments, the Ricardian equivalence is the third largest factor effecting saving patterns (McMorrow & Roeger, 2004, p. 32). If one talks about future saving patterns, especially linked to aging, one has to consider the equivalence proposition as it can effect saving patterns significantly.

The idea of an equivalence of household savings and governmental transfers goes back to the neoclassical economist David Ricardo. More present is the explanation by Robert Barro in the Journal of Political Economy (Barro, 1974). The **Ricardo–Barro equivalence proposition** postulates that foresight oriented households can deduce the consequences of present governmental transfers towards households if this is financed with an increase in public debt. The present public debt will be paid back with future taxes so that the today's national debt equals future taxes.

Figure 2.29 shows the effect within a standard diagram. One can see that a government induced increase in investments (step one) will lead to an increase in national savings. Directly thereafter an increase in the saving ratio follows (step two). If step two equals step one, than neither crowding-out nor crowding-in has occurred.

The Ricardian equivalence makes an important causal link, while taking demographic effects into account. The theory states that if a government sees the need for action to control the demographic transition process, it will induce a sudden response in households. Both **effects neutralize each other**. A shift of burden towards the future generation is, therefore, not possible. In the long run, deficit financing often increases the ratio of government outlays to the GDP. A decline in the investment ratio eventually causes the capital stock to decrease (Cezanne, 2005, pp. 460–461).

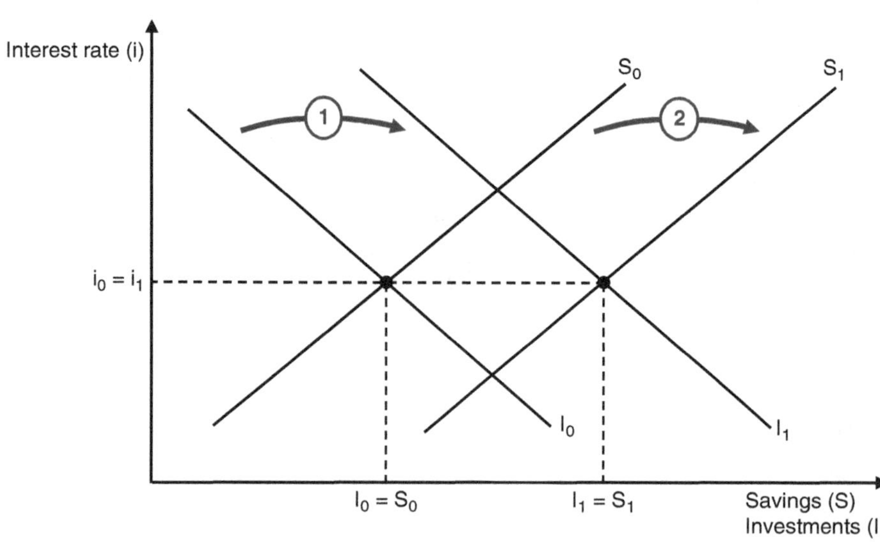

Fig. 2.29 Ricardian equivalence
Source: own figure

Section 2.3.1.1 stated that empirics do not show a negative saving ratio for elderly people. Another explanation for this lifecycle hypothesis, in a contradicting case, is when one assumes intergenerational, dynastic acting people. In this case, the Ricardian equivalence would demand that the economic subject raise the households saving ratio.

2.3.1.3 Rate of Return and Asset Meltdown Hypothesis

The role of capital markets is significant – especially in global aging – because capital moves across most countries without friction. International factor mobility diversifies demographic risks and is just as important as inter-temporal and intergenerational shift of resources (Börsch-Supan, 2004, pp. 26–27).

During a demographic transition, the returns on real capital and interests might decline. The index shares, and therefore the company value, may also **decrease substantially** (asset meltdown) on the stock market. Scientific literature, however, reveals no consensus regarding this effect (Börsch-Supan, 2004, p. 36). Expected returns proposed in the past will have to be adjusted downwards. Thus, a change towards higher stock shares in pension scheme portfolios can lead to lower return rates on assets than expected (Matthes & Römer, 2004, p. 303).

At the first glance, it seems obvious that under normal market conditions, with declining savings (capital supply), the real interest rates must rise, but as the behavior of the capital demand (investments) remains, it becomes unclear and the overall market reaction becomes difficult to determine (Matthes & Römer, 2004, p. 303).

A decline in real interest rates may follow from two considerations (Matthes & Römer, 2004, pp. 304–305):

- A declining population may lead to an obsolete capital stock, as it is not longer necessary to last machines, buildings or other facilities.
- The sales potential may decline with shrinking population. This is only to some extent implemented in neoclassical theories. Theoretically unutilized capital is easily rededicated to production factor labor.

The asset meltdown hypothesis assumes a declining rate on return for assets due to an **exceeding stock supply**. Thus, the stock prices will decline in the future. This is founded in the liquidation of portfolios in favor bond certificates to decrease price risks.

Conventionally, economists use closed-economy models to predict the effect of a possible asset meltdown. However, this overlooks the important fact of international capital flows under global aging (Börsch-Supan, 2004, p. 36). Thus, this perspective on the stock market may be too simplistic for the following reasons: (Matthes & Römer, 2004, p. 307):

- A change in **pension systems** may increase the saving ratio. This would lead to an additional stock demand.
- The **supply of stocks** alters depending on investing propensity or the costs of financing.

A valid prediction is therefore not possible, but eventually, the stock price depends on real economic price and the company value. However, if the demographic change affects the economy and thereby shrinks the earnings outlook, then the stock market may react with declining prices (Bräuninger, Gräf, Gruber, Neuhaus, & Schneider, 2002, p. 41). Capital markets will anticipate the demographic change, which will lead to gradually declining and noticeable effects on the capital markets (Matthes & Römer, 2004, p. 308).

If one talks about diversifying capital investments in order to overcome the demographic change, then one encounters the famous paradox of international capital investment – the **Feldstein–Horioka-Puzzle** (Feldstein & Horioka, 1980). Martin Feldstein and Charles Horioka analyzed domestic investments and national savings showing that about 90% of the domestic investments are financed by savings from the home country (Feldstein & Horioka, 1980, p. 321). Theoretically, in an open economy, capital is invested in countries with the highest return. This would be independent from geographical aspects. Later empirical analysis came to lower percentages, but the puzzle still exists and differs from textbook theories.

2.3.1.4 Trends

A decline in savings leads, by definition, to a decline in investments. This is true only for a closed economy. The link is disconnected in an open economy where capital is internationally mobile (Börsch-Supan, 2004, p. 30).

There are several mechanisms through which a population's age may affect private saving patterns. Mc Morrow and Roeger (2004, p. 35) distinguished the following:

- On the one hand **savings may increase** by forward looking households in working age. Also fewer dissaving of elderly people could support this.
- On the other hand **savings may decline** in the future because the share of low savings retirees increase or labor income is expected to be higher.

Nevertheless, the extrapolation of future saving patterns could be defective, because there is no reference mode for the unique event of demographic shifting (Matthes & Römer, 2004, p. 301). Therefore, the projection is only possible under the assumption of high uncertainty.

But savings also depends on interest rates. The overall net effect could easily be positive or negative depending on a change of the inter-temporal elasticity of substitution of period incomes (time preference) (Mc Morrow & Roeger, 2004, p. 35). Scientific literature shows different saving profiles for countries and that resaving is country specific and not a general phenomenon (Börsch-Supan, 2004, p. 32). Further reading on empirical effects of demographic change and saving behavior can be found in the article by James Poterba (2001).

The saving ratio will decline for OECD countries with an aging population. On the example from Germany, Boersch-Supan et al. (2002) showed in their model a leveling of the saving ratio. The effect of a lower saving ratio will take place 30 years from today (Börsch-Supan, Ludwig, & Winter, 2002, p. 79). Additionally, one must note that savings patterns may differ for models within closed economies.

The decline in the capital market can – even if it shows no demographic aging – be absorbed or withheld within an open capital market. This makes it possible to participate in countries with fewer demographic challenges. However, the investment in foreign countries may be associated with unpredictable risks (Matthes & Römer, 2004, p. 319).

2.3.2 *Labor Market*

When dealing with economic consequences of a demographic change, one comes, inevitably, into a discussion about the labor market. This section recalls some major facts and interdependencies of labor markets by analyzing the effects of labor demands and labor supplies. The effect on labor productivity and skills are elaborated in Sect. 2.3.3.

2.3.2.1 General Observations

By definition, the output of labor supply and population can be connected with the tautological expression (Leibfritz & Roeger, 2008, pp. 36–37; Cezanne, 2005, p. 502):

$$
\begin{aligned}
Y &\equiv Y \cdot \frac{L}{L} \cdot \frac{E}{E} \cdot \frac{N_{LF}}{N_{LF}} \cdot \frac{N_{WA}}{N_{WA}} \cdot \frac{N}{N} \\
Y &\equiv \underbrace{\frac{Y}{L}}_{p} \cdot \underbrace{\frac{L}{E}}_{h} \cdot \underbrace{\frac{E}{N_{LF}}}_{e} \cdot \underbrace{\frac{N_{LF}}{N_{WA}}}_{a} \cdot \underbrace{\frac{N_{WA}}{N}}_{d} \cdot N
\end{aligned}
\tag{2.21}
$$

with:

- $Y/L = p$ = labor productivity per hour
- $L/E = h$ = hours worked per worker
- $E/N_{LF} = e$ = employment rate
- $N_{LF}/N_{WA} = a$ = labor force participation rate (activity index)
- $N_{WA}/N = d$ = share of working age population in total population

By taking logs and derivation one can proxy the income growth in:

$$
\frac{\dot{Y}}{Y} = \frac{\dot{p}}{p} + \frac{\dot{h}}{h} + \frac{\dot{e}}{e} + \frac{\dot{a}}{a} + \frac{\dot{d}}{d} + \frac{\dot{N}}{N} \tag{2.22}
$$

Transposing to the growth rate of employment and minor rearranging delivers:

$$\frac{\dot{e}}{e} = \underbrace{\left(\frac{\dot{Y}}{Y} - \frac{\dot{p}}{p} - \frac{\dot{h}}{h}\right)}_{\textit{labor demand}} - \underbrace{\left(\frac{\dot{a}}{a} + \frac{\dot{d}}{d} + \frac{\dot{N}}{N}\right)}_{\textit{labor supply}} \tag{2.23}$$

According to Wolfgang Cezanne (2005, pp. 502–503), the employment rate changes if the growth in labor demand exceeds that of labor supply. **Labor demand** itself results positively if the growth rate of an economy – corrected by productivity increase and hours worked – is positive. Growth also generates employment. The second bracket term shows the growth of **labor force potential**. This term increases if the population, the share of working age, or the labor force participation increases. In general it is important to note, that all effects could compensate each other.

To evaluate the **demographic effect** one can analyze a simple tautological equation. As the society ages and shrinks one can assume that the growth rates of both d and N are negative. This implies that the labor force participation stays constant and the growth rate is zero, as long as there are no policy changes. Thus, the right bracket term will be negative and the total demand of labor force supply will decline. The left bracket term will probably fall around zero. This is due to the observed effect of low growth rates for industrialized countries and a low, but continuous productivity increase (The German Council of Economic Experts, 2007, p. 451). Both effects often compensate each other.

The **total effect on employment rate** will be positive, mainly because of the declining labor supply. This observation, of course, is very simplistic, particularly in regard to the high level of aggregation of different skills. The following section will address this in greater detail.

2.3.2.2 Labor Supply

The supply of labor is determined by a joint decision amongst family members from the same household. Each person must decide to either work or enjoy non-wage-paying alternatives. The aggregate supply is the sum of all households in an economy (Abel, Bernanke, & McNabb, 1998, p. 84). The neoclassical paradigm, with perfect competition, also assumes a price taking household. By choosing the appropriate labor supply, the household maximizes their utility, even under constraints. Mathematically, one can write (Wohltmann, 1994, pp. 309–311):

$$\begin{aligned} \max. \rightarrow U &= U\big(\overset{(+)}{F}, \overset{(+)}{Y}\big) \\ cond.\ W \cdot N_{LF} &= P \cdot Y \\ N_{LF} + F &= Z \end{aligned} \tag{2.24}$$

with:

- F = leisure
- Y = income
- W = nominal wage

- N_{LF} = labor supply
- P = price level
- Z = total available time

Solving the equation by using Lagrange algorithm one gets the well-known optimization condition:

$$\frac{\partial U/\partial F}{\partial U/\partial Y} = \frac{W}{P} \qquad (2.25)$$

If the **marginal rate of substitution equals that of the real wage**, than the labor supply has reached an optimum. Besides the challenges for corner solutions (negative correlation between wage and income) one can derive the aggregated labor supply curve for an economy in a real wage-labor-diagram. An increase in wage can lead to an increase in labor supply, because with a higher income, a higher indifference curve is possible.

Figure 2.30 represents the main dependencies in a combined diagram: On the left, a classical diagram of the labor market with a highlighted labor supply curve and on the right a causal-loop-diagram of the driving force behind. The major loop characterizes **labor-wage-connection**. If labor supply rises than the labor supply curve shifts to the right and wage decreases. But if wages increase than the burden to work declines and therefore labor supply increases.

Much more fascinating for the demographic analysis are the external factors. There are (Abel et al., 1998, pp. 85–88):

- Wealth
- Expected future wages
- Working-age-population
- Participation rate

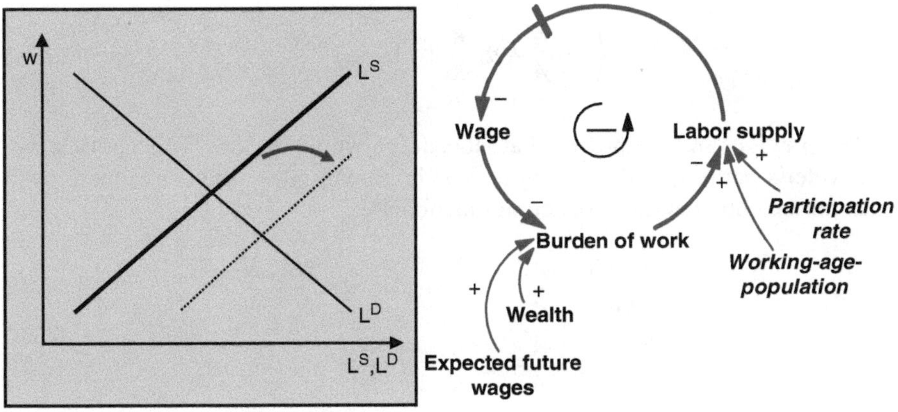

Fig. 2.30 Labor supply
Source: own figure

Demographics are connected with people's uncertainty about their future. Costs may rise (see Sect. 2.3.1.1 of this chapter). But a high uncertainty about future **wealth** (=low expected wealth) leads to a higher burden of work. This is easier to understand if one thinks of an "obligation to work". Therefore, the labor supply increases.

The domestic **working-age population** (without immigration) will decline. This is not only a question of retirement, but also a consequence of fewer young adults. When the participation rate does not change, then the labor supply declines as well. Only an increase in the participation rate could change the ratio between working age population (N_{WA}) and labor supply (N_{LF}).

Future wages also affect the current labor supply. The last paragraph outlined a possible decline of labor supply. This occurrence would imply a future increase in wages. This would make the households effectively wealthier and therefore would decrease the households' workload. The balancing loop closes with a link to an increasing labor supply.

The **major dominating effect** is therefore the decline in the working-age-population, so that the labor force decline induces rising wages. This effect, however, is not clear as the power of the other effects has not yet been analyzed in the scientific literature. Many authors simply focused on a declining workforce (see e.g. Schäfer & Seyda, 2004, p. 105; Nyce & Schieber, 2005, p. 159).

2.3.2.3 Labor Demand

The future labor demand depends on many factors, such as wage, prices, or capital stock. An insight as to how the future labor demand will change the economic outcome starts with the production function (Leibfritz & Roeger, 2008, p. 37):

$$Y = A \cdot K^{\alpha} \cdot N^{(1-\alpha)} \tag{2.26}$$

Transforming into growth rates yields:

$$\underset{(-)}{\frac{\dot{Y}}{Y}} = \frac{\dot{A}}{A} + \alpha \cdot \frac{\dot{K}}{K} + (1-\alpha) \cdot \underset{(-)}{\frac{\dot{N}}{N}} \tag{2.27}$$

The previous section proved that labor force would decline. This cutback will lead, ceteris paribus, to decreasing economic growth rates. The per capita growth rates for a Cobb-Douglas production function are:

$$\begin{aligned} \left(\frac{\dot{Y}}{N}\right) &= \frac{\dot{A}}{A} + \alpha \cdot \frac{\dot{K}}{K} + (1-\alpha) \cdot \frac{\dot{N}}{N} - \frac{\dot{N}}{N} \\ \frac{\dot{Y}}{Y} - \underset{(-)}{\frac{\dot{N}}{N}} &= \frac{\dot{A}}{A} + \alpha \cdot \frac{\dot{K}}{K} - \alpha \cdot \underset{(-)}{\frac{\dot{N}}{N}} \end{aligned} \tag{2.28}$$

The shrinking population turns the subtrahends on both sides of the equation into summands. The labor force decline will therefore increase the per capita income.

This is standard and intuitively understandable because a constant outcome divided by fewer people raises the per capita income.

One can achieve a deeper understanding of the connection between population and economic growth if the labor force and the population are treated differently. First, one assumes:

$$N_{LF} = \underbrace{\frac{N_{LF}}{N_{WA}}}_{a} \cdot \underbrace{\frac{N_{WA}}{N}}_{d} \cdot N \tag{2.29}$$

The per capita growth rates from (2.28) now become:

$$\underset{(-)}{\frac{\dot{Y}}{Y}} - \underset{(-)}{\frac{\dot{N}}{N}} = \frac{\dot{A}}{A} + \alpha \cdot \frac{\dot{K}}{K} + (1-\alpha) \cdot \underset{(-)}{\frac{\dot{N}_{LF}}{N_{LF}}} - \underset{(-)}{\frac{\dot{N}}{N}} \tag{2.30}$$

The negative population growth directly affects both sides and – again – increases the per capita income. However, the shrinking effect on labor force from the production function brings about a different aspect. The labor force is only a fraction of the total population, and the ratios for working age (d) and participation (a) may vary over time. Particularly the working age ratio to total population can change and depends only on the population structure. Three options are possible:

1. $(1-\alpha) \cdot \frac{\dot{N}_{LF}}{N_{LF}} < \frac{\dot{N}}{N}$: In this case the ratios stay more or less constant over time and because of $\alpha < 1$ the growth decline of the labor force is lower as of the population. $\frac{\dot{Y}}{Y} < \frac{\dot{N}}{N}$ leads to a **per capita increase**.
2. $(1-\alpha) \cdot \frac{\dot{N}_{LF}}{N_{LF}} > \frac{\dot{N}}{N}$: In this scenario the adjusted labor force ages faster than the population declines. People retire but still enjoy life. Fewer workers have to support the whole population. This means $\frac{\dot{Y}}{Y} > \frac{\dot{N}}{N}$ and the **per capita income will decline.**
3. $(1-\alpha) \cdot \frac{\dot{N}_{LF}}{N_{LF}} = \frac{\dot{N}}{N}$: The last scenario is more theoretical because in practice it rarely meets both growth rates. The labor force declines faster than the population, but the adjustment with (1-α) shrinks the growth rate exactly to the population growth rate. The **per capita income would stay constant** as $\frac{\dot{Y}}{Y} = \frac{\dot{N}}{N}$.

Another way to analyze future labor force demand is based on the assumption of individual profit maximizing firms. Companies are price taking and they have to decide how many people to employ. Workers are alike; there is no differentiation of skills (Abel et al., 1998, p. 77).

If one focuses more on the variable factors instead of the produced quantity for the firms profit than one can follow the input–output-rule for characterizing the profit maximum. The input–output-rule postulates that in profit maximum the marginal factor costs equal the total marginal costs, which equal the product price (Blum, 1994, p. 136). Concluding this, the wage and the product price are exogenous for the company. The firm must decide how much capital and labor it will use to maximize their profits. One can write (Heertje & Wenzel, 1997, p. 142):

$$\begin{aligned} \pi &= revenue - costs \\ \pi &= P \cdot Y - W \cdot N_{LF} - i \cdot K \\ Y &= \frac{\pi}{P} - \frac{W}{P} \cdot N_{LF} - \frac{i}{P} \cdot K \end{aligned} \tag{2.31}$$

The production function in a (Y;N_{LF})-diagram must be tangent to the iso-profit-line. Therefore, the marginal product of labor equals the marginal revenue of labor, expressed as:

$$\frac{\delta Y}{\delta N_{LF}} = \frac{W}{P} \tag{2.32}$$

Rearranging the variables reveals the **marginal revenue product of labor:**

$$W = \frac{\delta Y}{\delta N_{LF}} \cdot P \tag{2.33}$$

In profit maximum the marginal revenue product of labor equals the wage. An extra unit of labor contributes the profit by the corresponding amount. And an increase in wages turns the iso-profit-line upwards. Thus, the new tangent on the production function will lower labor. For the aggregated labor demand one can find the standard diagram on the right in Fig. 2.31.

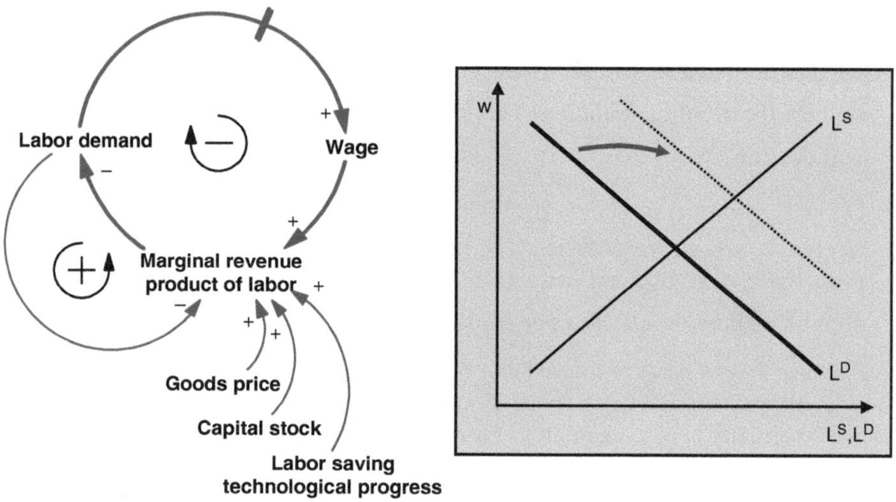

Fig. 2.31 Labor demand
Source: own figure

As in the Sect. 2.3.2.2 the labor supply, this diagram shows the labor demand in the same fashion. On the left, one sees the causal-loop explanation for the driving forces behind the labor demand. The marginal revenue product of labor depends on wages and on the product price but also – over the production technology – on the capital stock and on the labor saving technological progress. The connection of wages on labor demand is as expected. Raising wages decrease the demand for labor, whereas an increase in labor demand shifts the wages upwards.

How will demographic change affect labor demand? Companies adjust their production and therefore their labor demand to consumer needs. Because in a polypoly, firms are price-taking and depend on wages and on interest rates (not specifically specified here). In the previous section it was shown that wages might rise. This would lead to a decline in labor demand, as long as no adjustment in the production process is made.

Holger Schaefer and Susanne Seyda (2004, p. 108) argued that productivity increases with a constant rate. But if this is the total factor productivity then it will be independent from the amount of provided labor. The output increase does not affect the labor demand. One can see a productivity increase as labor induced. In this case it would be an increase in labor saving technology. Schaefer and Seyda indirectly showed, in addition to the causal-loop-diagram, that there are many factors, which interact (feedback). Thus, the demand also depends on factor prices and technological progress. Willi Leibfritz and Werner Roeger stated correctly, that these **determinants are almost unpredictable** (Leibfritz & Roeger, 2008, p. 99). Therefore, stating a total effect is not plausible, because the labor market has too many interacting factors. Some consumer trends may show directions for future behavior. This, however, will be outlined in the Sect. 2.3.4.1. The next Sect. 2.3.3 discusses the effects on skills, productivity, and innovation in an aging work force.

2.3.2.4 Trends

The major trend for industrialized countries will be a declining workforce coexisting with a shrinking population. If and how this will change the per capita income will be addressed in Chap. 5 From a theoretical point of view, there are many interacting variables and time depending external factors. The previous subsections discussing labor supply and labor demand presented an isolated view by neglecting the counterpart. Figure 2.32 explains, from a graphical point of view, the dependence of the labor market as a whole. One can see the interacting balancing loops of labor demand and labor supply. Both support the tendency to reach a stable equilibrium at a certain wage. The other diagram in this Figure shows this continuous approaching of the equilibrium point around the stable point. It is fairly obvious that all external factors continually change the steady state as they depend on time.

The next section will present a small example of two different skills and their impact on the labor market. All factors together and the assumption of a non-aggregate labor market in reality create fuzziness about a future trend.

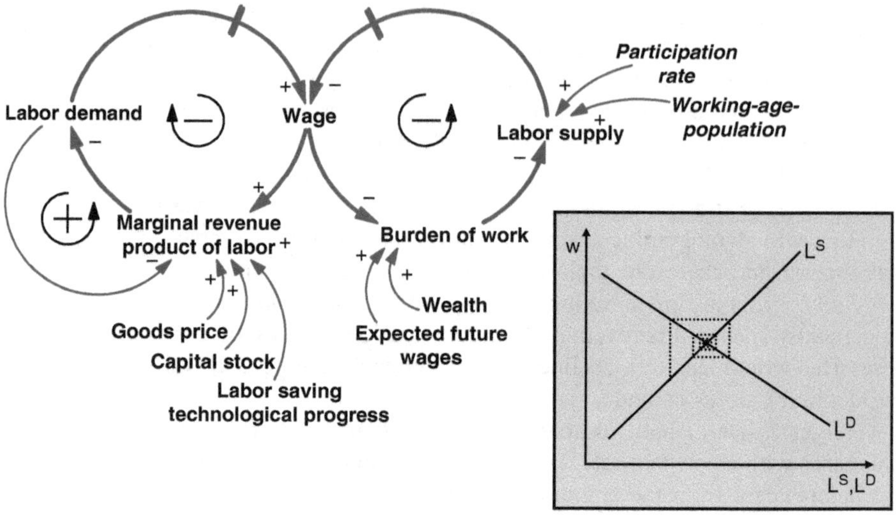

Fig. 2.32 Labor market
Source: own figure

The sector structure of the labor market depends on a number of various major factors. This trend creates the future adaption processes on the labor market. Christian Lutz et al. (Lutz, Meyer, Schnur, & Zika, 2002, pp. 321–322) named the following:

- The technical and **technological development** is connected with a high intensity of research and development.
- **Globalization** and internationalization intensify the competition and accelerate the R&D effort.
- **Ecological focusing** will increase market potential in recycle industry.
- **Demographic change** may increase the demand for healthcare products and wellness industry, but also for education.
- The shift towards the **tertiary sector** will continue.
- The **female participation rate** may increase and lead to an raising demand for houshold services.

To overcome, adopt or strengthen this trend policy-makers will have several variables to adjust and redirect. The following list names the important ones (Leibfritz & Roeger, 2008, p. 42; Schäfer & Seyda, 2004, pp. 110–116):

- Share of labor force (participation rate)
- Participation of older worker
- Unemployment (employment rate)
- Average number of hours worked per worker
- Activation of low skilled worker
- Immigration

Hans-Werner Sinn correctly drew the attention also on the company's side and not only on labor supply (Sinn, 2003, p. 25). He argued that a demographic decline of the population also **affects the employer and entrepreneurs**. New companies are usually founded by young entrepreneurs. Sinn assumed, therefore, a decline in entrepreneurs. Thus, the continuous aging and shrinking of society does not reduce unemployment rates, but rather intensifies the problem as the number of companies particularly new ones, will also decline. Sinn quoted (2003, p. 25, translated into English):

> It is an absurd and naïve idea that a country of old men will have a lower unemployment than a country of young, employable people.

2.3.3 R&D Sector

This section highlights different skills of labor, with a change in labor productivity and the innovational attitude of labor force in different age cohorts.

2.3.3.1 Skills

In the previous section, the effect of a shrinking labor supply was demonstrated. Usually, the labor market is treated as an aggregated market, mainly to keep the general explanation simple. But for understanding of the later modeled R&D sector and the demographic effects, one has also to consider a **split labor market** with two different labor skills. In an aggregated labor market, the labor force decline will lead to a rise in wages. But this effect would be different if the labor force – differentiated into high and low skilled labor – changed independently, e.g. through unequal fertility rates. This skilled biased labor supply will have effects on the sectors where the labor force is employed, on the income, and therefore also on the amount of consumption. Skill-biased labor supply is explained in Andrew Abel et al. (1998, pp. 93–96), John Bound and George Johnson (1992), and Stephan Nickell and Brian Bell (1995). The following paragraphs are excerpts from their works, however the application to demographic changes is new, as are the graphs.

As mentioned, labor demand splits into high-skilled and low-skilled labor demand. Workers are no longer identical. The production function now changes to:

$$Y = F(A, K, N_H, N_L) \tag{2.34}$$

For the first analysis one may assume a constant labor supply of skilled and unskilled workers. In Fig. 2.33 one can see, on the left, the underlying causal-loop structure. The top loop represents the labor demand for high-skilled workers. It is identical to the labor market diagram (shown in Fig. 2.32) in an aggregated labor sector, however, since the labor supply is constant, the labor supply loop is missing. As before, the driving force for labor demand is the marginal revenue product of

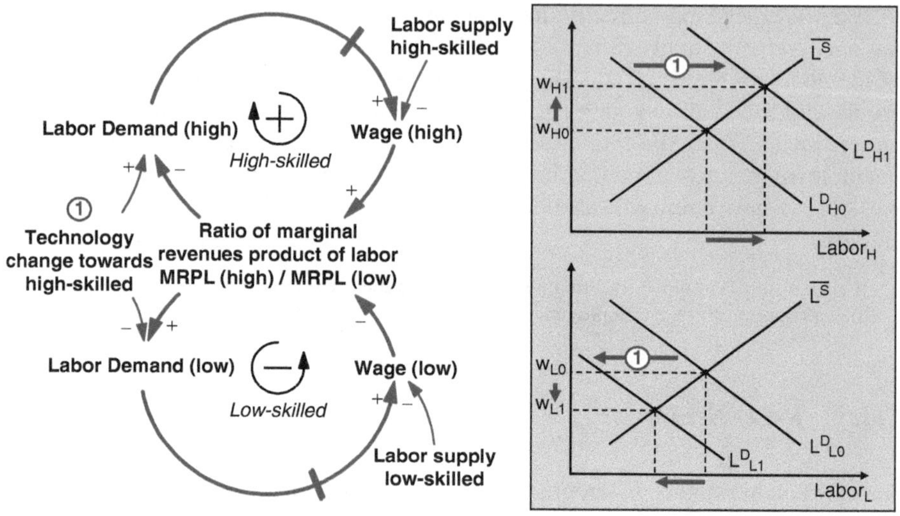

Fig. 2.33 Skill-biased technological change
Source: own figure

labor (MRPL). Unique to this diagram is the mirrored low-skilled labor demand loop. Both circles are connected by a ratio of the marginal revenue product of labor. Note, that the polarities for the low-skilled loop from and to the **MRPL ratio** change as the low-skilled MRPL is the divisor. Both markets are in equilibrium. Now, a skill-biased technological change increases (capital saving technological progress with spill over to high-skilled labor) the demand for high-skilled labor by introducing new machines, and the demand for low-skilled labor declines – rationalization investment. The diagram on the right, in Fig. 2.33, presents the standard supply and demand cross. The shift in the demand lines symbolizes the technology shock. From the delayed link the wages for high-skilled labor will rise and the low-skilled wages will decline. A permanent increase in technology will move the wages away from each other.

Now, consider a **declining labor force** instead of a technology shock. If both labor supply sources decline with the same rate, then the pressure on wages will be the same for both loops. But what if the high-skilled labor force declines more than the low-skilled labor force? In this case, the labor decline urges the wages to rise; however, high-skilled wages increase more, so the ratio of the marginal revenue product of labor increases as well. This leads to a decline in high-skilled labor demand and to a raising demand for low-skilled labor. This shift to a more labor-intensive production might be possible, but a more realistic scenario would be a shift to more automation (substituting labor with capital). The third loop, which is identical to the low-skilled-labor loop, is not explicitly drawn here. The underlying message is clear – a shrinking workforce increases the pressure for technological increase or substitutions.

The effect of an **inhomogeneous labor market** does not only work for skill discrepancies, but also differences in ages. Especially in a market with highly skilled and well educated this problem could arise. Zimmermann et al. described this problem in their book about unemployment (Zimmermann, Bauer, Bonin, Fahr, & Hinte, 2002, pp. 36–38). The basis for their age-biased-labor-market model is the assumption that expert knowledge is mainly accumulated through schooling, whereas it declines in later periods of working. Without any training the half-life of knowledge would force the expert knowledge to decline. That means that if new 'know-how' is added to the stock of firm's knowledge base only through recruitment then older employees (with seniority) and younger employees are not fully substitutable. In this case, a slightly modified causal-loop-diagram would apply. In comparison to older employees the demand for a younger labor force can lead to a wage differentiation.

With respect to the split labor market, one can doubt that a change in the demography could bring about a decline in unemployment within industrialized countries (Arnds & Bonin, 2003, p. 136). In fact, it might be more conceivable that the opposite will occur.

2.3.3.2 Labor Productivity

Labor productivity is founded on individual performance parameters. One can argue that these parameters change throughout a lifetime. With an aging workforce this individual effect presents a macro perspective. Joy Guilford was one of the first who approximated the average age of highest performance over a life time. According to this, scientists usually reach their maximum productivity at the age of 35 (Guilford, 1967; Sinn, 2005, p. 64). Biomedical research cannot support the thesis of a general performance decline throughout a working age (**deficit model**). Many factors and interdependencies with the environment and the specific task constitute the personal performance (**competence model**). More observable is a variation of performance in specific age groups – older and younger (Arnds & Bonin, 2003, p. 141).

Growth can only evolve from an individual productivity increase. This does not imply a future with less productive aged societies than today, but it forces the societies to reconsider the qualification of future labor force (Rürup, 2000, pp. 100–101):

- With regard to **experience knowledge**, cooperation and communication abilities and social competences, older employees should not have any disadvantage.
- Older worker might have a comperative advantage at **social abilites**.
- Experience knowledge accumulates over time and increases the **individuell performance**. It is available till the worker retires.
- Older employees might take longer for **learning new techniques** and for processing new knowledge.

Both the younger and older workforces are partly substitutable. Especially, spill-over effects of accumulated knowledge from the older workforce to the younger ones can support learning-by-doing of younger employees (Plünnecke & Seyda, 2004, p. 128). Berhard Boockmann and Viktor Steiner (2000, p. 136) analyzed the changes in labor productivity with an aging society. They found evidence to support that a longer education and professional trainings bring about a positive return in wages.

Birgit Verworn and Christiane Hipp analyzed several studies regarding the innovative capabilities of workforces. They concluded that a **decline in innovation is highly unrealistic**, especially for engineers (Verworn & Hipp, 2008, pp. 379–382). Taking their statement into account, one can conclude that growth rate parameters of the R&D stock will not change with an aging workforce.

2.3.3.3 Innovation

Industrialized countries face different velocities in structural changes towards a knowledge economy. These economies have the ability to scrutinize knowledge and handle the new production factor information. This development demands higher education, technical and scientific qualifications, mobility and self-learning and innovative personalities (Krey & Meier, 2004, p. 146).

The DB-Research group (Bräuninger et al., 2002) found two main effects of innovation. On the one hand, shrinking workforces could **shorten employees' and entrepreneurs' innovative ability**. But, on the other hand, this expected shortage can **create corresponding incentives** to increase the innovative capabilities. In addition, Verworn and Hipp did not find any significant empirical support for the decline in a company's formation (Verworn & Hipp, 2008, p. 384).

Especially the processes of invention, innovation, and diffusion depend on human capital. The technical progress is the result of learning and experience processes, however this progress devaluates knowledge. Horst Siebert argued (2002, pp. 1–4):

- Older workers will have accumulated experience, which becomes obsolete more quickly. Some of the employees could find it difficult to aquire needed skills or to cope with new technologies.
- The workforce may be more risk-averse. Less daring entrepreneurs would be a consequence and product innovation thus becomes more difficult.
- The demand for new products could weaken and their acceptance could decline. This may hamper the diffusion of new technologies.
- The adoption for innovation could decrease, because the older workforce might challenge new technologies either as consumers or employees.

Complex innovations, usually conducted in expert teams, consist of different disciplines and cultures. This creates a need for communication, coordination, experience, problem structuring – usually abilities one attributes to older employees (Krey & Meier, 2004, p. 162).

2.3.3.4 Trends

An aging workforce and the continuation of the technological progress will lead to a continuous demand for a highly qualified labor force. This might accelerate the split between the demand for highly skilled and lower skilled employees increasing the wage differentiation. The qualifications demanded to successfully meet future job requirements (knowledge-society) are highly incorporated with skills, which especially older workers can provide. But as there are many interacting factors a further research is necessary. There is evidence that a purposeful training will contribute to the decline intra-age-group differences in performance. So far, one can summarize that there is positive correlation between age and experience, and a negative correlation between age and physical as well as cognitive abilities. A good education could foster positive connections and it seems that experience has an influence on cognitive abilities (Börsch-Supan, Düzgün, & Weiss, 2005, p. 6). The age-depending negative outcomes must ceteris paribus have a negative effect on the productivity. Demanding tasks regarding power, agility or response time in the secondary sector might be therefore substituted by automation (Rürup, 2000, p. 102). In economic growth terms this would be a technological increase and thus, the ratio of capital to labor (capital intensity) would increase as fewer people were needed for the given stock of capital.

2.3.4 Other Effects

This subchapter lists other possible effects for demographic change. As most of them have only minor implications for the further demographic model of this work it is done more for the sake of completeness. But this does not mean that these effects are negligible.

2.3.4.1 Final Goods Sector: Consumption Pattern

To predict future consumption, forecasters questioned whether young cohorts, as they grow older, will adopt the products of their parents groups or will they assume new habits. Often it is assumed that a growth market will result when a new group enters the primary age for the product. In this case, the new group adopts the same patterns set by his/her parents. But often groups behave differently from the previous ones (Schnaars, 1989, p. 115). Valid forecasts for **consumption patterns** are difficult, not just because of the counteracting effects, but also due to the period effects. Longitudinal studies are necessary to control cohort-effects (Rürup, 2000, p. 93).

The aggregated demand for consumption goods depends not only on the number of people living in an economy, but also on the number of households. Elderly people live mostly in one- or two-person-households. The consumption rate of such households is usually higher than that of other households (Rürup, 2000, pp. 90–91). One has to distinguish between a population size effect and a population structure effect. The total consumption will fall due to the declining population, but also within the consumption there will be shifts towards different product categories (Nyce & Schieber, 2005, pp. 170–171). Which effect dominates is not predictable.

Other qualitative changes in demand can result from the following (Rürup, 2000, pp. 92–93; Lührmann, 2006, p. 63):

- Senior citizens do not fully adjust their living space to the change in household members. This leads to an increase in expenditures per person for habitation.
- Biological changes lead to an increase in demand for healthcare and nursing and to a decline in costs for mobility.
- The expenditures for press, TV or traveling might increase as the leisure time raises.
- Advertising may increase the demand for specific consumption goods, because elderly people become more and more a target group of advertising.

Aging alone will not change consumption patterns significantly. However, economic growth, consumer preferences, relative prices and level of expenditures will. The growing silver economy will, nevertheless, be an important factor as the shift in consumer preferences will affect the entertainment sector, healthcare sector, demands for "intelligent homes" and companies, which would be well advised to adjust their portfolio in advance (Schaffnit-Chatterjee, 2007, p. 6).

2.3.4.2 Social Security Sector: Health and Long-Term Care

The probability of needing help increases with the age. The factor behind healthcare spending is the health status and not age. Generally, the healthcare costs around the world will rise faster than the average rate of economic growth. Over time, this leads to an increase in demand for healthcare services and products (Office for Official Publications of the European Communities, 2007, p. 70).

On average, older people will consume considerably more healthcare than younger ones. Healthcare, however, tends to cluster disproportionally in a brief period before death. The period of frailty and disability increases sharply at older ages and very old ages (Office for Official Publications of the European Communities, 2007, p. 70). Contrary to the general assumption that healthcare costs rise in aging societies, Peter Zweifel and colleagues (Zweifel, Felder, & Meiers, 1999) found evidence that the costs of the last 2 years of life had no effect on health costs despite the increase of life expectancy over the past decades. The study concluded that healthcare expenditures would contribute much less to the cost increase than most observers previously claimed. All in all, the cost increase could be induced by half-way-technologies. This type of medical progress does not cure the diseases, but does sustain life (Nyce & Schieber, 2005, p. 177).

Additionally, not only **aging-related developments** will play a key role in healthcare and nursing, but also future technological developments which can support nursing. Personal healthcare is very labor intensive, thus there will be little room for technological improvements (Office for Official Publications of the European Communities, 2007, p. 71).

Uwe Reinhardt summarized healthcare effects, as follows (2002, pp. 259–260):

- Healthcare will grow because health services of any age group increase through technological progress.
- The percentage of health expenditures per GDP is extremely uncertain, as it depends on variables whose values are also dependent of time.
- Aging is only a relatively minor factor on healthcare costs because it affects any age group.
- A control of healthcare through a great reliance on market forces is certain to fail.
- Prefund healthcare for elderly trough individual financial contracts are likely to face political obstacles.

2.3.4.3 Social Security Sector: Pension Systems

Public and private spending ensures the decoupling of being old and poor. Provisions of public spending mainly achieved this. Despite trends for more private precautions, an adequate retirement income will become a public responsibility. All projections of the EU countries show an **increase in public spending on pensions** (Office for Official Publications of the European Communities, 2007, p. 67). The future income replacement level will depend on the development in labor markets and on the maturation of pension schemes. In certain cases, current levels turn out to be low compared to current earnings. Therefore, scientists suggest reforming the statutory schemes to reduce the replacement rates. This can stop the trend to a less generous pension outcome (Office for Official Publications of the European Communities, 2007, p. 68).

A pension reform towards "**pay as you go systems**" may increase the decline of the return on capital stock, because capital stock increases as the private savings increase, which leads to a higher supply of capital compared to fully funded pension systems (Matthes & Römer, 2004, p. 305). The change in pension schemes may have quantitative effects on labor supply. The income effect will increase labor supply as people anticipate a reduction in their pensions. This implies that the population will need to work more in order to maintain a certain standard of living. The substitution effect will reduce labor supply, as labor taxes will increase to finance statutory pensions. The power of these effects depends on the institutional framework and the adjustment for individual aging (Saint-Paul, 2002, p. 129).

Funded pension systems almost always result in higher saving ratios than "pay-as-you-go systems". However, the savings also depend on various demographic circumstances and could become negative in cases with strong population aging. Even countries that are moving forward to a funded system could face negative saving ratios. To replace the existing system with funded plans, policy-makers have to either pay off or reduce liabilities. Many industrialized countries do not have a fiscal surplus. Therefore, paying liabilities in a relatively short time period is hardly imaginable (Nyce & Schieber, 2005, pp. 125–127).

According to this information, the saving ratios for elderly people could decline in the near future. This depends on several factors and could explain positive saving patterns in OECD countries with aging challenges. As they are (Börsch-Supan & Essig, 2002, pp. 11–13):

- High pension payments in industrialized countries with strong social security systems lead to an **oversupply for older people**. Changes in pensions systems will increase the need for private pension schemes. This could increase the spread between savings during working age and dissaving later on, as savings and dissavings have to increase.
- Postwar generations may have **higher saving ratios** due to their habits which they keep also for higher ages. Future retirees probably will change their values.
- Individual home care and commercial nursing homes could lead to **accerlerated dissaving** of elderly people.

One method of **adjusting the extending lifetime to retirement systems** was presented by Warren Sanderson and Sergei Scherbov (2005). They divided entire lifetimes into separate periods of life, such as childhood, employment period and retirement period. If these periods are calculated as relative ratios to the total lifespan it would be possible to adjust these periods to the extending lifespan. Thus, retirement age would not be fixed anymore and this would overcome the phenomenon of extending periods of retirement and their costs for social security systems compared to years of paying into the system.

2.3.4.4 Political Sector: Fiscal Policy

Public budgets will be affected significantly through the demographic change. Whereas federal budgets have to carry most of the demographic burden, political subdivisions and local corporations may experience an expenditure decline when they properly adjust their budgets (Seitz, 2008, pp. 161–162).

The demographic change will have different regional effects on local authorities. Therefore, it is only with high uncertainty predictable. The **directly linked costs** to the demographic change are child-orientated transfers and educational expenditures. While these may decline, pension costs for public official will rise. Tax revenues are mainly incorporated into private income. This may lead to a decline in total tax revenues that cannot be withheld by corporate taxes (Brügelmann, 2004, p. 236).

2.3.4.5 Political Sector: Transport Infrastructure

Transport infrastructure is essential in an open economy. For exchanging goods and the mobility of labor force, a sustained transport system is imminent important. The costs of mobility, economic growth and technological progress are determinants for infrastructure. All will change over time. The declining population will mainly **affect individual traffic**. The degree of mobility for older people is lower, but may increase over time. Together with a shrinking population, this age-effect will lead to a decline in transportation demand. But one has to consider a spatial aspect, thus the population density is a crucial point for forecast the transport infrastructure (Just, 2007, pp. 39–41). Shrinking passenger transport will disburden road infrastructure. However, at the same time, the freight traffic will increase, thereby compensating for this effect (Just, 2004, p. 11).

2.3.4.6 Political Sector: Election and Governance

A changing dependency ratio may have an effect on election outcomes. Participation in voting usually increases with age. Voting for certain parties is highly individual, but every age cohort favors political decisions for their own age group. So, one can assume that rational acting subjects will not vote for a concept that will negatively affect them. Therefore, reforms are only feasible when they get support from the electorate. The **concept of median voter** enables scientists to forecast when people of higher ages could dominate younger voters. In the case of Germany, Hans-Werner Sinn and Silke Uebelmesser (2001) and Veit Schulz (2008) found evidence that in the near future the system could lock itself by preventing the current electorate of self constraining reforms. The results are transferable to all industrialized countries. This makes economic reforms impossible, if they burden only today's generation.

2.3.4.7 Real Estate Sector: Housing Demand

Especially, the housing and real estate market will be affected by a decline in the population. Franz-Xaver Kaufmann saw mainly **shrinking prices for real estates** and a declining credit rating for area municipalities (political subdivisions) (Kaufmann, 2005, p. 91). But these effects will be regionally distributed. Annette Mayer (2008, p. 453) identified three trends for a future demand in housing:

1. The cumulative demand for housing will increase and reach a peak with a delay to the demographic change.
2. The demand for specialized housing will increase, especially for elderly and very high aged people.
3. There will be regional disparities for projections through spatial determinants. This will lead to synchronic construction and deconstruction of real estate.

2.3.5 Summary and Conclusion

This section is dedicated the effects of the demographic change. So, the economic interdependencies of aging and shrinking are a particular focus. To cluster the manifold interactions this section focuses on the financial, labor and R&D sectors. Other noticeable economic effects are collected in the subsection "Other Effects".

Starting with the **lifecycle hypothesis** in the **financial sector**, the main focus is on the consequence of private saving rate. Figure 2.34 represents major outcomes from the financial sector analysis. The utility maximization for households is the underlying decision concept for households. To maximize consumption – and with it the utility – households must save a variable ratio of their income over a lifetime. Time preferences, bequests, buffer stocks and future labor expectations effect the calculation of the household consumption. Various modifications of the lifecycle hypothesis stress the importance of different determinants. Nevertheless, all augmentations unify the connection between income and saving rate and the statement that the demographic change will probably decrease the total national saving.

Continuing with the **Ricardian equivalence**, the focus is placed on foresight driven, rational acting subjects and their counteracting behavior, if the government would like to overcome undesired consequences of the demographic change. It can be shown that the saving ratio might rise, due to the increase in saving ratio in order to overcome later negative effects of tax increases.

The **asset meltdown hypothesis** is presented as a third major concern. Some authors argued that the stock price will fall when a significant number of workforces retire. This is based on the assumption of an exceeding stock supply. Pension systems and their changes will have an impact on this, but in an open economy this effect will be much lower than proposed.

After general information about the labor market, research has primarily focused on the labor demand and labor supply. Figure 2.35 shows the main influencing factors on this market.

The Sect. 2.3.2.1 presents **main growth drivers** for income from a labor market perspective, on the basis of a tautological expression. The factors were labor productivity, labor force participation rate and the share of working age population. Based on the fact that **labor supply** is mainly a maximization decision of the household, the causal loop for the labor supply was presented and analyzed on a demographic impact. Wealth, expected future wages, participation rate and the working age population were the main drivers besides the wage for supplying labor.

Labor demand is affected by the demographic change and a decline in labor supply via the wages. However, the marginal revenue product of labor determines the labor demand and, as a major decision indicator, it depends on the price of goods and other production factors. Interestingly, the per capita income is an output indicator for the production factor, which is affected via two labor supply channels. One connection is the direct effect of population and the second channel is the labor force itself as production factor. Since the labor force and the total population are linked, the overall effect depends on ratios such as participation.

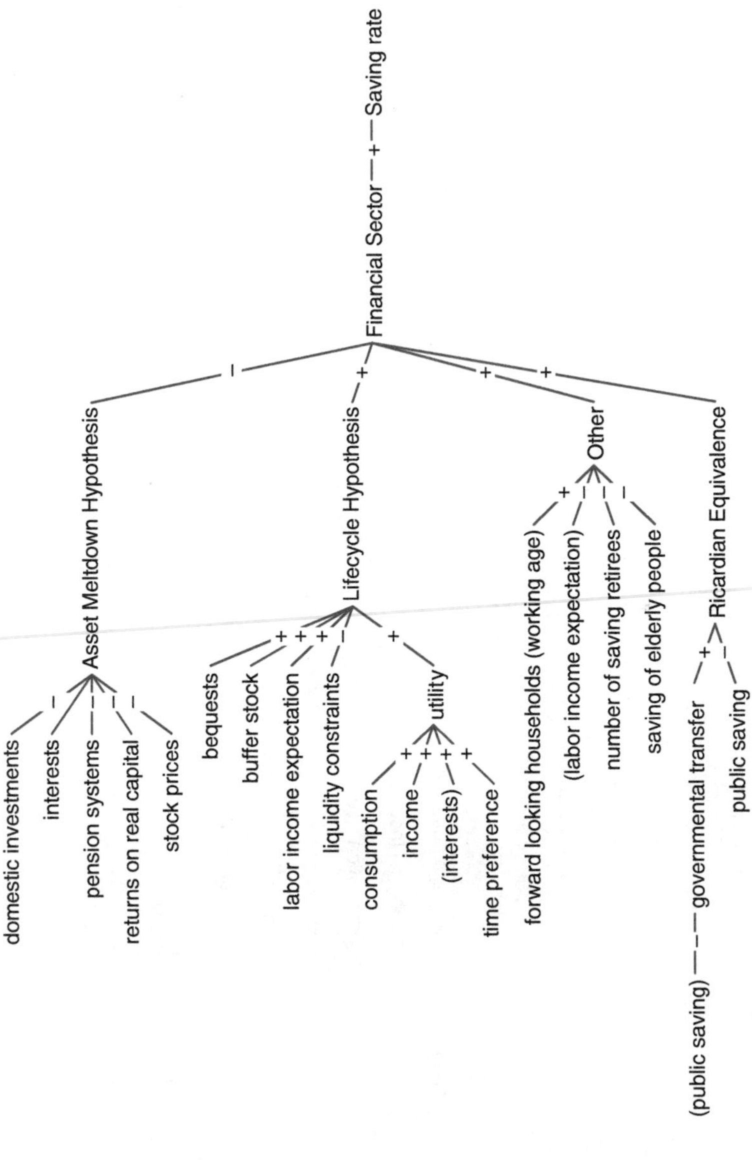

Fig. 2.34 Conclusion financial sector
Source: own figure

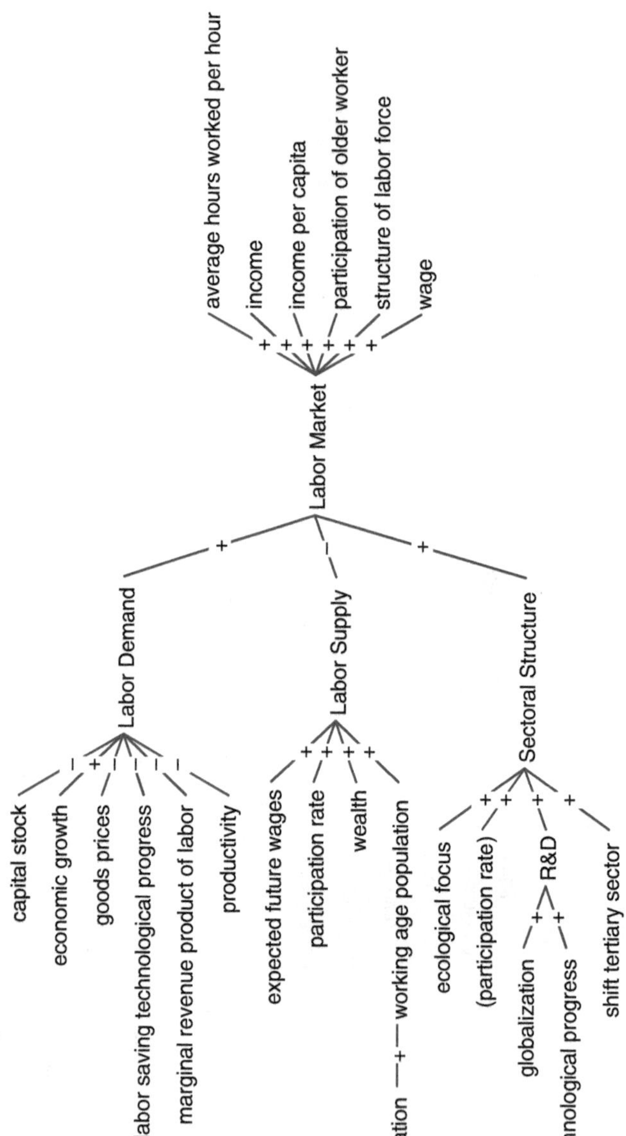

Fig. 2.35 Conclusion labor market
Source: own figure

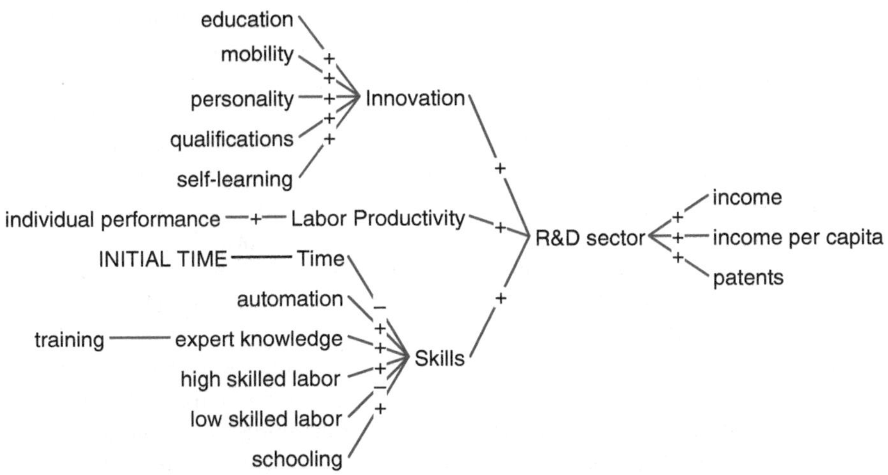

Fig. 2.36 Conclusion R&D sector
Source: own figure

The **labor market** as a whole is presented in Sect. 2.3.2.4. It is emphasized that many factors interact within the labor market. Additionally, most of them depend on time and are not constant. This makes it almost impossible to predict a future demand, since most factors also change over time.

The **research and development sector** adds to the labor market, but specifies the innovation of labor force, their productivity and their skills. Figure 2.36 shows these main factors.

If the labor market is separated into high and low skilled labor, the demand for labor is different to a general observation. One can explain wage differentiation in connection with the demographic change. Research on innovation and productivity has shown that the individual performance and the personality determine these factors dominantly.

Other economic aspects that may be influenced by aging and shrinking societies include the consumption sector, healthcare and long-term care, pension systems, real estate and housing market and the political sector. The challenges with "pay as you go" pension schemes are important, however, outlining them in great detail, goes beyond the scope of this work.

2.4 Chapter Summary

This chapter lays the groundwork for a new, self-developed model. It investigates the **major impacts of demographic change**. In doing this, the chapter is organized into two subchapters. While the first subchapter analyzes the influencing determinants on the demographic factors – fertility, mortality, migration, and population structure – the second subchapter concentrates on the consequences of a change in these factors and their impact on economic growth.

The overall trend for industrialized countries is fairly obvious. **Fertility is below the replacement level** and there is currently no promising sign of an upward trend. The economic theory of fertility (Becker/Barro) could explain the decline partly. A very promising approach is the biographic theory (Birg). A biographic lock-in effect hampers women to bear a first child. For those who decide to have a child, there is a high probability that the child will grow up without brothers and sisters. A population will only stabilize if in average two children per women are born. Having only one descendant will not stop the population shrinking.

With better technology and healthcare, the life expectancy rate increases and the mortality rate declines. This is the effect of an aging society. The population structure changes. More non-working people (very young and very old) depend on the working population. This increases the additional costs for the working population, supported by the increasing dependency ratios in industrialized countries.

As a shortcut, to overcome this effect of population aging and shrinking, policy-makers often request a more **open migration policy**. Unfortunately, no present theory – gravity models or behavioral models – can explain the migration process in a great detail. All the theories are more ex-post orientated. One could argue, with a specific econometric analysis the forecast would be robust, but as the whole the migration process depends on political decisions. The past trend is only a weak supporter of future development. Nevertheless, the major problem is that migration would be only the second best solution, as it does not cure the major problem of fertility below the replacement level.

After showing that industrialized countries face both a declining and aging process, in subchapter 1.3 the effects of such development on economic growth are investigated. For clarity reasons, the effects are analyzed in several economic sectors – financial, labor, research and development and others – but always in focus of the later model. Thus, not all effects can be outlaid here.

The **effect on the saving pattern** is of major interest, as this is a key variable in growth models. The lifecycle theory suggests a decline in this pattern. Also the labor market and the R&D sector are sensitive to demographic effects. A decline in workforce leads to different effects. One effect is the substitution to a more capital-intensive production. And the other is a change in labor productivity. If and how the skills of worker may decline is – regarding the empirical research and theories – a question of general and company individual policies. In addition, they discussed how the deficit model does not hold the empirics. It is replaced by the **modern competence approach**. Variation of performance is therefore not a question of aging rather a question of individual abilities.

The entire chapter shows that a single cause and effect chain does not exist if one talks about demographic change and their economic challenges. This goes hand-in-hand with the introduction of this work, where it is argued that economic systems are complex systems. In addition, the demographic process is not a singular event. The term names a period where certain effects occur simultaneously. This however, does not change patterns of economic systems – the analysis must be embedded into real and traditional economic theories. The next chapter focuses on major economic growth models as the foundation for later model building.

Chapter 3
Neoclassical Growth Theories

For almost two decades, from the early 1950s through the late 1960s, growth theory dominated economic theory, and Bob Solow dominated growth theory.
(Stiglitz, 1993, p. 50)

This chapter provides a detailed description of the current neoclassical growth theories. Beginning with a short introduction on exponential growth patterns, the following sections present three different model types: Exogenous, Endogenous and Semi-endogenous growth. The individual sub-chapters conclude with an analysis of demographic components within the model.

3.1 Introduction

3.1.1 Stylized Facts and the Power of Growth

The growth theory was re-established in the 1990s. The so-called 'new growth theory' mainly criticizes the neoclassic growth theory for three reasons:

1. The growth rate of the per-capita outcome was not determined by the long time saving and investment behavior.
2. Technical progress was only exogenous.
3. Empirical results do not fit with the theoretical models (Lucas, 1990; Barro, 1991).

One of the most surprising approaches to economic growth models is entitled: "*Population Growth and Technological Change One Million B.C. to 1990*"; published by Michael Kremer in the Quarterly Journal of Economics (Kremer, 1993). Kremer showed that long-run growth is consistent with the population implication of endogenous growth models. Figure 3.1 shows the exponential increase of the population for an extremely long time-frame (time on the x-axis) (Note: the scale is not linear).

L. Weber, *Demographic Change and Economic Growth*, Contributions to Economics,
DOI 10.1007/978-3-7908-2590-9_3, © Springer-Verlag Berlin Heidelberg 2010

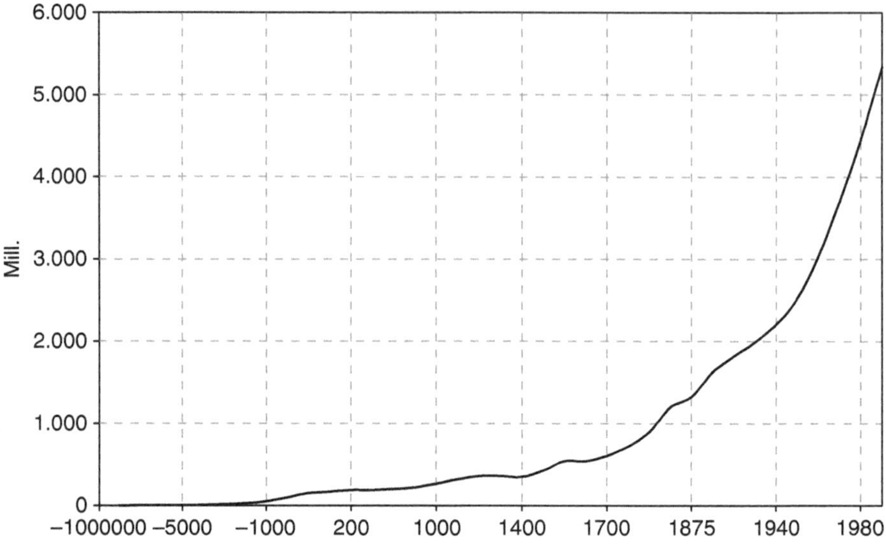

Fig. 3.1 World population growth
Source: own figure; data: Kremer, 1993, p. 682

The underlying growth pattern is very simple. When one assumes infinite small time steps in continuous time then it follows:

$$Population_t = Population_0 \cdot e^{growth\,rate \cdot t} \tag{3.1}$$

The corresponding stock and flow graph is presented in Fig. 3.2. Over the course of time the new stock evolves from the previous stock increased by a fraction. The population accumulates exponentially over time. In addition, one can see, on the right of the graph four simulations with different growth rates.

Thus, it can be observed that a small change in the growth rate has tremendous consequences for the absolute outcome – both in a short and prolonged generation. This pattern also works for national income or income per capita; which are integral key variables for economists and the population itself. Thus, small inter-country differences in growth rates per capita income have significant effects on a nation's standard of living (Snowdon & Vane, 2006, p. 589).

The structure driving the economic growth – capital accumulation – remains the same. However, various authors present different degrees of explanation. The main incentive of them is to broaden the knowledge on the growth rate itself as it vary over time with the above mentioned consequences for growth. In order to develop a deeper understanding of the systemic structure in exponential growth patterns, one must shed some light on different aspects of the growth theory. The following section highlights various growth models. In particular, the Solow-model, the Romer-model and the Jones-model are presented.

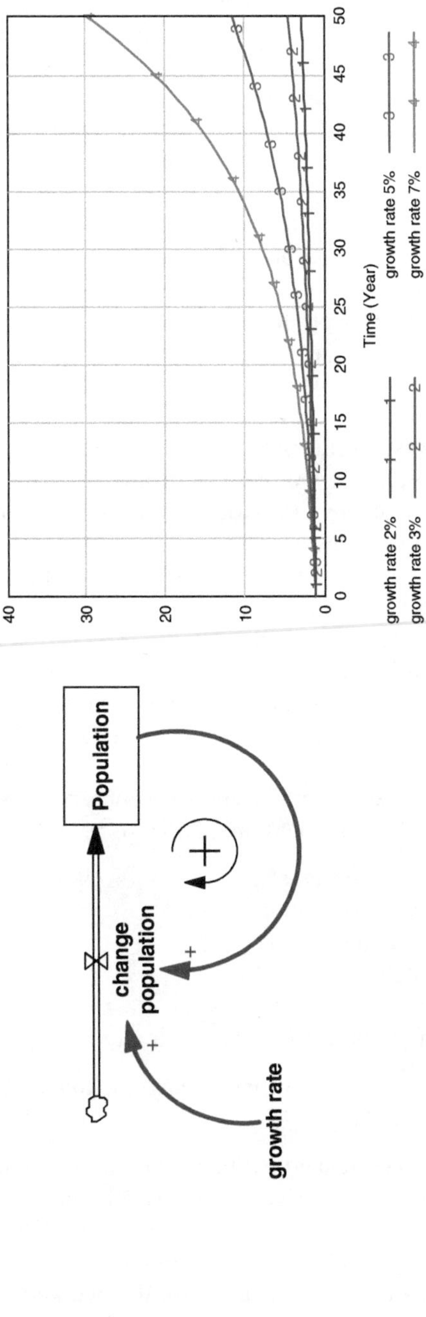

Fig. 3.2 Exponential growth pattern
Source: own simulation

3.1.2 Short Overview

Figure 3.3 illustrates the stream of economic growth theory. The grey highlighted boxes describe major steps in the growth theory, which are investigated later in this work. The description will follow a chronological order since every model evolved as a consequence of previous theoretical explanation about growth.

Chapter 3.2 begins with the foundation for all neoclassical growth models – the original Solow-model. It remains the standard growth theory, taught repeatedly in textbooks. Robert M. Solow described, as the first economist, the importance of capital intensity (K/L), which earned him a Nobel Prize in economics. Solow's paper (1956) is divided into subsections. He begins with a general model, without a specification of the production function and without a technology increase. Later Solow developed several extensions. Solow's work was ground breaking because he implemented labor force as a production factor into growth theory. Although there have been major changes in the growth theory, especially in regard to endogenizing technology, the Solow-type models still explain important behaviors and empirical results of economic growth.

The second section presents the first real endogenous growth model – the Romer-model (Romer, 1990). In 1990, Paul M. Romer published a model with an endogenized technology parameter. Previously, all models explained the importance of continuous technological increases, however failed to implement them within the model. Current empirical research has proven that results of the Romer-type models do not reflect the real growth data. Romer's growth model builds on special assumptions for certain parameters.

Charles Jones, in his semi-endogenous growth model, overcame this by extending the Romer-model to a more general case. Additionally, he could prove a more consistent theory with empirics. The Jones-model is described in more detail in the last section of this chapter.

Nicolas Kaldor summarized the main empirical observations about economic growth in his 1961 paper (Snowdon & Vane, 2006, p. 595):

- Output per capita grows continuously
- Capital labor ratio grows also continuously
- Stable rate of return on capital
- Capital output ratio is stable
- Constant share of labor
- Significant variation in the productivity growth rate between countries

As seen below, these observations were extended by Romer (1989) and by Jones (2001) (Snowdon & Vane, 2006, p. 595):

- Average growth rate is uncorrelated with the level of per capita income (Romer)
- International trade correlates positively with growth rates (Romer)
- Population growth is negatively correlated with growth (Romer)
- Growth accounting always finds residuals (Romer)
- High income countries attract skilled and unskilled workers (Romer)

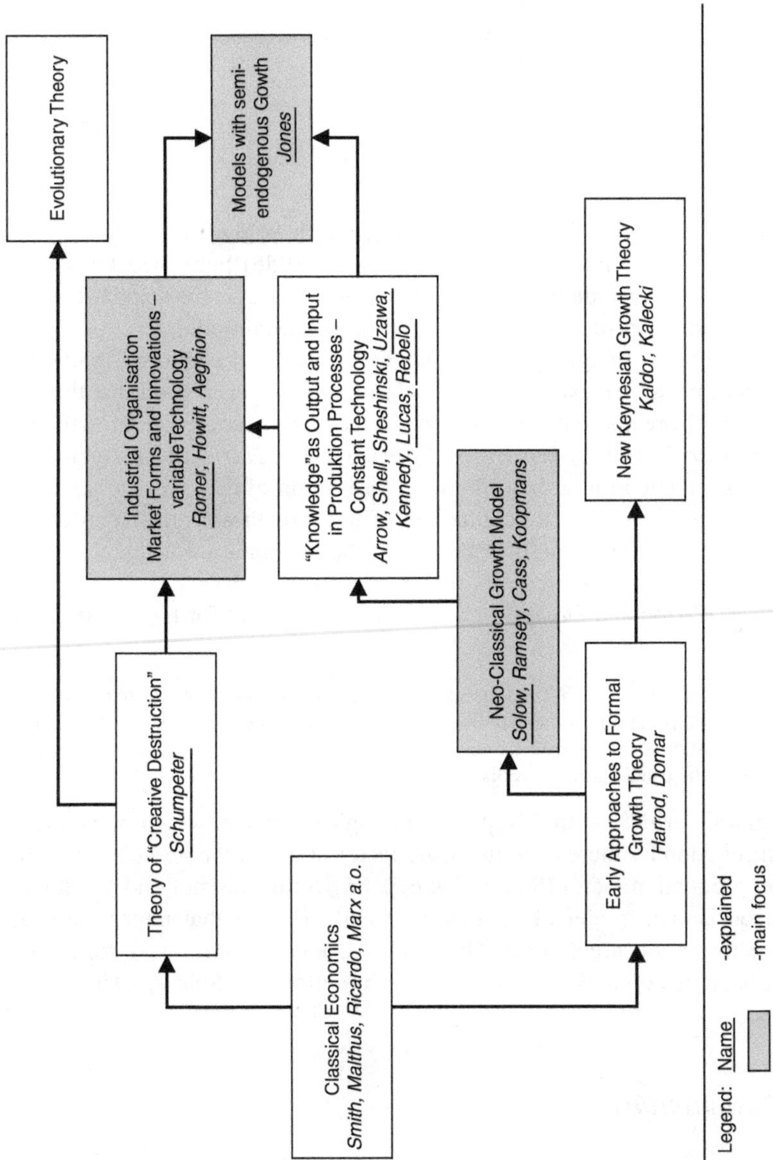

Fig. 3.3 History of economic growth theory
Source: own figure according to Bretschger, 1999, p. 9

- Income per capita differs enormous between countries (Jones)
- Growth rates for the world and for single countries vary over time (Jones)
- The position in the income distribution table of a country can change (Jones)

Thus this chapter presents and examines the evolution of neoclassical growth theories to found the work-specific semi-endogenous model of demographic growth.

3.2 Exogenous Growth Model (Solow, 1956)

A new chapter in the growth theory was opened with Solow's pioneering work in 1956. Almost at the same time Trevor W. Swan (1956) published his ideas on economic growth almost identical to Solow's. For this reason the standard neoclassical growth model is also referred to as the Solow-Swan-model.

Earlier schools of thought primarily neglected ideas of economic growth and explained them mostly as exogenous. Neoclassics, however, argued that the determinants of growth are not really accounted within the post-keynesian growth theory from Roy F. *Harrod* (1966) and Evsey *Domar (*1946*). Harrod* investigated business cycles as a fluctuation around the long-term trend of demand. *Domar's* main interest was the production factor capital (K). Thus, growth was only a consequence to accomplish full employment. In both models the orientation was mainly short- or mid-term (Frenkel & Hemmer, 1999, p. 27).

Solow used Harrod and *Domar's ideas* as a starting point for his article (Solow, 1956, p. 66):

> The "crucial assumption [of the] production takes place under conditions of fixed proportions. There is no possibility of substituting labor for capital in production. ... A remarkable characteristic of the Harrod-Domar-model is that it consistently studies long-run problems with the usual short-run tools.

Solow mainly criticized the simple technological change, which multiplies the production function by increasing the scale factor and also the absence of labor as an essential production factor (Solow, 1956, p. 85). Solow did not find much reality in the Harrod-Domar-model of economic growth. He felt that under the crucial assumptions the results are suspect. The Harrod-Domar-model is even for the long-run at best balanced on a "knife-edge equilibrium growth" (Solow, 1956, p. 65).

3.2.1 Assumptions

To introduce this section, the main assumptions of the basic Solow-model are the following:

- There are two production factors capital K(t) and labor L(t) and also technological progress as a third factor A(t) with $Y(t) = F[K(t), A(t)L(t)]$

- A constant fractions of output Y(t) is saved
- The capital stock K(t) takes a form of composite commodities
- Net investment is the rate of increase K(t) with $\dot{K} = I^N = sY$
- Output is understood as net output after depreciation of capital
- The production function is homogenous at the first degree – constant return to scales
- Full employment of the available stock of capital (Solow, 1956, p. 67)

These assumptions are outlined in the following sections in greater detail.

3.2.1.1 Production Function

At the core of every growth analysis is the production function. Solow's first introductory production function follows two simple production factors – capital K(t) and labor L(t) with Y(t) = F[K(t), L(t)]. Later in his paper this is extended to a function with technological progress, expressed as: Y(t) = F[K(t),A(t)L(t)]. In general, a function is well behaved when it follows the so-called Inada-conditions.

In 1963, the Japanese economist Ken-Ichi Inada clarified the assumptions made by Solow and Uzawa. He explained that a production function must fulfill the conditions for other factors (Inada, 1963):

1. Differentiable twice and therefore concave
2. Their marginal productivities must be positive and decreasing $\partial F(K,AL)/\partial K>0>\partial^2 F(K,AL)/\partial K^2$and $\partial F(K,AL)/\partial L>0>\partial^2 F(K,AL)/\partial L^2$
3. All factors are essential $F(K,0) = 0$ and $F(0,AL) = 0$
4. Their marginal productivities in the origin must be positive infinite $\lim_{K\to 0} F(K,AL)/\partial K = \infty$ and $\lim_{L\to 0} F(K,AL)/\partial L = \infty$
5. Unlimited input leads to unlimited output $\lim_{K\to\infty} F(K,AL) = \infty$ and $\lim_{L\to\infty} F(K,AL) = \infty$
6. Their marginal productivities in the point of infinity must be infinite $\lim_{K\to\infty} \partial F(K,AL)/\partial K = 0$ and $\lim_{L\to\infty} \partial F(K,AL)/\partial L = 0$
7. Finally, the constant returns to scale with $F(\lambda K, \lambda AL) = \lambda F(K,AL)$

Although Solow's paper describes a general version of the growth model for different production functions, similar to the Harrod-Domar-model with limited input-factors, this work concentrates only on a production function, known as the Cobb-Douglas-type. The primary reason for this is that in both the neoclassical and the later endogenous growth models Cobb-Douglas functions are a quasi-standard; Charles Cobb and Paul Douglas presented this function as a result of their empirical research (Cobb & Douglas, 1928). All textbook examples and numerous papers from leading authors such as Romer (1990), Gylfason (2003), Jones (2001), Barro and Sala-i-Martin (2004) and Arnold (1997) concentrate on the Cobb-Douglas functions in order to simplify the mathematical proof. Nevertheless, this type of function is consistent with the empirics (see i.e. Mankiw, Romer & Weil, 1992).

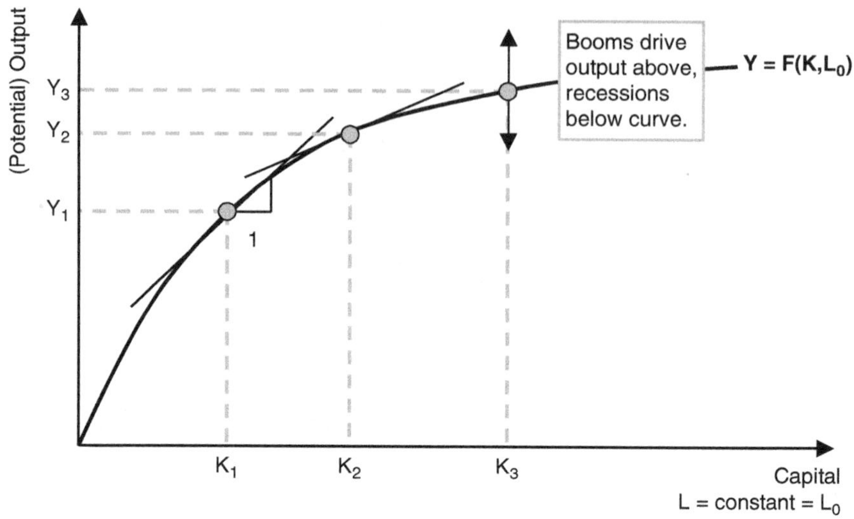

Fig. 3.4 Partial production function
Source: own figure according to Gaertner, 2003, p. 225

Economic growth models are long-term oriented. Therefore, short-term ups and downs of general business cycles are ignored. As it follows, Y represents a potential output, seen in Fig. 3.4.

The population's income Y is a *Cobb-Douglas-production function* with $Y = K^{\alpha} \cdot L^{1-\alpha}$. According to the Wicksell-Johnson-Theorem the level of elasticity in the production function equals one and is the sum of the partial production factor elasticity. $\alpha + (1 - \alpha) = 1$ (Frenkel & Hemmer, 1999, p. 39).

3.2.1.2 Labor Force

The labor supply grows exogenous and exponentially with the rate n and follows:

$$L = L_0 \cdot e^{n \cdot t} \tag{3.2}$$

Assuming the full employment of an available stock capital, one can see that the growth of L is represented in population growth (Solow, 1956, p. 67).

3.2.1.3 Closed Economy

The standard model assumes a closed economy. There are several augmentations of Solow's model, which explain in detail the consequences of an open economy.

Closed models often used to ease this understanding. By opening the model, a new interacting variable (foreign sector) is introduced, which complicates often the understanding of the main structure.

3.2.1.4 Savings

People consume a fraction c out of their current income (Y). This leads to C = c · Y. The amount, which is not consumed, is obviously saved. Thus, the fraction is s = 1−c (Gaertner, 2003, p. 230). Savings are assumed as a constant fraction for the output Y and follows with S = s · Y.

3.2.1.5 Investments

Solow's model observes output "as net output after making good the depreciation of capital" (Solow, 1956, p. 66). Therefore, all variables of this model are included in depreciations implicitly, i.e. investments are regarded as net investments.

This implies that net investment is just the rate of increase of this capital stock $\dot{K} = \frac{dK}{dt}$, so the basic identity at every instant of time is $\dot{K} = I^n =$ s · Y (Solow, 1956, p. 66).

From the circular flow model it follows that in equilibrium all planned spending equal income. Therefore, it is expressed as:

$$S - I + T - G + IM - EX = 0 \tag{3.3}$$

With T = government taxes, G = government spending, IM = imports and EX = exports. In the simplest case is IM = EX = T = G = 0 (Gaertner, 2003, p. 230), so that S = I.

3.2.1.6 Technological Progress

In general, a Cobb-Douglas production function can be expressed as Y(t) = F[A(t), S(t)K(t),H(t)L(t)] with A(t) as disembodied technology progress (Hicks-neutral), S(t) as capital saving technology progress (Solow-neutral), and H(t) as labor saving technology increase (Harrod-neutral).

One can also distinguish several determinates of growth and differentiate these factors within a classical production function (Cezanne, 2005, p. 499):

- The quantitative increase of the production factors
- The qualitative increase of the production factors
- Independent technological progress, and finally
- The change in the partial production elasticities

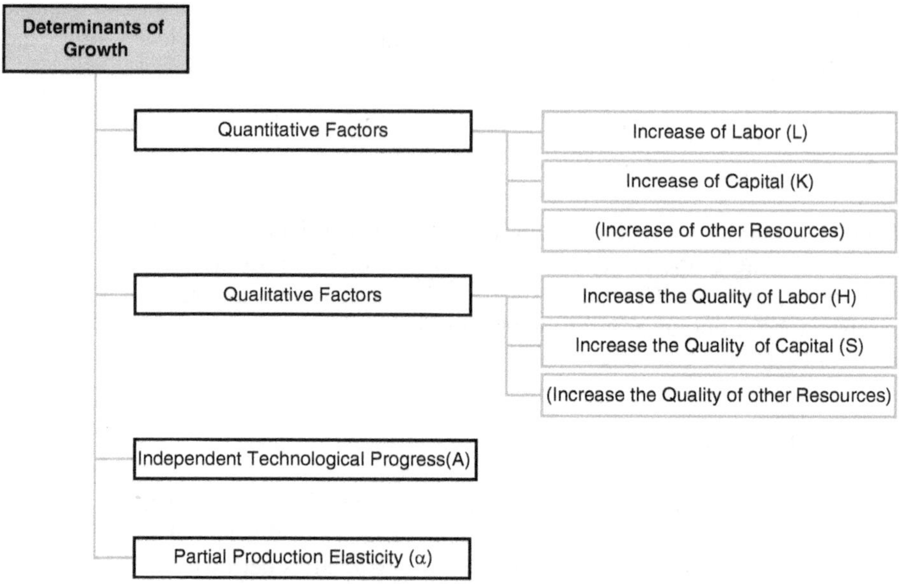

Fig. 3.5 Determinants of growth
Source: own figure according to Cezanne, 2005, p. 499

In Fig. 3.5 these previous listings are adapted into a neoclassical production function. Michael Frenkel and Hans-Rimbert Hemmer explained the technological progress as an innovation in new products or qualitative improved goods (Frenkel & Hemmer, 1999, pp. 109–110). This paper, however, focuses on the process of innovation – the same factor input leads to a higher factor output.

When technological progress does not change the marginal productivity of both factors, then it is referred to as the Hicks-neutral technological progress. In addition, the factor price ratio stays constant. The marginal rate of substitution is therefore only a function of the factor ratio and not the technology (Frenkel & Hemmer, 1999, pp. 115–116). This is expressed by:

$$\begin{aligned} Y(t) &= F[A(t), S(t)K(t), H(t)L(t)], \quad \text{with S(t) = H(t) = 1 and } \frac{dA}{dt} > 0 \\ &= A(t) \cdot F[K(t), L(t)] \end{aligned} \tag{3.4}$$

The progress is a factor of augmentation and product orientation. Assuming that A is increasing over time, then the isoquants Y_1, Y_2, Y_3 move upwards and angles α_1, α_2, α_3 are equal and constant, as seen in Fig. 3.6. Therefore, a technological change is neutral if the ratio of the marginal products stays constant for a given capital-labor proportion (Hicks, 1932).

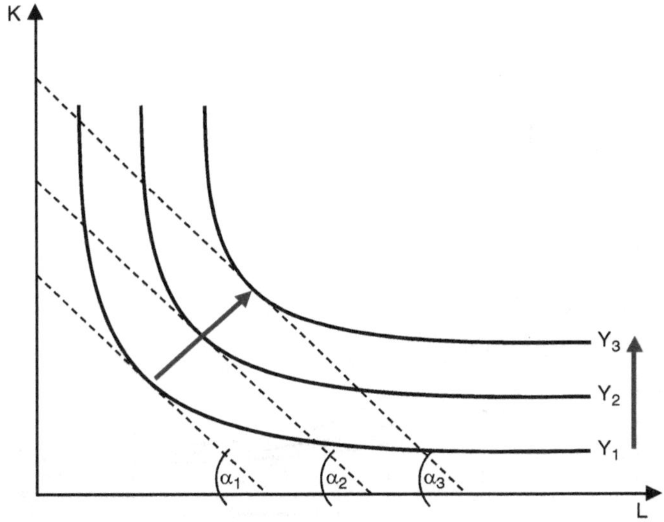

Fig. 3.6 Hicks-neutral growth
Source: own figure according to Frenkel & Hemmer, 1999, pp. 115–116

Harrod based his understanding of the technological progress on empiric research. He theorized that the interest rate and the capital coefficient are more stable than wage. His neutrality assumption follows that the capital coefficient stays constant over time only when capital K and output Y grow with the same rate. Therefore, it follows that technological progress has to be labor saving (Frenkel & Hemmer, 1999, pp. 119–120).

As seen in:

$$\begin{aligned} Y(t) &= F[A(t), S(t) \cdot K(t), H(t) \cdot L(t)], \quad \text{with A(t)} = \text{S(t)} = 1 \text{ and } \frac{dH}{dt} > 0 \\ &= F[K(t), H(t) \cdot L(t)] \end{aligned} \tag{3.5}$$

Figure 3.7 illustrates that an increasing Y leads to declining tangent angles α, hence is $\alpha_1 > \alpha_{2,} > \alpha_3$. A technological change is neutral if the input-factor-share remains unchanged over time, diving way to a capital output ratio (Harrod, 1966). Thus, the standard Solow-Model is a type of Harrod-neutral technological progress.

The last case is the capital saving technological progress. It is also named Solow-neutral. For the sake of completeness, one can write:

$$\begin{aligned} Y(t) &= F[A(t), S(t) \cdot K(t), H(t) \cdot L(t)], \quad \text{with A(t)} = \text{H(t)} = 1 \text{ and } \frac{dS}{dt} > 0 \\ &= F[S(t) \cdot K(t), L(t)] \end{aligned} \tag{3.6}$$

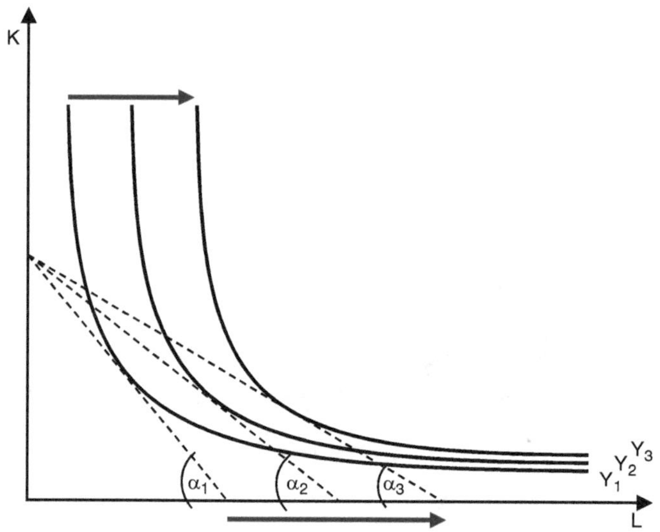

Fig. 3.7 Harrod-neutral growth
Source: own figure according to Frenkel & Hemmer, 1999, pp. 115–116

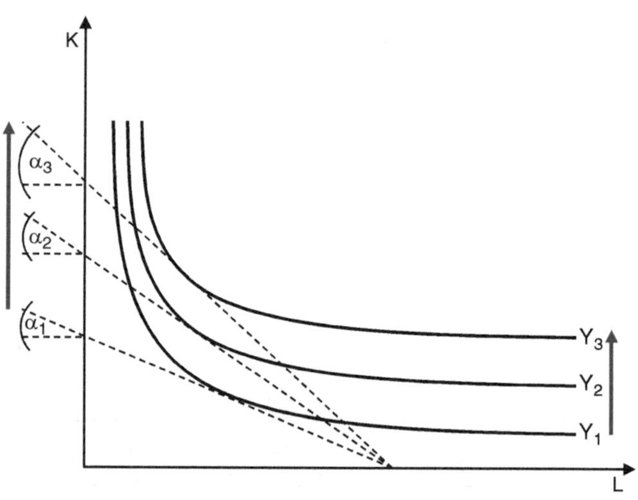

Fig. 3.8 Solow-neutral growth
Source: own figure

This specification represents the opposite of the Harrod-neutral technological progress. It is important to note that although it is named after Solow, it is not the technological progress that is usually implemented in Solow's growth model. Figure 3.8 explains the effect of an increasing S over time. The tangent angles α increases, hence $\alpha_1 < \alpha_{2,} < \alpha_3$.

3.2.2 *Structure*

3.2.2.1 Stock-Flow-Diagram

Based on the model assumption one can determine Solow's growth model with:

$$Y = K^{\alpha} \cdot (A \cdot L)^{(1-\alpha)} \tag{3.7}$$

$$\dot{K} = I^N = S \tag{3.8}$$

$$S + C = Y \tag{3.9}$$

$$S = s \cdot Y \tag{3.10}$$

$$C = (1 - s) \cdot Y \tag{3.11}$$

$$L = L_0 \cdot e^{n \cdot t} \tag{3.12}$$

$$A = A_0 \cdot e^{g \cdot t} \tag{3.13}$$

Note the symbolic changes. In the previous section, the Harrod-neutral technological progress was named H instead of A. Thus, there is an opportunity to add the Hicks-neutral and the Solow-neutral technological growth to the model, but for simplification they are set to 1.

Figure 3.9 shows the stock and flow consistent representation of the mathematical formulas. The model consists of three stocks – *capital K, labor L and technology A*. Every stock has a net-inflow, whereas "I net", "delta L" and "delta A" are the change over time from period t to t+1. The auxiliary variables are outcome (Y), savings (S) and consumption (C). The exogenous factors (constants) are the partial production elasticity of capital (α), the saving ratio (s), the labor force growth rate (n) and the technological progress growth rate (g).

The model includes *exponential growth patterns* at three places:

- The technology loop with the length one and *A – delta A – A*
- The labor loop with the length one and *L – delta L – L*
- The investment loop with the length three and *K – Y – S – I – K*

3.2.2.2 Phase Plot

The formulation of the capital stock is diverted out of the model. Depreciations are thereby considered within the net investments. This is different from many standard examples, where depreciations in the basic model are explicit.

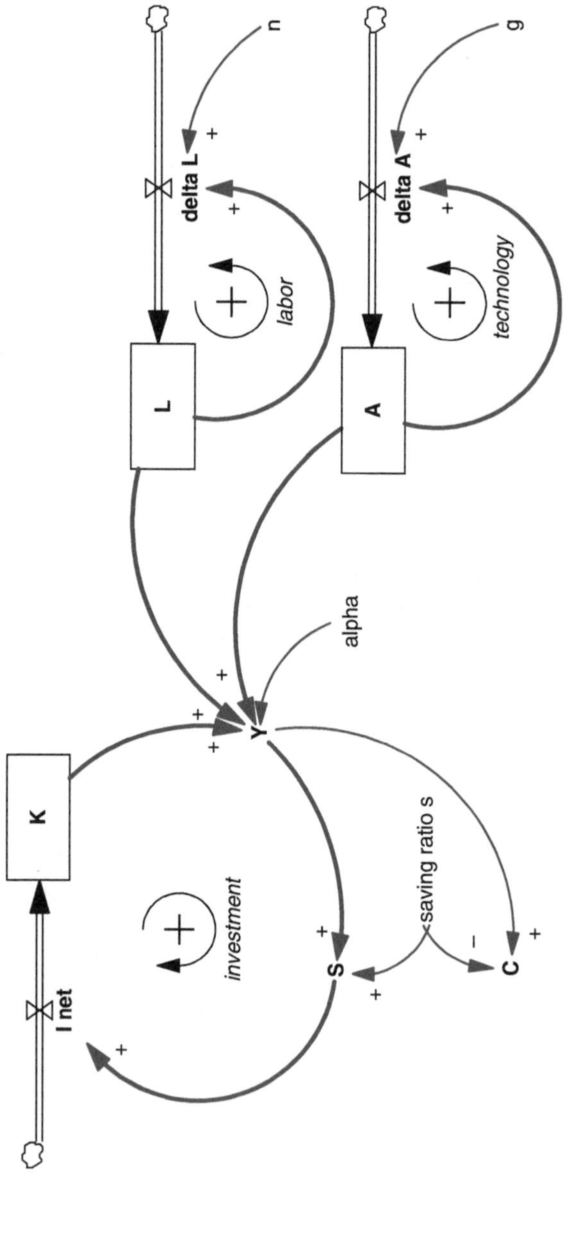

Fig. 3.9 Solow-model
Source: own figure

The capital per efficient unit of labor (k) is one of the central topics in the neoclassical growth theory. It is defined as the relationship of capital (K) to labor (L) and labor saving technological progress (A):

$$k = \frac{K}{AL} \tag{3.14}$$

The transposing into the intensive form of the output (Y), taking into consideration the standardization of effective labor force, delivers the equation:

$$f(k) = \frac{Y}{AL} = \left(\frac{K}{AL}\right)^a = k^a \tag{3.15}$$

If the capital per efficient unit of labor rises, then the income per effective capita (*Y/AL*) increases as well, but with decreasing growth rates. This is due to the fact that the capital share of output (α) is smaller than 1.

Furthermore, the capital per efficient unit of labor $k = \frac{K}{AL}$ diverts with time, thus:

$$\begin{aligned} \dot{k} &= \frac{\partial \frac{K}{AL}}{\partial t} = \frac{\dot{K} \cdot (AL) - K \cdot \left(\dot{AL}\right)}{(AL)^2} \\ &= \frac{\dot{K}}{AL} - \frac{K \cdot \left(\dot{AL}\right)}{(AL)^2} = \frac{\dot{K}}{AL} - \frac{K \cdot (\dot{A}L + \dot{L}A)}{(AL)^2} \end{aligned} \tag{3.16}$$

$$\begin{aligned} &= \frac{\dot{K}}{AL} - \frac{K\dot{L}A}{(AL)^2} - \frac{K\dot{A}L}{(AL)^2} \\ &= \frac{\dot{K}}{K} \cdot \frac{K}{AL} - \frac{\dot{L}}{L} \cdot \frac{K}{AL} - \frac{\dot{A}}{A} \cdot \frac{K}{AL} \\ &= \frac{I^n}{K} \cdot \frac{K}{AL} - n \cdot \frac{K}{AL} - g \cdot \frac{K}{AL} \\ &= \frac{I^n}{AL} - (n+g) \cdot k \end{aligned} \tag{3.17}$$

After the substitution of $I^n = S = s \cdot Y$ and $f(k) = \frac{Y}{AL} = k^\alpha$ one comes to Solow's famous fundamental equation:

$$\dot{k} = s \cdot f(k) - (n+g) \cdot k \tag{3.18}$$

This equation is the fundamental bases for almost all growth-theoretical analysis (see i.e. Auerbach & Kotlikoff, 1999; Mankiw, 2007; Barro & Sala-i-Martin, 2004).

Putting this all together one can create a phase plot with k on the abscissa and three functions on the ordinate: income per effective capita (*Y/AL*), the net investments $s \cdot f(k)$ and the requirement line with $(n+g) \cdot k$ (see Fig. 3.10).

If k is smaller than k* than, over the course of time, the capital intensity will continue to increase. Because *f(k)* is based on a function with decreasing marginal

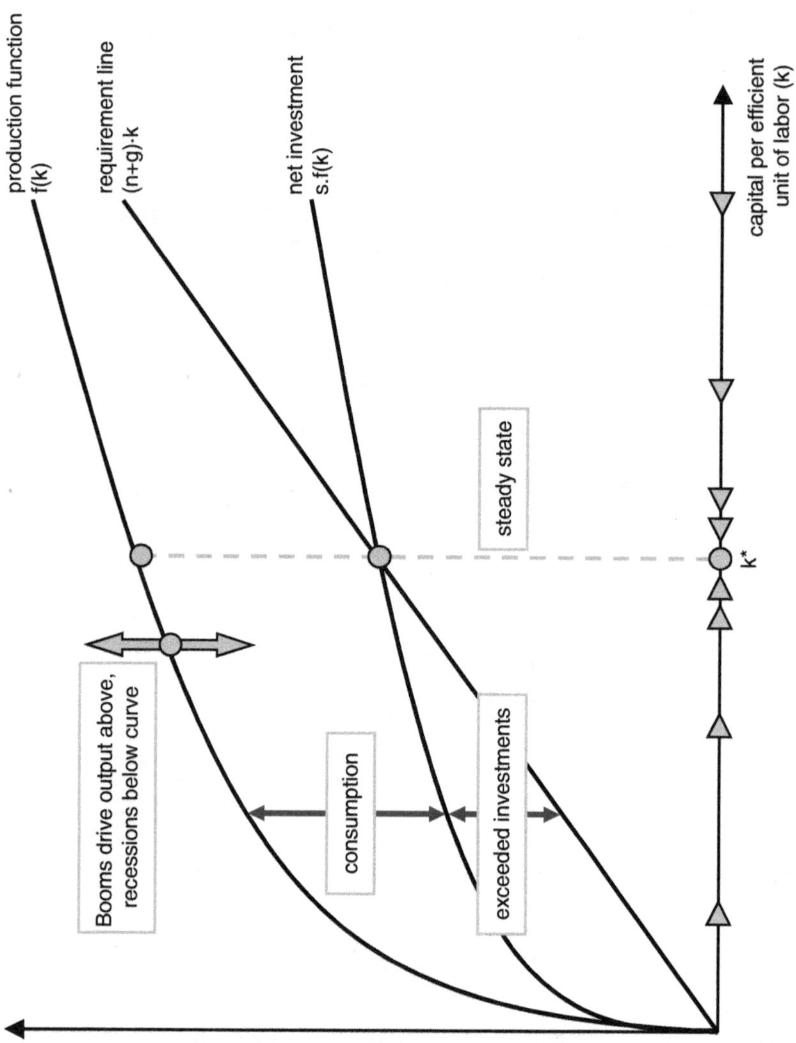

Fig. 3.10 Solow-model: phase plot
Source: own figure according to Gaertner, 2003, p. 231

productivity, the increase is continually declining. The curve $(n+g) \cdot k$ indicates which net investments are necessary per capita, so that the effective capital intensity can be maintained with a growing population and continual technological progress. The curve $s \cdot f(k)$ describes the actual net investments per capita. As long as $s \cdot f(k)$ is larger than the required investments $(n+g) \cdot k$ the effective capital intensity per output labor will increase (exceeding investments).

3.2.2.3 Long-Term Equilibrium

In the post-keynesian tradition, a steady state is defined as periodic equilibrium if:

- Planed investments equals planed savings (independently set up)
- The production capacity is fully utilized (Frenkel & Hemmer, 1999, p. 37)

In this neoclassical world, however, the equilibrium provides for the goods, the labor and the capital market. This means that:

- All produced goods will be sold (Investments = Savings)
- All capital goods are utilized
- All labor supply is employed (Frenkel & Hemmer, 1999, pp. 37–38)

All of this is defined within the assumptions presented by the neoclassical model. To evaluate the stable point in the Solow-model, Solow provided the major model with the variable k. The model aims for a related steady state in $k = \frac{K}{A \cdot L}$. When the steady state is achieved, k* stays constant over time with $\frac{\partial k}{\partial t} = 0$. In this case, investments, which are required to support the technological progress and the population growth, equal that of the net investments. One can formulate this:

$$\frac{\partial k}{\partial t} = 0 = s \cdot f(k) - (n+g) \cdot k \tag{3.19}$$

Leading to:

$$s \cdot f(k) = (n+g) \cdot k \tag{3.20}$$

The steady state k* follows with:

$$\frac{s}{(n+g)} = \frac{k}{f(k)} = \frac{k}{k^{\alpha}} = k^{1-\alpha} \tag{3.21}$$

$$k^* = \left(\frac{s}{(n+g)}\right)^{\frac{1}{1-\alpha}} \tag{3.22}$$

The capital stock grows at an equal rate to both the population and the technological progress. Hence, this follows:

$$k = \frac{K}{A \cdot L} = \text{constant} \tag{3.23}$$

$$\frac{\dot{K}}{K} = \frac{\dot{L}}{L} + \frac{\dot{A}}{A} = n + g \tag{3.24}$$

One can show that the equilibrium of Y and K grows, with the growth rates of the technical progress and population growth:

$$\frac{\dot{Y}}{Y} = \frac{I^n}{K} = \frac{\dot{L}}{L} + \frac{\dot{A}}{A} = n + g \tag{3.25}$$

Interestingly, the per-capita income, within the steady state, grows at the same rate as the technical progress. Seen here as:

$$\dot{\left(\frac{Y}{L}\right)} \Big/ \left(\frac{Y}{L}\right) = \frac{\dot{A}}{A} = g \tag{3.26}$$

The variables grow exponentially, however the ratio $k = \frac{K}{A \cdot L}$ remains constant with k*. Note that the equilibrium point is independent from the initial level of K, L or A. It contains the growth rates of the population and technology as well as the saving ratio. The statement is quite clear: increasing steady wealth growth happens only through technical progress. And it is only a question of time, and not of wealth, for countries to achieve the same steady state.

3.2.3 Dynamics

3.2.3.1 Transitional Dynamics

An economy with a capital intensity smaller than k^*, produces net investments which are larger per capita than the necessary net investments per capita to maintain the capital intensity for a growing population and technological progress. The capital intensity increases. This process takes place until a steady state is reached. At this point, s corresponds $s \cdot f(k)$, and is necessary to maintain for investments resulting from an increasing population and the growing technology. The balanced capital intensity is k^*.

By using Solow's fundamental equation $\dot{k} = s \cdot f(k) - (n + g) \cdot k$ one can show that the change in capital stock depends on the exceeded investments above the required investments. Figure 3.11 illustrates how the capital per effective unit of labor changes when the capital per effective unit of labor emerges. There are three functions:

1. $s \cdot f(k)$
2. $(n + g) \cdot k$
3. Resulting $\dot{k}$ after subtraction (1) and (2)

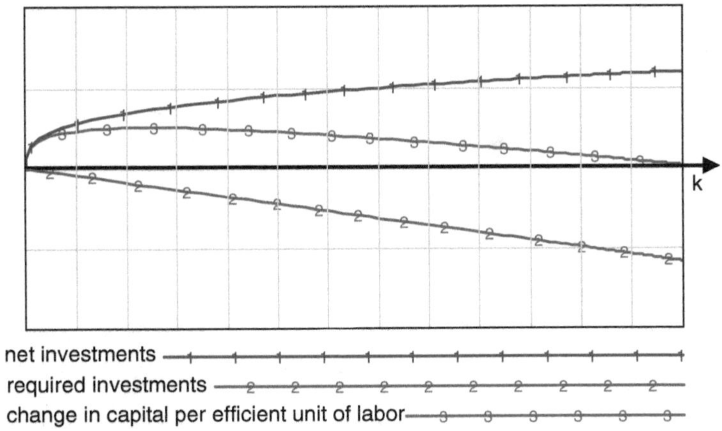

Fig. 3.11 Change in capital per efficient unit of labor
Source: own simulation

One can recognize that the resulting $\dot{k}$ increases with growing k until the required investments equal the net investment. After the maximum point k grows, in correlation to the declining growth rate, until the steady state k* is attained.

If one compares two countries with different initial values of the capital stock, then it follows that the capital stocks will approach each other over time. When the growth rate of the population and the technical progress are equally large and the saving ratio s is identical, then the steady state will be the same. This is referred to as: *absolute convergence*. When the saving ratios or the growth rates of the population or technical progress differ, then they simply approach each other. This is called: *relative convergence*. Therefore, it is only a matter of time before the wealth of these countries adjusts itself. This is due to the decreasing marginal productivities in the production factors. In 1992, Mankiw, Romer and Weil (Mankiw et al., 1992) presented a famous study, which empirically examined this approach and confirmed the core statements of the Solow-model.

3.2.3.2 Approaching Velocity

Another way to illustrate the transition towards the steady state is the approaching velocity. The previous section argued a long-term equilibrium. This section highlights velocity and answers the question: Is it increasing or decreasing over time when it comes to the steady state? Figure 3.12 shows that the velocity declines with growing k. Technically, the long-term steady state is reached in infinity with decline approaching velocity. This is represented in the graph with dotted lines; each dot represents a step in time. The negative acceleration leads to the shrinking distance between dots.

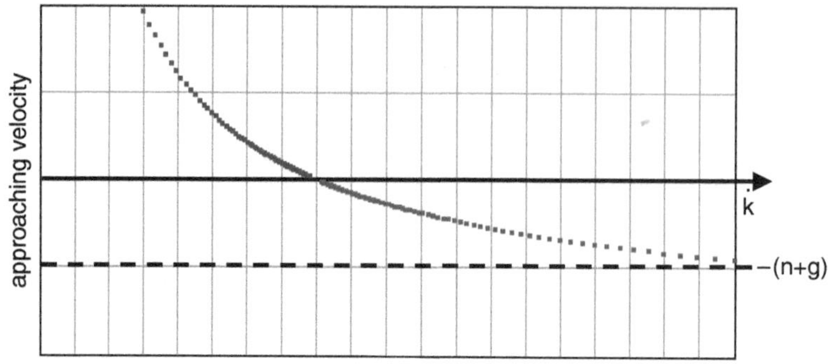

Fig. 3.12 Velocity of capital intensity per effective unit labor
Source: own simulation

Mathematically, the formula for the approaching velocity is derived from the equation:

$$\dot{k} = s \cdot f(k) - (n+g) \cdot k \tag{3.27}$$

Dividing by k gives the growth rate of k:

$$\frac{\dot{k}}{k} = s \cdot \frac{f(k)}{k} - (n+g) \tag{3.28}$$

3.2.3.3 Golden Rule of Accumulation

The so-called 'Golden Rule of Accumulation' goes back to a paper from Edmund Phelps in the American Economic Review (Phelps, 1961). He explained a simple way to investigate the optimal saving rate. This would be to measure the maximization of the total inter-temporal consumption. Phelps stated:

> By a golden age I shall mean a dynamic equilibrium in which output and capital grow exponentially at the same rate so that the capital-output ratio is stationary over time (Phelps, 1961, p. 639).

In Phelps' model, the economy is already in a steady state and the capital per efficient labor stays constant over time, the net investments are zero and all required investments are due to technological progress and population growth. This is presented in the equation:

$$s \cdot f(k) = (n+g) \cdot k \tag{3.29}$$

Phelps suggested a simple policy. The investment is a constant proportion of the output and has an endogenized saving rate (Phelps, 1961, p. 639).

But how much weight should be put on current and future consumption (Gaertner, 2003, p. 237)? A way to evaluate this could be to maximize the inter-temporal consumption. The relevant optimization function is:

$$C = Y - S \overset{!}{=} \max. \tag{3.30}$$

Given the consumption per effective labor with $c = \frac{C}{AL}$ the maximization function can be changed to:

$$c = f(k) - s \cdot f(k) \overset{!}{=} \max. \tag{3.31}$$

Inserting this in equation (3.29), it leads to:

$$c = f(k) - (n + g) \cdot k \overset{!}{=} \max. \tag{3.32}$$

C maximizes where the first derivative equals zero $\frac{\delta c}{\delta k} = 0$ and the second derivative is less than zero $\frac{\delta c}{\delta^2 k} < 0$ with $c'' = f''(k) < 0$. Insertion gives the following:

$$c' = f'(k) - (n + g) = 0 \tag{3.33}$$

$$c' = a\left(\frac{K}{AL}\right)^{a-1} - (n + g) = 0 \tag{3.34}$$

$$a\left(\frac{K}{AL}\right)^{a-1} = (n + g) \tag{3.35}$$

As seen in Sect. 3.2.2.3, the condition for a constant capital on efficient labor is known by:

$$k^* = \frac{K}{AL} = \left(\frac{n + g}{s}\right)^{\frac{1}{a-1}} \tag{3.36}$$

Insertion in (3.35) delivers:

$$a \cdot \left(\left(\frac{n + g}{s}\right)^{\frac{1}{a-1}}\right)^{a-1} = (n + g) \tag{3.37}$$

$$a \cdot \frac{n + g}{s} = (n + g) \tag{3.38}$$

$$a = s \tag{3.39}$$

The solution indicates that maximum consumption is possible, if the capital coefficient alpha of the production functions equals that of the saving rate s. As Phelps described it:

> We may call [the] relation [...] the golden rule of accumulation, and with good reason. In a golden age governed by the golden rule, each generation invests on behalf of future generations that share of income which [...] it would have to had past generations invest on behalf of it. We have shown that, among golden-age paths of natural growth, that golden age is best which practices the golden rule (Phelps, 1961, p. 642).

3.2.3.4 Dynamic Efficiency and Dynamic Inefficiency

The Golden Rule states that if the current saving rate is not equal to the golden saving rate, then consumption does not maximize inter-temporary. Assuming that the saving rate is too high, lowering the saving ratio would instantaneously increase consumption C over time. This is the situation for *dynamic inefficiency*. More interesting for policy-makers, however, is the situation with too low savings rates. This is referred to as *dynamically efficient*. Raising it would provide a higher consumption in the future, but the immediate effect would be a lowered consumption, which later, rises above the previous consumption levels. All in all, policy-makers have to decide whether this generation (today) or the future generation (long run) should gain an advantage of higher consumption (Gaertner, 2003, p. 237).

Figure 3.13 presents both cases. On the left is the situation of $s > s_{gold}$. On the right side is $s < s_{gold}$. At time $t = 10$ the saving rate switches to $s = s_{gold}$. The consumption per effective capita is marked as line 3. The long run and new steady state are both higher than the initial one. However, in dynamically efficient cases C/AL drops below the initial value before it increases. The path of long run higher consumption can only be obtained at the cost of today's lower consumption. Remarkably, in the case of dynamically inefficiency (left graph) the per capita income dramatically declines. As the income Y/L was not part of the maximization it drops with a shrinking saving ratio s.

3.2.4 Policy Experiments

This section examines the demographic determinations used by Solow within the neoclassical growth model. Chapter 2 identified and discussed the main points:

1. Population
2. Population Structure
3. Fertility

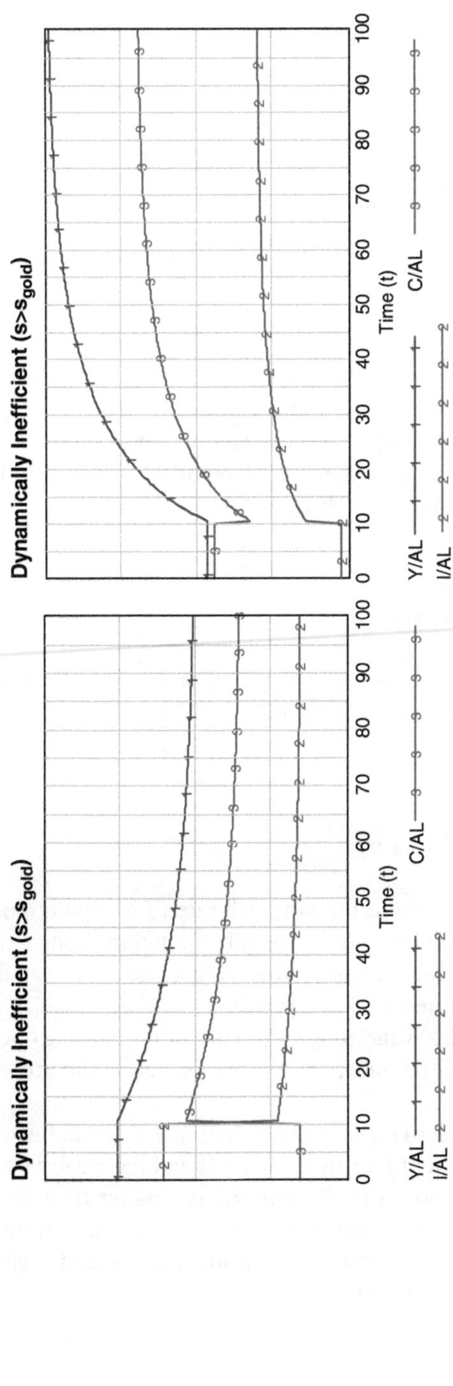

Fig. 3.13 Golden rule of accumulation
Source: own simulation

4. Mortality
5. Migration

The Solow-model consists of several constant factors:

- Initial value of capital (K_0), labor (L_0) and technology (A_0)
- Saving ratio (s)
- Labor growth (n)
- Technological progress (g)

Demographic determinants can either be integrated into external factors or implemented into the model structure as endogenized factors.

3.2.4.1 Population

The Solow-model represents only the labor force, which means that only the working citizens are considered in the economy. But the neoclassical theory assumes flexibility in both wages and the labor market. Thus, this assumption of full employment leads to a linkage between labor force and population. The stock of labor force (L) is an adequate substitute for the population.

3.2.4.2 Population Structure

The labor stock is the aggregation of the total workforce. It does not distinguish between working and non-working population. Thus, a population structure is not explicitly embodied and does not imply an age structure effect.

3.2.4.3 Fertility and Mortality

Fertility and mortality add up to the net birth rate of a population. Section 3.2.1.2 shows the connection between labor force and population. Hence, the growth rate of labor force and population are the same. A decline in a population implies a population size effect (Gruescu, 2006, p. 32).

As shown in Sect. 3.2.2.3 the long-term capital output ratio per efficiency unit does not depend on the initial values of the stocks, but on the growth rates of L and A and on the saving ratio s.

The phase plot in Fig. 3.14 shows how an increase in g and n would influence the steady state. The requirement line shifts upward and the steady state capital output ratio per efficiency unit moves to the left. K_1 is smaller than k_0. A lower steady state per capita income follows directly from this, due to a higher amount of the net-investments needed to support the continuous labor and technology increase. Mathematically, this is expressed:

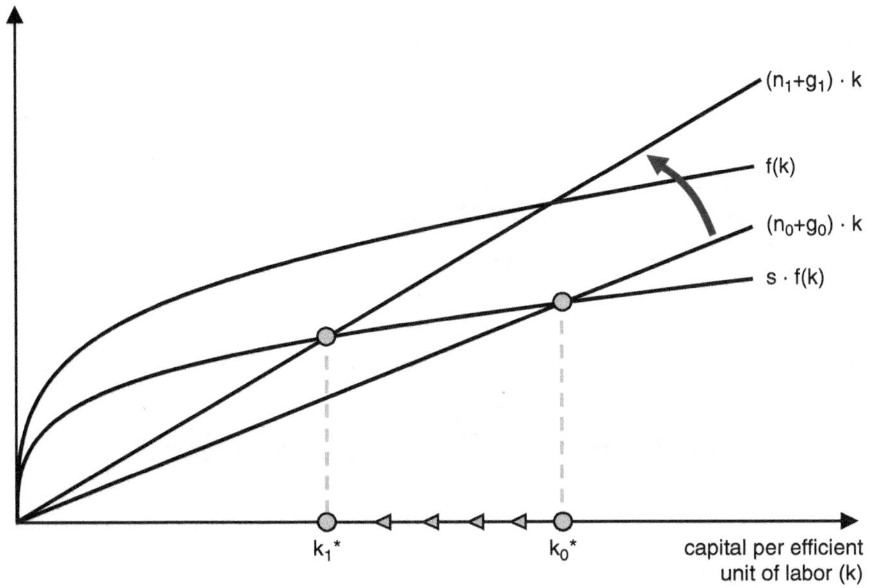

Fig. 3.14 Policy experiments: required investments
Source: own figure

$$
\begin{aligned}
k^* &= const. \\
\frac{dk}{dt} &= 0 \\
\frac{\dot{K}}{K} &= \frac{\dot{L}}{L} + \frac{\dot{A}}{A} \\
\frac{\dot{K}}{K} &= n + g
\end{aligned}
\tag{3.40}
$$

This is different from the basic scenario shown in Fig. 3.15. The increase in the technology growth rate accelerates the exponential growth of stock A (grey scenario runs are above base scenario); similar to the labor force (L) but with the growth rate n. From the Cobb-Douglas function F(K, AL) one can see that an increase in A and L also leads to a higher output Y (all sensitivity runs are above the base scenario). Because the proportion s of the output Y, is invested in K, one can consequently conclude that the capital stocks also must accelerate in their exponential growth.

The variables effective in capital intensity and income per effective capita do have a new and lower steady state value in the scenario run than in the base run. However, the capital intensity and the income per capita increase because both of them are growing with the rate g or formally:

$$
\dot{\left(\frac{K}{L}\right)} \Big/ \frac{K}{L} = \dot{\left(\frac{Y}{L}\right)} \Big/ \frac{Y}{L} = g \tag{3.41}
$$

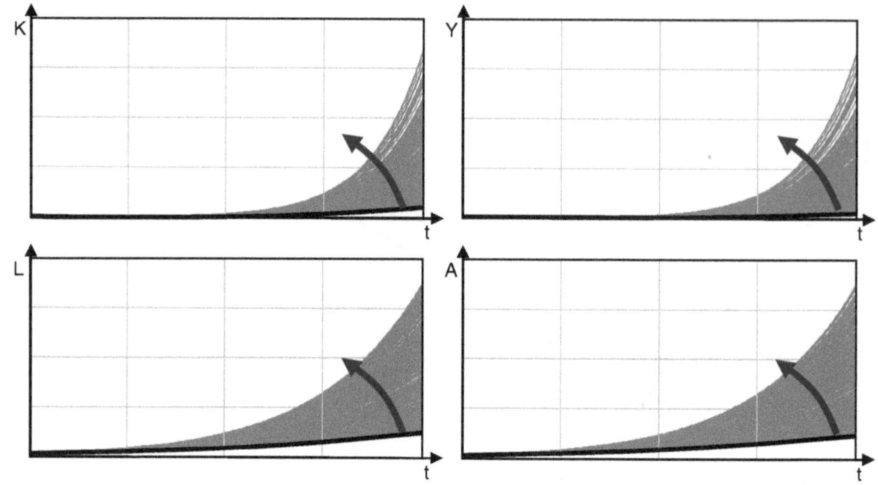

Fig. 3.15 Sensitivity run: K, L, Y, A
Source: own simulation

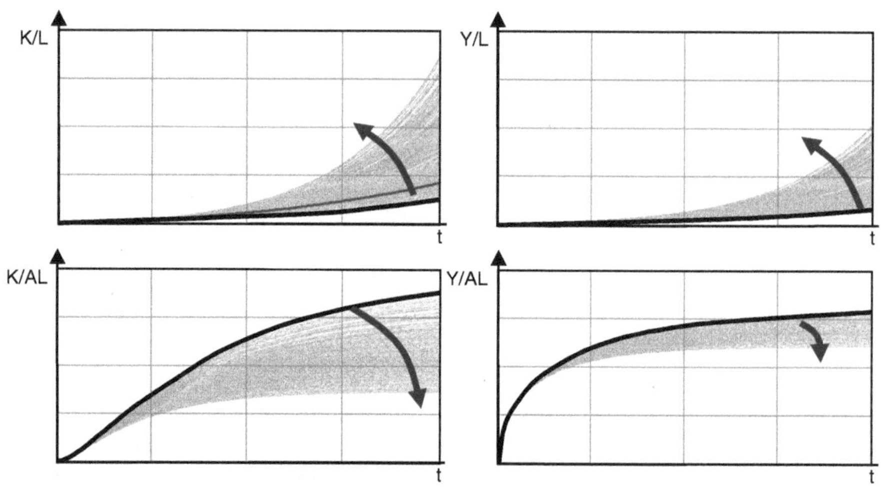

Fig. 3.16 Sensitivity run: K/L, K/AL, Y/L, Y/AL
Source: own figure

The behavior is also shown in Fig. 3.16.

A decline in the population growth rate n, such as how it appears through a demographic change, will first be problematic when $n \leqslant 0$ and $|n| \geqslant g$. In this case, the growth rate from n+g and the requirement line are both negative. Graphically, there is not intersection with the investment, and the new steady state capital intensity per effective unit of labor (k) is zero. All real investments, in this case, rise above the required investments.

Last but not least, it must be commented that the growth rate n is constant. Thus, in this case it is not possible to reflect on how the population changes and grows over time.

3.2.4.4 Migration

Migration is not considered in the model, as it implies a closed economy. Indirectly a constant, migration is based on the labor force stock and is possible if one assumes that the growth rate of migration is embodied in the growth rate of the labor stock (n).

3.2.4.5 Other Factors

A change in the savings ratio s would shift the net investments upward, defined as sf (k) and displayed in Fig. 3.17. The new steady state k_1 moves right, towards a higher effective capital intensity. This results in a higher capital stock and outcome of Y. As there are more savings S the net investments increase. In addition, the capital stock and the outcome Y grow faster.

Figures 3.18 and 3.19 present this behavior – seen in the constant growth rates of g and n compared to the base run. The stocks of labor and technology are identical

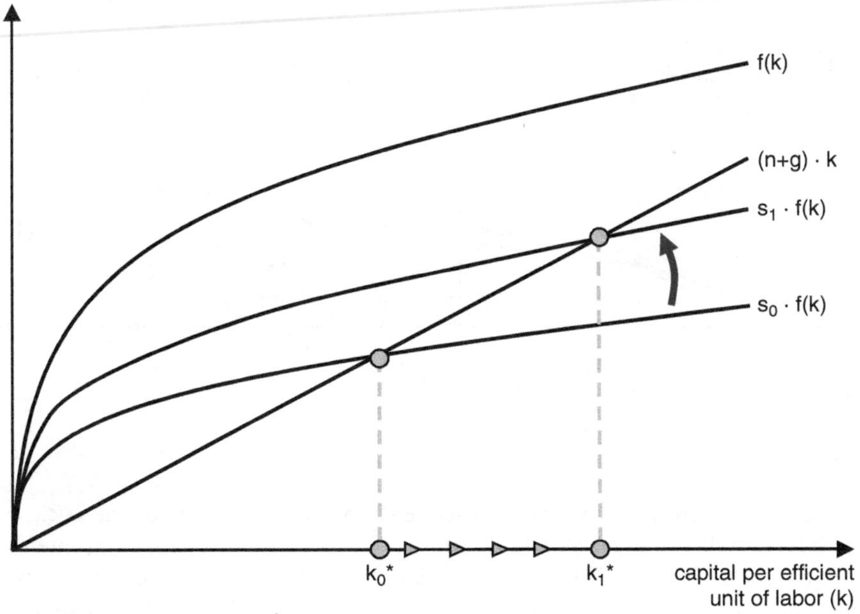

Fig. 3.17 Policy experiments: net-investments
Source: own figure

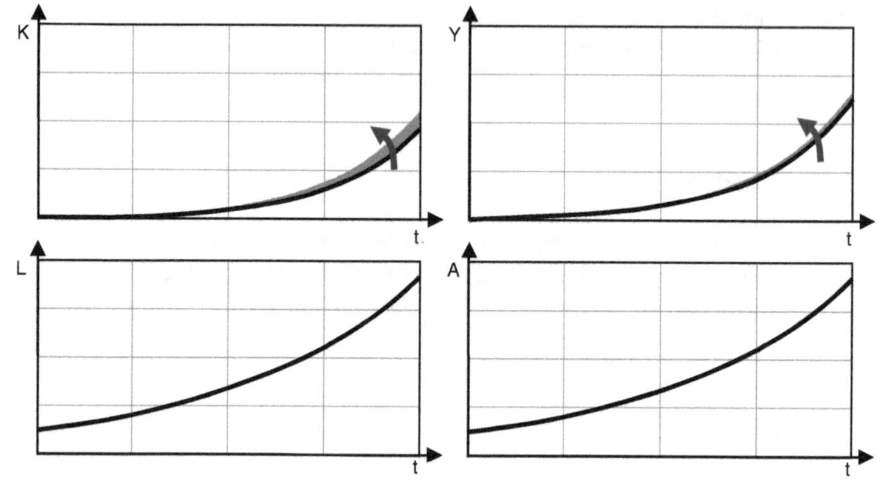

Fig. 3.18 Sensitivity run: K, L, Y, A
Source: own figure

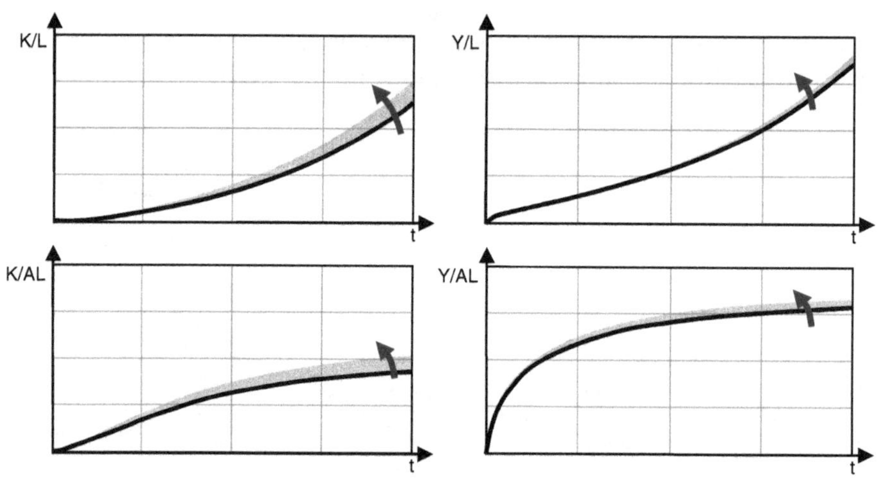

Fig. 3.19 Sensitivity run: K/L, K/AL, Y/L, Y/AL
Source: own figure

to the base run. These are a direct consequence of the increasing capital stock, but still, adequate labor and technology growth enable the effective capital intensity and the effective income per capita to achieve a higher value compared to the base run. Due to the increase in capital, both the capital intensity and the income per capita increase.

3.2.5 Augmentation

The Solow-model does not represent important demographic components within the equation. Thus, various authors have expanded upon the basic model and have published detailed observations about demographic changes. The following three sub-sections will discuss these findings.

3.2.5.1 Model of "Silver Growth" (Gruescu, 2006)

In 2006, Sandra Gruescu expanded the growth model with a self-introduced dependency ratio. This ratio made it possible to explicitly connect labor force (L) and population (N). Normally, in the neoclassical model there is a direct relationship between these two factors, usually within the first rule. This implies, of course, that the model does not take unemployment into consideration.

The dependency ratio is defined with (Gruescu, 2006, p. 96):

$$D = \frac{N - L}{L} \tag{3.42}$$

The nominator implies the non-working population and the denominator refers to the labor force. D symbolizes the number of non-workers as a part of a total worker composition. Gruescu addressed the idea that age structure will effect growth in numerous different models. An example of this can be found in the neoclassical growth model with a constant saving ratio. In this thesis, the Gruescu-model is technically advanced from the Solow-model; however, Gruescu's paper does not take this progress into account. In addition, the model begins with depreciation. In addition, the model is not consistent with the already presented original Solow-Model. A modification is seen below:

Replacing D and L, is reflected in:

$$L = \frac{N}{1 + D} \tag{3.43}$$

Inserting into the Cobb-Douglas production function gives:

$$Y = K^{\alpha} \cdot \left(A \cdot \frac{N}{1 + D}\right)^{1-\alpha} \tag{3.44}$$

Per effective capita delivers than:

$$\frac{Y}{AN} = \frac{1}{(1 + D)^{1-\alpha}} \cdot k^{\alpha} \tag{3.45}$$

The growth rates of the labor force and the population are both exogenous and constant. The introduced dependency ratio can substitute the labor force in the main equation as the population itself. If the growth rates of L and N are equal, then it follows constant D. If the labor force growth is smaller than the population growth, it implies that D is rising, which is also an indicator of an aging society.

Figure 3.20 presents the stock-flow-diagram for the Gruescu-model. The new components of this model, compared to the Solow-Model, are highlighted. The population stock N consists of a reinforced loop, with the growth rate p. The dependency ratio is calculated of N and L.

The steady state k=K/AL is derived from non-changing k over time (Gruescu, 2006, pp. 99–101):

$$s \cdot k^{\alpha} = (x + g) \cdot k \cdot (1 + D)^{1-\alpha} \tag{3.46}$$

(x = labor force growth rate; in the previous Solow-model marked with n)

$$k^* = \frac{K}{AL} = \left(\frac{s}{n+g}\right)^{\frac{1}{1-a}} \cdot \frac{1}{1+D} \tag{3.47}$$

One can replace $\frac{1}{1+D} = \frac{L}{N}$, showing clearly that the steady-state capital intensity per effective labor depends on the difference between L and N.

A large population N and a low proportion of working people (L) would lead to a low k* compared to Solow's model. From this, one can conclude that a population with a higher share of elderly people has lower income per capita (Gruescu, 2006, p. 101):

$$\frac{Y}{AL} = \left(\frac{s}{n+g}\right)^{\frac{\alpha}{1-a}} \cdot \frac{1}{1+D} \tag{3.48}$$

That the steady-state values from D are dependent must be implicitly accepted – D is constant. This, however, is only the case when the growth rate for labor force L and population N are the same and act as constants.

In conclusion, Gruescu's work makes it possible to consider age-quotas for education, such that, one can distinguish between the working and non-working population. The implications of this added the factor of unemployment in various concepts and brought unemployment to the light within economic research. In spite of this, Gruescu's ideas, in many situations, require specific conditions:

1. The dependency ration must be constant. A dynamic simulation of an aging population is observable only when a steady state is rejected.
2. The growth rates from L and N are exogenous.
3. Following this, the dependency ratio between the L and N relationship is established, but withdrawn later, in order to serve as a production function.

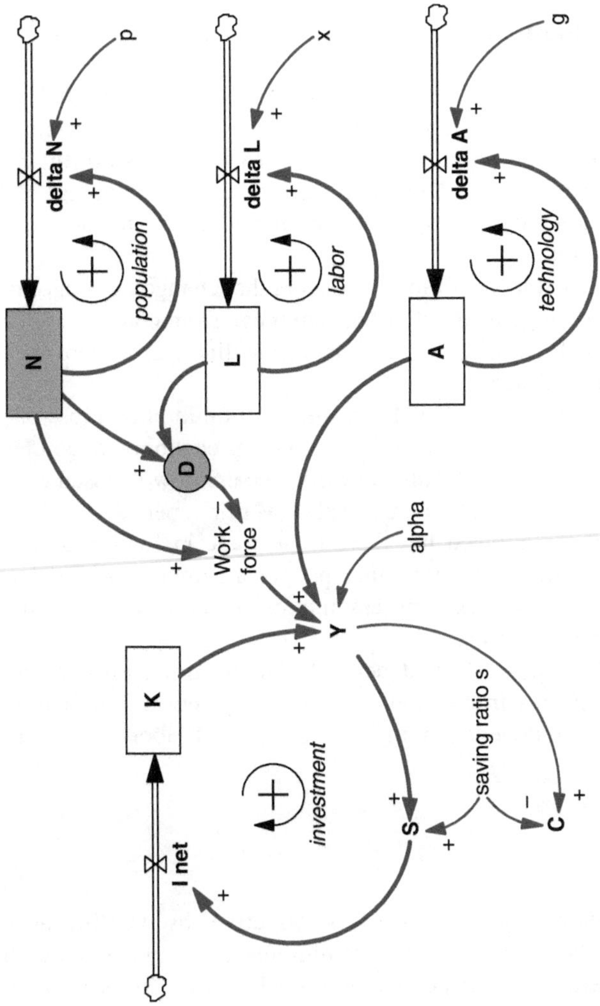

Fig. 3.20 Gruescu-model
Source: own figure

Ideally, labor force (L) would be a part of the function L = F(N(t),D(t)). If this occurred, L would serve as a complete substitute for production function. And the dependency ratio would be time sensitive. With this, one could more effectively and accurately restructure the age dynamic.

3.2.5.2 Model with Migration (Barro/Sala-i-Martin, 2004)

In Robert Barro and Xavier Sala-i-Martin's approach (2004, p. 383) several augmentations are taken into account, thereby improving the Solow-Model to address the changing demographic more accurately. Barro and Sala-i-Martin took a closer look at migration components. This implementation is based mainly on their 2004 work, and is slightly modified in order to fit within the themes and symbolic presented in this work.

Both emigration and immigration are factors that change an economy's population and labor force. In general, labor tends to move from countries with low wage rates to those with high wage rates. Labor mobility can hasten an economy's convergence toward its steady state.

Migration operates in two ways. First, immigration implies a loss of population in the home country and a gain in the host country's economy. Second, emigration brings a domestic economy a decline on work force. Solow's closed economy does not include migration, but Barro and Sala-i-Martin opened it to some extent. Mobility of persons is allowed but there is no trade in foreign goods or assets. That is, the unrealistic assumption that people are more mobile than physical capital. Although this is an extreme assumption, it serves to illustrate the power of migration in a growth model.

Migration M(t) is positive and depends on the time, thus, there can be a greater flow of migrants into a domestic economy. For simplification, one can assume that migration depends on the current stock of labor force and the migration ratio:

$$m = \frac{M}{L} \tag{3.49}$$

The more a country presents itself as attractive, by creating an open market for workers, the more migrants/immigrants the country will attract. The labor force changes over time; population growth and migration can be expressed as:

$$\dot{L} = (n + m) \cdot L \tag{3.50}$$

The quantity of capital each migrant brings along is κ(t) and the new element κ(t)M(t) contributes to the capital stock K. One can easily show that this is based on

Solow's fundamental equation, where the new capital intensity per effective worker over time is:

$$\dot{k} = s \cdot f(k) + m \cdot \hat{\kappa} - (g + n + m) \cdot k \tag{3.51}$$

with $\hat{\kappa}$ as capital per effective migrant.

Barro and Sala-i-Martin (2004) explained the term $m \cdot \hat{\kappa} + (g + n + m) \cdot k$ as the "new" requirement line and $m \cdot (k - \hat{\kappa})$ as the augmentation. Here, it is important to stress this new extension because their interpretation of the migration might be misleading. For this purpose, see Fig. 3.21, which shows in detail a stock-flow-model for this augmentation. Now capital stock has two inflows. One is identified as a net investment and the other is capital brought by immigrants. In addition, the labor force stock increases not only with population growth, but also due to immigration.

Capital brought by the migrants from their country of origin is considered as investments, however are not required or dependent on the previous national income. Thus, the term $m \cdot \hat{\kappa}$ is better treated as additional real investments comparable with $s \cdot f(k)$ instead of required investments. But an increase in the population due to migration $m \cdot k$ has an additional effect on the required investment.

Another major factor of additional capital from immigrants is that it can counteract the growth of the effective capital intensity and move it above a steady state. Barro et al. did not mention this phenomenon (Barro & Sala-i-Martin, 2004). Figure 3.22 presents, on the left side, the standard case with low migration rates. Real investments consist of $s \cdot f(k) + m \cdot \hat{\kappa}$ and are higher than in the standard Solow-model. The right graph in Fig. 3.22 shows the theoretical case of "over-investment". This situation happens if the capital brought by immigrants, within one period, is too high and if the periodic change of the effective capital intensity adds up above the steady state.

3.2.5.3 Model with Variable Population Growth (Solow, 1956)

The core idea of variable population growth goes back to Solow itself (Solow, 1956, pp. 90–91). The major point is presented here, with minor changes to be consistent with the previous sections.

Instead of treating the relative rate of population increase (n) as a constant; one can more classically make it an endogenous variable of the system. In particular, if one supposes that $\frac{\dot{L}}{L}$ depends only on the level of per capita income or consumption, or for that matter on the real wage rate, the generalization is especially easy to carry out.

Since the effective per capita income is given by $\frac{Y}{AL} = f(k)$, one can easily surmise that the growth rate of the labor force becomes a function of the effective capital-labor ratio alone with $n(k)$. The basic differential equation becomes:

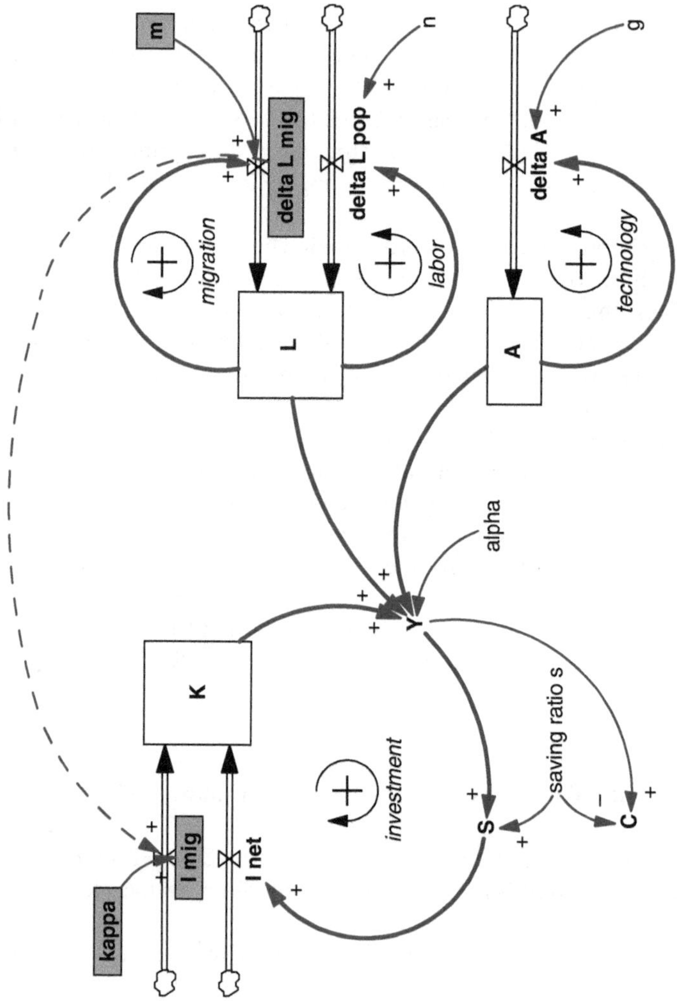

Fig. 3.21 Barro-Sala-i-Martin-model
Source: own figure

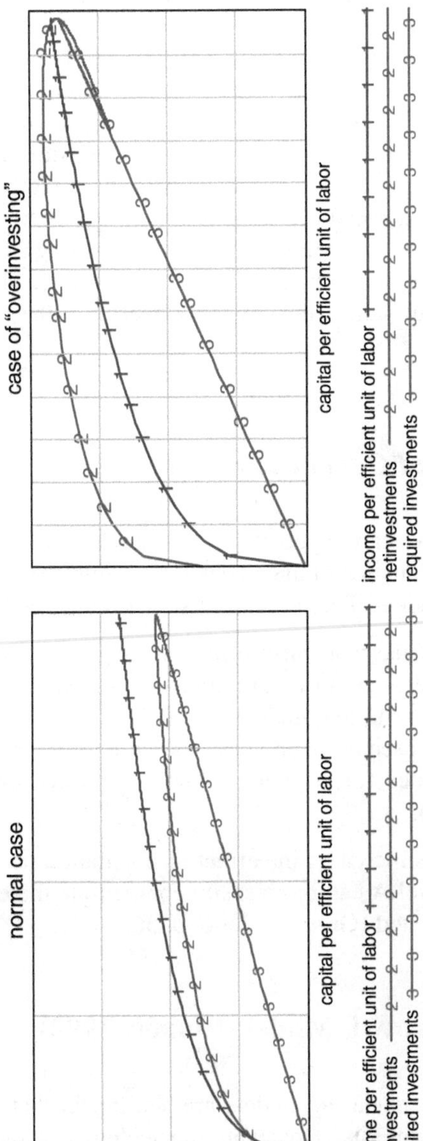

Fig. 3.22 Barro–Sala-i-Martin-model: phase plot
Source: own simulation

$$\dot{k} = sf(k) - (n(k) + g) \cdot k \tag{3.52}$$

The requirement line twists into a curve. Its shape depends on the exact mathematical relationship between population growth (n) and capital per efficient unit of labor (k).

Figure 3.23 shows the new augmented Solow-model. The endogenized population growth rate n is now influenced by three factors: capital, labor and technology. Two new loops exist in this augmentation. Labor changes with delta L over time. The stock of labor goes into the population growth rate with negative effects: An increase in L decreases n due the denomination in the effective capital intensity (population loop). More powerful with a reinforcing effect is the new capital growth loop; both loops are highlighted in Fig. 3.23. As long as the capital growth loop deploys its power, the requirement line twists upwards. The population loop becomes stronger over time and balances this effect until the new steady state is reached.

3.2.6 Discussion and Conclusion

The Solow-model was the starting point for the neoclassical growth theory. This thesis has provided an explanation of the model and has investigated the demographic determinants within the model. The main results are summarized as follows:

- A declining labor force has a negative effect on the growth rate of income Y and a positive effect on the growth rate of the income per capita.
- There is no age structure in the model.
- Because labor force is used as an adequate variable for the population the cases of different growth rates for population and labor force cannot be analyzed (Gruescu, 2006, p. 46).

Technological progress increases the effect of population decline. An economy with a low technology level A can more easily compensate the effects of the labor force as they are incorporated (Gruescu, 2006, p. 56).

3.3 Endogenous Growth Model (Romer, 1990)

Thus far, all previously introduced models are similar, in that they offer a good explanation for growth patterns. However, the technical progress A is always exogenous. The work of Gene M. Grossman and Elhanan Helpman (1995) changed this. They incorporated an intermediate-goods sector with monopolistic competition, which was borrowed from Avinash K. Dixit and Joseph E. Stiglitz (1977). In 1990, Romer published the Grossman-Helpman-model and connected their ideas with an extension of the Solow-model, thereby overcoming the decreasing rate on

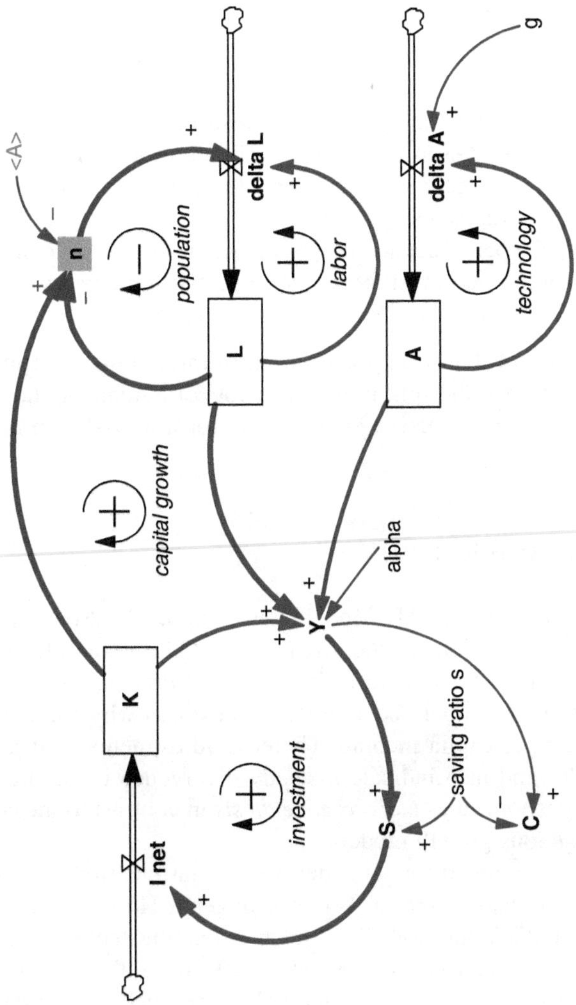

Fig. 3.23 Solow-model with variable population growth
Source: own figure

return. This founded the Romer-model – explaining the divergence between growth rates of countries. In addition, there are other models, which belong to the same branch of models as Romer's does. The basic idea behind this R&D models is that research and development sets stimuli for economic growth.

3.3.1 *Precursor of the Model*

The Romer-model grasps several ideas. Starting from the Solow-model, Romer focused on endogenized technology in the Research-and-Development-Sector (R&D). He combined the idea of monopolistic competition with the main idea of Joseph A. Schumpeter's "Creative Destruction". In addition, Romer's multi-sector model splits the labor-force stock, similar to Uzawa-Lucas, in two different labor groups. To achieve a deeper understanding of the Romer-model in connection with demographic parameters, one must stress the important precursors of the growth theory. These are:

1. Rebelos AK-model for the overcome of diminishing returns to capital
2. Uzawa-Lucas-model for the split into two sectors of human capital
3. Schumpeter's theory of "Creative Destruction" for a new stream on economic growth theory

3.3.1.1 AK-Model (Rebelo, 1991)

The Rebelo-model also called AK-Model, builds upon the Solow-model. It is presented here as one example of the AK-models. Other examples of this type can be found in Romer (1987) or Lucas (1988). The *decreasing marginal productivities* of the input factors should be overcome to explain why some countries do not converge in their per-capita income. Thereby, adjustments of these countries would be explicable, and also indicate a steady divergence or be prone to overtaking. The drift is designated as a *divergence thesis* in contrast to the convergence ideas from the exogenous growth models.

Sergio T. Rebelo accounted for some decisive variations from the Solow basic model. First, the technical progress A is no longer a Harrod-neutral or labor-saving, but rather a Hicks-neutral. This means that the technical progress no longer functions as a productivity factor for work L, but rather as a total productivity factor. Secondly, a human capital factor H is introduced. It takes the place of the technical progress for the Harrod-neutral. Thus, the new production function reads:

$$Y = A \cdot K^{\alpha} \cdot (H \cdot L)^{1-\alpha} \tag{3.53}$$

This is similar to the Solow-model. However, the decisive step is the determination of the human capital factor. It is no longer exogenous, but rather becomes endogenous and is described in the model with:

$$H = \frac{K}{L} \tag{3.54}$$

This means that the efficiency of the production factor L is determined by factor H. When the capital intensity grows, H increases. For example, through the uses of a computer (K) at a workplace (L) the output of the work can be increased. The use of $H = \frac{K}{L}$ in the new and summarized production function includes:

$$Y = A \cdot K \tag{3.55}$$

And dividing by labor force L gives the per capita income with:

$$f(k) = \frac{Y}{L} = A \cdot k \tag{3.56}$$

Other equations, like the growth of A and L or the movement equation of the capital stock are identical to the Solow-model.

Figure 3.24 shows the structure of the AK-model. The newly introduced variables are highlighted. Preceding this, the Solow-model indicates, through its new calculations, the difference in human capital. The loops "technology" and "labor" are already known. The capital stock K is *dually reinforced* by both the "Investment"-loop and the "Human Capital"-loop. This overcomes the decreasing of the marginal productivity of the capital and the model no longer indicates a steady state. Figure 3.25 provides the standard phase plot (Note: in this case, k represents the capital intensity and not the capital intensity per effective labor). The picture differs from the previous Solow-model. The real investments (indicated by a 2) permanently exceed the required investments (labeled 3) so that the function of the capital intensity (marked 1) grows continuously.

The AK-model is attributed the endogenous growth theory. Upon first glance, this is remarkable, due to the new approach to the technical progress. A is still declared exogenous and reinforces only the accumulation process. However, the AK-model attempts to get around the decreasing marginal productivity of capital and thus, for the first time, the meaning of the human capital are underlined. Although the human capital cannot yet be calculated, it nevertheless shows that a connection with the capital stock exits. It can be explained that the capital stock is composed of real and human capital. Presenting this here illustrates the idea of overcoming the constant returns to scale. Also, the model explains why some countries cannot approach others, such as in the Solow-model.

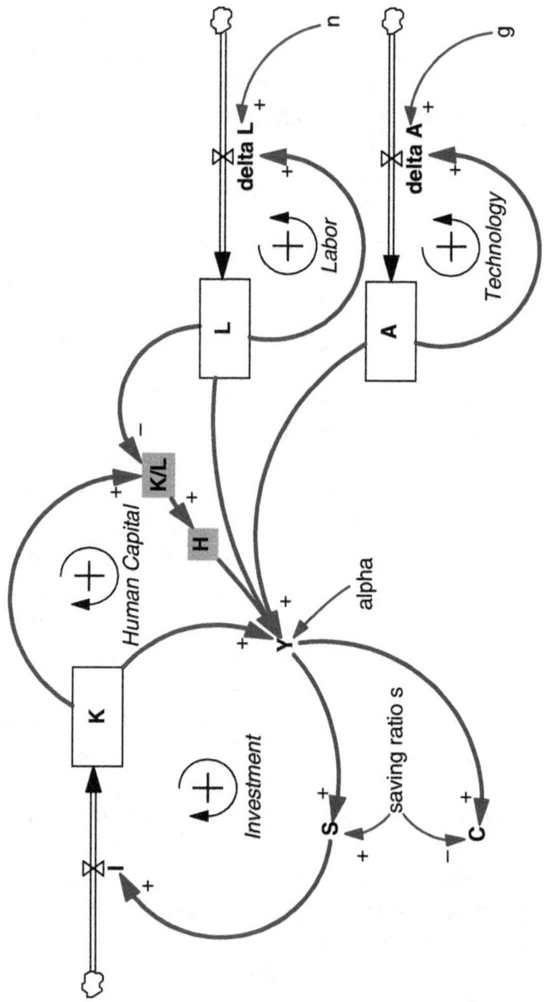

Fig. 3.24 Rebelo-model
Source: own figure

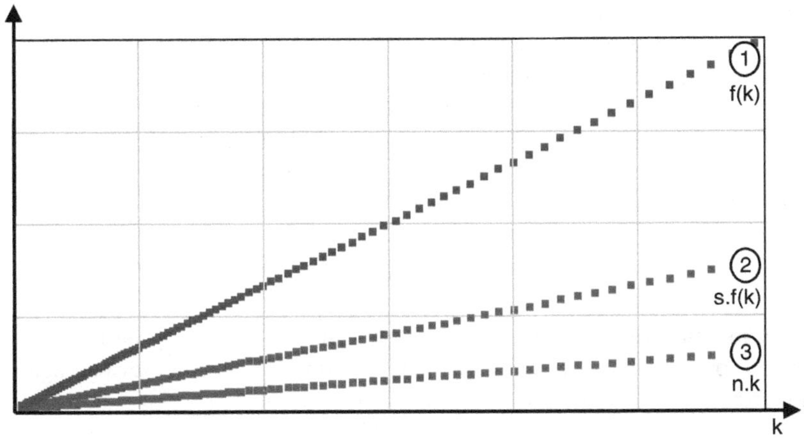

Fig. 3.25 Rebelo-model: phase plot
Source: own simulation

3.3.1.2 Uzawa-Lucas-Model (1988)

Basing on a model from Hirofumi Uzawa (1965), Robert E. Lucas presented a two-sector model on human capital (Lucas, 1988), the so-called Uzawa-Lucas-model. This model does not integrate the human capital as a proxy of the stocks K or L, but rather it models them directly as their own stock. The weakness of the AK-Model is that the human capital is not directly accumulative. It is presented here briefly as it is the first model that uses human capital as a stock and that splits the labor force into two different labor groups. The main explanation was taken out of Frenkel and Hemmer (1999, pp. 209–211).

The capital stock increases through net investments. However, how can one increase human capital? The answer is simple: through investments in education. The labor force supply L is replaced by the human capital. The labor force supply is described quantitatively and is no longer qualitative. Therefore, it is no longer an absolute quantity for labor forces, but rather a quality. Macro-economically, the human capital H is the labor force supply weighted with the average qualification level. By doing this, the working hours (u) of an average worker can now be calculated into the production sector (Y) and in (1–u) for the advanced education divide. Thus, the amount of education enlarges the human capital stock and appears with:

$$H = u \cdot H + (1 - u) \cdot H \tag{3.57}$$

By splitting the human capital, Uzawa and Lucas created a two-sector-model with a consumption good sector and an education sector. The variation of the human capital stock results from:

$$\dot{H} = (1 - u) \cdot H \cdot B \tag{3.58}$$

B is a technology parameter of the education sector. A high productivity of B yields a faster increase in human capital H. This can also be seen as a ratio for time budget constraint if B<1. The original model includes the depreciation of the human capital, for example, through the retirement from professional life or outward migration from the economic system. This is not explicitly observed in this contribution, however, but $\dot{H}$ is rather understood as a net increase. The human capital stock grows consequently exponentially with:

$$H_t = H_0 \cdot e^{B \cdot (1-u) \cdot t} \tag{3.59}$$

The remaining time u of the human capital flows, as already indicated, moves toward the production sector. The people's income Y can be described again in a similar form to the Cobb-Douglas-production function:

$$Y = A \cdot K^{\alpha} \cdot (u \cdot H)^{1-\alpha} \tag{3.60}$$

A constant component s, refers to the people's income as regulated through identity I = S. The increase in the capital stock is shown:

$$\dot{K} = I = s \cdot Y \tag{3.61}$$

The technical progress A is Hicks-neutral and grows exponentially in accordance with:

$$A_t = A_0 \cdot e^{g \cdot t} \tag{3.62}$$

Figure 3.26 graphically represents the Uzawa-Lucas-model. Again, there is a basic resemblance to the previously presented models – *three stocks K, H and A lead to the growth of Y*. All three grow exponentially. The model includes an education sector and a consumption good sector. It is important to note that the growth of the human capital is still exogenous. This is determined through the size of (1–u) and is variable, thus, u is still exogenous. However, u becomes endogenous through the amount of time spent. Each economy can determine how much time is designated to education. Lastly, the entire human capital is the power that determines the per-capita-wealth Y/H.

The growth rate of the capital stock derives out of the goods market equilibrium with:

$$A \cdot K^{\alpha} \cdot (u \cdot H)^{1-\alpha} = C + I \tag{3.63}$$

Rearranging to change of the capital stock and dividing with K gives:

$$\frac{\dot{K}}{K} = \frac{A}{K^{1-\alpha}} \cdot (u \cdot H)^{1-\alpha} - \frac{C}{K} \tag{3.64}$$

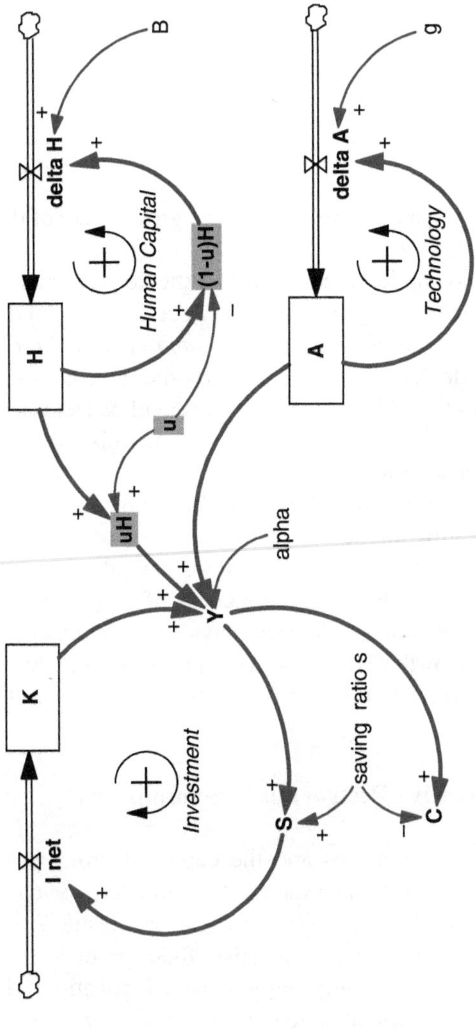

Fig. 3.26 Uzawa-Lucas-model
Source: own figure

For the growth of the human capital stock follows:

$$\frac{\dot{H}}{H} = B \cdot (1 - u) \tag{3.65}$$

The growth rate of the human capital intensity can be obtained by subtracting both growth rates to:

$$\dot{\left(\frac{K}{H}\right)} \Big/ \left(\frac{K}{H}\right) = \frac{A}{K^{1-\alpha}} \cdot (u \cdot H)^{1-\alpha} - \frac{C}{K} - B \cdot (1 - u) \tag{3.66}$$

One can see that a decreasing u slows down the growth rate of the human capital intensity.

With the Uzawa-Lucas-model, the absence in the convergence of the countries can also be explained (see convergence thesis in Sect. 3.2.3.1 and divergence thesis in Sect. 3.3.1.1). This is due to the fact that the *human capital stock is too slight* or the growth of H is too little. Countries could overcome the consequence of too little capital more easily than missed human capital (Frenkel & Hemmer, 1999, p. 211). This new knowledge comes from the AK-model. In this model the absence of convergence is due to the savings.

Human capital takes over the role of exogenous technical progress in the Solow-model. To sustain steady growth, the human capital stock has to grow exponentially. This, however, is only plausible if new generations can adopt the previous stock of knowledge (Arnold, 1997, p. 109). The uniqueness of this model derives from the assumption that endogenous time is allocated between the production and the education sector. Endogenous growth results in a constant marginal, which in turn, returns on human capital in the production sector (Frenkel & Hemmer, 1999, p. 219).

3.3.1.3 Theory of "Creative Destruction" (Schumpeter)

Schumpeter analyzed business cycles and the capitalist order and concluded that capitalism is an inherently unstable system (Schumpeter, 1996a; Schumpeter & Seifert, 1993). He argued that economic fluctuations result from technological innovations. Profit-maximizing agents improve their products or processes and business cycles result from continually implemented innovations (Barnett & Rose, 2001, p. 188). Schumpeter explained that competition represents a sequence of innovation and transfer processes (Schumpeter, 1996a, p. 228). Firms support research and development in order to secure themselves by creating a *monopoly over time*. Through a *transfer process*, they encourage customers from other companies to try their new product. By doing so, they enable the disbursement of R&D costs and have both a pioneering and a competitive advantage in comparison to other companies. This generates spillovers to other firms; their lure of profits inspires others to follow. Companies that cannot adapt will lose market shares and might disappear. Others change successfully to survive with new standard practices and may also *generate innovation* for positive transfer processes (Barnett & Rose, 2001, p. 189).

This creative destruction accounts in Schumpeter's view for the capitalism success. Without this instability there would be no development or improvement (Barnett & Rose, 2001, p. 190). Or as Schumpeter wrote in his book "Capitalism, Socialism, and Democracy" (Schumpeter & Seifert, 1993, pp. 137–138):

> The fundamental impulse that sets and keeps the capitalist regime in motion comes from the new consumers' goods, the new methods of production or transportation, the new markets, the new forms of industrial organizations that capitalist enterprise creates. . . . The opening up . . . illustrates the same process of industrial mutation – if I may use this biological term – that incessantly revolutionizes the economic structure from within, incessantly destroying the old one, incessantly creating a new one. This process of Creative Destruction is the essential fact about capitalism.

Khalid Saeed (2008, pp. 32–39) presented a model of Schumpeter's theory and based it on an exact outline in Benjamin Higgins (1968, pp. 88–105). Saeed publically mentioned that Schumpeter introduced a concept of "saving up"; this constitutes the part of output that is not invested and not consumed. Figure 3.27 presents a simplified causal-loop-diagram of Saeed's model without neglecting the important key issues of innovation and transfer processes (Saeed, 2008, p. 35).

The relevant stocks are marked as boxes, representing *capital*, *labor* and *entrepreneurs*. All of these change over the course of time in relation to their net-flows. The figure consists of several loops. In order to create a cyclical behavior one needs at least two time lags and one balancing loop. Double crossed lines in the causal links mark delays or time lags. The "Saving up"-loop represents withheld investments, which grow as the output grows. Investments arise from new technologies. In turn they depend positively on entrepreneurs, which derive out of a number of potential entrepreneurs. The potential to become an entrepreneur (*entrepreneurial spirit*) increases as the background of a friendly entrepreneur al climate evolves and the expectation of a high profit rate increases (see Schumpeter, 1996b). Both factors, however, depend on wages. Constraints in the labor market influence the climate and the profits negatively and take away the very elements of the entrepreneurial environment (Saeed, 2008, p. 39). The two loops referring to these effects are negative and the only possibility for higher profits can be stimulated in this model, within the profit-loop. The entire model shows an expanding circular behavior through the innovation and transfer processes of the entrepreneurs.

3.3.2 Assumptions

The following section is based on Romer's original article (1990), and Schmidt (2003), who gave a wonderful explanation of the dynamics for the growth model. Additional points were taken from Frenkel and Hemmer (1999). Some rearranging of the notation was done for putting it in the stream of this work.

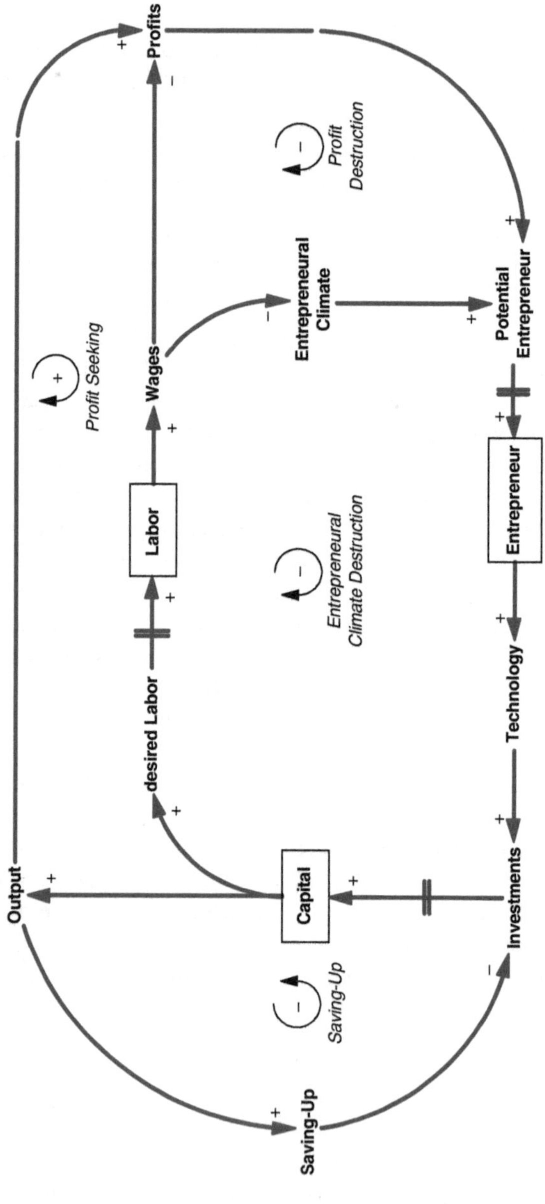

Fig. 3.27 Schumpeter's "Creative Destruction"
Source: own figure

Romer was not the first to address an incomplete excludability, non-rivalry, market power, externalities, increasing return or the accumulation of knowledge, but he was the first one who brought all those ideas together (Schmidt, 2003, p. 460). Romer based his paper on three premises (1990, p. S72):

1. Technical change is the foundation of economic growth: Technical change and capital accumulation account for much of the increase in output per capita.
2. Technical change arises mainly from the incentive actions taken by people: Agents respond to the market and therefore technological progress is rather endogenous than exogenous.
3. Instructions for working with raw materials are different from other economic goods: Once the set of instructions is occurred it can be used with no additional costs.

All of the previous models rely on price-taking behavior, but taking these premises into consideration, it follows that the equilibrium comes without price taking.

One can summarize Romer's main assumptions as follow (Schmidt, 2003, p. 460):

1. Labor supply is constant
2. Total stock of human capital is fixed
3. Designs are divisible
4. The research process is deterministic
5. Human capital is the only production factor in the R&D sector to show the importance of this factor
6. Innovation is capital-widening
7. No adjustment costs for capital
8. No erosion of the monopoly power of the producers
9. Research creates only new intermediate goods not new consumer goods
10. The economy is closed

3.3.2.1 Ideas as a Public Good

Goods are distinguished by two fundamental attributes: excludability and rivalry in consumption (Samuelson, 1954, p. 387). Private goods are characterized with both attributes; however, pure public goods do not have either of them. As private goods are tradable within competitive markets, problems may occur for pure or partly public goods (Cezanne, 2005, pp. 49–53). The question for growth theory is the non-rival yet excludable case, as the third premises of Romer implies that technology is a non-rival input. The second premise mandates that the action of individuals must benefit them. Hence, technology improvements must be at least partly excludable. Finally, Romer's first premise connotes that growth is driven by partially excludable, non-rival goods (Romer, 1990, p. S74). *Human capital* and *knowledge* are different, in that human capital is tied to the person. Here, one can assume that people decide about themselves. Knowledge, however, manifests itself in the Schumpeterian understanding for new products and is registered through the patents in abstract form. Thus, the *non-excludability* no longer works automatically, but rather becomes accessible for a larger group. Knowledge, therefore, is marked with *external effects* (spillover).

The marginal costs of knowledge are not dependable; knowledge can be excluded by patent protection. The feature of knowledge has *no rival in consumption*. Non-rival goods involve fixed cost of production, which are often substantial for the process of creating new ideas. Once this has been created, there are zero marginal costs for the further use of this design. For this reason the mechanism of patent and copyrights exists in order to guarantee the entrepreneurs rights, at least for certain time, so they can earn a reward (Snowdon & Vane, 1999, p. 80). Comprehensively, according to Schumpeter's characteristics, knowledge also serves a public good.

This non-rivalry has three implications for Romer's growth theory (Romer, 1990, p. S75):

1. Non-rival goods accumulate without bound on the per capita basis
2. Human capital accumulates with bound on the per capita basis
3. Non-rivalry of knowledge allows knowledge spillovers

Alone from the issue of treating knowledge, at least as a partly public good, it follows that the growth function does not have a constant return to scale.

3.3.2.2 Final-Goods Sector

The final-goods sector uses labor, human capital and intermediate goods and is modeled as Cobb-Douglas function with

$$Y = {H_Y}^{\alpha} \cdot L^{\beta} \cdot \int_0^A x(i)^{1-\alpha-\beta} di \tag{3.67}$$

The function exhibits overall constant return to scale. The homogenous production function enables one to describe the output as actions of a single, aggregate, price-taking firm. In addition, it expresses that the output is a separable function of all different types of capital goods. One marginal unit has no effect on the marginal productivity (Romer, 1990, p. S81). Thus, it follows that intermediate goods do not complete with other production factors. They are neither substitutes, nor complements (Frenkel & Hemmer, 1999, p. 243).

Again this implies that the share (s) from the people's income is saved and that the identity of the capital stock S = I increases. The movement of the capital stock is given by:

$$\dot{K} = s \cdot Y \tag{3.68}$$

Following the Euler theorem, all factors can be paid to their marginal products so that the wage of employees is distributed as follows (Schmidt, 2003, p. 75):

- Human capital in the final-goods sector $w_Y = \alpha \cdot H_Y{}^{\alpha-1} \cdot L^\beta \cdot A \cdot \int_0^A x(i)^{1-\alpha-\beta} \cdot di$
- Labor $w_L = \beta \cdot H_Y{}^{\alpha} \cdot L^{\beta-1} \cdot A \cdot \int_0^A x(i)^{1-\alpha-\beta} \cdot di$

3.3.2.3 Intermediate-Goods Sector

The intermediate-goods sector does not have a representative firm. Each intermediate good (i) describes a distinct firm (i), which, before they start production, must purchase a design for their good (i). Once a firm has produced a specific design it can obtain a patent for life (Romer, 1990, p. S81). The value of the design is the discounted value of the rental income. Monopoly power is, nevertheless, restricted by the possibility of entering new agents into the market – especially through free entry (Schmidt, 2003, p. 39).

The decisive step in Romer's model is the linking of knowledge to the consumption goods sector. It is supposed that with knowledge procedure innovations are carried out, i.e. the manufacturing of a product occurs through the specialization of singular intermediate good. The amount of the intermediate goods x_i is identical to the knowledge A.

In symmetry, the equation follows:

$$\bar{x} = \frac{K}{A} \tag{3.69}$$

and therefore

$$\int_0^A x(i)^{1-\alpha-\beta} \cdot di = A \cdot \frac{K}{A} \quad \text{(Arnold, 1997, p.142).} \tag{3.70}$$

This accumulation specifies potential consumption embodied in intermediate goods (Schmidt, 2003, p. 37).

3.3.2.4 Research Sector

For simplicity, Romer suggested treating designs as:

> idealized goods that are not tied to any physical good and can be replicated without additional costs, but nothing hinges on whether this is literally true or merely close to being true (Romer, 1990, p. S75).

The research sector is specialized for capital equipment and designs; they never become obsolete (Schmidt, 2003, p. 35). Frenkel and Hemmer mentioned that the sector has two important characteristics (1999, p. 243):

1. Producing designs and innovations for specific products
2. Creating new knowledge for further research

Romer assumed that anyone who works in the R&D sector has free access to the entire knowledge stock. This is only feasible while knowledge is not a rival input factor. The aggregate stock of knowledge evolves over time as:

$$\dot{A} = \rho \cdot H_A \cdot A \tag{3.71}$$

The productivity parameter is ρ. The rate of new designs directly depends on the number of human capital working in the R&D sector. Also, larger stock of knowledge creates higher worker productivity (Romer, 1990, p. S85). The relatively intense use of human capital and existing knowledge is specified as singular inputs. If this situation was actualized, this sector one would have to implement other essential factors, such as capital equipment. This also points out that information is not only a result of activity, but that it is an input factor (Schmidt, 2003, p. 35).

The growth of the knowledge follows the well-known exponential growth scheme:

$$A = A_0 \cdot e^{\rho \cdot H_A \cdot t} \tag{3.72}$$

Within this model, price discrimination is not possible (Romer, 1990, p. S87). The productivity of the human capital is an increasing function of the knowledge stock. This leads to declining costs of production for new designs (Schmidt, 2003, p. 35). Summarizing, Romer's three premises (see beginning Sect. 3.3) have two important implications in the research sector:

1. Ideas can be accumulated without limit on the per capita basis.
2. Knowledge creation involves a spillover of benefits, which cannot be captured by producers (Snowdon & Vane, 1999, p. 80).

3.3.2.5 Labor Force

For simplification, a constant is used as an input for human capital H and labor L. It is seen as $H = H_0$ and $L = L_0$. The human capital can be used in two sectors. Either in the R&D-sector (A) or in the final product sector (Y): $H = H_Y + H_A$. At the same time, the variable s_R determines the fixed share of work in the R&D-sector and $(1-s_R)$ shows the remaining share in work for the final-goods sector free:

$$H_A = s_R \cdot H \tag{3.73}$$

$$H_Y = (1 - s_R) \cdot H \tag{3.74}$$

This formula neglects the fact that L and H are supplied together. Here, one can think of two different types of workers – some of them specialize in human capital accumulation, the others in labor.

The growth rate of the R&D-sector is determined through the supply of human capital (i.e. engineers). And the consumption goods sector Y and the R&D-sector A competes for the human capital H.

3.3.3 *Structure*

Romer's model consists of four basic input factors – capital, labor, human capital and level of technology, which are divided into three sectors:

- A *research sector A*
- A *intermediate-goods sector x*
- A *final-goods sector Y*

3.3.3.1 Stock-Flow-Diagram

Before presenting the stock-flow-diagram, one can determine the Romer-model with the following equations:

$$Y = {H_Y}^{\alpha} \cdot L^{\beta} \cdot \int_0^A x(i)^{1-\alpha-\beta} di \tag{3.75}$$

$$A = A_0 \cdot e^{\rho \cdot H_A \cdot t} \tag{3.76}$$

$$x(i) = \bar{x} = \frac{K}{A} \tag{3.77}$$

$$\dot{K} = I^N = S \tag{3.78}$$

$$S + C = Y \tag{3.79}$$

$$S = s \cdot Y \tag{3.80}$$

$$C = (1 - s) \cdot Y \tag{3.81}$$

$$H = \bar{H} = H_A + H_Y \tag{3.82}$$

$$L = \bar{L} \tag{3.83}$$

The output of goods is not only the production in this economy. Namely, the research sector produces designs and the intermediate-goods sector changes capital with the help of the designs into durables. The final-goods sector output is created with the usage of durable, labor and human capital. The output adds partly to the capital stocks.

Figure 3.28 shows the total Romer-model as a stock-flow-diagram. The Romer-model consists of only two stocks, the knowledge A and the capital stock K, while the labor force offers L as a constant and an exogenous human capital H. The intermediate-goods sector is marked with x, and leads directly into the final-goods sector. Again, the exponential growth pattern of the two stocks is clear. The behavior remains comparable to the other models, but nevertheless the explanation for exponential growth is unrelated.

3.3.3.2 Phase Plot

The model combines the ideas of the Solow-model, where A is exogenously, and the Uzawa-Lucas-model, where allocation of labor determines the evolving of human capital. Logically, the Romer-model behaves similarly to the two models.

Figure 3.29 presents the standard phase plot, known from the Solow-model. The characteristics and the explanation are therefore comparable. The capital intensity per effective human capital rises until a steady state is achieved. As long as k is below that point the real investments exceed the required investments. This phase plot is only similar to Solow if share of human capital dedicated to R&D (s_R) is constant.

3.3.3.3 Long-Term Equilibrium

In the Romer-model equilibrium, prices and quantities will be influenced by (Romer, 1990, p. S88):

- Consumers who take the interest rate as given
- Holders of human capital who decide to work in the research or in the final goods market
- Human capital that takes the stock of knowledge A, the price of designs P_A, and the wage w_A as given
- The final-goods sector where producers choose the amount of production factor
- Each firm because they set the price to miximize their profits and decide about their entry of producing intermediate goods
- The supply of each good as it is equal to demand

All durable goods are supplied at an equal level $\bar{x}$. If they were not producers, then their profits could increase in the intermediate-goods sector by reducing the

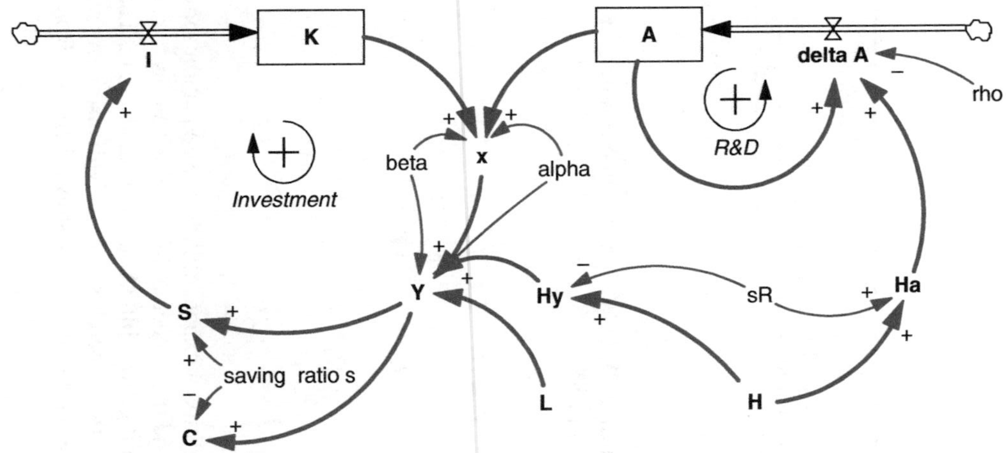

Fig. 3.28 Romer-model
Source: own figure

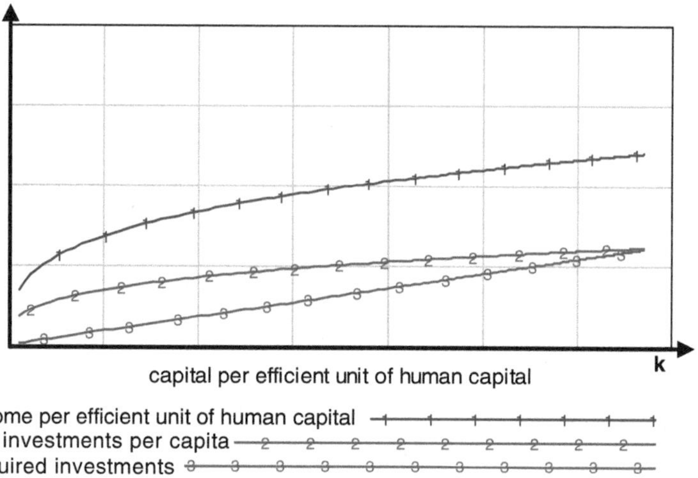

Fig. 3.29 Romer-model: phase plot
Source: own simulation

output of high output firms. With $K = A\bar{x} = A \cdot \frac{K}{A}$ one can rewrite the output equation Y (Romer, 1990, p. S88)

$$\begin{aligned} Y &= {H_Y}^{\alpha} \cdot L^{\beta} \cdot \int_0^A x(i)^{1-\alpha-\beta} di \\ Y &= {H_Y}^{\alpha} \cdot L^{\beta} \cdot A\bar{x}^{1-\alpha-\beta} \\ Y &= {H_Y}^{\alpha} \cdot L^{\beta} \cdot A\left(\frac{K}{A}\right)^{1-\alpha-\beta} \\ Y &= (H_Y A)^{\alpha}(LA)^{\beta} K^{1-\alpha-\beta} \end{aligned} \tag{3.84}$$

Even if there is an additional exponent β, the last equation shows a formulation comparable to Solow's and the expected diminishing returns to capital. If A grows exogenously then K would grow with gA into the steady state. The productivity of human capital working in the research-sector H_A will also grow with gA. From the profit maximization function (not explicitly shown here, see Romer, 1990, p. S87 for details) comes

$$\pi = (\alpha + \beta)\bar{p} \cdot \bar{x} \tag{3.85}$$

And the discounted present value of the profits must equal the design price P_A it follows:

$$P_A = \frac{1}{r}\pi = \frac{\alpha + \beta}{r}\bar{p} \cdot \bar{x} = \frac{\alpha + \beta}{r} \cdot (1 - \alpha - \beta){H_Y}^{\alpha} \cdot L^{\beta} \cdot \bar{x}^{1-\alpha-\beta} \tag{3.86}$$

The design price derives from the willingness to pay of patents buyers. As long as their monopoly rents are positive, the capital goods producers compete against each other for the patents. The intermediate goods are sold on a monopolistic market and the producer can set the price according to their marginal costs, with consideration of quantity-price-relationships. According to the Chamberlin Rule, the price is set as a mark up above the marginal costs. The mark up follows the elasticity of demand (Frenkel & Hemmer, 1999, p. 247). Romer showed that this means a price for designs with:

$$P_A = \frac{\varepsilon}{1-\alpha-\beta} \tag{3.87}$$

The long-term steady state capital intensity per effective unit human capital does not changes over time. So one could formulate:

$$\begin{aligned}
\frac{\delta k}{\delta t} &= const. \Rightarrow \frac{\dot{A}}{A} + \frac{\dot{H}}{H} = \frac{\dot{K}}{K} \\
\frac{\rho \cdot s_R \cdot H \cdot A}{A} + 0 &= \frac{s \cdot \left(H_A{}^{\alpha} \cdot L^{\beta} \cdot \int_0^A x(i)^{1-\alpha-\beta} \right)}{K} \\
\rho \cdot s_R \cdot H &= s \cdot H_A{}^{\alpha} \cdot L^{\beta} \cdot A \cdot \left(\frac{K}{A}\right)^{1-\alpha-\beta} \cdot K^{-1} \\
\rho \cdot s_R \cdot H &= s \cdot (1-s_R)^{\alpha} \cdot L^{\beta} \cdot H^{\alpha} \cdot K^{-\alpha-\beta} \cdot A^{\alpha+\beta} \qquad (3.88) \\
\left(\frac{K}{A}\right)^{\alpha+\beta} &= \frac{s \cdot (1-s_R)^{\alpha}}{\rho \cdot s_R \cdot H} \cdot L^{\beta} \cdot H^{-\beta} \cdot H^{\beta} \cdot H^{\alpha} \\
\left(\frac{K}{AH}\right)^{\alpha+\beta} &= \frac{s \cdot (1-s_R)^{\alpha}}{\rho \cdot s_R \cdot H} \cdot \left(\frac{L}{H}\right)^{\beta} \\
\frac{K}{AH} &= \left[\frac{s \cdot (1-s_R)^{\alpha}}{\rho \cdot s_R \cdot H} \cdot \left(\frac{L}{H}\right)^{\beta} \right]^{\frac{1}{\alpha+\beta}}
\end{aligned}$$

The final equation is similar to the Solow steady state, where no initial values of the stocks determine the long-term steady state. The capital intensity depends on the saving ratio s, the growth rate of the R&D-stock and on the ratio between human capital and labor.

3.3.4 Dynamics

In the Romer-model a continuous structural change evolves. This specialization is associated with a constant, frictionless reallocation of human capital (Ruschinski, 1996, pp. 119–120), where no transaction costs exist.

From the research sector, one knows that the wage for the human capital employed is $w_H = P_A \cdot \rho \cdot A$. One also knows the price of a design with

$P_A = \frac{\alpha+\beta}{1-\alpha-\beta}$. To equalize the marginal products from the sectors, the wages for human capital and the final-goods sector must be the same.

So it follows that:

$$w_H = w_Y \tag{3.89}$$

$$\frac{\alpha+\beta}{1-\alpha-\beta} \cdot \rho \cdot A \cdot x_i = \frac{\alpha+\beta}{(1-\alpha-\beta)^2} \cdot \frac{A \cdot x_i}{H_Y} r \tag{3.90}$$

The growth rate of A comes with:

$$\frac{\dot{A}}{A} = \rho H_A \tag{3.91}$$

And in the steady state all growth rates for capital and income must equal this:

$$\frac{\dot{A}}{A} = \rho H_A = \frac{\dot{K}}{K} = \frac{\dot{Y}}{Y} \tag{3.92}$$

The model exercises how the growth rate could differ between countries (see convergence thesis in the Solow subchapter 3.2.3.1). It is useful for an economy to have a specific stock of human capital and thereby high productivity in the R&D sector, because this leads to high growth rates of capital and income.

3.3.5 Policy Experiments

As in the previous section about policy experiments with the Solow-model, one can do the same analysis for the Romer-model.

The five major demographic determinants include:

(1) Population
(2) Population Structure
(3) Fertility
(4) Mortality
(5) Migration

The Romer-model, unlike the Solow-model, is composed with the following constant, exogenous factors:

- Initial value of capital (K_0) and technology (A_0)
- Technology parameter ρ
- Partial production elasticities α and β
- Saving ratio (s)
- Ratio of human capital employed in R&D (s_R)
- The fixed values of labor in the final-goods sector (L) and human capital (H)

Demographic determinants can be implemented in the model structure or operate within the above listed constants. The following sections analyze to what extent demographic features are implemented in the structure of the Romer-model.

3.3.5.1 Population

As in the previous Solow-model, the Romer-model assumes full employment and sets the population and work force identical. However, Romer measures the labor force L as 'skills' such as a coordination and human capital H as the 'cumulative effect of activities' (Romer, 1990, p. S79). This predicts the population itself. So the population is neither embodied into the model nor deductible.

3.3.5.2 Population Structure

One can see a fraction of labor force and human capital as the population structure. However, without knowing the skills or qualification factors, one cannot calculate the population.

3.3.5.3 Fertility and Mortality

For mathematical reasons, Romer did not implement population growth. Therefore, fertility and mortality cannot be simulated.

3.3.5.4 Migration

As the model does not imply any exchange with foreign countries, this model cannot simulate migration. Unfortunately, Romer's model has a fixed labor force and human capital, thus, migration cannot be simulated.

3.3.5.5 Other Factors

Two different factors come to mind when analyzing the impact of certain important and model specific factors. One is the fixed labor skill, particularly in the final-goods sector and the other is the human capital. The constant factor L goes with power of β in the main final goods equation. An increase in L leads therefore directly to an increase in Y.

More interestingly, the human capital is twofold: on the one hand it builds up the growth rate of the R&D sector and on the other hand it goes into the final-good sector. If the level of human capital is too small, a very low growth may arise as the growth rate of the knowledge stock would be too little and stagnation occurs.

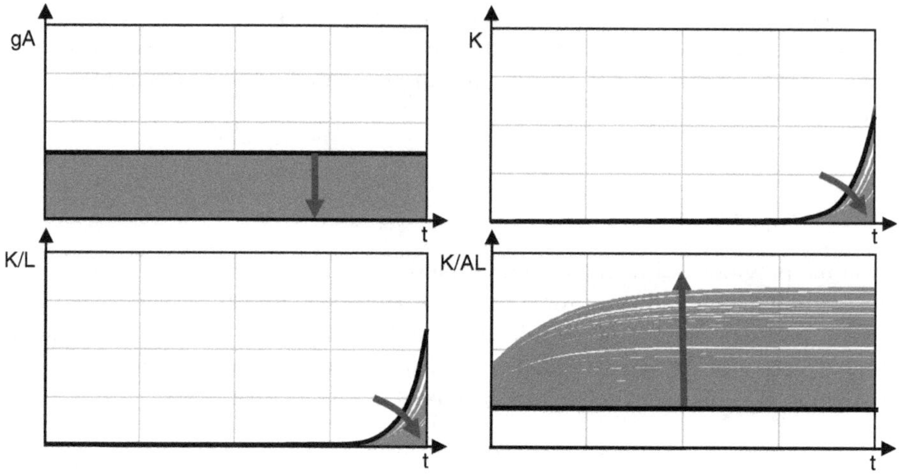

Fig. 3.30 Sensitivity run: decline in human capital
Source: own simulation

Research has shown that the reason for this is due to positive external effects (Romer, 1990, p. S96).

The model is in steady state and grows along the balance growth path with gA. The first simulation is a decline in the human capital stock. With the fix ratio s_R this will have consequences for the R&D sector and also for the final good sector. Figure 3.30 shows the effect of such a decline.

First, one can notice that a decline in human capital leads to a permanent decline in the growth rate gA. The per capita capital stock and per effective capita is displayed prominently. The requirement line in the standard phase plot shifts downwards and a new steady state occurs at a higher level of the capital intensity (see also in the graph at lower right). This arises at the cost of a slower growth for the capital stock and the capital intensity, which one can see in Fig. 3.30. The effect in the shift for the ratio s_R between human capital employed in the final-goods sector and employed in the R&D sector towards the final goods sector would be the same as H_A is only a fraction of H.

3.3.6 Discussion and Conclusion

For the first time, the Romer-model explains how innovations can influence an economic system through an increase in productivity. While the innovation process is explained in the model, the Schumpeterian transfer process is not yet implemented, because older technologies are not squeezed out of the market. Thus, the model accepts the existence of imperfect markets and introduces monopolistic competition. This represents an inconsistency with the neo-classical acceptance of *perfect competition*, but it is more realistic.

Most interesting is the positive implication for human capital. A larger stock will yield higher growth rates (Romer, 1990, p. S99). If one assumes that the human capital stock grows – as it has been seen in most countries – the limits showing the growth rate of the final-goods sector is n (Christiaans, 2004, p. 205).

The model indicates two market failures: *research and monopoly price setting.* Research creates positive spillover. And monopoly price setting instead of marginal cost price setting, leads to an intermediate-goods sector. For these reasons the government needs to implement two policies:

- R&D subsidies for internalising the spill over
- Product subsidies for to overcome the too little production capacity (Arnold, 1997, p. 147)

This leaves space for policy implications, however, it will be shown in the next subchapter that the Romer-model is based on a special case of the research function and is not empirically supported. For this reason the Jones-model is presented.

3.4 Semi-Endogenous Growth Model (Jones, 1995)

Despite the brilliance of Romer's theoretical extensions, it is difficult to find empirical proof for the validity of the theory. Between the growth of the knowledge and the number employed in the R&D-sector, a connection between the two would have to exist according to Romer's idea. Jones criticized that this cannot happen (1995a). If the level or resources in the R&D sector is doubled, the per capita growth of the output Y doubles as well. Lutz Arnold summarized this general problem as follows (Arnold, 1997, p. 222, translated from German into English):

> The basic problem is that we have an implausible model with appropriate empirical implications (the Uzawa-Lucas-model with growth through human accumulation) and a plausible model with doubtful empirical implications (the Grossman-Helpman-Romer-model with growth through R&D).

Moreover, the problem exists that the R&D-sector's constant returns to scales are present. Usually, neo-classical models assume decreasing return of scales. Jones (1995a) presented a model of a semi-endogenous growth, thereby combining the Romer-model with an increasingly growing population and decreasing returns to scale. This refinement, however, still generates long-run growth of profit-maximizing agents. However, it is not endogenous as it was in the AK models, where policy-makers can change the long-term growth effects.

The following sections are diverted from Jones (2001, pp. 96–122; 1995a) and Arnold (2006, 1997, pp. 153–160). There are several models, which extend or vary the idea of Jones (Dinopoulos & Thompson, 1998; Segerstrom, 1998; Li, 2000; Young, 1998). Chol-Won Li (2000), for example, showed that semi-endogenous growth is more general than endogenous growth in a two-R&D-sector growth model. Endogenous growth requires 'razor-edge' conditions within certain parameters. But all of these new models are based on Jones' theory.

3.4.1 Assumptions

In general the Jones-model basis on the following assumptions:

- There are three sectors: final-goods-, intermediate and R&D-sector
- There are two production factors in the final-goods sector: intermediate products x and labor L(t)
- There are two production factors in the intermediate-goods sector: capital K(t) and technology A(t).
- The R&D sector depends on a ratio of workers L
- A constant fraction s of output Y(t) is saved
- The capital stock K(t) takes a form of composite commodities
- It is a closed economy
- Net investment is the rate of increase K(t) with $\dot{K} = I^N = sY$
- Output is understood as net output after depreciation of capital
- There is full employment

Some minor changes in the notations were done to avoid misunderstandings and to make it comparable with the other sections of this thesis. The following sections analyze the different sectors in greater detail.

3.4.1.1 Final-Goods Sector

The sector is very much like the final-goods sector of the Solow-model. A homogenous output-good Y is produced by a large number of perfectly competitive firms. A constant ratio of labor L_Y, produces final goods out of intermediate goods x_j with:

$$Y = L_Y{}^{1-\alpha} \cdot \sum_{j=1}^{A} x_j{}^{\alpha} \tag{3.93}$$

A measures the number of capital goods that are available for the final-goods sector. Firms in the end-product sector take the number of intermediate goods as given. One can easily analyze the model by replacing the summation with an integral. The production function changes from a discrete function to a continuous one:

$$Y = L_Y{}^{1-\alpha} \cdot \int_0^A x_j{}^{\alpha} dj \tag{3.94}$$

A measures the range of goods that are discretionary in the final-goods sector. The price is normalized to one and firms have to decide how much labor and how much of capital goods they use to produce the output Y. The profit maximization problem is therefore:

$$\max_{L_Y, x_j} L_Y{}^{1-\alpha} \cdot \int_0^A x_j{}^{\alpha} \cdot dj - w \cdot L_Y - \int_0^A p_j \cdot x_j \cdot dj \tag{3.95}$$

W is the wage paid to labor in this model and p_j is the rental price for the capital good. There are two first order conditions to this problem.

$$w = (1 - \alpha)\frac{Y}{L_Y} \tag{3.96}$$

This means that firms hire until the marginal product of labor equals wage. The following second condition implies that firms rent capital goods until the marginal product of capital equals the rental price.

$$p_j = \alpha L_Y{}^{1-\alpha} x_j{}^{\alpha-1} \tag{3.97}$$

3.4.1.2 Intermediate-Goods Sector

Monopolists produce capital goods which are sold in the final-goods sector. These firms purchase the designs, for a specific capital good, from the research sector. Due to patent protection, only one firm manufactures each capital good. Once the design has been bought at a fixed cost, the intermediate sector firms produce the capital good with a very simple function: one unit of raw capital is translated into on unit of the capital good. The profit maximization problem is represented by:

$$\max_{x_j} \pi_j = p_j(x_j) \cdot x_j - r \cdot x_j \tag{3.98}$$

The term $p_j(x_j)$ is the demand function. Rewriting the first order condition one yields:

$$p_j{}'(x) \cdot \frac{x}{p_j} + 1 = \frac{r}{p_j} \tag{3.99}$$

The price p_j is then:

$$p_j = \frac{1}{1 + \frac{p_j{}'(x) \cdot x}{p_j}} \cdot r \tag{3.100}$$

The elasticity $\frac{p_j{}'(x) \cdot x}{p_j}$ is equal to $\alpha - 1$ and can be calculated from the demand curve equation. The price p_j is then simply a markup over the marginal costs r with:

$$p_j = \frac{1}{\alpha} \cdot r \tag{3.101}$$

All monopolists sell for the same price. Because the demand functions are equal for all firms, each capital good is introduced in the final-goods sector with the same amount $x_j = x$. Every firm earns the same profit and this is given by:

$$\pi = \alpha \cdot (1 - \alpha) \cdot \frac{Y}{A} \tag{3.102}$$

Also the total demand for capital from the firms must equal the total stock of capital in the economy:

$$\int_0^A x_j \cdot dj = K \tag{3.103}$$

The capital goods are used in the same amount x, so that one can determine x also with $x = \frac{K}{A}$.

3.4.1.3 Research Sector

As in the Romer-model, the research sector is a key factor. Anyone is free to propose new ideas. Ideas are new designs, which generate new capital goods. For the new design, the investor receives a patent to exclusively produce these capital goods. In both models – Romer's and Jones' – it is implied and simplified that the patent last forever. The inventor sells the patent to the intermediate goods sector.

The Jones-model describes advanced countries of the world (Jones, 2001, p. 97). This is in contrast to Solow's neoclassical model, which is applicable to different countries.

The stock of knowledge (A) evolves over time and can be seen as the technological course of history. The stock changes with $\dot{A}$ as a number of ideas at a period of time. This change of stock is equal to the number of people who research for new ideas (L_A) multiplied by the invention rate $\bar{\rho}$:

$$\dot{A} = \bar{\rho} \cdot L_A \tag{3.104}$$

In the simplest version these discover rates are constant, but Jones (and also Romer, as mentioned earlier) saw it depending on the stock of previously found ideas. Jones expected that the rate of discovering new ideas is a function of the amount of knowledge in an economy (Jones, 1995a, p. 765). This implies that new ideas increase researcher's productivity. But one could also say that the simplest ideas were discovered first and it get harder and harder to discover new ones. These two approaches lead to the modeling idea of:

$$\bar{\rho} = \rho \cdot A^{\phi} \tag{3.105}$$

Rho and phi are constants. The first variable works as a multiplier for new ideas like a Hicks-neutral technology increase. One can see it also as undetermined variable. Phi could have separate interesting values:

1. $\phi > 1$ indicates that the productivity increases the R&D stock. This case is called 'standing on shoulders'. The presence of increasing returns to scale results from the non-rivalry of ideas (Jones, 2001, p. 98).
2. $\phi < 1$ is referred as 'fishing-out' and means it becomes harder over time to develop new ideas.
3. $\phi = 1$ shows the 'Romer' case where phi is completely arbitrary degree of returns and was presented in Sect. 3.3.
4. $\phi = 0$ indicates that the stock of knowledge independently growths from previous ideas (no productivity increase). As Romer (1990) argued that it is more a philosophical question whether it is increasing or diminishing returns.

Jones falsified the Romer prediction of a proportion between an economy's growth rate and the labor force growth rate (Jones, 1995b). Over time, the size of the labor force grows immensely, however in this new model growth rates are seen to be relatively constant or even declining. Figure 3.31 presents this in detail for Germany, France, USA and Japan.

One could also think that the change in stock of knowledge depends on the number of people searching for new ideas. It might be that a duplication of efforts is more likely when there are more scientists engaged in the R&D sector. Or as Samuel Kortum (1993) and Nancy Stockey (1995) considered an overlap in research reduces the total number of innovations produced by the scientists. Introducing the exponent λ for L_A gives the possibility to do so. The parameter λ can vary between 0 and infinity. Putting this all together, one expresses the change in the stock of knowledge as:

$$\dot{A} = \rho \cdot {L_A}^{\lambda} \cdot A^{\phi} \tag{3.106}$$

Now as one can see how the stock of knowledge changes over time and might ask: what is the price for this knowledge (on the market as patent)? Economically, it is the present discounted value of the profits to be earned by the intermediate companies. In equilibrium the arbitrage equation must state that the return on profits equals earnings with the interest rate r (Jones, 2001, p. 116):

$$r \cdot P_A = \pi + \dot{P}_A \tag{3.107}$$

R is constant on a balanced growth path. π and $\dot{P}_A$ have to grow with the same rate so that follows:

$$P_A = \frac{\pi}{r - n} \quad \text{as } \pi \text{ is proportional to Y/A, which grows with gA = n.} \tag{3.108}$$

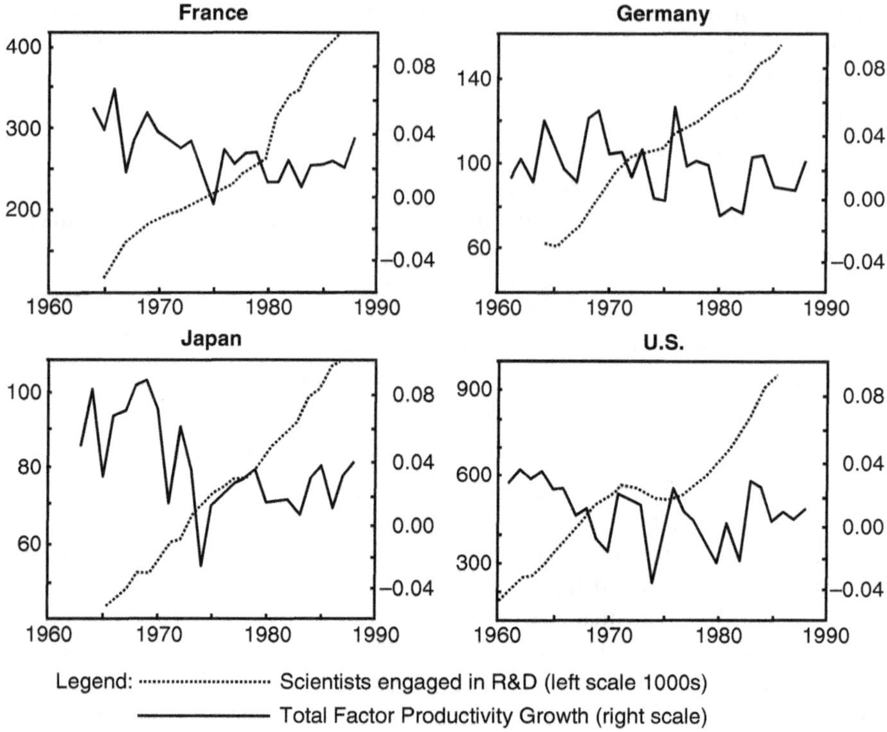

Fig. 3.31 R&D scientists and TFP growth
Source: own figure based on Jones, 1995b, pp. 517–518

3.4.1.4 Labor Force

Instead of assuming a constant labor force supply as in the Romer-model, Jones modeled the sector explicitly. In the Romer-model, one can see that the stock is defined by human capital and not by labor supply. This, however, is inconsistent since micro-foundations imply that new ideas are tied to persons (Jones, 1995a, pp. 762–763). The stock of labor L grows over time with the rate n. Similar to the Solow-model the absence of unemployment is assumed and therefore the labor stock is equivalent to the population itself. The benevolent planner has to decide how much labor work in the final-goods sector and how much produce new ideas. So the stock of labor splits into two activities with:

$$L = L_Y + L_A \tag{3.109}$$

The fraction of labor working in the R&D sector is s_R with $0 < s_R < 1$.

3.4.2 Structure

3.4.2.1 Stock-Flow-Diagram

The Jones-model is determined by the following equations:

$$Y = {L_Y}^{1-\alpha} \cdot \int_0^A {x_j}^{\alpha} dj \tag{3.110}$$

$$A = \left({A_0}^{1-\phi} + \frac{\rho}{1-\phi} L^{\lambda} t \right)^{\frac{1}{1-\phi}} \tag{3.111}$$

$$x_j = x \tag{3.112}$$

$$x = \frac{K}{A} \tag{3.113}$$

$$\dot{K} = I^N = S \tag{3.114}$$

$$S + C = Y \tag{3.115}$$

$$S = s \cdot Y \tag{3.116}$$

$$C = (1 - s) \cdot Y \tag{3.117}$$

$$L = L_0 \cdot e^{n \cdot t} \tag{3.118}$$

$$L = L_Y + L_A \tag{3.119}$$

The standard Jones-model is usually presented with a depreciation. However, for uniformity the investments are considered as net investments. Figure 3.32 presents the model in stock-flow-consistent style.

One can clearly recognize the affinity to the Romer-model, with one major difference – the labor sector grows exponentially. In addition, the difference in φ is not visible in the structure. The model consists of three exponential loops:

1. Investment-Loop
2. R&D-Loop
3. Labor-Loop

All three loops are reinforced and therefore accelerate the growth. A steady state is only attainable if they all grow with the same rate, as there are linked together. The origin of all is the labor sector, which is determined by the growth rate n.

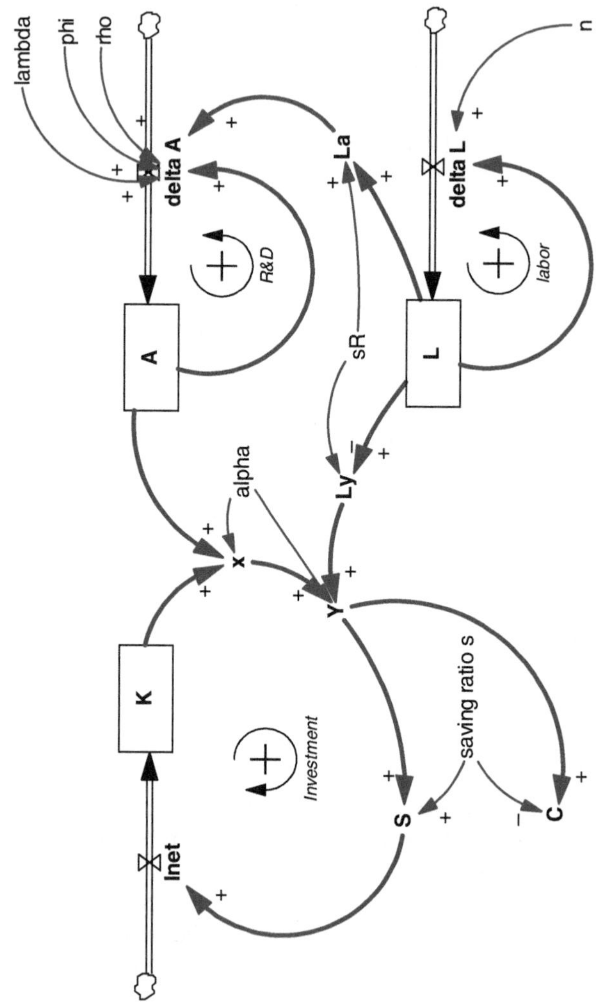

Fig. 3.32 Jones-model
Source: own figure

The R&D sector consists of the constants λ, φ and ρ and the Investment-Loop (with intermediate-goods sector and final-goods sector) is driven also by the constants α and s.

3.4.2.2 Phase Plot

As already mentioned, the Jones-model belongs to the group of semi-endogenous models. One could therefore assume that elements from both categories – endogenous models and exogenous models – should be found in it. Figure 3.33 presents the differences.

The left chart exhibits the relationship exogenous model. With a population growth greater than zero, the model evolves to a steady state. As long as the real investments sf(k) exceed the required investments (n+gA)k, the capital intensity per effective worker will grow over time. The difference between the two shrinks until equilibrium is reached. However, the same model can produce the behavior of a non-decreasing rate to return. This is shown in the right chart. With n = 0, the real investments always exceed the required investments. This means that the capital intensity is continuously growing without reaching any stable point.

3.4.2.3 Long-Term Equilibrium

Along the balanced growth path this model follows as all neoclassical models: the capital intensity per efficient unit of labor stays constant over time. The long run growth rate is constant so that Solow-model algebra applies. Then the capital intensity per effective worker is:

$$
\begin{aligned}
\frac{\delta k}{\delta t} &= const. \Rightarrow \frac{\dot{A}}{A} + \frac{\dot{L}}{L} = \frac{\dot{K}}{K} \\
gA + n &= \frac{s \cdot \left({L_Y}^{1-\alpha} \cdot \int\limits_0^A x(i)^\alpha \right)}{K} \\
gA + n &= s \cdot {L_Y}^{1-\alpha} \cdot A \cdot \left(\frac{K}{A}\right)^\alpha \cdot K^{-1} \\
gA + n &= s \cdot (1 - s_R)^{1-\alpha} \cdot (AL)^{1-\alpha} \cdot K^{-1+\alpha} \\
\left(\frac{K}{AL}\right)^{1-\alpha} &= \frac{s}{gA + n} \cdot (1 - s_R)^{1-\alpha} \\
\frac{K}{AL} &= \left[\frac{s}{gA + n}\right]^{\frac{1}{1-\alpha}} \cdot (1 - s_R)
\end{aligned}
\tag{3.120}
$$

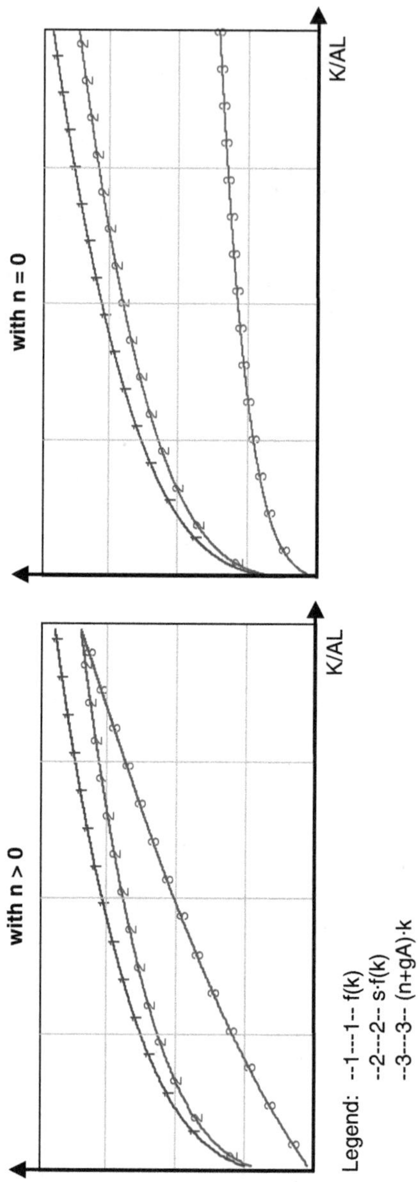

Fig. 3.33 Jones-model: phase plot
Source: own simulation

As $f(k) = k^{\alpha}$, the per effective capita income follows with:

$$\frac{Y}{AL} = \left(\frac{s}{n + gA}\right)^{\frac{\alpha}{1-\alpha}} \cdot (1 - s_R) \tag{3.121}$$

The main difference to equation (3.22) is the term $(1-s_R)$, which adjusts to the difference between L_Y and L.

As the stock of knowledge is now endogenized, distinguishing itself from the Solow-model, one can calculate the growth rate gA. The change of stock A is projected:

$$\dot{A} = \rho \cdot L_A{}^{\lambda} \cdot A^{\phi} \tag{3.122}$$

Therefore, the growth rate gA for any point in time is:

$$\frac{\dot{A}}{A} = \rho \cdot L_A{}^{\lambda} \cdot A^{\phi-1} \tag{3.123}$$

Along the steady state growth path, gA is constant; however this only occurs if the numerator and denominator grow at the same rate. Taking logs and derivatives of both sides it follows:

$$0 = \lambda \cdot \frac{\dot{L}_A}{L_A} - (1 - \phi)\frac{\dot{A}}{A} \tag{3.124}$$

$$gA = \frac{\dot{A}}{A} = \frac{\lambda \cdot n}{(1 - \phi)} \tag{3.125}$$

Usually the Jones-model is assumed with $\lambda = 1$ and $\varphi = 0$, so that the growth rate of the number of researchers follows easily with n. If the researchers' growth rate would be higher because of different values of λ and φ it could eventually exceed the population, which is not realistic.

Lastly, one must solve the allocation of labor between the intermediate-goods sector and the research sector. One could assume s_R as an exogenous constant, which would work well for achieving any steady state. But in order to find the optimum s_R has to be endogenized.

Workers in the final-goods sector earn a wage w_Y which is equal to the marginal product of that sector:

$$w_Y = (1 - \alpha) \cdot \frac{Y}{L_Y} \tag{3.126}$$

In this model, researchers' income is based on the value of the designs they create. It is assumed that they do not recognize that the productivity may decline as labor floods the sector. Also, they do not internalize the knowledge spillover. Therefore, the wage is equal to the marginal product and the value of new ideas:

$$w_A = \bar{\rho} \cdot P_A \tag{3.127}$$

Free entry from both sectors ensures that the wage must be the same $w_Y = w_A$.

$$\bar{\rho} \cdot P_A = (1 - \alpha) \cdot \frac{Y}{L_Y} \tag{3.128}$$

Substitution of $P_A = \frac{\pi}{r-n}$ from equation (3.108) and recalling that π is proportional to Y/A:

$$\bar{\rho} \cdot \frac{\alpha \cdot (1 - \alpha) \cdot \frac{Y}{A}}{r - n} = (1 - \alpha) \cdot \frac{Y}{L_Y} \tag{3.129}$$

Canceling and leaving:

$$\frac{\bar{\rho}}{A} \cdot \frac{\alpha}{r - n} = \frac{1}{L_Y} \tag{3.130}$$

Also notice that $\frac{\dot{A}}{A} = \frac{\bar{\rho} \cdot L_A}{A}$ and $\frac{L_A}{L_Y} = \frac{s_R}{(1 - s_R)}$ reveal:

$$s_R = \frac{1}{1 + \frac{r-n}{\alpha \cdot gA}} \tag{3.131}$$

This equation shows that the faster the economy grows the higher is the fraction s_R.

To summarize, the long run growth rate of the economy is determined by the population's growth rate and parameters of production function.

3.4.3 Dynamics

If the stock of researchers stopped growing, as the model implies, economic growth would eventually halt. A constant research effort cannot sustain the needed increase in the stock of ideas in order to generate long-run growth (Jones, 2001, p. 104). The endogenous growth model of the Romer-type can show permanent increases in an economy's growth rates. This will lead to an acceleration in population growth over time. Jones (1995a) eliminated this defect.

In order to analyze the effect of permanent increases in the population of the working R&D sector, it is assumed that $\lambda = 1$ and $\varphi = 0$. This will not change any result qualitatively. One can write:

$$\frac{\dot{A}}{A} = \rho \cdot \frac{L_A}{A} = \rho \cdot \frac{s_R L}{A} \tag{3.132}$$

As shown in Fig. 3.34, the economy travels a steady state growth path. At time $t = 40$ the number of researchers increases as s_R increases. L_A/A jumps to a higher level. As a consequence, the number of researchers affects the production of new ideas; but the technological progress exceeds the population growth n and therefore L_A/A declines until the economy returns to the balanced growth path.

The stock of knowledge grows along the balanced growth path. A change in s_R increases the level of technology but levels very quickly on a new but higher level. Figure 3.35 shows this level effect on a logarithmic scale. This is different from both the Solow-model and the Romer-model. Notice that the transition itself takes place at a very quick rate.

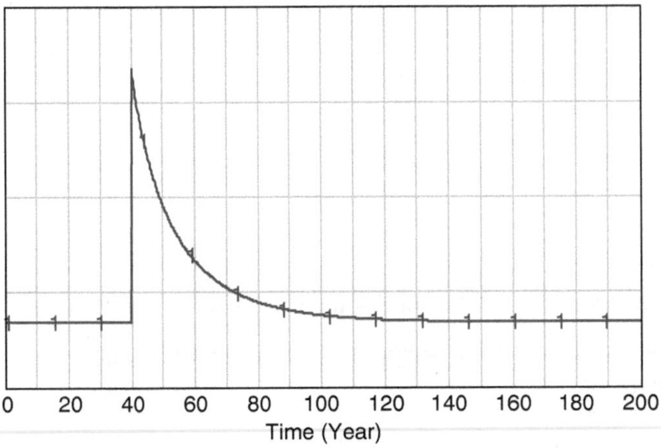

Fig. 3.34 Increase in R&D share: technology growth rate
Source: own simulation

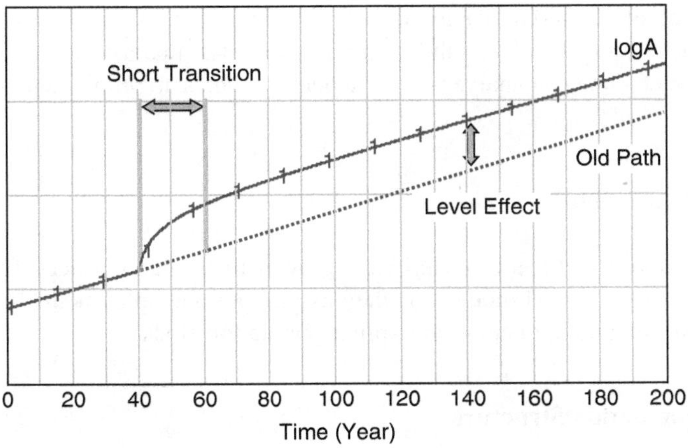

Fig. 3.35 Increase in R&D share: stock of technology
Source: own simulation

The effect on the per capita income and the income per effective worker is presented in Fig. 3.36. It is remarkable that the power of exponential growth almost overcomes the declining effect of an increase in the technology stock (see the left figure). The right graph represents the drop in income per effective worker. The very short transition between $t = 40$ and $t = 60$ is almost negligible.

To summarize, the main result yields a permanent increase in s_R, in turn, having no permanent effect on the growth rate.

3.4.4 Policy Experiments

By starting capital intensity below the steady state, one can investigate the effects of the following demographic factors:

(1) Population
(2) Population structure
(3) Fertility
(4) Mortality
(5) Migration

And also one knows that the Jones-model consists of several constant factors:

- Initial value of capital (K_0), labor (L_0) and technology (A_0)
- Saving ratio (s)
- Labor growth (n)
- The amount of labor working in R&D (s_R)
- The specific constants to determine the change of knowledge (ρ, φ, λ)
- The partial production elasticity of capital (α)

For simplification, one assumes $\lambda = 1$ (no decreasing return on workers) and $\rho = 1$ (no accelerating factor) and $\varphi = 0$ (no scale effect on existing knowledge).

With these two modules – the demographic determinants and the exogenous growth factors – one can analyze how the demographics are implemented in Jones' model.

3.4.4.1 Population

The population growth is modeled as a growth in the labor force. This is very typically for neoclassical models, as they assume no unemployment. But this also implies a missing component – an explicit population stock.

3.4.4.2 Population Structure

All previous models, such as the Jones-model, do not distinguish between the working and the non-working population. Therefore, a population structure is not explicitly embodied. This does not imply an age structure effect.

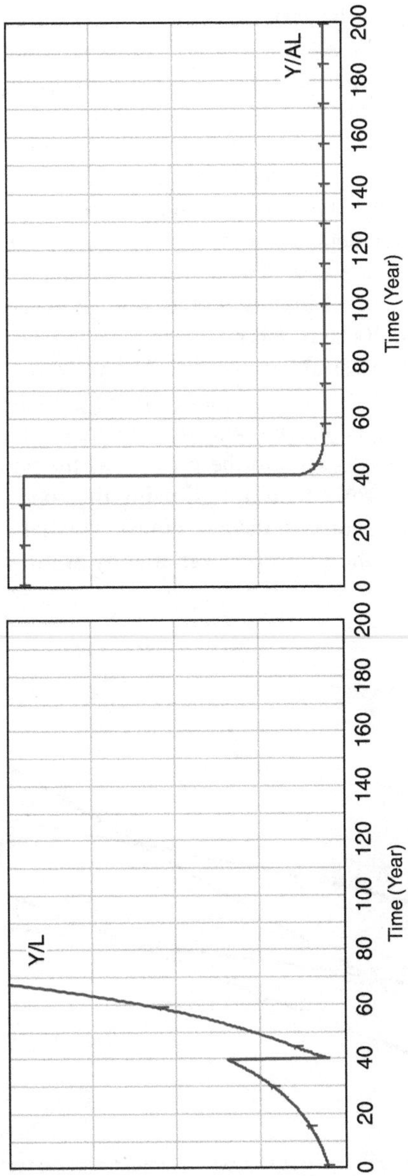

Fig. 3.36 Increase in R&D share: behavior Y/L and Y/AL
Source: own simulation

3.4.4.3 Fertility and Mortality

Fertility and mortality are indirectly included in the model, with the net growth rate of the population n. Figure 3.37 shows the effect of a declining, but still positive growth rate in a phase plot for the Jones-model.

The requirement lines shift downwards and the steady-state capital per efficiency unit of labor moves to the right. K_1 is bigger than k_0. Figures 3.38 and 3.39 present the consequences for certain important variables.

Following common sense – if the growth rate of a population is so important for economic growth in the model, then a declining growth rate would lead to shrinking values for most of the variables. This phenomenon is observed in Fig. 3.38. Capital stock, income and technology depend on the stock of labor. The labor stock grows slower with smaller growth rate n so that the exponential growth slows down. If population or the number of researchers would stop growing, then the long-run growth would cease (Jones, 2001, p. 104).

The effect on the per capita variables and per effective worker variables is shown in Fig. 3.39. As one may probably assume, a declining growth rate slows both the capital intensity and the per capita income. However, both variables still have positive growth rates gA. This is seen in the growth, as the nominator grows with n+gA and the denominator grows with n. Following this, one can see that the per effective worker variables presented in the chart must eventually achieve a new and higher steady state. Dividing the per capita variable by A produces the values per

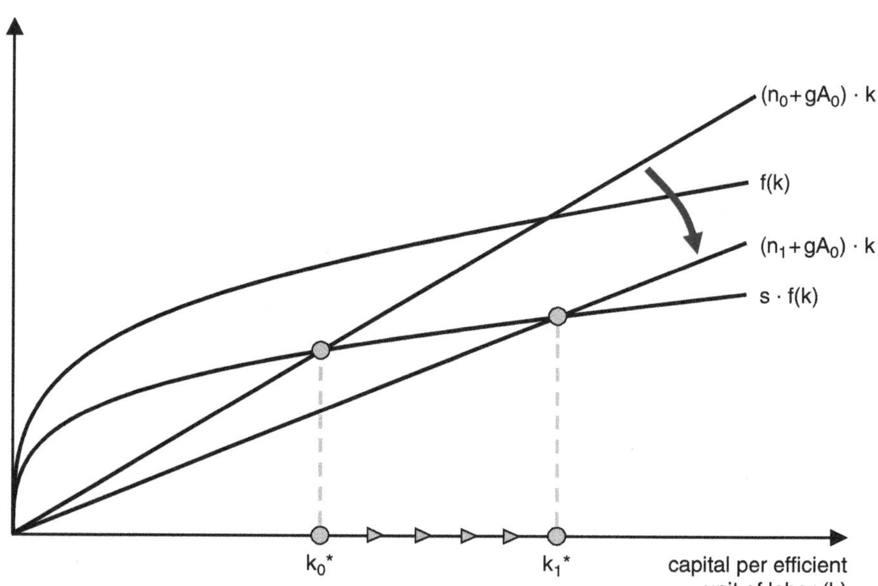

Fig. 3.37 Policy experiments: population growth rate
Source: own figure

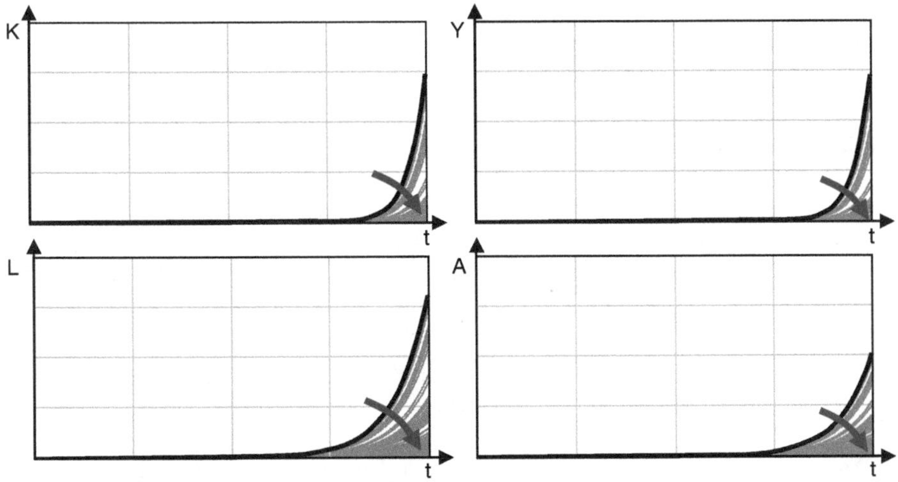

Fig. 3.38 Sensitivity run: K, L, Y, A
Source: own simulation

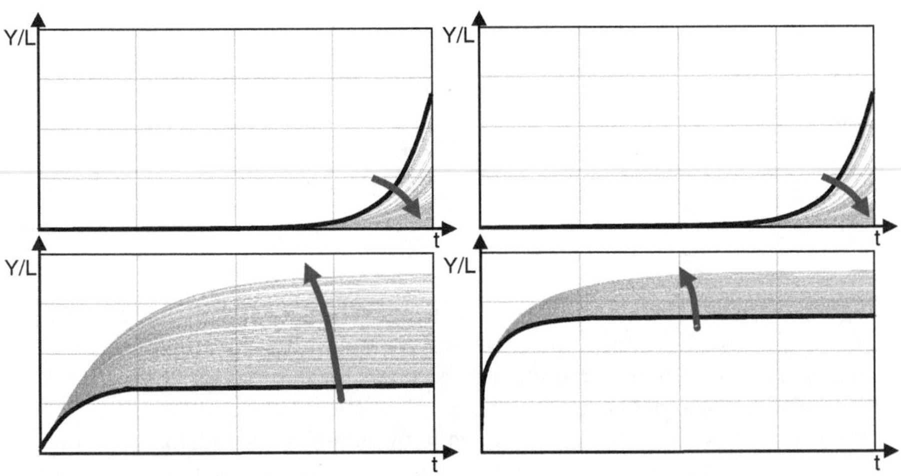

Fig. 3.39 Sensitivity run: K/L, K/AL, Y/L, Y/AL
Source: own simulation

effective worker; the growth rate gA is eliminated and the per effective workers values equalize.

3.4.4.4 Migration

The Jones-model focuses on an economy with no foreign trade. It is a closed model for which the foreign sector is not a determining factor. Therefore, migration is not considered within the model. A change in the labor growth rate n already shows some indirect influences.

3.4.4.5 Other Factors

One interesting factor is the ratio s_R, which determines the split between the labor force, the final-goods sector and the R&D sector. In this case, the steady state is already reached. The steady state income per effective worker can be seen in the equation (3.121):

$$\frac{Y}{AL} = \left(\frac{s}{n + gA}\right)^{\frac{\alpha}{1-\alpha}} \cdot (1 - s_R) \tag{3.133}$$

An increase in s_R would lead directly to a decline in the income per effective capita. This also means that lower capital intensity per effective worker is needed to support the balanced growth. Much more interesting, however, is the income per capita – which derives out of this equation by multiplying with A.

$$\frac{Y}{L} = \left(\frac{s}{n + gA}\right)^{\frac{\alpha}{1-\alpha}} \cdot (1 - s_R) \cdot A \tag{3.134}$$

Now knowing that $A = \rho \cdot L_A{}^{\lambda} \cdot A^{\phi}$ and replacing $L_A = s_R \cdot L$ yields:

$$\frac{Y}{L} = \left(\frac{s}{n + gA}\right)^{\frac{\alpha}{1-\alpha}} \cdot (1 - s_R) \cdot \rho \cdot (s_R \cdot L)^{\lambda} \cdot A^{\phi} \tag{3.135}$$

S_R occurs twice. The first time it enters negatively and decreases the income per capita since more researchers mean fewer workers in the final-good sector. The second s_R is used to reflect that more researchers mean more ideas, which finally increases the income per capita.

So, which effect is stronger? A sequential Monte-Carlo simulation could prove this. Figure 3.40 shows the result of 200 simulation runs. Starting in a steady state, the constant s_R fluctuates with a uniform distribution around their equilibrium value.

On the left, one finds the values for the per effective worker income and the capital stock. An increase in s_R shifts the new steady state downwards. However, after a short transition period, a steady state is reached. On the right, one can see that the changes of s_R per capita values slope downwards. This can be evaluated well in Fig. 3.41

The transition process from the change of s_R goes mainly over the stock of knowledge. An increase in s_R, for example, forces the stock of R&D-knowledge to grow, thereby increasing gA suddenly. The higher number of researchers increases also L_A/A, which means there are too many researchers for the current stock of knowledge. The stock of knowledge is changing over time with the rate:

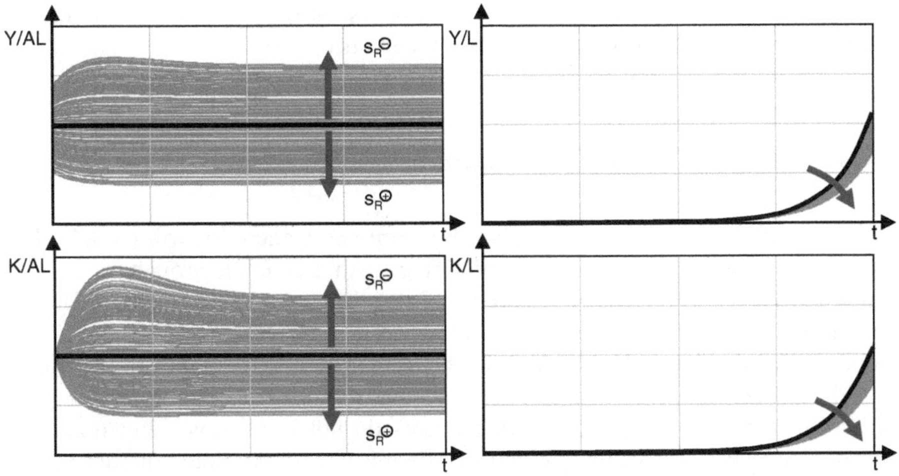

Fig. 3.40 Sensitivity run (Change in s_R): Y/AL, K/AL, Y/L, K/L
Source: own simulation

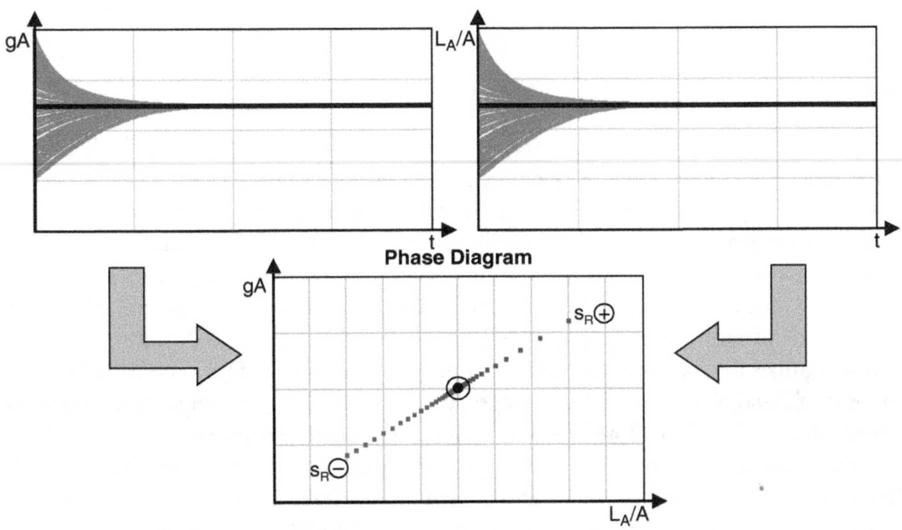

Fig. 3.41 Sensitivity run (Change in s_R): phase diagram gA-L_A/A
Source: own simulation

$$\dot{A} = \rho \cdot (s_R \cdot L)^{\lambda} \cdot A^{\phi} \tag{3.136}$$

As long as both charts in Fig. 3.41 are above the previous steady state, the stock value of knowledge is too little. The third chart in Fig. 3.41 shows the phase plot from this transition process. The dots mark simulation steps. One can see that the moving towards the steady state after the impulse slows down until it is finally reached. The case of a lowering s_R works vice versa.

3.4.5 Discussion and Conclusion

The Jones-model is the classic standard for semi-endogenous growth models. The growth driver in this model is the population growth. Economic growth is an entity which depends on new ideas of researchers. In addition, the Jones-model shows that growth relates to the effective number of researchers rather than to the population. It overcomes, therefore, the problems of the Romer-model. As in the Solow-model, subsidies R&D and capital accumulation have no substantial long-term effects along the transition path. Growth differences do not last forever, but transition dynamics can be very strong. A major difference from the Solow-model is that growth is generated endogenously, in the sense that new technologies are created out of profit maximizing agents (Jones, 1995a, pp. 777–778). But it still follows the policy invariance of the Solow-model and is therefore classified with respect to its behavior between the Solow and the Romer-model.

3.5 Chapter Summary

Although the Solow-Swan-model was revolutionary for its time, it does not completely explain economic growth. Specifically, the model fits well with certain countries empirically; however it does not implicitly explain long-term positive per capita growth. In addition, the technological production factor is only included into the model in that way, that it comes *as manna from heaven* (Robinson, 1971). In those types of models the technical progress is not fully explained, stating that one can recognize this because the technical progress surly influences the population's income Y, and yet no variable, except the growth rate g, changes the progress (Robinson, 1971). Therefore, growth is only explained exogenously.

One alternative to this approach is presented in the Romer-model. Romer took Schumpeter's idea of "Creative Destruction" and internalized technology in his model. New capital goods increase the productivity and the externality of knowledge able the model to show long-term per capita growth. Romer is credited with the implementation of monopolistic competition within an economic growth model. According to this model, if the population grows at a positive rate n, then the per capita income does not attain a steady state. This does also not hold with the empirics (Christiaans, 2004, pp. 252–253). Empirically, there is no correlation between economic growth and the growth rate of researchers.

Jones combined the main ideas of endogenous growth models of Romer-type with the Solow-model to overcome the special conditions. His model shows semi-endogenous growth with a politic invariance. Jones showed that only the population

Type	Exogenous	Endogenous	Semi-Endogenous
Model	Solow	Romer	Jones
Population Variable	L	L and H	L
Growth Rate	n	-	n
Populaton	indirect in labor force	not deducable	indirect in labor force
Population Structure	not embodied	as fraction of L and H	not embodied
Age Ratio	only in augmented models	-	-
Fertiliy	indirect in n	-	indirect in n
Mortality	indirect in n	-	indirect in n
Migration	only in augmented models	-	-

Fig. 3.42 Comparison of key growth models
Source: own figure

growth rate determines the long run steady state growth. But policy-makers do have the choice to strengthen level effects.

All models focus on the supply side of the market, which is similar to most of the economic growth literature. The economy is fully utilized and the demand follows the supply of goods. This also means that the demographic effects of the demand side were not analyzed in this chapter. The leaving demographic determinants from Chap. 2 will be investigated in Chap. 4 as it introduces a large-scale macroeconomic model founded on Jones' growth model.

As a brief summary Fig. 3.42 provides an overview on the three main models presented in this chapter.

This chapter clarified the need for a comprehensive universal demographic model, since most of the models do not halt with demographic factors. Even one of the latest attempts to implement these factors was presented in Sect. 3.2.5.1 – the Gruescu modeled a simple demographic change without optimal planning decision-making. Other concepts attempt to embody demographic factors, but are primarily based on micro-founded models (see for further reading Blackburn & Cipriani (1998), Becker, Murphy & Tamura (1990) or Braun (1993).

The next chapter introduces the simulation method before building the new demographic semi-endogenous growth model.

Chapter 4
Demographic Growth Model

> *"Some forecasts fail because they mistakenly assume the continuation of a long-standing demographic, social, or political trend. Often the opposite has occurred. Long-term trends can shift suddenly and unexpectedly."*
>
> (Schnaars, 1989, p. 97)

4.1 Introduction

This chapter consists of two major parts. In the first subchapter, the semi-endogenous demographic growth model is explained in detail. The model consists of four sectors – population, R&D, growth and utility. The paper is structured in this order, as the origin of growth is the population sector which influences the R&D sector and the growth sector. The utility sector adds to the growth sector and serves as indicator for the evaluation of policies. This subchapter concludes after the model is initialized and executable.

The second subchapter evaluates the model by conducting two behavioral tests. The first test examines a stable population, where the effects on major key variables of the other sectors are analyzed. The second test investigates population growth and analyzes whether the model converges towards a steady state or not. Semi-endogenous models present the growth of population stocks as the only source of convergence for the capital intensity per effective capita. Following these tests, the model is fully evaluated in regard to its structure and behavior. Continuing on this theme, the next chapter executes various scenarios for demographic change.

Before starting with the first subchapter, one should have a look at the modeling techniques for system dynamics. A full scientific comparison of system dynamics and other economic modeling and analyzing techniques would be beyond the scope of this work. Nevertheless, it is useful to outline a short description of system dynamics and its advantages and disadvantages compared to econometrics. Especially the study of econometrics has presented a quasi standard analysis tool for economic problems.

L. Weber, *Demographic Change and Economic Growth*, Contributions to Economics, DOI 10.1007/978-3-7908-2590-9_4,

Primarily developed by Jay Forrester, system dynamics came to the forefront in the mid 1950s. He set forth a guiding philosophy and representational techniques for the simulation of complex, non-linear, feedback systems (Meadows & Robinson, 2007). Originally applied to management systems, this methodology reached a broader audience when Forrester published the World Dynamics model (Forrester, 1971) and the, more popular science-orientated, companion book "Limits to Growth" (Meadows, 1972; Meadows, Randers, & Meadows, 2004). These works were the beginning of the discussion between economists and system dynamicists about the advantages and disadvantages of system dynamics and econometrics (see for example William Nordhaus Nordhaus, 1973 and Jay Forrester Forrester & Low, 1974).

Equilibrium modeling is the focus in most areas of economic analysis. But policy-makers are often more interested in the path taken by policy variables when reaching equilibrium. For this, system dynamics offers an accessible methodology. This approach is consistent with economic modeling of dynamic phenomena, but it uses different conventions and terminology (Smith & Ackere, 2002, pp. 1–2).

In general, econometrics analyses the correlations between input and output variables, whereas system dynamics tries to understand the underlying systems structure. The insight is not needed for econometricians, as long the model can transfer the reference behavior into the prediction period. In highly volatile and complex situations, this may not be the appropriate method, as this can only replicate experienced behavior patterns. System dynamics tries to overcome this by modeling the assumed systems structure. One can see this major difference in Fig. 4.1.

It is often claimed that econometrics and system dynamics differ in the time pattern (Frerichs & Kübler, 1980). Whereas econometrics focuses on short and mid-term perspectives, system dynamics focuses on long-term perspectives. But this is only partly true, because with the underlying structure of first order differential equations, system dynamics is very well suitable for short-term simulations too. However, one has to consider that system dynamics stresses the importance of feedback processes, and therefore it is more a question of frequency of the given data and not of the simulation period. In addition, some critics say that system dynamics would be rather qualitative orientated than quantitative orientated (Myrtveit,

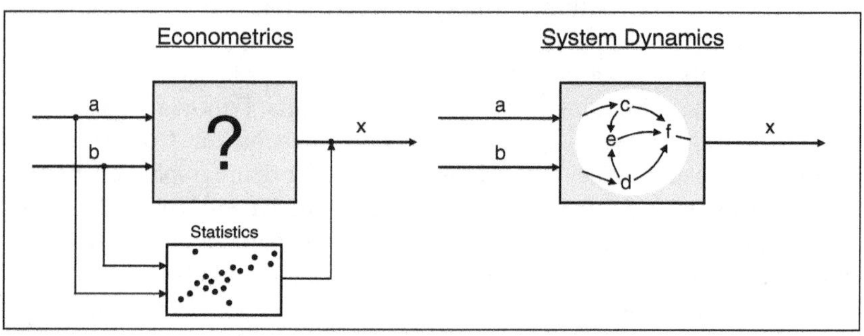

Fig. 4.1 Perspectives of econometrics and system dynamics
Source: own figure

Characteristics	System Dynamics	Econometrics
perspective	system	sub-system
model boundary	open, but causal closed (few exogenous variables)	open (few endogenous variables)
focus	structure - causality	data - correlation
model purpose	behavior modeling	prediction modeling
time horizon	(short-), mid- and long-term	short- and mid-term
data	more qualitative, but quantitative also	quantitative
policy simulation	policy change	decision change
policy evaluation	ex-ante for change in specifications	ex-ante for change in instruments
functional form	nonlinear parameters and variables	linear parameters and variables

Fig. 4.2 Comparison of econometrics and system dynamics
Source: own figure

2005, p. 26). This is also only true to some extent. System dynamics can handle both types of data, and is therefore not restricted to quantitative simulations.

Figure 4.2 presents an overview of major differences between system dynamics and econometrics (see Sommer, 1981, Sommer, 1984; Myrtveit, 2005; Frerichs & Kübler, 1980).

The modeling techniques are complimentary. Whereas system dynamics tries to enlighten systemic structures of observed economic systems, econometrics can provide analyzed data of exogenous input variables for simulation models. One can summarize that the major objections about a use of system dynamics in economics apply mainly to their inherent assumptions and not to the modeling technique itself. Often, system dynamics modeling coexists with so-called heterodox approaches of economics (Radzicki, 1994, Radzicki, 2003; Sterman, 1986, Sterman, 1989). However, this work proves that a use of system dynamics can also shed light on important aspects in the field of neoclassical economics.

4.2 Model Specifications

4.2.1 System Structure

4.2.1.1 Model Boundary

A dynamic model is a simplification of a real world system, which changes through time and space (Moffat, 1992, p. 7; Imboden & Koch, 2005, p. 7). Since a model can only present a picture of the reality, one has to define the *model boundary* as well as the included and excluded variables. The following Fig. 4.3 presents an overview of the key variables. For clarity, the different model parts are separated.

The subsequent simulations differ in some variable values of the exogenous constants, but not in the constants themselves. Also, the initial values of the stocks are equal, thereby keeping the simulation results comparable.

Model Part	Endogenous Variables	Exogenous Variables	Excluded Variables
Population Sector	age cohorts births deaths ratio high to low skilled	education ratio female ratio fractional death ratios migration of working age people total fertility ratio	infant mortality migration of non-working people shifting mortality rates very high ages over 90
R&D Sector	high skilled labor technology	accelerator degree of congestion in research return on stocks of ideas	quality improvements
Growth Sector	capital stock consumption demographic foreign direct investments income intermediate products investments low skilled labor production savings	capital broughtby immigrants production elasticity of capital saving ratio wage distribution	depreciation of capital exchange rates foreign direct investments inflation monetary sector unemployment
Utility Sector	accumulated utility per capita accumulated utility per effective capita consumption per capita consumption per effective capita utility per capita utility per effective capita	marginal utility reference time time preference	age specific utility function

Fig. 4.3 Demographic growth model: model boundary
Source: own figure

4.2.1.2 Integration Method and Error Test

Dynamic behavior arises from the integration of stocks within systems (Forrester, 1968, pp. 10–11). *Accumulation produces delays* between time periods and creates the dynamic system behavior. In a system dynamics model, the integration process is modeled as a first order difference equation. This is entirely equivalent to a continuous natural process in socio-economic systems if the solution interval is short enough (Forrester, 1968, pp. 6–11). Another reason for using difference equations for differential problems is based on the facts that observations are only done at certain points in time, yet the system is still continuous. Therefore, this is more a question of measurement and observations. With increasing measure points in time, the difference equation becomes more and more continuous.

The current state of a stock depends on its initial conditions and the sum of all inflows and outflows over time. In order to eliminate the influence of the time interval, the in- and outflows are expressed as units per time. Thus, the multiplication by the time interval delivers the correct unit dimension for the stock (Bossel, 1994, p. 95). From a mathematical point of view, stocks integrate their net flows and the net flow is a derivative of the stock (Sterman, 2004, p. 232)

Every simulation is the result of an experimental deduction, and represents partial solutions of the model. With certain probability, one can deduce the general solution; however, complex models often do not have an analytical solution. The restriction to numerical solutions often gives necessary model flexibility for detailed analysis (Hirschhäuser, 1981, p. 22). Figure 4.4 presents the process sequence for a dynamical simulation.

Figure 4.4 only provides a general overview about a simulation sequence. However, independently from the integration method for computational simulations, one can also write (points 2–6 for each time step) (Bossel, 1994, p. 109):

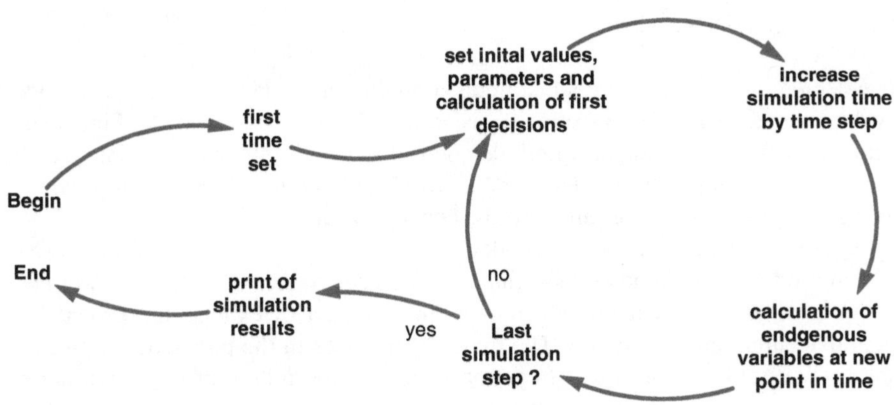

Fig. 4.4 Sequence of a dynamical simulation
Source: own figure according to Hirschhäuser, 1981, p. 23

1. *Specification of the initial conditions* for the stocks and all constants as vector $z_0 = [z_1(t_0), z_2(t_0), \ldots, z_n(t_0)]$
2. *Determination of the system influences* of the current input variables as vector $u(t)$
3. *Determination of possible time-dependent parameters*
4. *Calculation of the flows* for the stocks: $dz/dt = f(z(t), u(t), t)$
5. *Numerical integration* of the flows to determine the stocks: $z(t) = z_0 + \int_0^t (dz/dt) \cdot dt$
6. *Computation of the output vector*: $v(t) = g(z(t), u(t), t)$

The typical integration method for numerical simulations is of *Euler type*. As a rule of thumb for Euler integration methods, Forrester suggests the appropriate length of the solution interval:

> "The solution interval should be half or less of the shortest first-order delay in the system." (Forrester, 1968, pp. 6–3)

In Forrester's time, computerization was just beginning, thus it was introduced to save the computer time. With today's possibilities, it is recommended to decline the integration step until the model behavior does not change anymore. Especially in the case of very complex and non-linear models, the simulation results would be faulty, with a huge integration step. Integration techniques that are newer than the Euler approach increase the accuracy without declining the time step. If either the small time step slows down the simulation, or the system is highly changing, the *Runge–Kutta integration method* might be a better solution. This advanced technique interpolates between two time steps (for further reading see Bossel, 1994, p. 104; Sterman, 2004, p. 902). Although the Runge–Kutta method requires more computer power, the accuracy is much higher than Euler's method (Sterman, 2004, p. 908). Therefore, the demographic growth model uses the Runge–Kutta integration method with a time step dt = 1.

4.2.1.3 Model Overview

The demographic growth model is founded on the semi-endogenous growth model by Jones (see Sect. 3.4), but some decisive additional steps are made. Firstly, the population sector is much more detailed than a simple exponential growth approach. Secondly, the model part "Utility" will provide variables to evaluate increasing or shrinking welfare with the concept of utility.

Figure 4.5 presents the whole model in the highest aggregated form. It consists of four model parts. Some of them can be recognized as related to the Jones-model.

As in all neoclassical growth models, the concept of exponential growth via capital accumulation is central. The major differences in the population sector are not explicitly visible in this aggregation level, but the inflow of migration is one new aspect. Also, the stock of capital can now be increased by immigration capital. The accumulation of net present discounted utility to compare different simulation results is new, too.

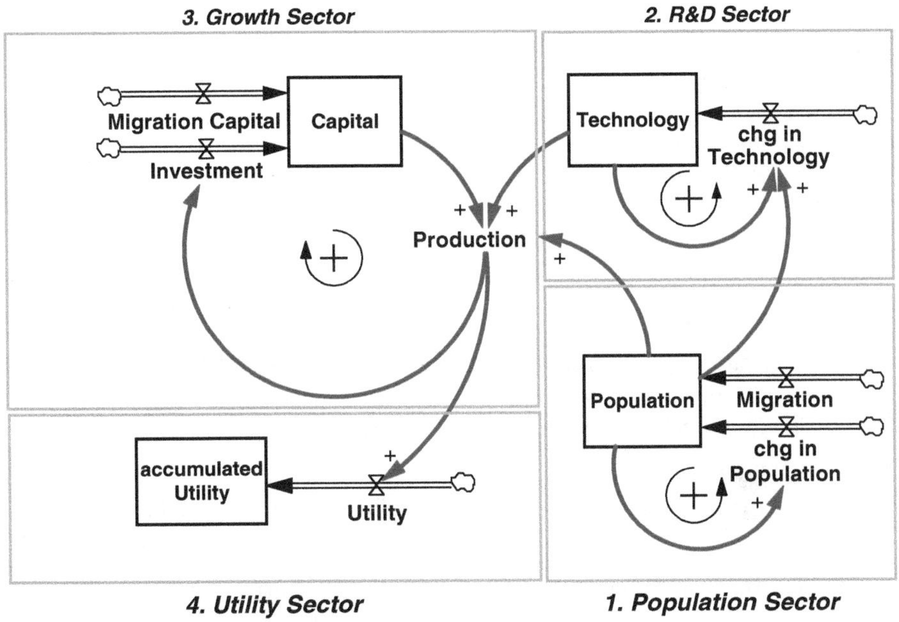

Fig. 4.5 Demographic growth model: model overview
Source: own figure

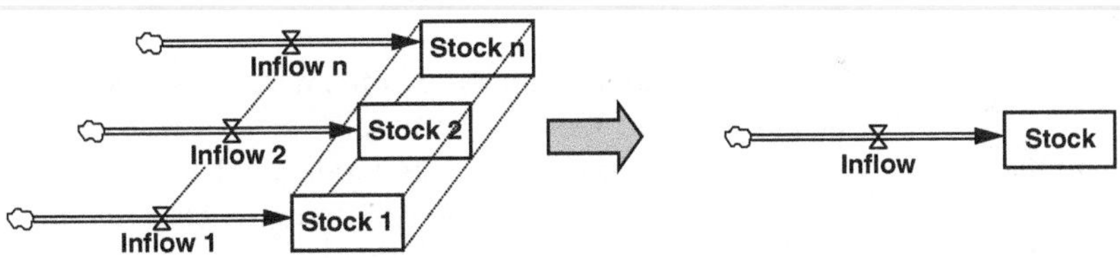

$$\begin{aligned} Stock\ 1_{t+1} &= Stock\ 1_t + Inflow\ 1_t \\ Stock\ 2_{t+1} &= Stock\ 2_t + Inflow\ 2_t \\ Stock\ n_{t+1} &= Stock\ n_t + Inflow\ n_t \end{aligned}$$

$$Stock_{t+1} = \begin{pmatrix} Stock\ 1_{t+1} \\ Stock\ 2_{t+1} \\ Stock\ n_{t+1} \end{pmatrix} = \begin{pmatrix} Stock\ 1_t \\ Stock\ 2_t \\ Stock\ n_t \end{pmatrix} + \begin{pmatrix} Inflow\ 1_t \\ Inflow\ 2_t \\ Inflow\ n_t \end{pmatrix}$$

Fig. 4.6 Concept of subscripts
Source: own figure

The explanations of the model parts follow the order as shown in Fig. 4.5; however, a few remarks have to be made to introduce the model. Some variables are distinguished in *different layers*, which transform the variable into a vector or matrix (in the modeling language called "subscript"). The model structure for every vector would be the same. For the sake of clarity, the model structure only shows the general structure. Figure 4.6 shows this concept in detail.

Some later model variables are be two-dimensional, creating a matrix. As an example, one can think of a company with a certain number of employees. The first dimension to differentiate could be the department level (research, sales, human resources, etc.), and the second dimension could be level of experience (manager, assistant, associate, partner, etc.).

In the model, one subscript describes different age groups. Although the age groups in the population sector are explicitly visible, some variables of other model parts are distinguished invisibly (subscript) in four age cohorts with:

age: age0014, age1539, age4064, age6589
Comment: age cohorts

The other subscript describes different skills. High-skilled labor refers to the R&D sector, whereas the low-skilled labor works for the production of consumption goods in the final good sector.

skill: high, low
Comment: high skilled labor to work in R&D; low skilled labor to work in final goods sector

The subscripts can be combined to create a 4 × 2-Matrix with:

$$\begin{pmatrix} age0014, high & age0014, low \\ age1539, high & age1539, low \\ age4064, high & age4064, low \\ age6589, high & age6589, low \end{pmatrix}$$

Additionally, some variables will be introduced into the model, in order to keep the *structure dimensionally consistent*. One has to modify some equations. Such modifications are required if one has to calculate an exponential function with a fraction exponent. In these cases, the basis must be dimensionless. When this occurs, a unit "dummy" is introduced into the model. In addition, some production functions consist of fractional exponents. In some cases – e.g. in Cobb–Douglas production function – all exponents add to one. To avoid the unit confusion for the production factors, one can argue that the production function is only a statistical approximation for real world behavior and not a "real" production function. The unit dummies are shown in the Annex of this work.

4.2.2 Part "Population"

4.2.2.1 Basic Structure

As in Fig. 4.5 (model overview) shown, the aggregated population stock will be explicitly formulated in this section. The population sector consists of four stocks.

Each stock covers a certain period of life for a human. Whereas the first stock ranges from birth until 15 years of age, all of the following stocks cover 25 years of life. The stocks (age cohort = ac) are:

ac0014[skill], ac1539[skill], ac4064[skill], ac6589[skill]

It would be possible to disaggregate in greater detail, but with these four groups, most of the important life aspects can be covered. The variable ac0014 represents childhood and adolescence. The variable ac1539 represents the next period of life, including younger workers, and, more importantly, childbearing ages. Older employers, who are not of childbearing age, are represented by the variable ac4064. Finally, retirees are represented by the variable ac6589.

The squared brackets characterize the subscript. The whole aging chain is differentiated into high- and low-skilled labor. This actually creates two totally separated lives streams of high- and low-skilled workers with eight stocks in total.

The fundamental demographic equation, as referenced in (2.11), is represented as:

$$\Delta P_t = (B_t - D_t) + M_t \tag{4.1}$$

The population in total, as well as every single population stock, changes over time according to its inflows and outflows. Figure 4.7 shows the ac0014 as example for all cohorts. Births increase the stock. Migration can work two ways (bi-flow), and their direction depends on the value. Deaths and aging people decrease the stock.

Mathematically, the course over time is:

$$P_{t+1} = P_t + \Delta P_t = P_t + (B_t - D_t) + M_t \tag{4.2}$$

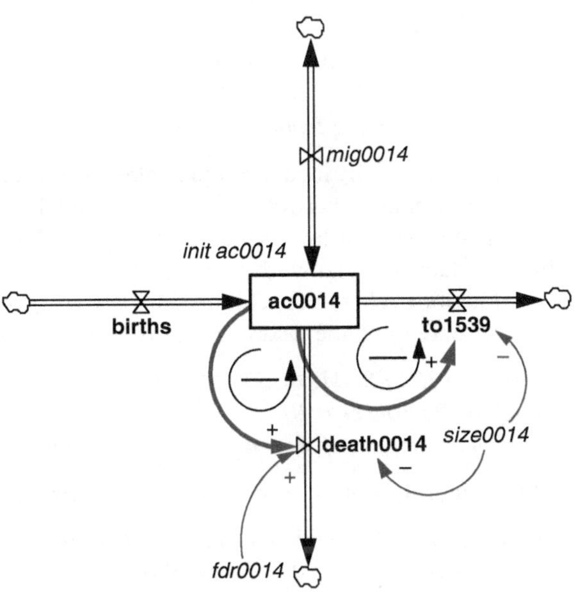

Fig. 4.7 Demographic growth model: population stock
Source: own figure

For all four stocks, the formulation therefore is:

ac0014[skill] = INTEG(births[skill] + mig0014[skill] - death0014[skill] - to1539 [skill], init ac0014[skill])
ac1539[skill] = INTEG(to work[skill] + mig1539[skill] - death1539[skill] - to4064[skill], init ac1539[skill])
ac4064[skill] = INTEG(to4064[skill]+ mig4064[skill] - death4064[skill] - to retire[skill], init ac4064[skill])
ac6589[skill] = INTEG(to retire[skill] + mig6589[skill] - death6589[skill] - to9000[skill], init ac6590[skill])
Unit: Person [0,?]
Comment: age cohort

The term "INTEG" stands for the integration of the flows, and the "init acxxxx [skill]" notifies the initial value of the simulation for each stock.

4.2.2.2 Aging

Jones presented the total population as only one stock. With assumed uniform distribution, every change (growing or shrinking) in the stock will instantaneously take place. To model the continuous process of aging more precisely, one has to assume different age stages. Thus, the total population is represented as an *aging chain*. In this structure, aging represents the transfer from one stock to another. Every transfer increases the order of the material delay, so that the population in the demographic growth model is a fourth order material delay with an average delay of 90 years.

The first stock, ac0014, has a size of 15 years. This is the average time for a person to go through the stock (residence time). The number of people that age from 14 to 15 is:

to1539[skill] = ac0014[skill]/size0014
Unit: Person/Year [0,?,10]
Comment: aging from 14 to15

At this point in the model, people enter work life. As previously mentioned, the model differentiates between high-skilled and low-skilled workers. Children of both high-skilled and low-skilled parents have the same probability of achieving a higher education, and working for their whole work life in this sector (no social discrimination). Therefore, children of both groups must be added together, and then distributed into the next age cohort (ac1539) with respect to their skills:

skilled ac15 = SUM (to1539[skill!])
Unit: Person/Year [0,?]
Comment: sum of skilled young population

Then entering work life, with respect to their education:

*to work[high] = education ratio * skilled ac15*
*to work[low] = (1 - education ratio) * skilled ac15*

Unit: Person/Year [0,?]
Comment: enter in working age with respect to education (high and low skilled)

After 25 years of work life, the people enter the second work-phase as experienced workers. This also marks the end of the childbearing age. The amount of people moving into the cohort ac4064 is:

to 4064[skill] = ac1539[skill]/size1539
Unit: Person/Year [0,?,10]
Comment: aging from 39 to 40

By the age of 65, the work life ends and all people (both high-skilled and low-skilled) move into the retirement period through the end of their lives with

to retire[skill] = ac4064[skill]/size4064
Unit: Person/Year [0,?,10]
Comment: aging from 64 to 65 (retirement)

Usually, aging models assume an open right boundary. This means that the last stock of life span is open until people die (Sterman, 2004). Unfortunately, this creates a challenge when calculating the correct number of people in the stock. This problem increases with the stock size, because the fractional death rate for every point in time in this stock is equal. However, one can easily imagine that the probability of dying is much higher for a 100-year old person than for a 65-year old. To keep this miscalculation small, the highest stock is *closed on the right boundary*, which implicitly means that people leave the stock (and the model focus) at the age of 90. This creates a failure, but it dramatically increases the correct behavior of the last stock. Therefore, the neglecting of very high-aged people is acceptable. The mathematical formulation is:

to 9000[skill] = ac6589[skill]/size6589
Unit: Person/Year [0,?,10]
Comment: aging from XX to XX

4.2.2.3 Births

Births are calculated from the total fertility rate of the age group ac1539. Only women of childbearing age can have children. The number of children that a woman can have during her life is expressed in the synthetic variable total fertility rate, and differs from country to country. Since the stock does not differentiate between sexes, the exogenous given female ratio is valid for the whole model. This constant can vary theoretically between 0 and 1. The total number of births per year is:

*births[skill] = ac1539[skill]/size1539 * female ratio * TFR*
Unit: Person/Year [0,?]
Comment: births per year

It is worth noting that the births and the first stock are distinguished in children born from the high-skilled and born from the low-skilled, or more accurately, in children born from the highly educated or the less educated. The stock ac0014 represents children from high-skilled and low-skilled parents.

It is also worth noting that, with regards to marriage status, this model does not consider who the father of the newborns is. It is only important to have at least one male in the population. This can be assumed, as long as a minimum of two persons is in the stock ac1539.

4.2.2.4 Deaths

People can die within any age cohort, but the probability of this occurrence differs. In general, the risk increases over time, and with increasing age.

Infant mortality is not specifically taken into account, but is accounted indirectly by including this mortality into the calculations of the first stock. For the stocks, the number of deaths per time period can be calculated with:

*death0014[skill] = fdr0014/size0014 * ac0014[skill]*
*death1539[skill] = fdr1539/size1539 * ac1539[skill]*
*death4064[skill] = fdr4064/size4064 * ac4064[skill]*
*death6589[skill] = fdr6589/size6589 * ac6589[skill]*
Unit: Person/Year [0,?]
Comment: dead persons in cohort 00 to 89

The total number of deaths depends on the amount of people per stock, and the fractional death rate (fdr). The fraction does not differ with the skills of the person in the stocks, but rather differs with the age. The rate is derived out of life tables.

The structure represents an *exponential decay*, and is similar to aging. In infinity, the stock would reach zero if inflows equal zero.

In the presented case, the total outflow of every stock is the outflow of aging to the next stock, as well as the outflow through deaths. In the case of the level variable ac0014[skill], it is:

total outflow ac0014[skill] = to1539[skill] + death0014[skill]
*= ac0014[skill]/size0014 + fdr0014/size0014 * ac0014[skill]*

In this situation, deaths continuously remove people from the age cohort (Sterman, 2004, p. 479). The average time per cohort is than less 1/cohort size as people also die. Another way to model the net outflows is if the maturing and the dying people add up exactly to first order formulation. Applied to the example of the age cohort ac0014[skill], it is:

total outflow ac0014[skill] = to1539[skill] + death0014[skill]
*= (1- fdr0014)/size0014 * ac0014[skill] + fdr0014/size0014 * ac0014[skill]*
*=1/size0014 * ac0014[skill]*

In this case, the first order exponential outflow is split into two flows and the fractional death rate is the "valve" to control the flows. This expression implies that the average time per cohort is constant. Often, this is used in models where people are not defined by age, but rather by categories. The last method is appropriate for populations with little change. The first presented alternative is better suited for increasing or shrinking cases, because of the distribution of the population in each cohort. In this case, it is more hyper-exponential than exponential (Sterman, 2004, p. 479).

4.2.2.5 Migration

Migration is very essential for the dynamics of the population. Over a specific period of time, every stock of the aging chain is increased or decreased by a certain exogenous amount of people. As this model demonstrates the problem of demographic change in industrialized countries, migration is mainly seen as immigration (inflow) to the stock. Each stock differentiates the migration with respect to their skills. The formulation is given with:

mig0014[skill] = CONSTANT
mig1539[skill] = CONSTANT
mig4064[skill] = CONSTANT
mig6589[skill] = CONSTANT)
Unit: Person/Year [0,?,10]
Comment: migration cohort from 0 to 89

The amount of migration is a politically set exogenous factor. The migration is therefore decoupled from the associated stock.

One must also consider that children do not usually migrate alone. Moreover, senior citizens rarely move permanently. For these two reasons, and to keep the model small, it is assumed that only childless, working people immigrate. The immigration to the stock ac0014[skill] and ac6589[skill] will be zero.

4.2.2.6 Total Population Sector

Figure 4.8 shows the population sector in greater detail. Auxiliary calculations are to be found in the annex of this work. People age from the left to the right of this Figure.

There is only one *reinforcing loop* in this sector; starting at the stock ac1539 and goes to births. Newborns age over 15 years in the stock ac0014 until they reach the childbearing age, which is the stock ac1539. Two *delays slow this acceleration* process. The first delay is the inflow in the stock ac0014 (births) and the second one is the inflow in the stock ac1539 (to work). One can infer that it takes time until a newborn girl can become a mother. These delays will significantly influence the behavior of the stock, as the risk of amplification may occur. A comparable

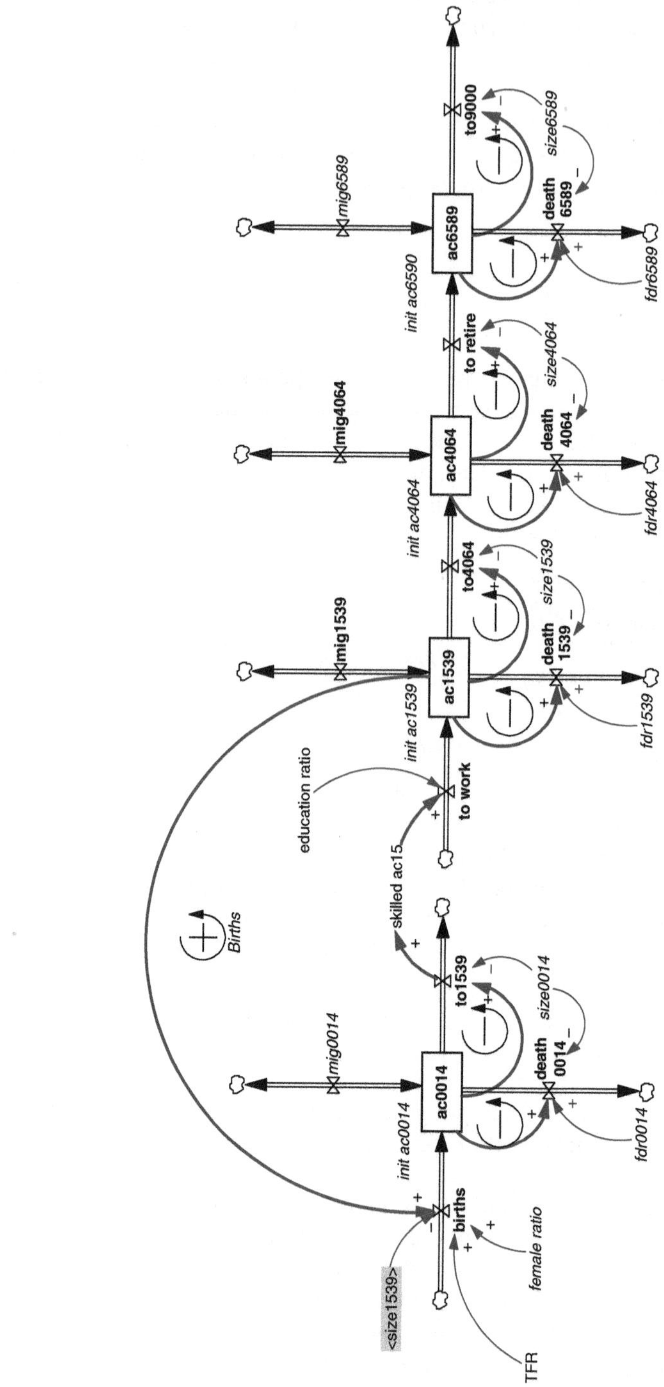

Fig. 4.8 Demographic growth model: population sector
Source: own figure

situation is found in supply-chain management. Forrester named this effect the "bullwhip effect" (Forrester, 1999, pp. 137–186; Sterman, 2004, pp. 684–694).

Several *balancing loops* are visible in this structure. Each stock consists of two balancing outflows. One is the loop that calculates the amount of people who died. The other one is the number of people who age in the next stock, or those at the right end of the aging chain who leave the system.

The aging structure is divided amongst stocks ac0014 and ac1539. As mentioned in the section about the aging process, this is necessary in order to provide high-skilled and low-skilled workers for the working life stocks, independent from their social origin. Only the constant "education ratio" splits the flow into the different subscripts.

4.2.3 Part "Research & Development"

This part of the model is totally consistent with the research and development sector in Jones' semi-endogenous growth model (see Sect. 3.4). To recapitulate, the following equation illustrates how the patent stock changes over time (see (3.106):

$$\dot{A} = \rho \cdot {L_A}^{\lambda} \cdot A^{\phi} \tag{4.3}$$

The corresponding equation in the model is:

*delta A = rho * ((Lh/unit Person) ^ lambda) * ((A/unit Patent) ^ (phi))*
Unit: Patent/Year [0,?]
Comment: change in R&D sector

If one removes the parameters for unit consistency, one can see the equivalent structure. The patent or R&D stock is then:

A = INTEG(delta A, init A)
Unit: Patent [0,?]
Comment: current stock of patents

The amount of labor (Lh) doing research in the R&D sector comes from the interface to the population sector, and is the sum of all workers of the high-skilled sector, or

Lh = ac1539[high] + ac4064[high]
Unit: Person [0,?]
Comment: total number of high skilled workers

The input of human capital is connected to the person itself. If this person leaves the system, then the knowledge is lost as well. However, the output of the R&D sector is accumulative (Rürup, 2000, p. 97).

This sector is the smallest, but is nevertheless a very important sector, as it reflects the endogenous growth of technology. Figure 4.9 shows the structure in detail.

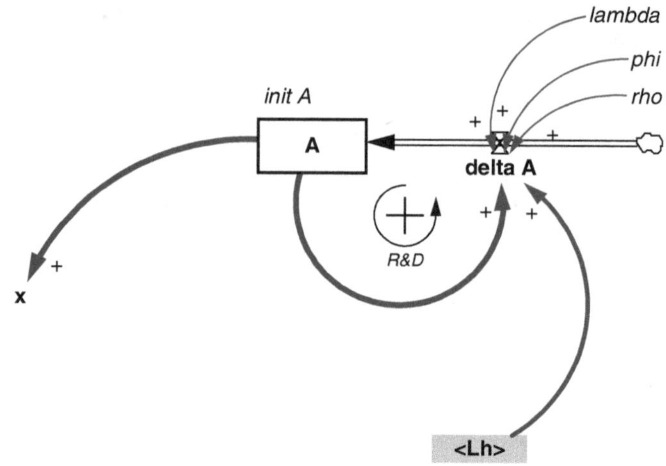

Fig. 4.9 Demographic growth model: R&D sector
Source: own figure

The standard exponential growth structure with the reinforcing loop, "R&D", is evident. An increase of any constant will increase the growth rate of the loop. The high-skilled labor (Lh) connects the population sector with the R&D sector, whereas the patent stock (A) goes into the intermediate goods sector (x), which will be explained in the next section.

4.2.4 Part "Growth"

This part of the model is based mainly on the Jones-model, but with important augmentations. The next section outlines this part step-by-step. As a starting point, Fig. 4.10 presents this sector in general.

In general, all subscripted variables in the model figures are round shaped for better distinction to normal auxiliaries.

4.2.4.1 Intermediate Goods and Final Goods Sector

Beginning with the *intermediate goods sector* already known from Sect. 3.4.2.1, one writes:

*x = (K/unit Euro) ^ (alpha) * (A/unit Patent) ^ (1 - alpha) * unit Euro per Year*
Unit: Euro/Year [0,?]
Comment: Intermediate goods sector

Canceling out the dummy variables for unit consistency, one observes that the intermediate goods sector follows a Cobb-Douglas production function. The connection to the R&D sector comes with the patent stock A.

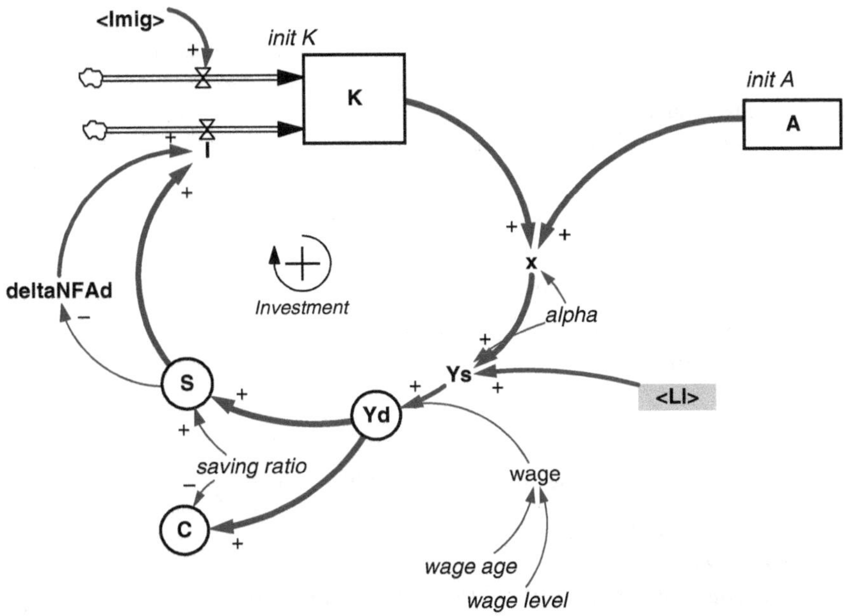

Fig. 4.10 Demographic growth model: growth sector
Source: own figure

The *final goods sector* uses the produced intermediate products, and creates final goods for consumption, with the help of labor. One writes for the supply of the production:

*Ys = (x) * ((Ll/unit Person) ^ (1 - alpha))*
Unit: Euro/Year [0,?]
Comment: production (supply final goods sector)

The variable Ll stands for the sum of low-skilled workers coming from the population sector with:

Ll = ac1539[low] + ac4064[low]
Unit: Person [0,?]
Comment: total number of low skilled workers

One observes that the units from the capital stock, labor stock, and the patent stocks are independent from time, whereas the production Y^s and the produced intermediate goods x are auxiliaries which depend on time with the unit Euro/Year.

4.2.4.2 Demand for Goods

The demand for goods equals the production in the Jones-model, but is not explicitly shown in that model. The demographic growth model takes this concept of supply equals demand, but with a major augmentation. With the detailed description of the population stock, the model can *distinguish different income and age groups*. The personal income distribution is not based on households, but rather on individuals.

The production is distributed to the income by the 4 × 2 matrix (wage), with respect to age and skill:

*Yd[age,skill] = wage[age,skill] * Ys*
Unit: Euro/Year [0,?]
Comment: income (demand final goods sector)

The wage-matrix normalizes different income levels. Two exogenous constants formulate this matrix:

wage age[age] = CONSTANT
Unit: Dmnl [0,?]
Comment: wage age distribution for all cohorts

wage level = CONSTANT
Unit: Dmnl [1,2,0.1]
Comment: wage level of high skilled worker to low skilled worker

Whereas the wage age yields the distribution over the age cohorts, the wage level provides the factor that high-skilled workers earn, compared to low-skilled workers. The dimensionless standardized wage is thus derived with:

*wage[age0014,high] = (wage level/(1 + wage level)) * (wage age[age0014]/ SUM (wage age[age!]))*
*wage[age1539,high] = (wage level/(1 + wage level)) * (wage age[age1539]/ SUM (wage age[age!]))*
*wage[age4064,high] = (wage level/(1 + wage level)) * (wage age[age4064]/ SUM (wage age[age!]))*
*wage[age6589,high] = (wage level/(1 + wage level)) * (wage age[age6589]/ SUM (wage age[age!]))*
*wage[age0014,low] = (1/(1 + wage level)) * (wage age[age0014]/SUM (wage age [age!]))*
*wage[age1539,low] = (1/(1 + wage level)) * (wage age[age1539]/SUM (wage age [age!]))*
*wage[age4064,low] = (1/(1 + wage level)) * (wage age[age4064]//SUM (wage age [age!]))*
*wage[age6589,low] = (1/(1 + wage level)) * (wage age[age6589]/SUM (wage age [age!]))*
Unit: Dmnl [0,2,0.1]
Comment: low skilled wage always 100%, high skilled wage in % of low skilled wage, wage age distribution as external provided

The summarized result for Y^d is therefore:

$$\text{Yd[age, skill]} = \begin{pmatrix} Yd[age0014, high] & Yd[age0014, low] \\ Yd[age1539, high] & Yd[age1539, low] \\ Yd[age4064, high] & Yd[age4064, low] \\ Yd[age6589, high] & Yd[age6589, low] \end{pmatrix}$$

4.2.4.3 Saving and Consumption

The subdivided income, Y^d, from the previous section enables the saving and consumption variables to be itemized as well. This enables the calculation and simulation of the *individual consumption* and the *individual saving* for a median people of each age cohort with respect to their skills.

The saving ratio splits the income into consumption and savings. In the model, the saving ratio is a 4×2 matrix, with individual saving rates between 0 and 1. One thus writes:

$$\text{saving ratio[age, skill]} = \begin{pmatrix} s.ratio[age0014, high] & s.ratio[age0014, low] \\ s.ratio[age1539, high] & s.ratio[age1539, low] \\ s.ratio[age4064, high] & s.ratio[age4064, low] \\ s.ratio[age6589, high] & s.ratio[age6589, low] \end{pmatrix}$$

With this matrix, one introduces the *lifecycle hypothesis of consumption* into a growth model, by giving different saving ratios with respect to age. The individual ratios are provided externally.

The according saving is:

*S[age,skill] = saving ratio[age,skill] * Yd[age,skill]*
Unit: Euro/Year [0,?]
Comment: saved income

The consumption is than given with:

*C[age,skill] = (1 - saving ratio[age,skill]) * Yd[age,skill]*
Unit: Euro/Year [0,?]
Comment: current consumption

The consumption connects the growth model part with the utility model part, and is explained later. The next section closes the growth loop.

4.2.4.4 Investment and Capital Stock

From the circular flow of income and the national account system, one can assert that for a closed economy:

$$S = I \tag{4.4}$$

For an open economy, this formula changes to (Cezanne, 2005, p. 241)

$$S = I + \Delta NFA \tag{4.5}$$

The *change in net foreign assets (NFA)* equals the current account. The idea of capital transfer from foreign countries is adopted in this model, but only to some extent. The model opens partly, first by allowing migration, and second by allowing capital inflow. However, the capital inflow is not fully utilized, because it only allows capital that is necessary to even out negative savings because of the demographic changes. One can thus imagine the case where the total savings of the economy become negative. In this case, the investment is negative as well, if the economy is closed. A partial openness for capital imports can withhold negative investments.

deltaNFAd = IF (SUM (S[age!,skill!]) < 0, - SUM (S[age!,skill!]), 0)
Unit: Euro/Year [0,?]
Comment: amount of change in net foreign assets due to demographic change to set investments to zero.

The investments are usually positive and equal the sum of all individual savings. In the worst case, the savings and the net change in foreign investments adds to zero.

I = SUM (S[age!,skill!]) + deltaNFAd
Unit: Euro/Year [0,?]
Comment: investments equal spending and change in net foreign assets

Based on the population sector one knows that migration is possible. Every immigrant might move to the domestic country and bring additional capital. This idea follows the Barros–Sala-i-Martins-model from Chap. 3 (see Sect. 3.2.5.2). The amount per migrant is exogenous, so that:

*Imig skill[skill] = (mig0014[skill] + mig1539[skill] + mig4064[skill] + mig6589[skill]) * mig capital[skill]*
Unit: Euro/Year [0,?]
Comment: capital that brought by immigrants with respect to skills

With the two investment inflows, the growth loop is closed. The whole loop follows the exponential growth pattern. It is the *major causal loop of the model,* and the core of every neoclassical growth model since Solow. With the decisive augmentation explained thusly, this standard pattern will reveal more insight than the standard and well know variations.

4.2.5 Part "Utility"

Although consumption, consumption per capita, or consumption per effective capita are good indicators to value the social welfare of an economic system, one might also think of *utility as an appropriate measurement*. The maximization of households' utility function is found in growth models with endogenous saving rates that are based on their utility standard. The idea of *inter-temporal maximization* goes back to a brilliant paper by Frank Ramsey (Ramsey, 1928). Specifications were done by David Cass (Cass, 1966) and Tjalling Koopman (Koopmans, 1963). Today, this model approach is called Rasmey–Cass–Koopman model. Before outlining the utility sector of the demographic growth model, the basic idea of utility functions is introduced.

There is a large number of households (H). Each member of the household consumes C(t) at time t. N(t) names the total population. Each household has to save or consume the earned income at each point in time and seek to maximize its lifetime utility (Romer, 2006, p. 49). The utility function of the household then takes the form:

$$U = \int_{t=0}^{\infty} e^{-\sigma \cdot t} u(C(t)) \cdot \frac{N(t)}{H} \cdot dt \tag{4.6}$$

The *instantaneous utility function* u(C(t)) projects the personal utility of each member. Sigma is the discount rate for future utility, and an indicator for the time preference (Arnold, 1997, p. 56). An increased sigma leads to a decreased value of future consumption to the current state (Romer, 2006, p. 49).

The instantaneous utility function u(C(t)) is usually presented as (Barro & Sala-i-Martin, 2004, p. 91)

$$u(C(t)) = \frac{C(t)^{1-\theta}}{1-\theta} \text{ with } 0 < \theta \text{ and } \theta <> 1 \tag{4.7}$$

This function is known as the *constant-relative-risk-aversion utility* (CRRA utility). The coefficient of relative risk aversion is theta, and therefore independent from the consumption. The coefficient determines the inverse of the inter-temporal elasticity of substitution (Aghion, Howitt, & García-Peúnalosa, 1999, p. 22). Theta also determines the willingness to shift the consumption between two periods (Romer, 2006, pp. 49–50). An increasing theta leads to a declining marginal utility of consumption. Hence, consumers will be less willing to shift today's consumption into the future (Arnold, 1997, p. 56). A theta value close to zero would lead to an almost linear correlation between consumption and utility. The household is then willing to allow large swings of the consumption, and takes advantage of small differences between discount rate sigma and the rate of return on saving (Romer, 2006, pp. 49–50).

Three additionally remarks on the utility function (Romer, 2006, p. 50):

1. The exponent 1-θ leads to increasing consumption if $\theta < 1$ but to a decreasing if $\theta > 1$. Dividing the consumption through $1 - \theta$ ensures that the whole term is positive regardless θ.
2. In the special case $\theta = 1$, the utility function simplifies to ln C (this is a special case and results of L'Hopitals rule Arnold, 1997, p. 56).

3. The time preference theta must be always greater than sigma. Otherwise, the household could maximize their utility by postponing its consumption till infinity.

The concept of an inter-temporal utility function is adopted in the demographic growth model. As no household structure is considered in the model, the utility function is changed into two different dimensions: first, as consumption per capita, and second, as consumption per effective capita. These types are deduced from the 4 × 2-matrix of the consumption variable with:

C per capita[age0014,skill] = C[age0014,skill]/ac0014[skill]
C per capita[age1539,skill] = C[age1539,skill]/ac1539[skill]
C per capita[age4064,skill] = C[age4064,skill]/ac4064[skill]
C per capita[age6589,skill] = C[age6589,skill]/ac6589[skill]
*Unit: Euro/(Person*Year) [0,?]*
Comment: consumption per capita with respect to age and skills

C per eff capita[age0014,skill] = C per capita[age0014,skill]/A0014[skill]
C per eff capita[age1539,skill] = C per capita[age1539,skill]/A1539[skill]
C per eff capita[age4064,skill] = C per capita[age4064,skill]/A4064[skill]
C per eff capita[age6589,skill] = C per capita[age6589,skill]/A6589[skill]
*Unit: Euro/(Person*Year*Patent) [0,?]*
Comment: consumption per effective capita with respect to age and skills

The model overview in Fig. 4.11 illustrates how the consumption leads to the different utility stocks.

Based on the exogenous constant, the utility and the marginal utility are calculated:

*U[age,skill] = IF (theta <> 1, ((C per capita[age,skill] * (unit Time * unit Person/unit Euro)) ^ (1 - theta))/(1 - theta), LN (C per capita[age,skill] * (unit Person * unit Time/unit Euro))) * (unit Utility/(unit Person * unit Time))*
*Unit: Utility/(Person*Year) [0,?]*
Comment: utility at current time

*effU[age,skill] = IF (theta <> 1, ((C per eff capita[age,skill] * (unit Time * unit Person * unit Patent/unit Euro)) ^ (1 - theta))//(1 - theta), LN (C per eff capita [age,skill] * unit Time * unit Person * unit Patent/unit Euro)) * (unit Utility/ (unit Time * unit Person * unit Patent))*
*Unit: Utility/(Person*Year*Patent) [0,?]*
Comment: utility per effective capita

Initially, the long formulation is based directly on (4.6). Again, the dummy variables are needed to handle the uneven exponents of the functions. Also, both formulas consists of an if-condition to compute the utility correctly for the case of $\theta <> 1$ and $\theta = 1$.

The next step discounts the future values of both the utility and the effective utility at a *reference point in time*. The reference point enables the model to discount the utility to special events during the simulation.

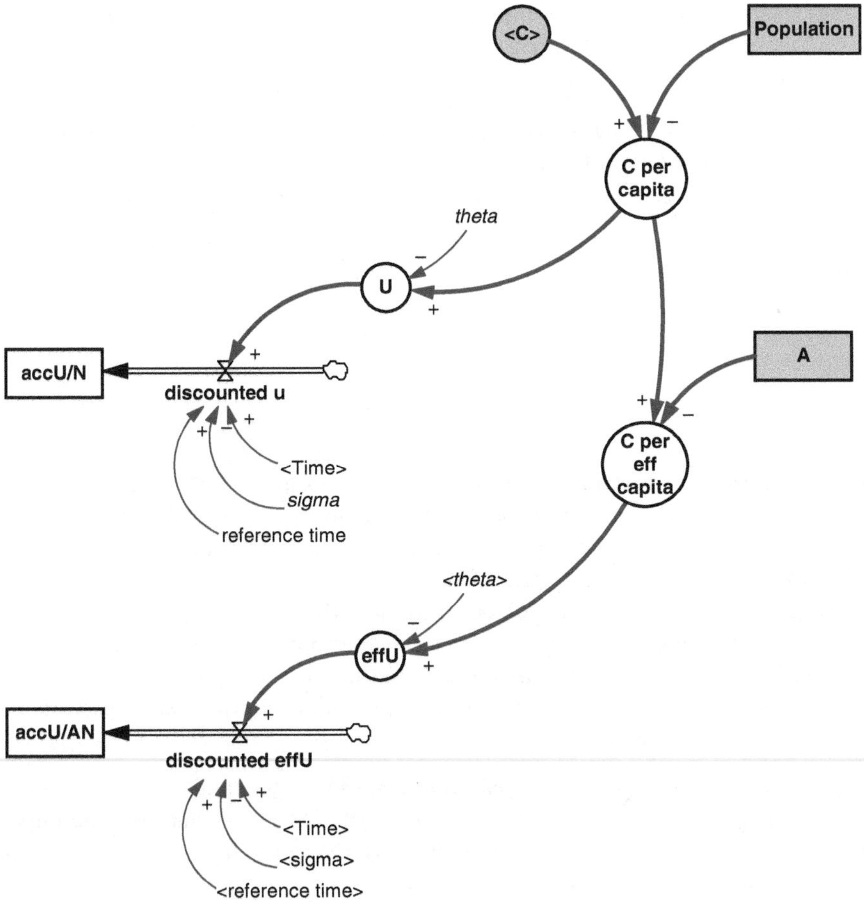

Fig. 4.11 Demographic growth model: utility sector
Source: own figure

*discounted u[age,skill] = IF (Time < reference time, 0, U[age,skill] * EXP (- sigma * (Time - reference time)/ unit Time))*
*Unit: Utility/(Person*Year) [0,?]*
Comment: discounted utility at point t in time

*discounted eff u[age,skill] = IF (Time < reference time, 0, effU[age,skill] * EXP (- sigma * (Time - reference time)/unit Time))*
*Unit: Utility/(Person*Patent*Year) [0,?]*
Comment: discounted effectice utility

One can see that the discounted values cumulate both the stock of the accumulated utility per capita and the stock of the accumulated utility per effective capita over time.

accU/AN[age,skill] = INTEG(discounted effU[age,skill], init U/AN[age,skill])
*Unit: Utility/(Person*Patent) [0,?]*
Comment: accumulated discounted utiltiy per effective capita

accU/N[age,skill] = INTEG(discounted u[age,skill], init U/N[age,skill])
Unit: Utility/Person [0,?]
Comment: accumulated discounted utility per capita

Later, these two indicators show directly what effect different policies will have on the welfare of the economy.

4.2.6 Initialization

The model should *start in equilibrium*. This eases the later evaluation of the simulation results, because the behavior must arise from the model structure, and not from any exogenous influence. Also, the effects of the changes in parameter values for policy testing can explicitly analyzed.

The equilibrium of the model depends directly on the initial values of all feedback stocks and the exogenous variables. From the model overview, and from the Jones-model, one surmises that everything is based on population sector. The R&D sector and the growth sector are sequentially initialized. Therefore, the following order must comply:

1. *Initialization of model part "Population"*: Basing on the total population (N) the initial in- and outflows (delta N) are calculated. With these numbers the important growth rate of the population stock (gN), the initial labor force (init L) and initial labor force ratio (sR) is derived.
2. *Initialization of model part "R&D Sector"*: The patent stock initializes with the variable init A. This adds up on important key variables from the population stock and the initial growth rate of the patent stock (gA).
3. *Initialization of model part "Growth"*: By using the initial wage distribution (wage) and the initial saving ratio, the steady state capital intensity per effective capita is calculated. Because in the steady state the capital intensity does not change, one can derive the value of the initial capital stock (init K), with the help of the initial patent stock (init A) and the initial total population (init N).

The utility sector is not initialized, as there is no endogenous structure with feedback loops. Every variable depends on the other three sectors. The process of initialization is explained in detail in the annex, with individual tables for each run.

All formulas are based on the growth chapter (see Chap. 3), where there are outlined theoretically. The *total number of people* is 1,000 in all cases. Different total fertility rates will lead to different growth rates of the population. Because of the specific death rates of the age cohorts, every growth rate of a population mirrors in a *specific population structure*. The age pyramid of a constant growing population is different to a constant population. Therefore, the initial values for the age cohort may differ between simulation runs.

4.2.7 Summary and Conclusion

This subchapter presented the author's own, extended model. The demographic growth model is founded on one of the latest branches of the endogenous growth theory. Jones' semi-endogenous model was adopted and decisively augmented. The total new population sector was outlined. By splitting the population stock in different age groups, and also differentiating in high-skilled and low-skilled labor, one can simulate demographic behavior.

The adopted and modified utility function will give more specific simulation results. Policy-makers can then figure out whether a policy will have a present effect or not.

With the initialization, the model is suitable for testing and evaluation in the next subchapter. To sum up, Fig. 4.12 presents the model in almost full description. Supplementary calculations and dummy variables are hidden for the sake of clarity.

4.3 Model Testing and Evaluation

This section evaluates the previous build model by taking tests. Eminently the model behavior test for a growing and stable population is important. Not all tests results in printable outcomes. Some tests are simply a part of the model process and are only explained, not sketched.

4.3.1 Model Validation Tests

A good model delivers results a policy-maker can trust. Following the *concept of critical rationalism* for a non-empirical problem, one has to execute rigorous model testing before trusting the results. Figure 4.13 presents the standard scheme for an empirical and non-empirical scientific approach.

This work aims to present new insights for demographic change in growth models. Therefore, the left causal-loop-diagram in the Fig. 4.13 is applied in this work. Further research of the model could and should be empirically tested with statistical data from various industrialized countries.

The different tests and their general explanation for the following paragraphs were taken out of Sterman (2004, pp. 858–889), Forrester and Senge (1980, pp. 209–228) and Forrester (1999, pp. 115–136).

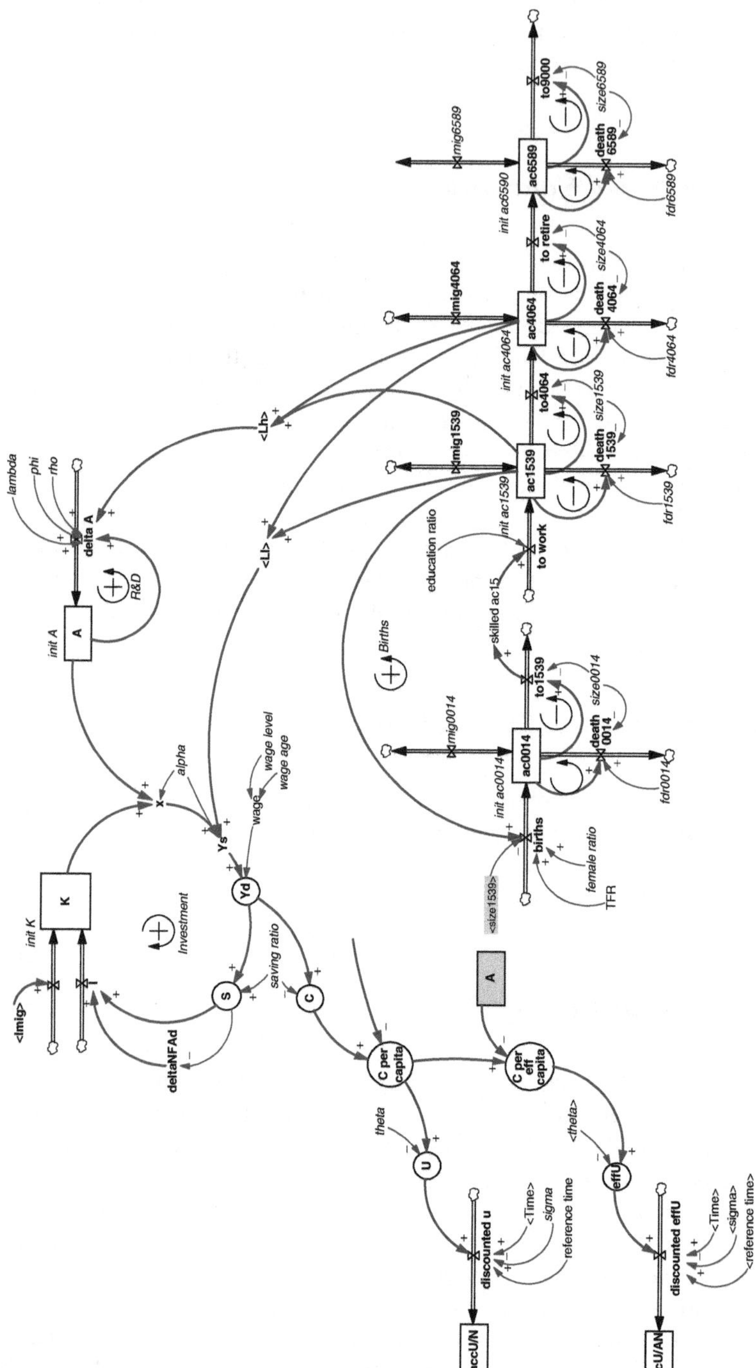

Fig. 4.12 Demographic growth model
Source: own figure

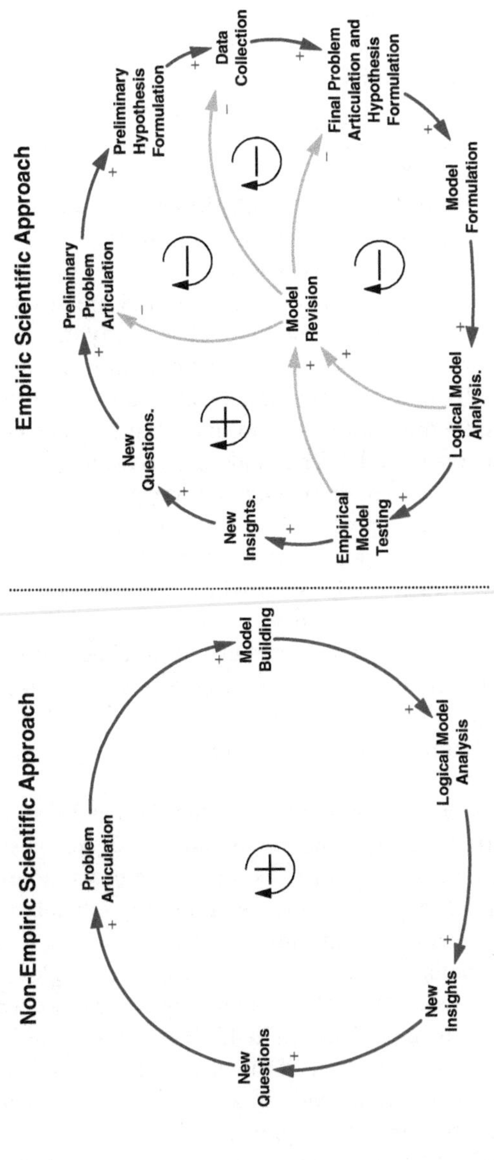

Fig. 4.13 Concept of critical rationalism
Source: own figure according to Kleinewefers & Jans, 1983, p. 16

Structure assessment, for example, looks for an appropriate level of aggregation; whether the model is constrained by underlying laws or not. This structural assessment is already completed, since the model adapts to the accepted model from Jones, and was only extended by explicitly formulating the population sector.

This model connects mathematical equations to real world variables. All terms in equation must be measured by dimensions (Forrester, 1968, pp. 6–1). In addition, social and economical variables also express dimensions. In mathematical software solutions, it is fairly typical, to neglect the *dimensional consistency*. For statistical software this might be appropriate since regressions only imitate system behaviors, however for systems modeling, a focus on dimensional consistency is very important (Imboden & Koch, 2005, pp. 20–22). To avoid mistakes, the modeler should check the units. Terms with different units within an equation will indicate inaccurate equation formulation (Forrester, 1968, pp. 6–2). The demographic growth model shows consistent units.

The *parameter assessment* and their value consistency are of interest for parameter sensitivity. The problem occurs at the limes. The utility function, for example, has a threshold value for $\theta = 1$. In this case the function is simplified. A reliable model may adopt this. All other variables are considered to be consistent with their real world counterparts. Saving ratios may normally have values between 0 and 1, but can be negative in an open model. The modeling software allows for these cases to input variable boundaries. These boundaries are part of the model and are presented in the annex or subchapter where the variables are explained. During simulation runs the software produces warnings if the boundaries do not hold. The presented demographic growth model runs without boundary warnings and produces also reliable values for critical inputs.

Another test is the *integration error test.* One has to choose the time step dt for the simulation carefully. Smaller time steps should not result in different model behavior. By using Runge-Kutta as integration method this risk declines dramatically. Additionally, smaller time steps were investigated, but the model time step of $dt = 1$ could be confirmed.

Sensitivity analysis is part of the model development and testing process. The focus is on the sensitivity of the model to numerical changes of exogenous constants. In Chap. 3 the sensitivity analysis for the major variables of the models from Solow, Romer and Jones was made. Nothing unpredictable was observed. Insofar, no additionally sensitivity runs are necessary.

Stepwise modeling is not a real test and therefore is often neglected. However, it is an important strategy, especially for large models because it prevents the modeler from structural mistakes. The model shown in this work was created by the stepwise technique, in that every new added part of the model was immediately tested after its introduction. Unknown behavior can so be revealed in the very early model stages and thereby eases the verification process.

All in all, the in the scientific literature recommended model tests were executed. The results show the expected behavior. In the next subchapters the single model sectors will be analyzed under certain conditions with a view to the plausibility of their behavior.

4.3.2 *Test Run 1 "Stable Population"*

4.3.2.1 Description

The first test run analyzes how the model behaves if the population is in a steady state. This means that for every period of time, the number of births is equal to the number of deaths. However, the total demographic growth model should not be in equilibrium, as one knows from Jones' model, this can only happen if the population grows. The hypothesis for this model behavior is therefore a growing stock of capital. The simulation runs for 100 time periods and the time step is dt = 1.

4.3.2.2 Initialization

The simulation values are defined in that way that the behavior of all model subscripts can be analyzed. This means that the variables do not intent to be extremely realistic.

The *population sector* consists of a total population of 1,000 people. Every population growth rate has a specific shape to the population structure. This and the following explanation are shown in Fig. 4.14. The initial values of the different stocks are calculated by simulations. The population is stable and does not change over time. The people per cohort are equal in both subscripts (high- and low-skilled) due to the education ratio at 0.5. The model is closed, therefore migration does not occur. The fractional death rates are derived from various life tables from European countries and are assumed to be an average for different industrialized countries. Like reality, they have the same structure from young to old age cohorts. The cohort size is fixed for all runs. It is important to note that the total fertility rate (TFR) is 2.08. Based on the life tables the sex ratio of the population at this TFR is stable.

The *growth sector* consists of the patent and capital stock. Both values are calculated based on the initialization process (see Fig. 4.15). The partial production elasticity of capital is set to 0.5 and no depreciation occurs. The constants for the patent stock are taken from Jones' suggestion. In order to avoid simplistic behavior, the wage distribution, the wage level and the saving ratios, do not equal zero.

Figure 4.16 presents the initial values for the *utility sector*. All accumulated utility stocks are set to one. The reference point for the accumulated utilities is t = 0. The elasticity of marginal utility and the time preference are very low and have an almost linear interdependence between consumption and utility.

4.3.2.3 Results

Beginning with the population sector one can see in the upper left graph of Fig. 4.17 that the *population does not change over time*. The in- and outflows of the

ModelPart "Population"				
Description	**Variable**	**Unit**	**high**	**low**
initial value 0 to14	init ac 0014	Person	102.30	102.30
initial value 15 to 39	init ac 1539	Person	164.74	164.74
initial value 40 to 64	init ac 4064	Person	149.77	149.77
initial value 65 to 89	init ac 6589	Person	83.19	83.19
migration 0 to 14	mig 0014	Person/Year	0	0
migration 15 to 39	mig 1539	Person/Year	0	0
migration 40 to 64	mig 4064	Person/Year	0	0
migration 65 to 89	mig 6589	Person/Year	0	0
capital per immigrant	mig capital	Euro/Person	0	0
Description	**Variable**	**Unit**	**Value**	
fractional death rate 0 to 14	fdr0014	Dmnl/Year	0.0050	
fractional death rate15 to 39	fdr1539	Dmnl/Year	0.0348	
fractional death rate 40 to 64	fdr4064	Dmnl/Year	0.1000	
fractional death rate 65 to 89	fdr6589	Dmnl/Year	0.8000	
cohort size 0 to 14	size0014	Year	15	
cohort size 15 to 39	size1539	Year	25	
cohort size 40 to 64	size4064	Year	25	
cohort size 65 to 89	size6589	Year	25	
total fertility rate	*TFR*	*Person/Person*	*2.08*	
sex ratio female	female ratio	Dmnl	0.5	
education ratio	education ratio	Dmnl	0.5	

Fig. 4.14 Test run 1: exogenous variables for the population sector
Source: own data

Model Part "Growth"				
Description	**Variable**	**Unit**	**Value**	
initial patent stock	*init A*	*Patent*	*9.682*	*calculated*
initial capital stock	*init K*	*Euro*	*92.934.205*	*calculated*
partial production elasticity of capital	alpha	Dmnl	0.5	
depletion rate	delta	Dmnl/Year	0	
degree of congestion	lambda	Dmnl	1	
return on stocks of ideas	phi	Dmnl	0	
accelerator	rho	Dmnl	1	
Description	**Variable**	**Unit**	**Value**	
wage age distribution	wage age [age0014]	Dmnl	0.75	
	wage age [age1539]	Dmnl	1.00	
	wage age [age4064]	Dmnl	1.50	
	wage age [age6589]	Dmnl	0.50	
Description	**Variable**	**Unit**	**high**	
wage level of high skilled worker	wage level	Dmnl	1.25	
Description	**Variable**	**Unit**	**high**	**low**
saving ratio	saving ratio [age0014]	Dmnl	0.10	0.15
	saving ratio [age1539]	Dmnl	0.20	0.25
	saving ratio [age4064]	Dmnl	0.30	0.35
	saving ratio [age6589]	Dmnl	0.40	0.45

Fig. 4.15 Test run 1: exogenous variables for the growth sector
Source: own data

Model Part "Utility"				
Description	**Variable**	**Unit**	**high**	**low**
initial accumulated utility stock	init U/N [age0014]	Utility/Person	1	1
per capita	init U/N [age1539]	Utility/Person	1	1
	init U/N [age4064]	Utility/Person	1	1
	init U/N [age6589]	Utility/Person	1	1
initial accumulated utility stock	init U/AN [age0014]	Utility/(Person*Patent)	1	1
per effective capita	init U/AN [age1539]	Utility/(Person*Patent)	1	1
	init U/AN [age4064]	Utility/(Person*Patent)	1	1
	init U/AN [age6589]	Utility/(Person*Patent)	1	1
Description	**Variable**	**Unit**	**Value**	
elasticity of marginal utility	theta	Dmnl	0.05	
time preference	sigma	Dmnl	0.05	
reference time	reference time	Year	0	

Fig. 4.16 Test run 1: exogenous variables for the utility sector
Source: own data

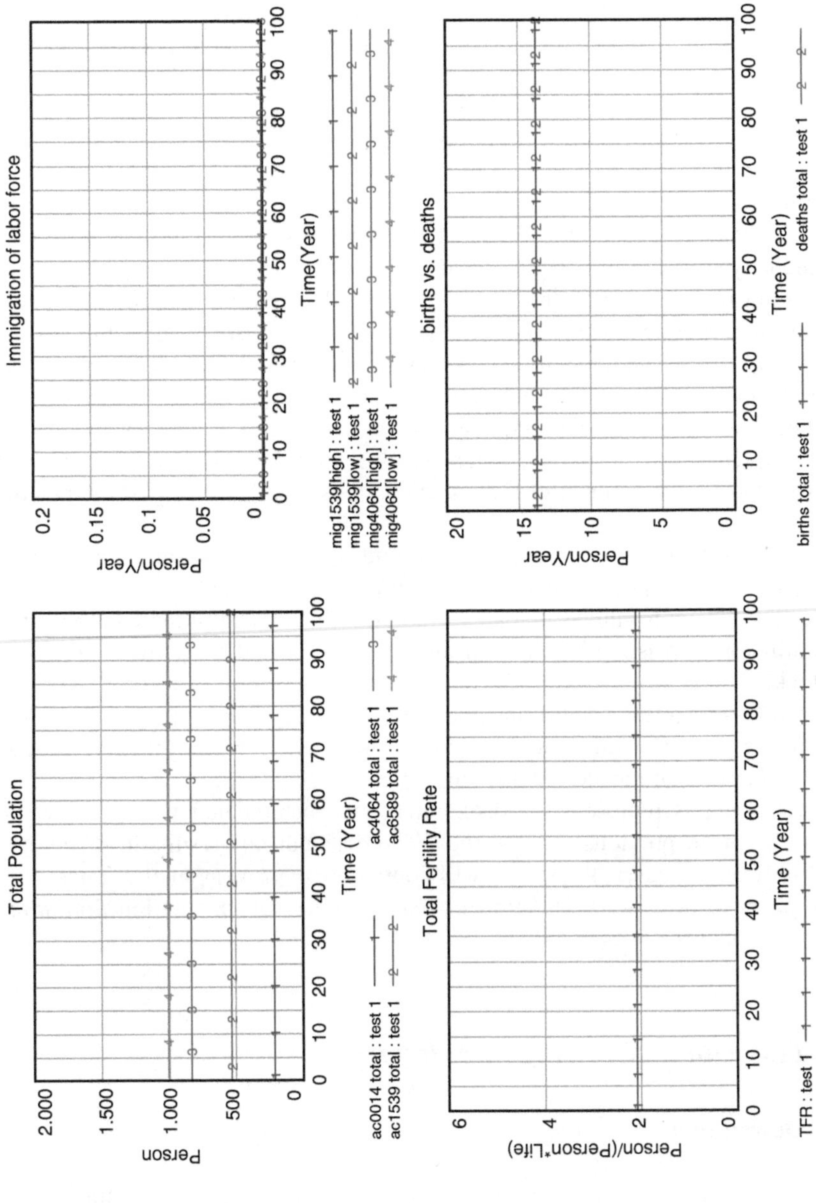

Fig. 4.17 Test run 1: results population sector
Source: own figure

population stocks are constant as births equal deaths and migration equals zero. The *TFR stays constant at 2.08* throughout the entire simulation. One can also show that the disaggregated age cohorts and their aging are constants.

In Fig. 4.18 one can see two important *demographic indicators*.

First, the dependency ratio provides the relationship between working and non-working population and is about 0.60 all time. This means more people working and fewer are either retired or in school. Second, the Billeter J indicates that more young people than old people exist, because the value is positive. Also, the working population can sustain the non-working population, which one can see on the close to zero value.

In the next section one can see the growth sector as a whole. First, one should evaluate the standard phase plot. Figure 4.19 represents the income per effective capital intensity as well as the required and the real investments. All variables grow with declining rates; however, the real investments exceed the required ones. No equilibrium will ever be reached. To the right, one can compare the growth rates of the important stocks. The population stays constant over time, therefore gN equals zero. The patent stock shows a continuing decline in its growth rate because the high-skilled workers are constant and, thus, the variable delta A does not change as well. The capital stock follows the patent stock with a delay because the growth loop gains power from two sources: the capital stock and the easing of the patent stock.

The next group of graphs in Fig. 4.20 provides an overview for per *effective capita variables*. Capital, income and consumption, as well as, savings all grow over time. The reason for this is that all variables in the numerator increase beyond the denominator, consisting of the constant population and the slower growing patent stock.

The last figure gives a short insight into the *utility sector* (Fig. 4.21). As consumption grows, the utility increases over time. The utility per effective capita slows down because of the slower growing patent stock.

The lower graphs represent the discounted and accumulated values at every point in time for all previous time periods. The discount rate results in shrinking marginal utilities, however, the stocks will continuously grow at smaller rates.

Every sector behaves well. The model behaves for a stable population similar to the ancestor model from Jones.

4.3.3 *Test Run 2 "Growing Population"*

4.3.3.1 Description

The second test aims to prove how the model behaves with a growing population. This is the one to one application of the core idea from Jones semi-endogenous growth model. The demographic model should deliver similar results. Although the population sector is growing the whole model will be n steady state for all important

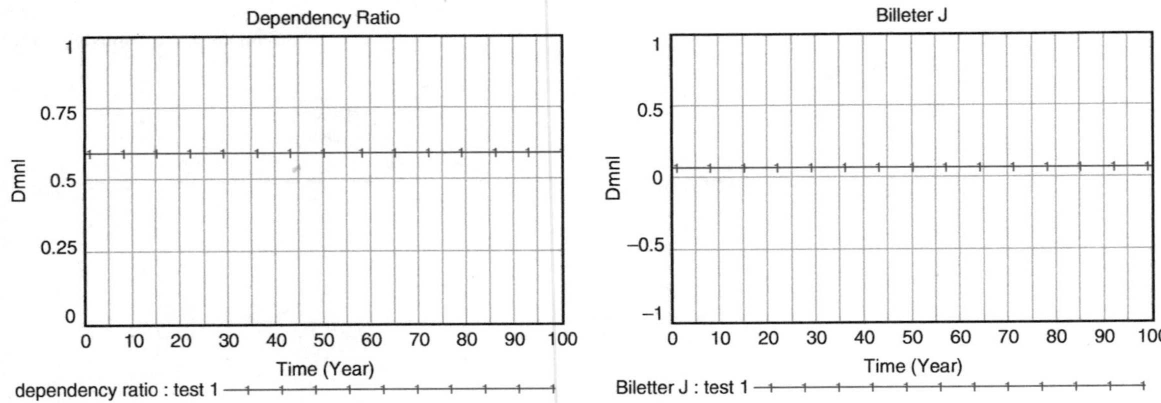

Fig. 4.18 Test run 1: results population indicators
Source: own figure

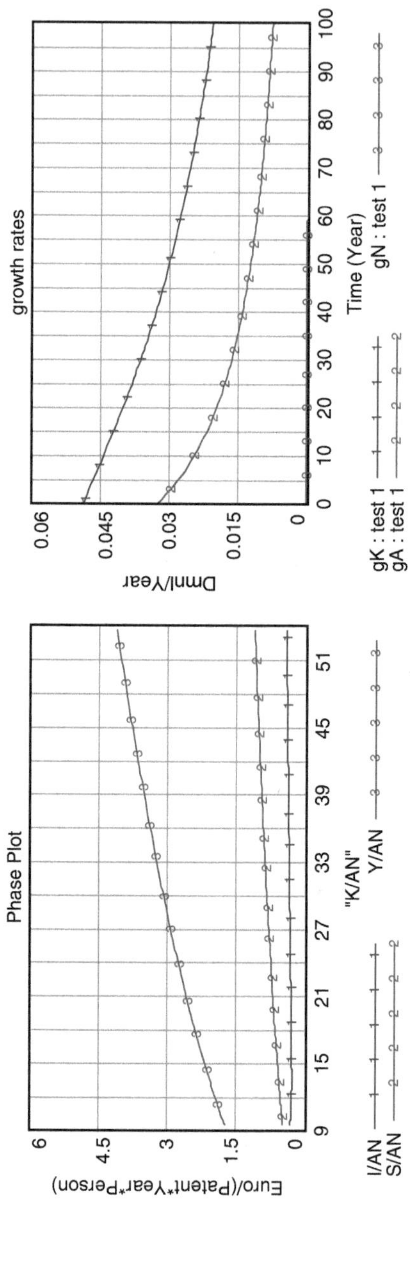

Fig. 4.19 Test run 1: results growth sector
Source: own figure

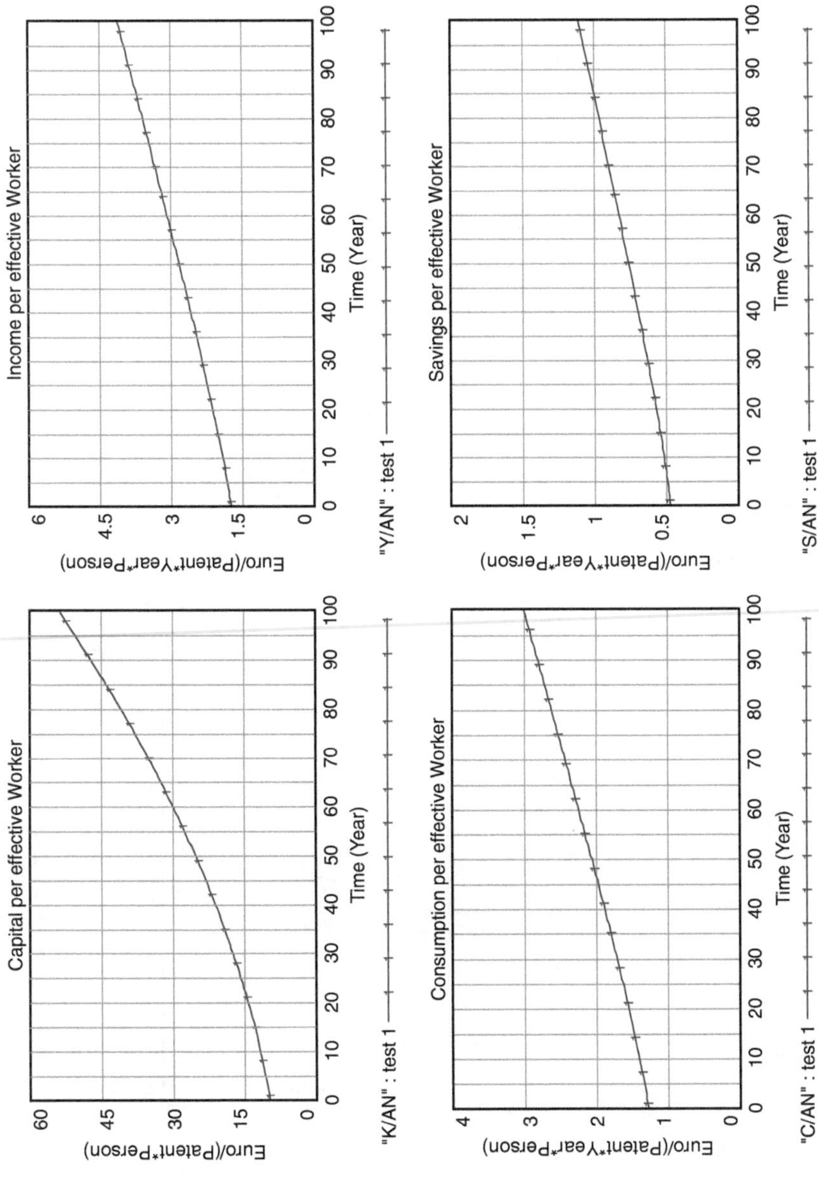

Fig. 4.20 Test run 1: results per effective capita variables
Source: own figure

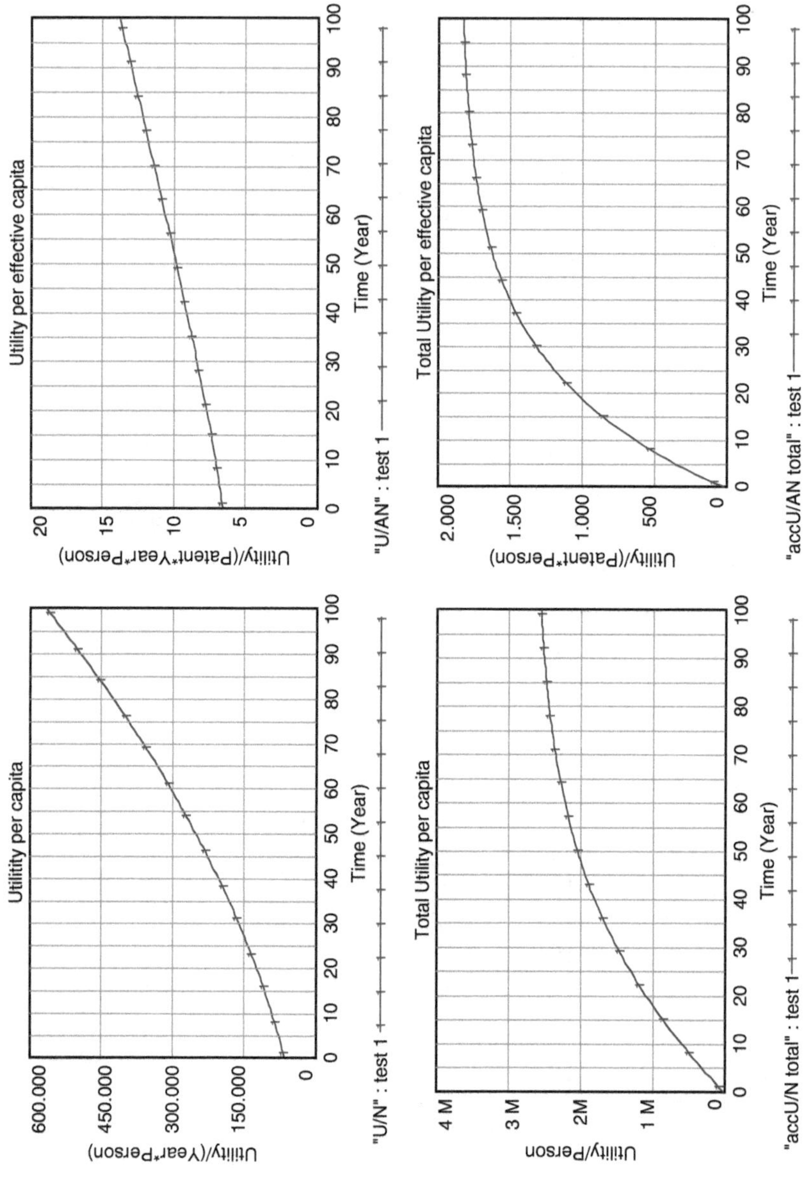

Fig. 4.21 Test run 1: results utility sector. Source: own figure

variables based on the per effective capita basis. Again, the simulation runs for 100 periods with a time step of dt = 1.

4.3.3.2 Initialization

The model initializes with almost the same exogenous data as test run 1, with two major differences.

First, the *structure of the population differs* although the number of total population is again 1,000 people. And second, the *increased total fertility rate* is five children per women per life. The growing population with a fixed growth rate indicates exponential growth and therefore the number of young people will exceed the older ones. The structure for the population is numerically estimated to provide, as in the first test run, a stable growth rate and a fixed age distribution. Figure 4.22 shows the exogenous variables of the population sector. The changed data are marked in italics.

4.3.3.3 Results

Starting this time with the population sector, one finds the results in Fig. 4.23.

The total population is increasing and grows exponentially. Because the total fertility is above the replacement level (5.0–2.08) the number of *births will always exceed the number of deaths*. This leads to a net inflow.

Figure 4.24 shows two important population indicators, one is the Billeter J and the other is the dependency ratio. The dependency ratio moves compared to the first test near to one. This means that the economic dependency is increased. This is mainly due to the increased number of young people. The Billeter J is still positive which indicates a greater number of young people compared to elderly people. The increased value shows that the population is growing.

The major figure for the growth model part is the *phase plot*. Figure 4.25 shows the phase plot on the left-hand and the three important growth rates on the right-hand.

As hypothesized, the model is in equilibrium. The straight line in the phase plot is the point of equilibrium, due to the scale of the abscissa. The real investments (S/AN) equals the required investments (I/AN). In this steady state, the growth rate of the population gN transfers to the R&D sector which grows with the same rate. Hence, gN = gA. The capital stock K grows at the sum of both rates, because the population and the patent stock eventually affect the final goods sector.

Figure 4.26 shows the per effective worker variables. All four graphs *quote the equilibrium,* because the value does not change over time. The small variations from a straight line are only due to the simulation accuracy of the rounded numbers. From the per effective worker variables, one can easily conclude that the per capita variables will grow with the rate gA.

Model Part "Population"				
Description	**Variable**	**Unit**	**high**	**low**
initial value 0 to 14	*init ac0014*	*Person*	*185.73*	*185.73*
initial value 15 to 39	*init ac1539*	*Person*	*177.27*	*177.27*
initial value 40 to 64	*init ac4064*	*Person*	*97.93*	*97.93*
initial value 65 to 89	*init ac6589*	*Person*	*39.09*	*39.09*
migration 0 to 14	mig0014	Person/Year	0	0
migration 15 to 39	mig1539	Person/Year	0	0
migration 40 to 64	mig4064	Person/Year	0	0
migration 65 to 89	mig6589	Person/Year	0	0
capital per immigrant	mig capital	Euro/Person	0	0
Description	**Variable**	**Unit**	**Value**	
fractional death rate 0 to 14	fdr0014	Dmnl/Year	0.0050	
fractional death rate15 to 39	fdr1539	Dmnl/Year	0.0348	
fractional death rate 40 to 64	fdr4064	Dmnl/Year	0.1000	
fractional death rate 65 to 89	fdr6589	Dmnl/Year	0.8000	
cohort size 0 to 14	size0014	Year	15	
cohort size 15 to 39	size1539	Year	25	
cohort size 40 to 64	size4064	Year	25	
cohort size 65 to 89	size6589	Year	25	
total fertility rate	*TFR*	*Person/Person*	*5*	
sex ratio female	female ratio	Dmnl	0.5	
education ratio	education ratio	Dmnl	0.5	

Fig. 4.22 Test run 2: exogenous variables for the population sector
Source: own data

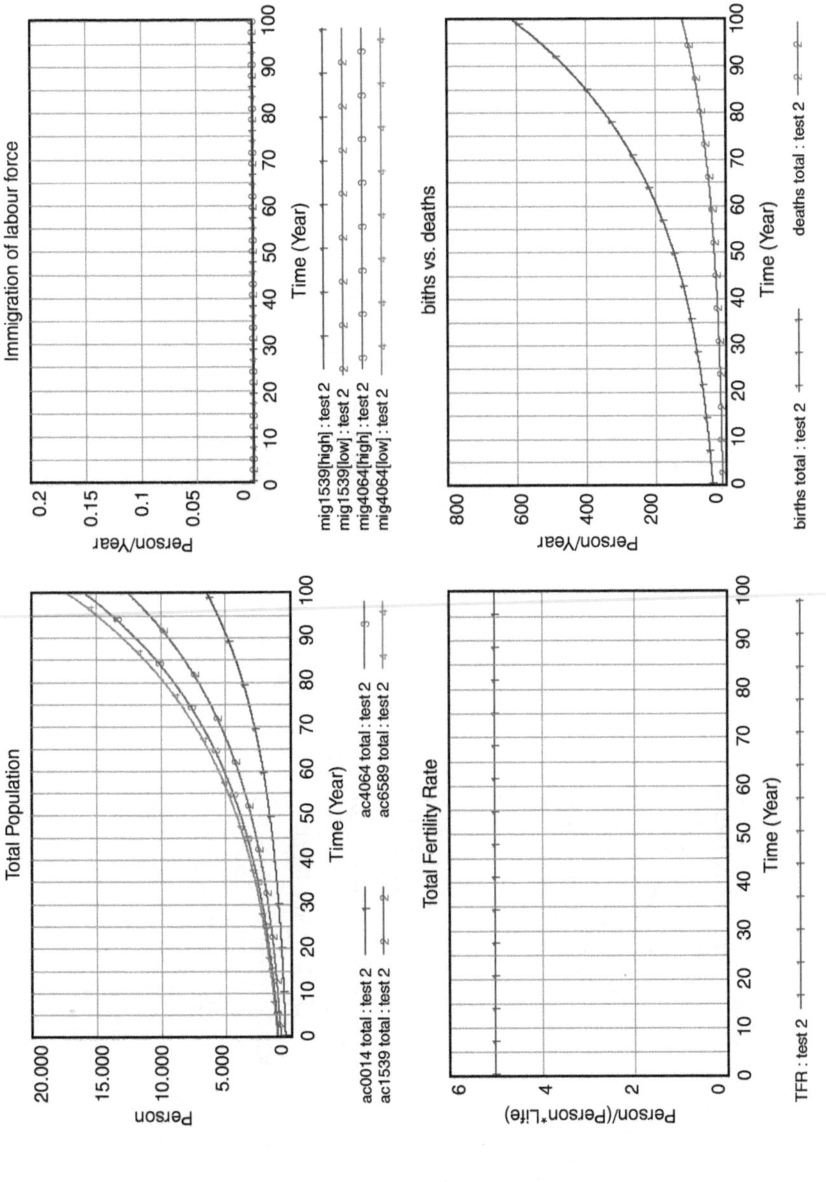

Fig. 4.23 Test run 2: results population sector
Source: own figure

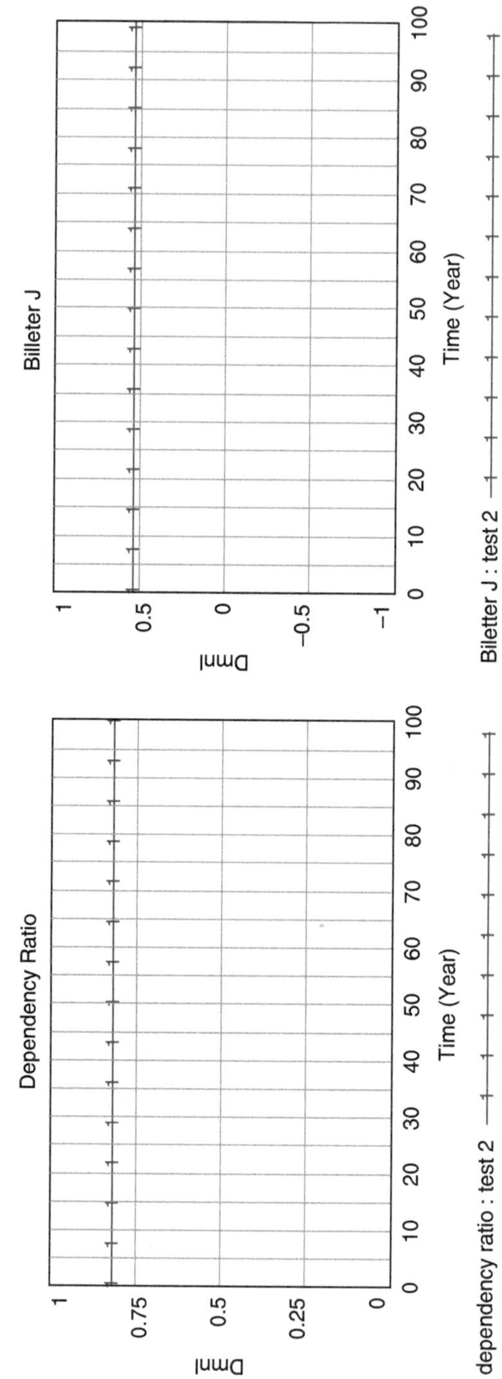

Fig. 4.24 Test run 2: results population indicators
Source: own figure

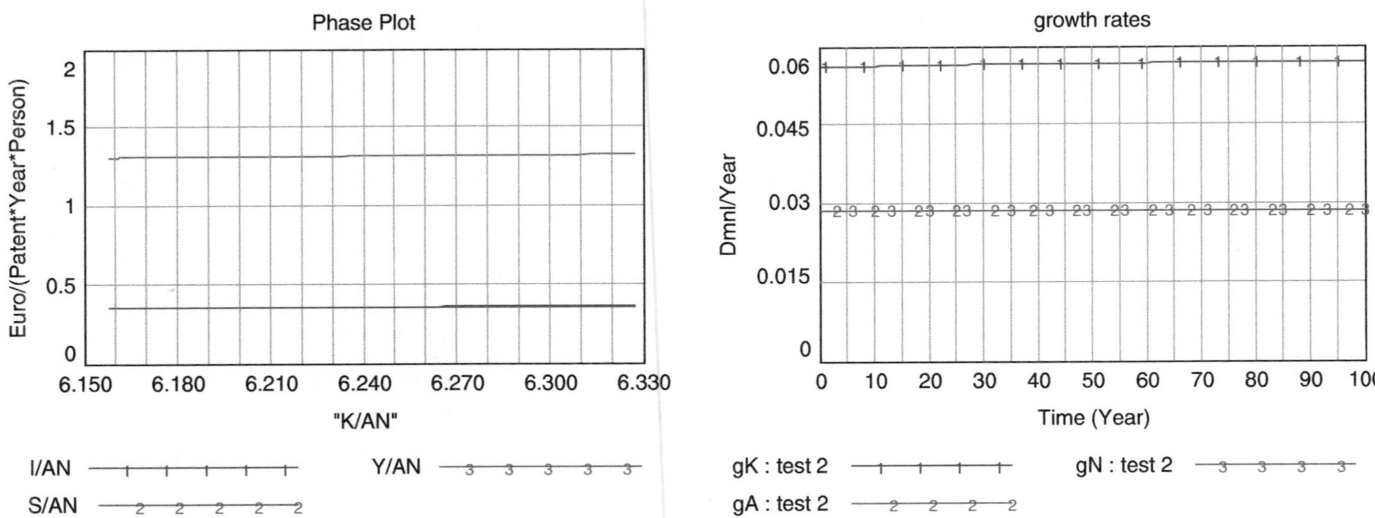

Fig. 4.25 Test run 2: results growth sector
Source: own figure

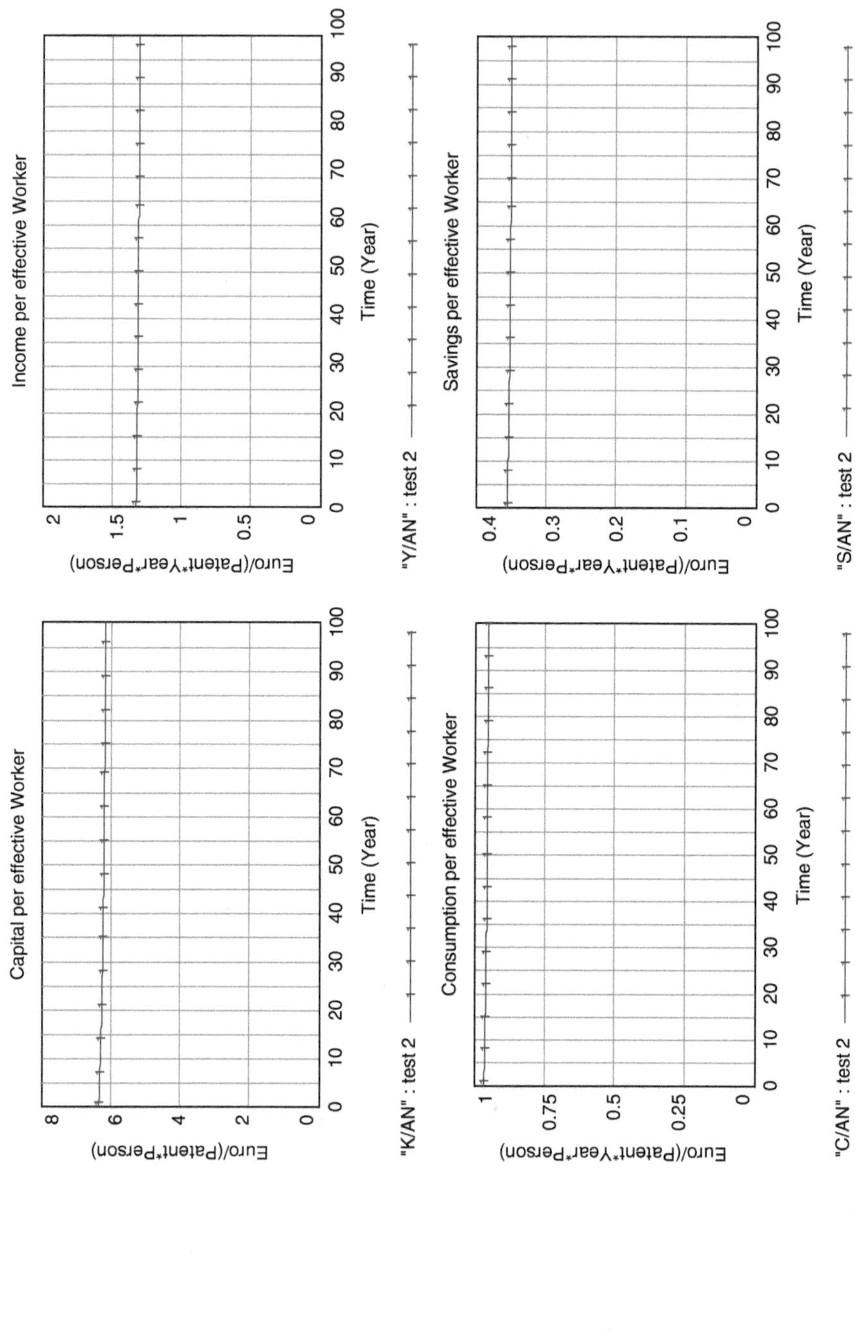

Fig. 4.26 Test run 2: results per effective capita variables
Source: own figure

The *utility sector projects very interesting results* (see Fig. 4.27). At first glance one notices the constant utility per effective capita in the upper right corner. This is consistent with the other per capita variables.

The resulting accumulated total utility is almost the same in number as in the test run 1, but one cannot compare these two figures. As the scale of the utility values is different, the total utility is comparable just by chance. The reason for this huge difference in the utility value is the power of the R&D sector which continues to grow. If one compares the utility per capita on the left for both runs, one can see that the test run 2, because of the growing patent stock, leads to a much higher increase than the test run 1. But this does not hold true for the accumulated utility per capita. This is due to the strength of the discount rate. Although the utility per capita increases more than in test run 1 it is until $t = 60$ below the values of the run 1. The later higher utility values will be discounted by sigma and does not add in such high amounts to the accumulated utility to keep up the earlier losses compared to test run 1. Or, one could just say, that time matters.

The test run 2 with a growing population shows very promising results. Every variable follows the theoretically predicted behavior.

4.3.4 Summary and Conclusion

This chapter part tested and validated the demographic growth model. First, the model went several tests: structural assessment, dimensional consistency tests, integration error test and parameter assessment. Second, two behavioral tests were conducted. The first test stressed the importance of a stable population in order to prove the population sector. The second test went a step further and evaluated if a growing population in the demographic model delivers comparable results as from semi-endogenous models demanded. All tests were successfully passed.

4.4 Chapter Summary

This chapter developed and tested a new semi-endogenous demographic growth model. The role of system dynamics and econometrics was also addressed. This was necessary because econometrics is nowadays a quasi standard for macroeconomists.

The first subchapter led the reader through the developing process of the demographic growth model. Beginning with the new population sector and the disaggregation of the population stock all inflows and outflows were outlined. Especially the feedback structure was surveyed. The following R&D sector equaled the already known Jones-model from Sect. 3.4. But the growth model part was augmented significantly. The concept of subscripts with their distinguishing between high- and low-skilled worker and four different age groups provides

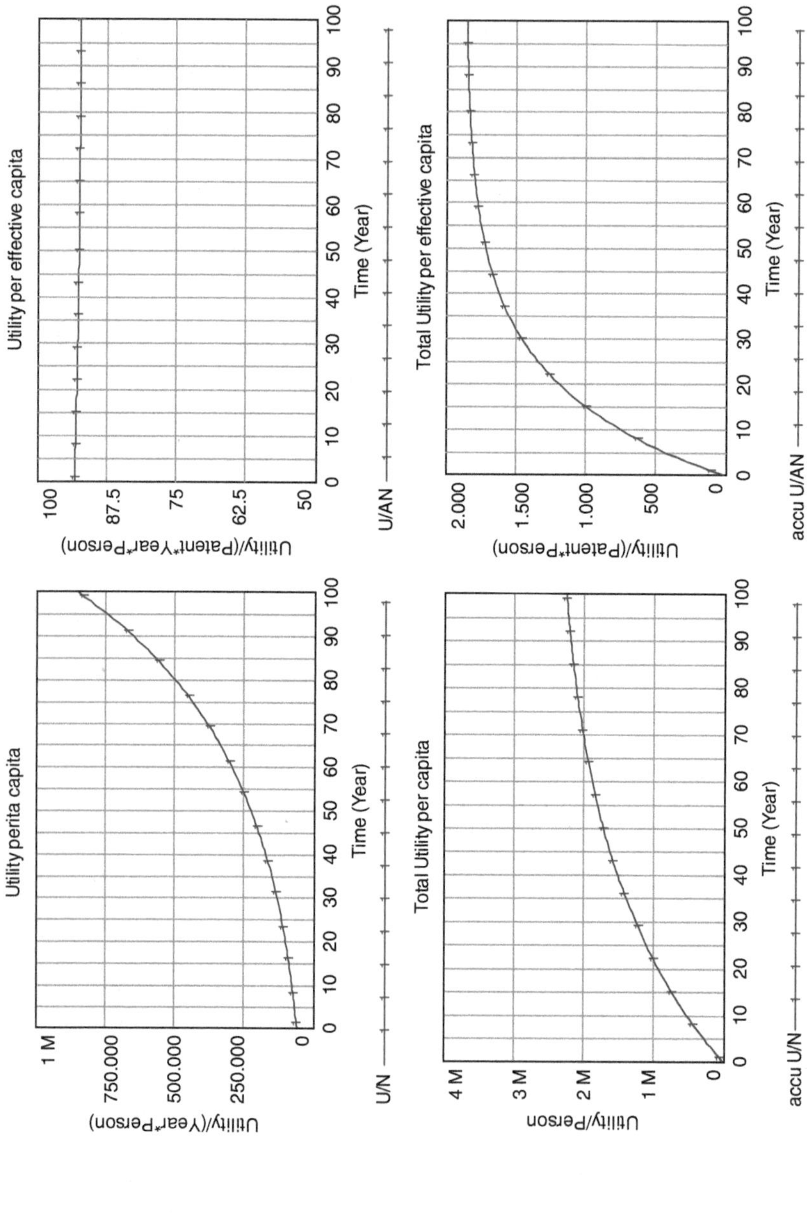

Fig. 4.27 Test run 2: results utility sector
Source: own figure

deeper insight in the standard growth loop of capital investment than previous models. By doing so, the lifecycle hypothesis of consumption can now be implemented into growth models. The new utility sector is based on the idea of the Ramsey–Cass–Koopmanns-model and is usually used to endogenize the saving ratios. But in this case it gives the scientists the chance to compare different policies.

Initialization is extremely important for the proper behavior of the model. By starting in equilibrium one prevents themselves from misreading the behavioral results. Because only with an equilibrium start one can be sure that the observed behavior derives out of the model structure and not out of exogenous parameter values.

The second subchapter mainly stressed the importance of tests to validate the model. Structural and behavioral tests were conducted. The dimensional consistency is as much important as the behavior tests. Stepwise modeling prevented already in the early modeling phase structural and logical mistakes. The final model itself is fully outlined in the annex for use. The first behavior test analyzed the population sector, whether is behaves well in equilibrium or not. All figures showed understandable behavior. But as semi-endogenous models needs a growing population for a steady state of the whole model and not only of the population sector, a second test run were performed. With a total fertility rate of 5.0 the number of births was above the replacement level of 2.08. The population showed stable growing behavior. A growing population led to a growing patent stock in the R&D sector. This causes the whole model into equilibrium. Several figures proved this.

The executable model can now be applied with theoretical founded but real world problems borrowed data. The next chapter analyzes the economic consequences for aging and shrinking societies.

Chapter 5
Scenario and Policy Analysis

Man lives and works within social systems. His scientific research is exposing the structure of nature's system. His technology has produced complex physical systems. But even so, the principles governing the behavior of systems are not widely understood.
(Forrester, 1968, p. 1)

In this chapter the author's semi-endogenous growth model is applied to various demographic problems. The presented scenarios are conceptual. Thus, general results and explanations for the case of aging and shrinking of economies are presented. In later empirical work one can estimate all exogenous variables for a full parameter adoption. Then the model delivers results – based on the neoclassical growth theory – on how a country will develop over time.

The chapter is structured into different scenarios, as one can see in Fig. 5.1. All of them are extreme scenarios which provide the bandwidth of possible behavior. Mixed scenarios can easily be created. The first subchapter provides the base run. It shows the economical development in an aging and declining society. From this base run all scenarios are derived. The second subchapter is entitled "Family Orientation". In this scenario, the shrinking population stabilizes at the replacement level at a specific point in time. The following subchapter "Education Orientation" combines two policies: First, the previous policy of stabilizing at the replacement level and second, a policy towards more education. With this it is aimed to overcome negative results of the base run scenario. At last, the third subchapter "Migration Orientation" examines a specific migration policy in conjunction with the family orientation policy.

For this, the simulation horizon is always 100 time periods. The base run starts the model at equilibrium, with a total fertility rate of 5.0. At $t = 10$ the fertility rate drops below the replacement level at 1.0 child per women per lifetime and simulates therefore a shrinking society. This development will be retained for a time period of 40 years which is slightly more than one generation. The three different scenarios will always start at $t = 50$. Thus, one can see for another period of 50 years, which is more than 1.5 generations, how these policies change the previous decline of the society as well as the resulting economic factors.

L. Weber, *Demographic Change and Economic Growth*, Contributions to Economics,
DOI 10.1007/978-3-7908-2590-9_5,

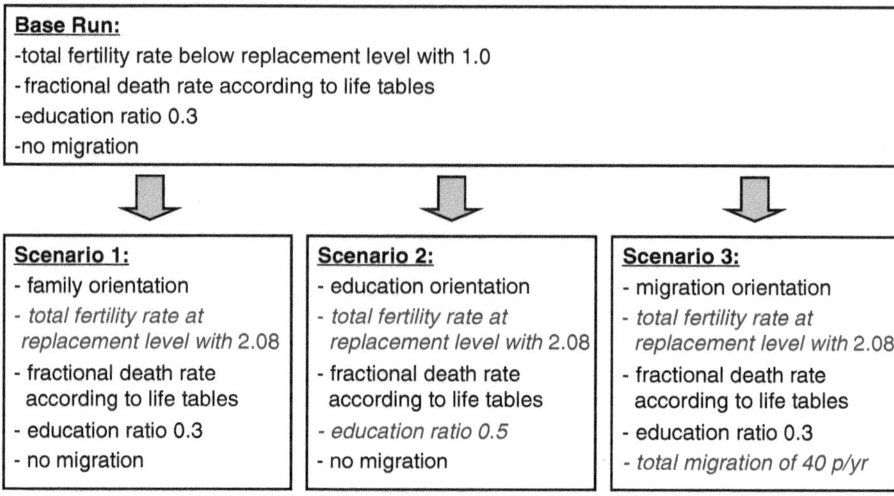

Fig. 5.1 Demographic growth model: scenario overview
Source: own figure

5.1 Base Run

5.1.1 Description

The base run is the foundation for all investigated scenarios. It reflects the upcoming period of demographic change for industrialized European countries. This run represents the change of a steady state economic growth into a aging and shrinking society. The change will take place at t = 10 and the decline will continue until the simulation ends at t = 100. Neither migration nor other changes occur.

This declining 90 year period is not realistic yet, but it should show:

1. How the model behaves over time for a declining society
2. Maximum effects for important key figures
3. The economic transition process

5.1.2 Initialization

The initialization starts in the population sector. The total number of people living in the hypothetical economy is 1,000. The structure of the population is again derived from the total fertility rate and their inflows and outflows. Projecting the difference between high- and low-skilled labor is not the differentiation into the secondary and tertiary sector. Highly-skilled workers reflect a greater level of education, independent of the workplace. As the percentage of high-skilled workers differs in industrialized countries it is assumed that this amounts 30% of the working-population. This different distribution of high- and low-skilled workers, in comparison to the test runs, explains the different number of people in each age cohort, as seen in Fig. 5.2. The Figure also shows the fractional death rates and the sex ratio. The total fertility, an important key variable in this run, is shown in italics.

Figure 5.3 presents all of the exogenous constants and initial values for the stocks in the growth model. The amount of capital and the number of initial patents are calculated based on mathematical initialization process (see Annex for a detailed description.

The partial production elasticity of capital is assumed with 0.3 and there is no depletion rate in the model. Currently the model is formulated in net-flows for investments; however it can also used in the consideration of gross-investments. The exogenous parameters for the patent stock are as usual.

The wage distribution between age groups and skill levels plays an important role in the consumption-saving-relation. From a theoretical view it is assumed that children (ac0014) do not have any own income. Beneficiary payments from the government are excluded and assumed to be in parent's monetary flow. The reference for all wages is the income of low-skilled workers in the age cohort of 15–39. High-skilled age cohorts in general are assumed to earn 25% more than the appropriate low-skilled age cohort. Senior workers (ac4064[skill]) are assumed to earn 50% more than the younger workers (ac1539[skill]). After retirement, one gets only 60% of appropriate income (ac1539[skill]). Note that this and the following saving ratios are theoretical and must not reflect reality.

The amount of income that can be saved is, in general higher, for high-skilled than for low-skilled worker. As children do not have any income they cannot save any money. The saving ratio increases over a lifetime and falls to a lower level during retirement (ac6489). One can also assume a negative saving ratio in the last age cohort, but this does not change the behavior. Also in Sect. 2.3.1 it was explained that the question about saving rates in late live periods differs between empirical studies.

The last model part to be initialized is the utility sector (see Fig. 5.4). In the beginning, all utility values are normalized to 1. The elasticity of the marginal utility is lower than the time preference, thus avoiding postponing consumption. The value is close to zero in order to create a strong connection with consumption. The time preference of 0.2 will bring only smaller discounted values than a higher time preference. Finally, the reference time is set to 10. This is the point at which the simulation changes from a growing to a shrinking population.

The next section outlines the simulation results, based on these initial values.

5.1.3 Results Population Sector

The population will decline fundamentally. The upper two graphs in Fig. 5.5 present the population structure at the time t=10 and t=100 for comparison. One

Model Part "Population"				
Description	**Variable**	**Unit**	**high**	**low**
initial value 0 to14	init ac0014	Person	111.44	260.02
initial value 15 to 39	init ac1539	Person	106.36	248.17
initial value 40 to 64	init ac4064	Person	58.76	137.10
initial value 65 to 89	init ac6589	Person	23.45	54.72
migration 0 to 14	mig0014	Person/Year	0	0
migration 15 to 39	mig1539	Person/Year	10	10
migration 40 to 64	mig4064	Person/Year	10	10
migration 65 to 89	mig6589	Person/Year	0	0
capital per immigrant	mig capital	Euro/Person	0	0
Description	**Variable**	**Unit**	**Value**	
fractional death rate 0 to 14	fdr0014	Dmnl/Year	0.0050	
fractional death rate15 to 39	fdr1539	Dmnl/Year	0.0348	
fractional death rate 40 to 64	fdr4064	Dmnl/Year	0.1000	
fractional death rate 65 to 89	fdr6589	Dmnl/Year	0.8000	
cohort size 0 to 14	size0014	Year	15	
cohort size 15 to 39	size1539	Year	25	
cohort size 40 to 64	size4064	Year	25	
cohort size 65 to 89	size6589	Year	25	
total fertility rate	*TFR*	*Person/Person*	1	
sex ratio female	female ratio	Dmnl	0.5	
education ratio	education ratio	Dmnl	0.3	

Fig. 5.2 Base run: initial values of the population sector
Source: own figure

Model Part "Growth"				
Description	**Variable**	**Unit**	**Value**	
initial patent stock	*init A*	*Patent*	5.809	*calculated*
initial capital stock	*init K*	*Euro*	10.228.816	*calculated*
partial production elasticity of capital	alpha	Dmnl	0.3	
depletion rate	delta	Dmnl/Year	0	
degree of congestion	lambda	Dmnl	1	
return on stocks of ideas	phi	Dmnl	0	
accelerator	rho	Dmnl	1	
Description	**Variable**	**Unit**	**Value**	
wage age distribution	wage age [age0014]	Dmnl	0.00	
	wage age [age1539]	Dmnl	1.00	
	wage age [age4064]	Dmnl	1.50	
	wage age [age6589]	Dmnl	0.60	
Description	**Variable**	**Unit**	**high**	
wage level of high skilled worker	wage level	Dmnl	1.25	
Description	**Variable**	**Unit**	**high**	**low**
saving ratio	saving ratio [age0014]	Dmnl	0.00	0.00
	saving ratio [age1539]	Dmnl	0.20	0.10
	saving ratio [age4064]	Dmnl	0.25	0.15
	saving ratio [age6589]	Dmnl	0.10	0.05

Fig. 5.3 Base run: initial values of the growth sector
Source: own figure

Model Part "Utility"				
Description	**Variable**	**Unit**	**high**	**low**
initial accumulated utility stock	init U/N[age0014]	Utility/Person	1	1
per capita	init U/N [age1539]	Utility/Person	1	1
	init U/N [age4064]	Utility/Person	1	1
	init U/N [age6589]	Utility/Person	1	1
initial accumulated utility stock	init U/AN [age0014]	Utility/(Person*Patent)	1	1
per effective capita	init U/AN [age1539]	Utility/(Person*Patent)	1	1
	init U/AN [age4064]	Utility/(Person*Patent)	1	1
	init U/AN [age6589]	Utility/(Person*Patent)	1	1
Description	**Variable**	**Unit**	**Value**	
elasticity of marginal utility	theta	Dmnl	0.10	
time preference	sigma	Dmnl	0.20	
reference time	*reference time*	*Year*	10	

Fig. 5.4 Base run: initial values of the utility sector
Source: own figure

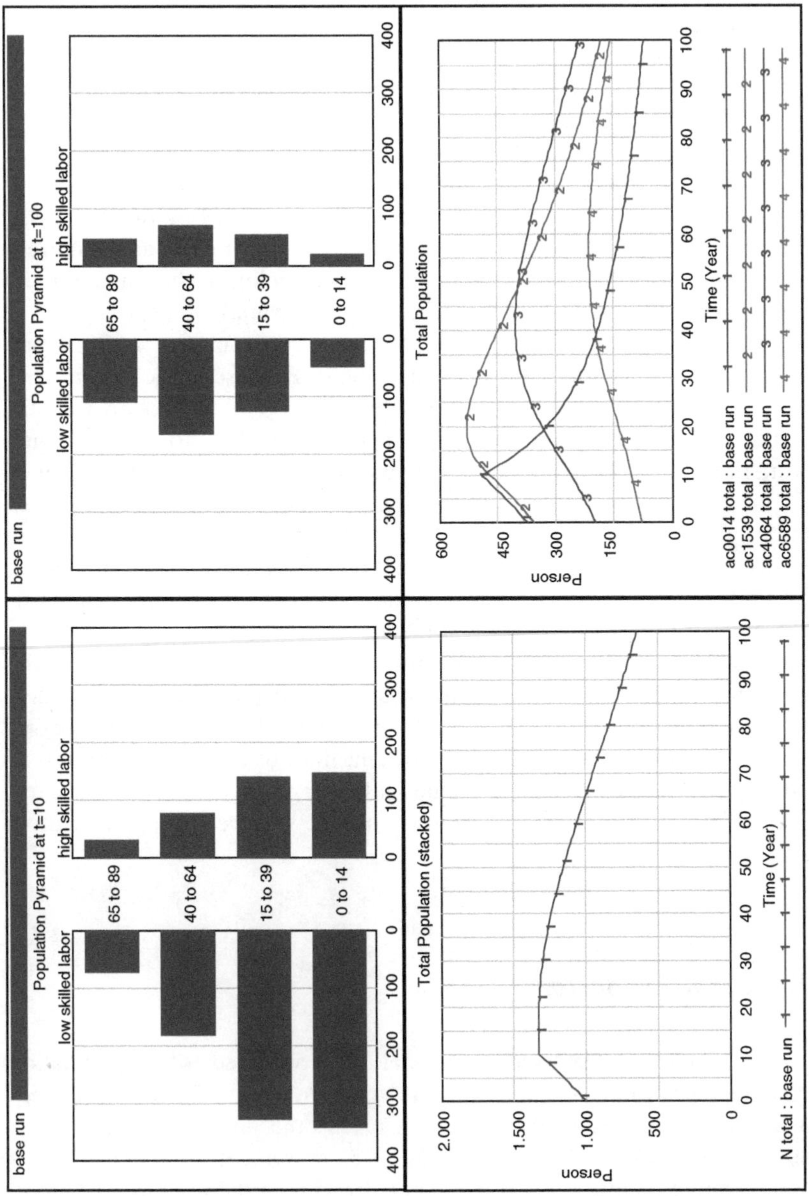

Fig. 5.5 Base run: results total population
Source: own figure

can see that not only the wideness of the population changed, but also the structure totally changed. Whereas at t = 10 the age cohort of 0 to 14 is the largest group, at t = 100 it is the smallest one. The total population (graph down left) declined from around 1,300 people in t = 10 to around 650 people at t = 100.

How the structure changed over time illustrates the lower right graph, where the total population is disaggregated into the different age cohorts. One can recognize the cohort 0014 (no. 1) and how it declines suddenly after the policy is switched. All other age cohort stocks behave like the youngest one and show the material delay pattern with declining and shifting peaks.

The change of a population occurs through their in- and outflows. Figure 5.6 shows the inflows, births and immigration, as well as the outflow of deaths. By chance, the birth rate declines at t = 10 to almost the same amount as the current deaths. As a consequence of this the population starts to decline as the amount of the outflow exceeds the inflows. This will continue until the simulation ends.

The dependency ratio shows the ratio between a non-working (ac0014 and ac6589) and working population (ac1539 and ac4064). Because of the low number of births the dependency ratio declines (see Fig. 5.7). This is due to the still increasing number of elderly people. They just aged into the last stock and finished their working life. At t = 40 the ratio reaches its lowest value where the number of workers is the highest compared to the number of non-working people. From t = 10 until t = 40 (more than one generation) the economic situation for the social security systems improves, although the population already declines. After t = 40 the situation worsen. The number of non-workers continuously increases whereas the number of working citizens shrinks.

However, the Billeter J is more meaningful than the dependency ratio. The nominator is the subtraction of the youngest age cohort (ac0014) by the oldest age cohort (ac6589). Hence, if the Billeter J turns negative, than the number of elderly people will exceed the youngest cohort. This must be equal to the minima in the dependency ratio. One advantage of the Billeter J is its function as an early indicator. It declines continuously and shows, from the very beginning, a negative outcome.

5.1.4 Results R&D Sector

The patent stock and the R&D sector, in total, are connected to the population sector by the number of high-skilled labor. A decline in the number of births does not affect this sector immediately, because it takes time until the stocks of the ac1539 and the ac4064 decline. The continuous retirement of older workers decreases the number of high-skilled workers (Lh). Due to the high-skilled labor, the change in patent stock is matched one to one (delta A). A will continue to grow but with smaller rates. Figure 5.8 shows the most important variables of the R&D sector.

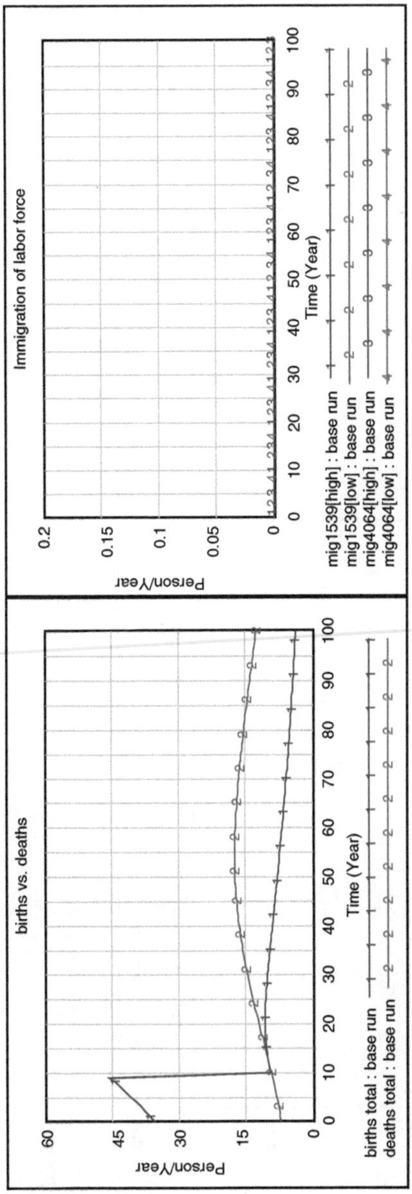

Fig. 5.6 Base run: results changes in population sector
Source: own figure

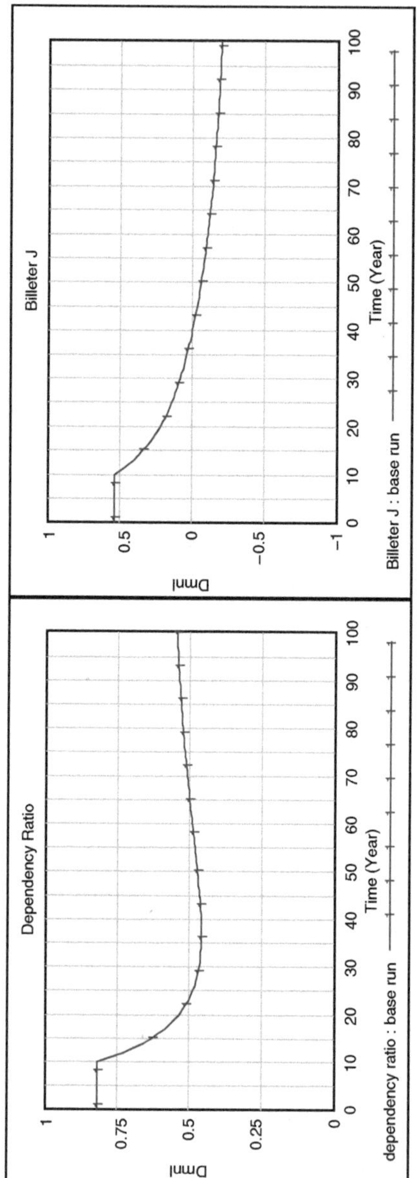

Fig. 5.7 Base run: results population indicators
Source: own figure

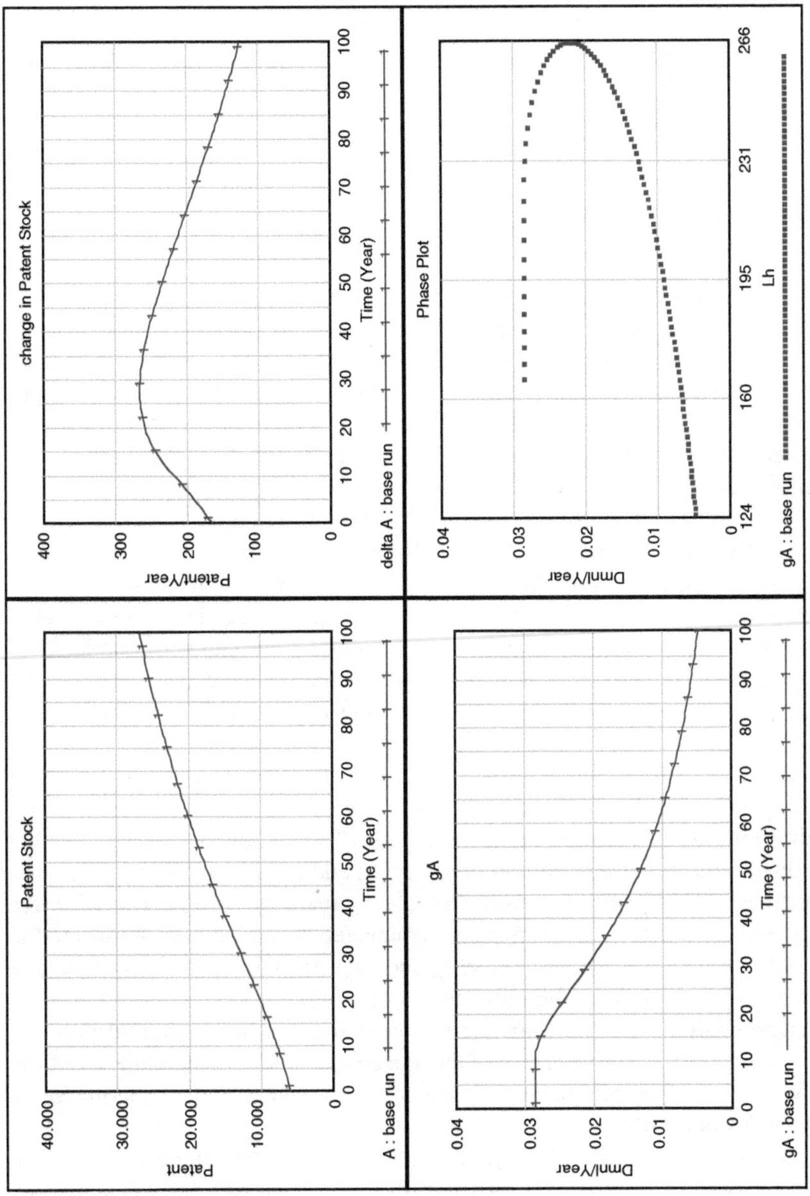

Fig. 5.8 Base run: results R&D sector
Source: own figure

The lower left graph in Fig. 5.8 represents the growth rate gA for the patent stock. The growth rate will decline to zero in infinity, when the working population fades. The fourth graph in this Figure represents the phase plot for the growth rate gA in relation to the number of high-skilled labor. One might remember that in the Jones-model in Sect. 3.4.4.5 the plotted line was straight. The bending now occurs due to delays in the population sector. The maximum point of the high-skilled labor forms the curve in the phase plot.

5.1.5 Results Growth Sector

The following results are of great importance. Figure 5.9 provides an overview of the growth sector behavior. The upper left graph shows the standard phase plot for all neoclassical growth models, with the capital intensity per effective capita (K/AN) on the x-axis. The simulation run starts in equilibrium, with capital intensity per effective capita around 2. The fertility decline pushes the model out of its steady state. The required investments suddenly decline. One can observe this in the lower left graph (no. 1).

The upper right graph presents the growth rates of the capital stock (gK), the population (gN), and the patent stock (gA). The continuing positive growth rate of the patent stock compensates for the negative growth in population and leads via the production function to a positive growth of the capital stock. This, additionally, reinforces itself. Summarizing this positive growth effect one can better understand why in the lower left graph the real investments increase. The consequence of the exceeding investments leads to an increase of the capital intensity (lower right graph).

The next set of graphs for the growth sector is shown in Fig. 5.10. It aims to provide insight on how income is split into consumption and savings. For recollection, the different saving rates are in the upper right. The income per effective capita must rise due to the increase in capital intensity. In addition, both consumption and savings increase. This happens because of the increase in income per effective capita and the both depending variables are connected by the fix saving ratio to the income. But this simple behavior is only the aggregation of the different age cohorts. A better insight gives therefore Fig. 5.11.

The disaggregation into the four age cohort delivers a differentiated point of view. The savings per effective capita of the age cohort of 15–39 increase over time because the number of people shrinks. Hence, the denominator of the equation S/AN let the whole fraction grow.

Due to the material delay in the population aging chain, this slope is delayed in all other. The savings per effective capita in the age cohort of 65–89 is somehow different. This is due to the above mentioned effects about the distribution of the patent stock. In the case of savings per effective capita, it follows:

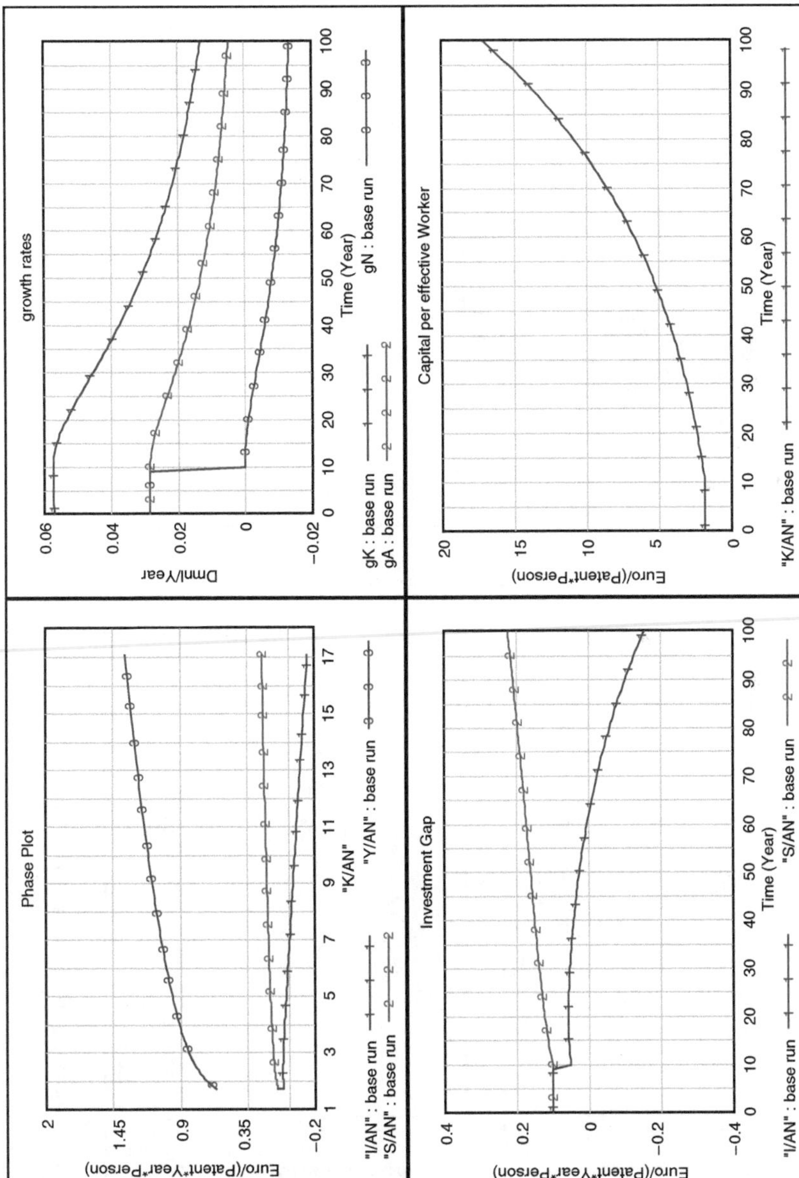

Fig. 5.9 Base run: results growth sector
Source: own figure

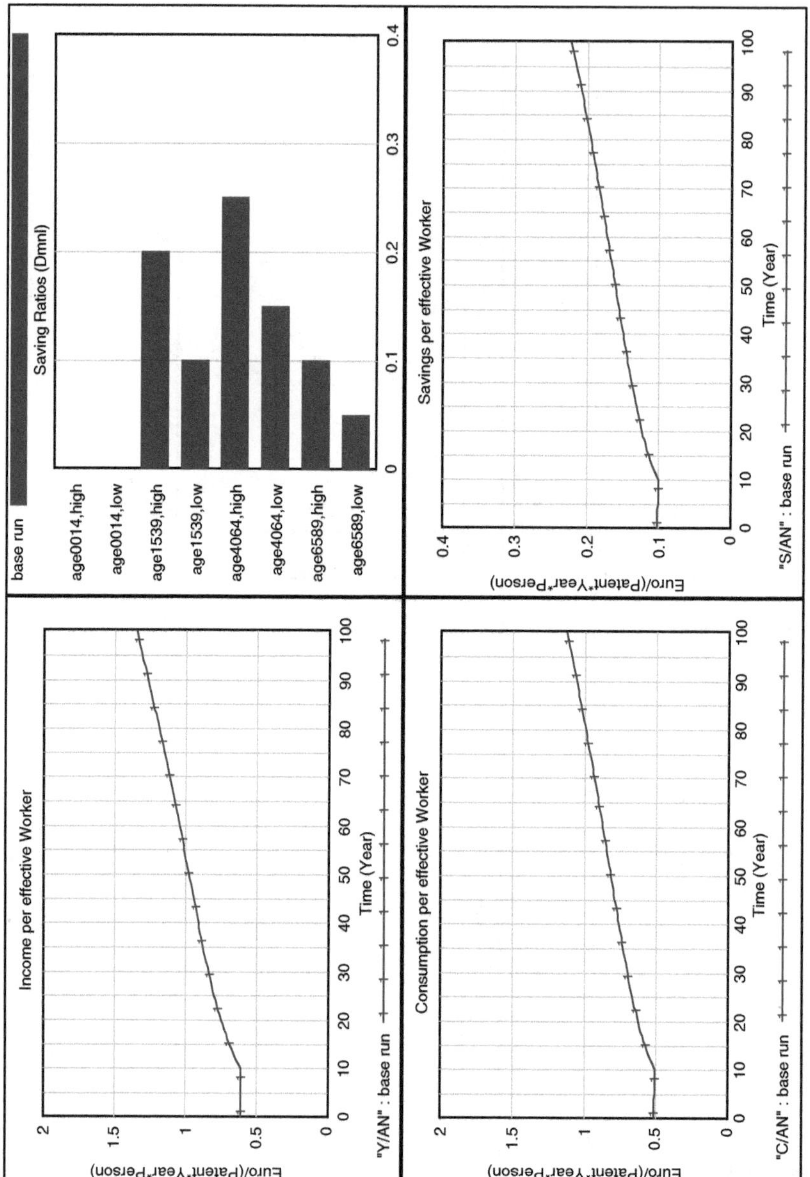

Fig. 5.10 Base run: results per effective capita variables
Source: own figure

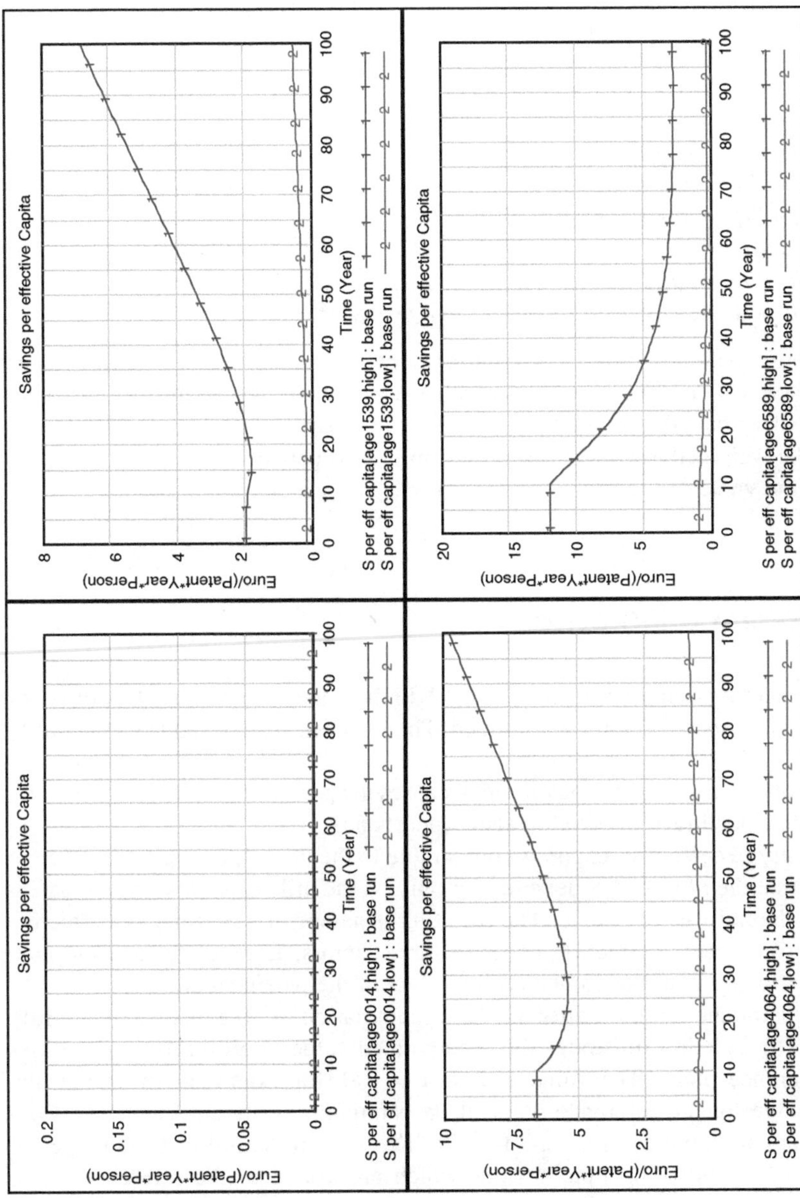

Fig. 5.11 Base run: results savings per effective capita
Source: own figure

S per eff capita[age0014,skill] = S per capita[age0014,skill]/A0014[skill]
S per eff capita[age1539,skill] = S per capita[age1539,skill]/A1539[skill]
S per eff capita[age4064,skill] = S per capita[age4064,skill]/A4064[skill]
S per eff capita[age6589,skill] = S per capita[age6589,skill]/A6589[skill]
*Unit: Euro/(Person*Year*Patent) [0,?]*
Comment: savings per effective capita

with

*A0014[skill] = A/N total * ac0014[skill]*
*A1539[skill] = A/N total * ac1539[skill]*
*A4064[skill] = A/N total * ac1539[skill]*
*A6589[skill] = A/N total * ac6589[skill]*
Unit: Patent [0,?]
Comment: R&D expenditures per age group

The consequence of this is that the amount of patents, belonging to the age cohort 6589, will rise in correlation with the decline of population in all other stocks. To distribute the originally single stock into partial patent stocks for the age cohorts, the weighted average is used. Shifting ratios between the age cohorts shift therefore the value of the partial patent stocks.

5.1.6 Results Utility Sector

The utility sector is summarized in Fig. 5.12. In the upper two graphs, the utility per capita and per effective capita is presented. These values are derived from the utility function.

The positive growth of the patent stock causes the per capita utility to continually increase. The decline in population also supports this.

The utility per effective capita is comparable to the utility per capita. One has to recapture that the ratio U/AN depends not only on the utility, but also on the patent stock and the number of people. The resulting behavior of the utility per effective capita is a complex interaction of these three factors. Eventually, consumption increases stronger than the compensating effect of the patent stock.

The accumulated total utility is the accumulation of the discounted utility function. The function illustrates the accumulated value of all discounted utilities to the reference point. The value at time $t = 100$, for example, shows the discounted value for the reference point, if the simulation lasts until $t = 100$. Both graphs reach an upper limit around $t = 50$. Increases in the utility beyond $t = 50$ get discounted from long time periods which are drawn to the reference point. Economically, one can say that future utility gains will only be implemented into today's decision if they are not too long-term oriented.

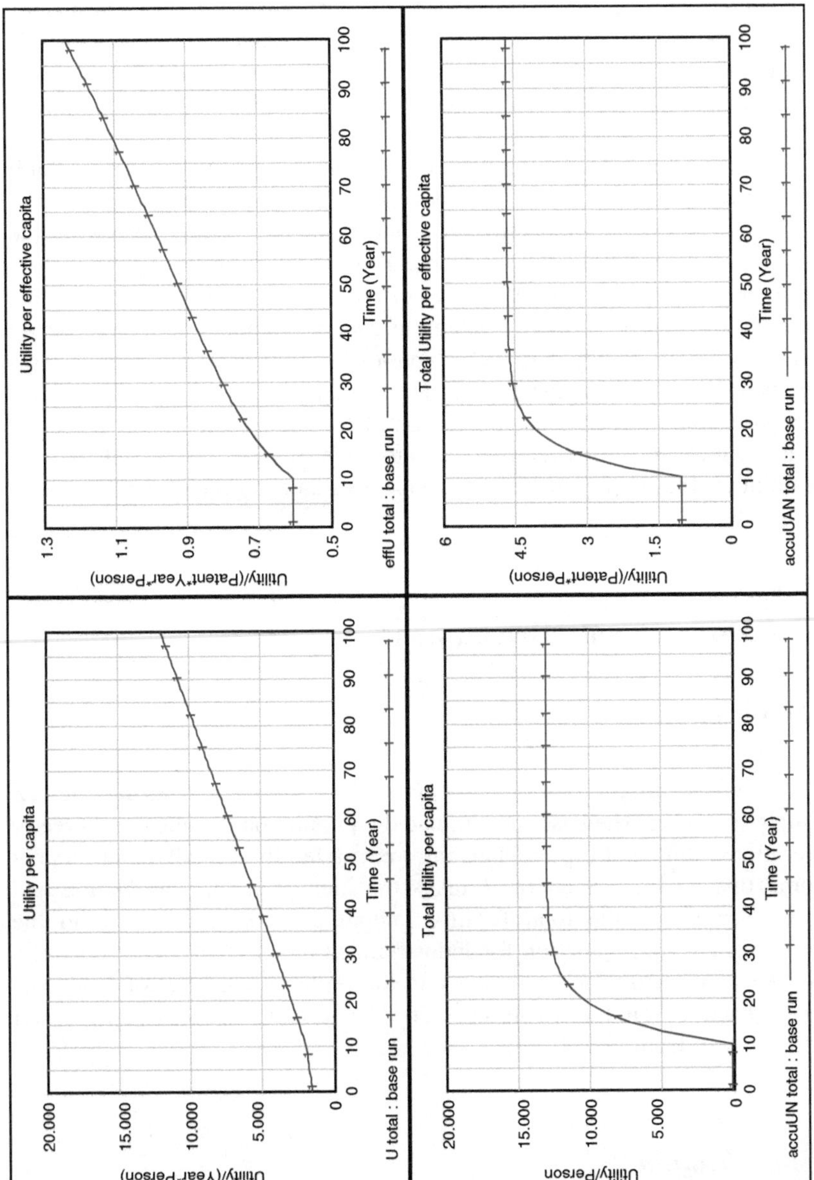

Fig. 5.12 Base run: results utility sector
Source: own figure

5.1.7 Summary and Conclusion

The base run revealed very interesting results. The population sector showed the expected behavior of a declining population. Indicators, such as the dependency ratio are not sufficient to present the whole population change. In these dynamic situations the Billeter J is better suited. The long delay between the total fertility decline and the first offshoots hide the fundamental population changes for almost one generation.

The R&D sector slows down after the above mentioned population decay, but it still contributes positively to the whole economy. The model in general shows positive growth rates. The capital intensity increases over time. Therefore, the indicator K/AN is a weak evaluation instrument for the entire economy. Consumption per effective capita and the savings per effective capita do not reveal perfect insight into the population change. Population changes demand the researcher to disaggregate the values to evaluate the behavior of the different age groups. This was done, as an example, for the savings per effective capita. The utility sector follows the consumption behavior. The accumulated values can serve as a good indicator for policy scenarios as well, because discounting future values to a reference point enables policy-makers to test and evaluate various strategies within a timeframe.

5.2 Scenario 1 "Family Orientation"

5.2.1 Description

Founding on the base run for a declining population, this scenario tests the effect of a stabilizing population. The base run simulated a population decline over three or more generations. But what if politicians introduce a family–friendly environment to overcome this decline? Scenario 1 takes the idea of family orientation and assumes an increase in the total fertility rate at $t = 50$. As outlined in the Sect. 2.4, an increasing population for industrialized countries is rather unlikely. Therefore, the total fertility increases only to the replacement level of 2.08. The base run is still active from $t = 10$ until $t = 50$. The variables of the scenario 1 start to affect the system from $t = 50$.

5.2.2 Initialization

The initialization of the population sector is comparable to the base run as one can see in Fig. 5.13. All exogenous variables, but the total fertility rate and the reference point, are identical to the base run.

Model Part "Population"				
Description	**Variable**	**Unit**	**high**	**low**
initial value 0 to 14	init ac0014	Person	111,44	260,02
initial value 15 to 39	init ac1539	Person	106,36	248,17
initial value 40 to 64	init ac4064	Person	58,76	137,10
initial value 65 to 89	init ac6589	Person	23,45	54,72
migration 0 to 14	mig0014	Person/Year	0	0
migration 15 to 39	mig1539	Person/Year	0	0
migration 40 to 64	mig4064	Person/Year	0	0
migration 65 to 89	mig6589	Person/Year	0	0
capital per immigrant	mig capital	Euro/Person	0	0
Description	**Variable**	**Unit**	**Value**	
fractional death rate 0 to 14	fdr0014	Dmnl/Year	0,0050	
fractional death rate 15 to 39	fdr1539	Dmnl/Year	0,0348	
fractional death rate 40 to 64	fdr4064	Dmnl/Year	0,1000	
fractional death rate 65 to 89	fdr6589	Dmnl/Year	0,8000	
cohort size 0 to 14	size0014	Year	15	
cohort size 15 to 39	size1539	Year	25	
cohort size 40 to 64	size4064	Year	25	
cohort size 65 to 89	size6589	Year	25	
total fertility rate at t=50	*TFR*	*Person/Person*	2.08	
sex ratio female	female ratio	Dmnl	0,5	
education ratio	education ratio	Dmnl	0,3	

Fig. 5.13 Scenario 1: initialization of the population sector
Source: own figure

The initial value of the TFR is 5.0 children per women per life and declines to 1.0 at t = 10. So far both runs are identical. Italics in Fig. 5.13 indicate the jump to the replacement level of TFR = 2.08 at t = 50.

The growth sector initial values do not differ to the base run. For the sake of completeness Fig. 5.14 illustrates this.

The initialization of the utility sector is represented in Fig. 5.15. The reference point shifts to t = 50 so that all scenarios will be comparable. This shift is necessary for practical considerations. Politicians have to decide at t = 50 whether the policy should be adopted or not. A reference point with t = 10 would be in the past and therefore not relevant.

5.2.3 Results Population Sector

The discussion of these scenario results will mainly focus on the behavior from t = 50 until the simulation horizon at t = 100, because earlier behavior is identical to the base run.

Figure 5.16 reflects the results for the population structure. The two population pyramids are snapshots from the policy decision point (t = 50) and the simulation end (t = 100). At t = 50 one can see how the structure changed from a growing population to an aging one. The people in the age cohort ac6489 exceed the amount of both high- and low-skilled young people. However, the total number of workers still dominates the system. These results are comparable with today's situation of industrialized countries. The increase of TFR changes the structure of the population. After 50 years (at t = 100) of this policy the stock of the youngest age cohort turns upward and almost becomes equal to the oldest age cohort. The stock of the working population almost stabilizes, albeit on a lower level than at t = 50. In the lower left graph one can see that despite the increase in fertility the total population still declines, but with slowing effect. If one simulates this policy for a longer period, one can see that it takes up to t = 140 until the population stabilizes. This means that the increase of the TFR needs almost three generations before the desired result is achieved.

Finally, the lower right graph in Fig. 5.16 shows how the different stocks evolve over time. From this, one can reason why stabilization takes so long. Births depend on the childbearing cohort ac1539. It takes almost a generation before this group stabilizes. The challenge, of course, is that potential mothers need to be born first. The two older stocks follow the behavior of the childbearing cohort with the usual material delay of the first or second order, which takes again time to adopt.

Figure 5.17 provides the behavior of the flows according to the stocks of the previous graphs in Fig. 5.16. As one can see, the TFR changes (top left-hand) and affects directly the number of births (down left-hand). Although the birth increase takes place suddenly, it does not reach the absolute number of deaths until the simulation ends. The population shrinks. The effect is explained above.

Model Part "Growth"				
Description	**Variable**	**Unit**	**Value**	
initial patent stock	*init A*	*Patent*	5.809	*calculated*
initial capital stock	*init K*	*Euro*	10.228.816	*calculated*
partial production elasticity of capital	alpha	Dmnl	0.3	
depletion rate	delta	Dmnl/Year	0	
degree of congestion	lambda	Dmnl	1	
return on stocks of ideas	phi	Dmnl	0	
accelerator	rho	Dmnl	1	
Description	**Variable**	**Unit**	**Value**	
wage age distribution	wage age [age0014]	Dmnl	0.00	
	wage age [age1539]	Dmnl	1.00	
	wage age [age4064]	Dmnl	1.50	
	wage age [age6589]	Dmnl	0.60	
Description	**Variable**	**Unit**	**high**	
wage levelof high skilled worker	wage level	Dmnl	1.25	
Description	**Variable**	**Unit**	**high**	**low**
saving ratio	saving ratio [age0014]	Dmnl	0.00	0.00
	saving ratio [age1539]	Dmnl	0.20	0.10
	saving ratio [age4064]	Dmnl	0.25	0.15
	saving ratio [age6589]	Dmnl	0.10	0.05

Fig. 5.14 Scenario 1: initialization of the growth sector
Source: own figure

Model Part "Utility"				
Description	**Variable**	**Unit**	**high**	**low**
initial accumulated utility stock	init U/N [age0014]	Utility/Person	1	1
per capita	init U/N [age1539]	Utility/Person	1	1
	init U/N [age4064]	Utility/Person	1	1
	init U/N [age6589]	Utility/Person	1	1
initial accumulated utility stock	init U/AN [age0014]	Utility/(Person*Patent)	1	1
per effective capita	init U/AN [age1539]	Utility/(Person*Patent)	1	1
	init U/AN [age4064]	Utility/(Person*Patent)	1	1
	init U/AN [age6589]	Utility/(Person*Patent)	1	1
Description	**Variable**	**Unit**	**Value**	
elasticity of marginal utility	theta	Dmnl	0.10	
time preference	sigma	Dmnl	0.20	
reference time	*reference time*	*Year*	50	

Fig. 5.15 Scenario 1: initialization of the utility sector
Source: own figure

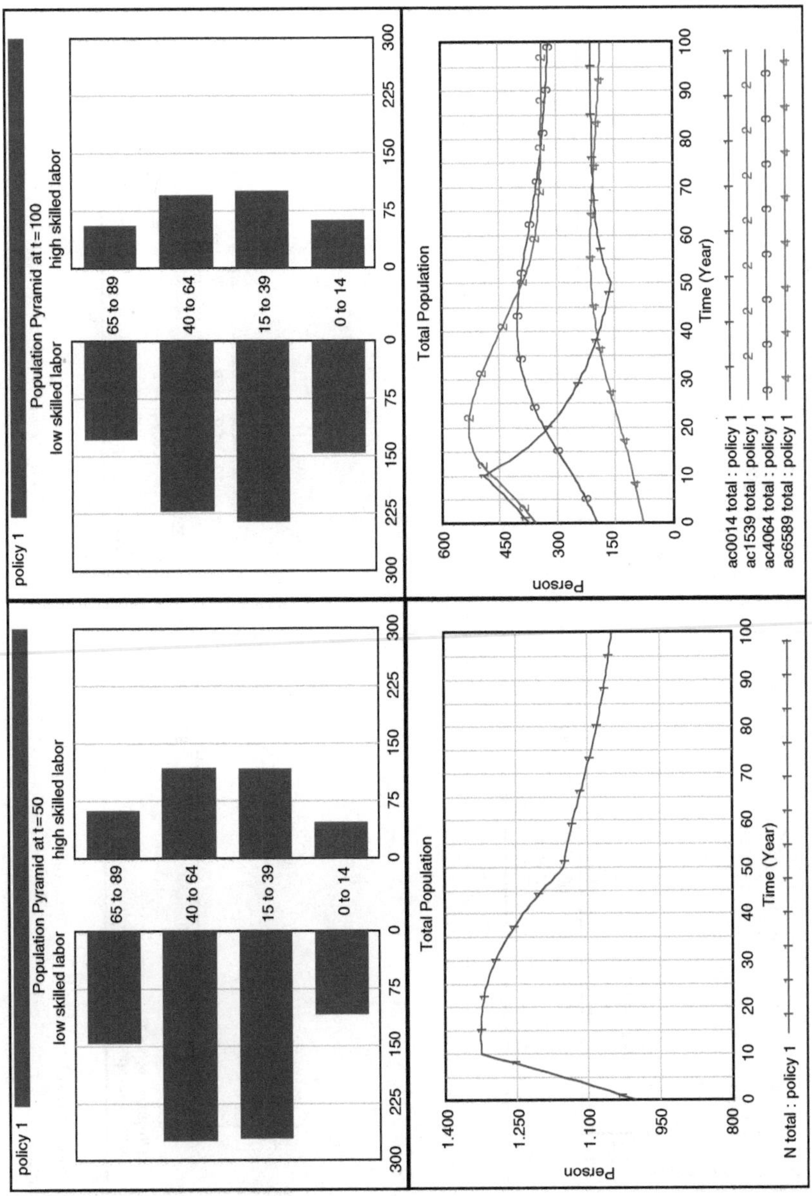

Fig. 5.16 Scenario 1: results total population
Source: own figure

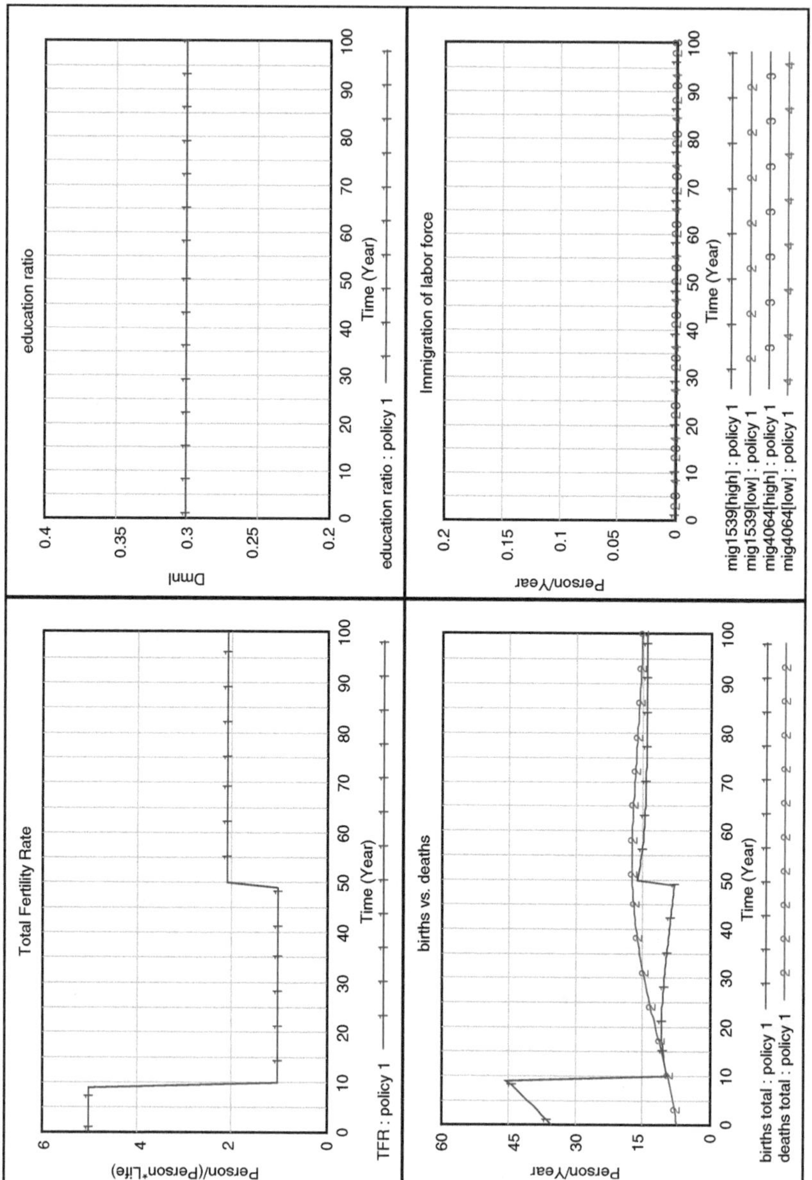

Fig. 5.17 Scenario 1: results changes in population sector
Source: own figure

The last set of graphs (Fig. 5.18) for the population sector shows again the dependency ratio and the Billeter J. The dependency ratio increases from t = 50 continuously and stabilizes around t = 80 at a level where three workers support two non-working people. As outlined earlier, the problem here is that the ratio indicates a stable relationship, whereas the population is still not in a steady state. This could be misleading.

The Billeter J shows that the deceptive stabilization of the dependency ratio is due to the outnumbering of young people compared to older ones, because it turns positive. It also indicates that the stabilization process is not finished yet, because it still rises (note, that the scale and the minor visible change could be misleading).

5.2.4 *Results R&D Sector*

The behavior of the patent stock does not differ much to the base run results (see Fig. 5.19). A minor difference can be seen at the right boundary of the simulation horizon. Due to the stabilization of the working population, the change in the patent stock levels out to a rate of 200 patents per year.

Nevertheless, the growth rate of the stock will continue to decline, because an increasing stock, feed by a constant value over time, leads to a decline of the ratio (delta A/A = gA). The phase plot in the lower right illustrates this. Each dot in the phase diagram indicates a time step. The slowing decline and following stabilization of high-skilled workers (Lh), decrease the space between two dots. If the simulation continued, one would see that the plotted-line runs vertically, parallel to the ordinate.

5.2.5 *Results Growth Sector*

The behavior of the important growth sector differs marginally to the base run. Taking the top left-hand graph in Fig. 5.20 one can recognize the still growing income per effective capita with increasing capital intensity per effective capita. Whereas a declining population leads to decelerating behavior, the now stable population induces the income per effective capita to accelerate the increase. This is due to the existing gap between real investments and required investments (lower left graph in Fig. 5.20). The needed investment increases after the rise of the total fertility rate, but not to the required level.

Theoretically, both the Jones-model and the author's constructed model are more general than Romer's endogenous growth model. Recapitulating theoretical aspects of Sect. 3.5, the Jones-model only shows a steady state for a growing population. In the case of a stable population Jones' model behaves like the Romer-model and does not show a steady state. Therefore, the Jones-model is called "semi-endogenous" to clarify the partial endogenity. One can conclude that

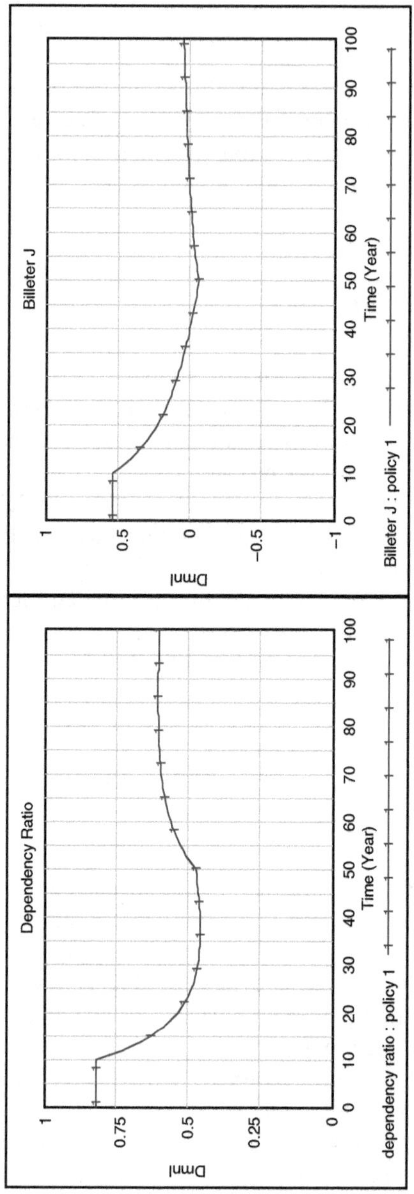

Fig. 5.18 Scenario 1: results population indicators
Source: own figure

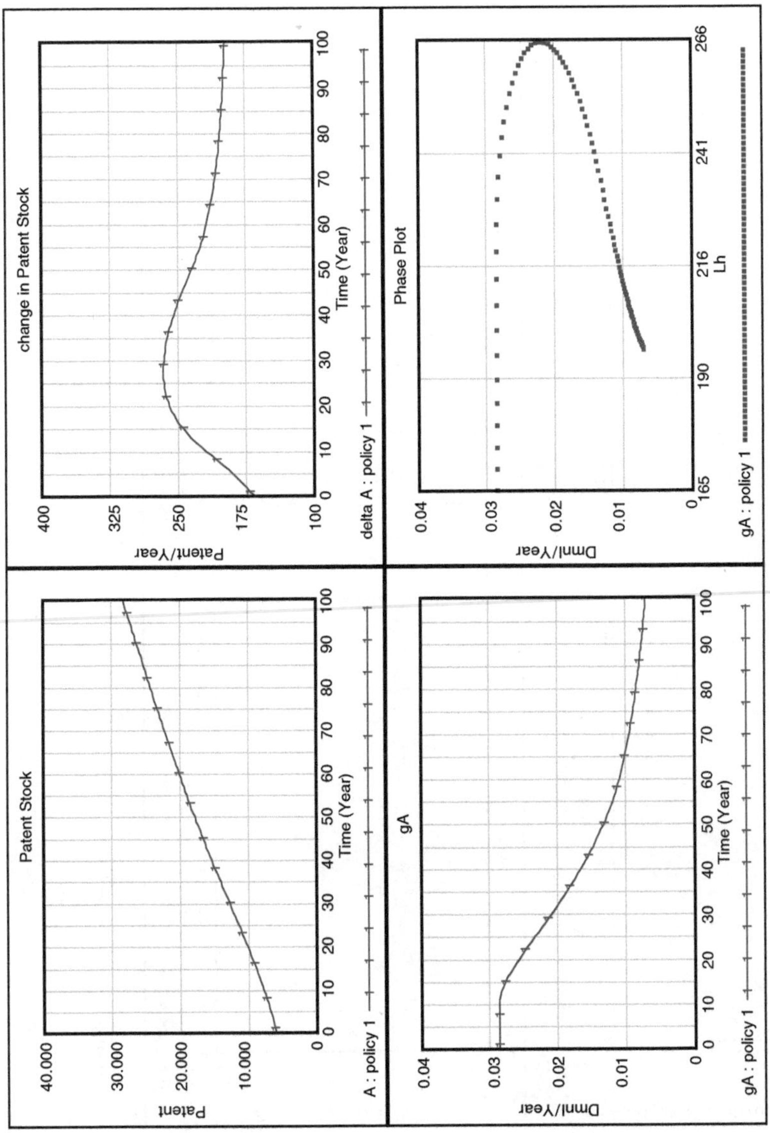

Fig. 5.19 Scenario 1: results R&D sector
Source: own figure

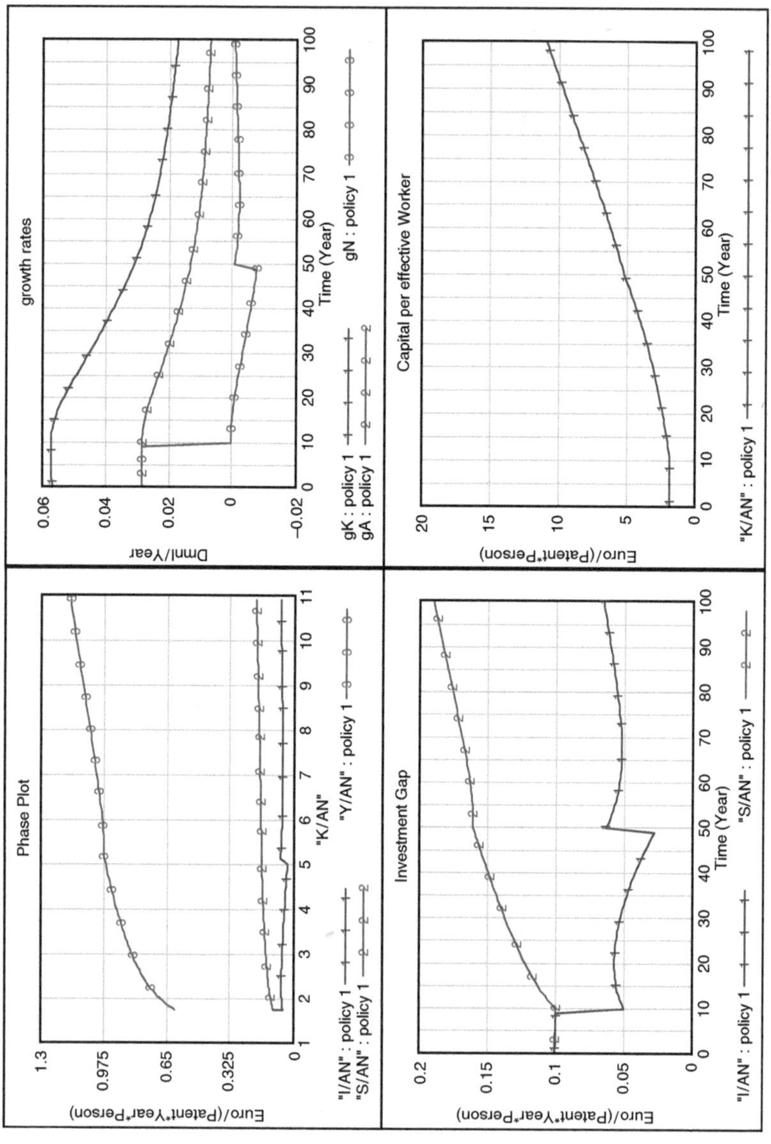

Fig. 5.20 Scenario 1: results growth sector
Source: own figure

the author's demographic growth model will not provide a steady state at all (top left-hand graph in Fig. 5.20).

Indeed, the growth rate of the population (gN) will increase to zero growth, but the patent stock growth rate (gA) will be positive in infinity. Thus, the whole model must grow (see gK in upper right graph). Hence, the capital intensity per effective labor will increase throughout the entire timeframe.

Figure 5.21 presents important per effective capita variables.

The decision point in t = 50 changes for all variables the marginal growth rate towards positive increasing. This means that stable populations will show an increase in all important growth sector variables similar to endogenous growth models.

For example, one can see the behavior of savings per effective capita in Fig. 5.22. The savings per age group behave differently. As in the base run the youngest age cohort shows zero savings. All other graphs have a turning point at t = 50 from accelerating to decelerating behavior. Longer simulation horizons reveal a short oscillating around a growing path above initial levels. This is due to the development in the population sector. It was previously mentioned that it takes longer than the simulation horizon to stabilize a population. The inherent delays in the population sector produce the oscillations.

5.2.6 *Results Utility Sector*

In the utility sector the changed reference point is visible in the accumulated total utility functions. Figure 5.23 presents these behaviors in the lower graphs. The discount of the utilities leads to an upper limit of the accumulated utility functions within the simulation period.

Both the utility per capita and the utility per effective capita rise with increasing rates after t = 50. The effect is comparable with the behavior of savings in the previous section. Thus, consumption increases over time, as there is no steady state. One divisor of the utility functions, namely the population, stabilizes and the other one, referred to as the patent stock, will continue with a smaller growth rate than the consumption. Hence, the ratio C/N and C/AN must increase.

5.2.7 *Summary and Conclusion*

In this section the first policy "family orientation" was introduced to overcome the population decline. This policy eventually stabilizes the population sector. However, it will take much longer than the simulation horizon. This leads to a dilemma for policy-makers: on the one hand, stabilization seems to be economically required, and on the other hand, they will not take credit for this policy during their incumbency (other positive aspects are neglected here). Positive effects of

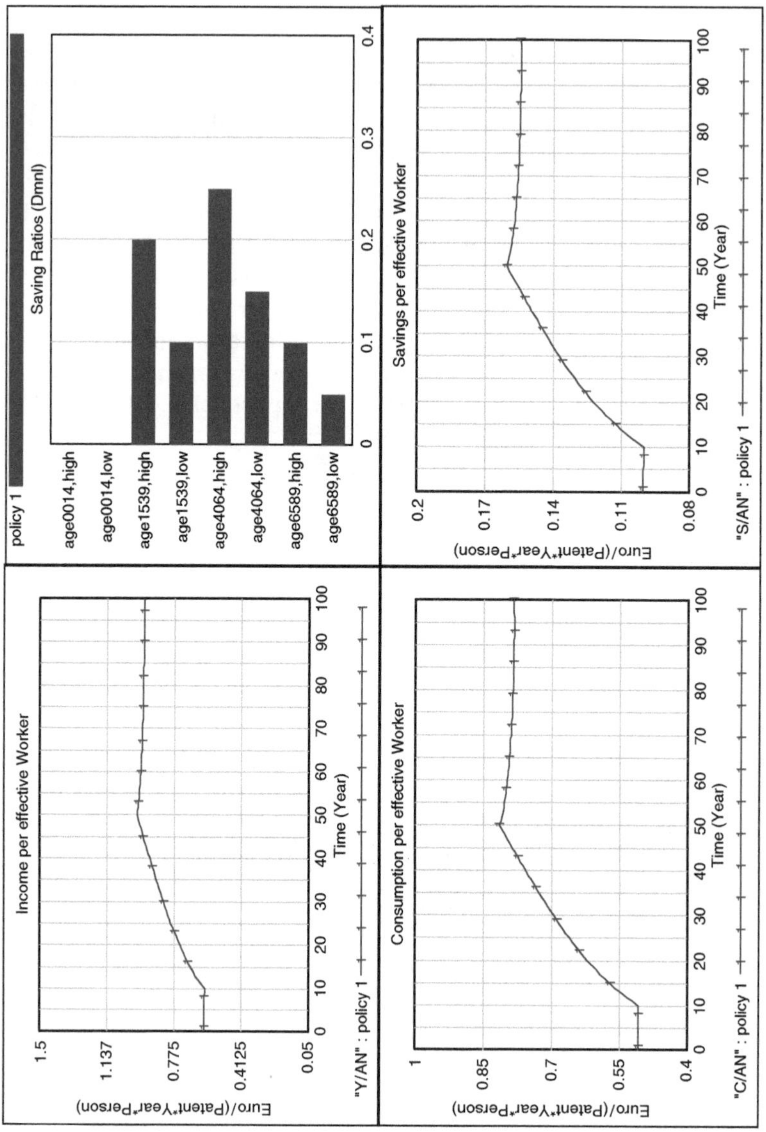

Fig. 5.21 Scenario 1: results per effective capita variables
Source: own figure

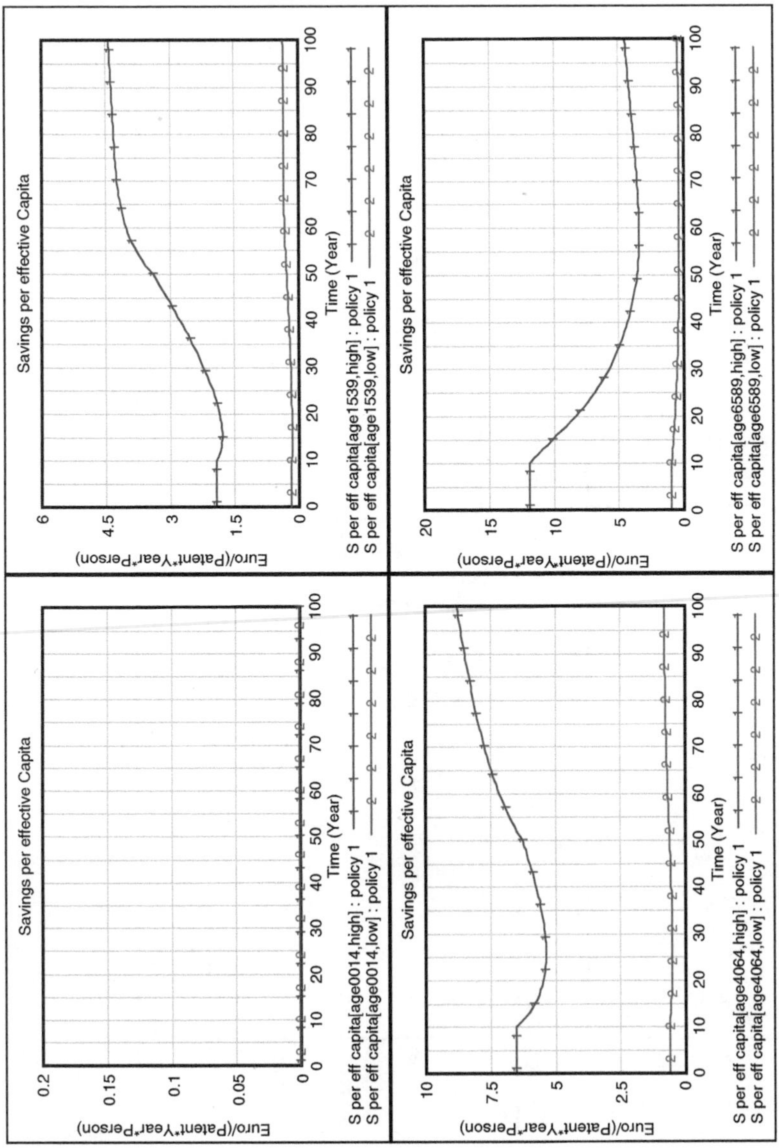

Fig. 5.22 Scenario 1: results savings per effective capita
Source: own figure

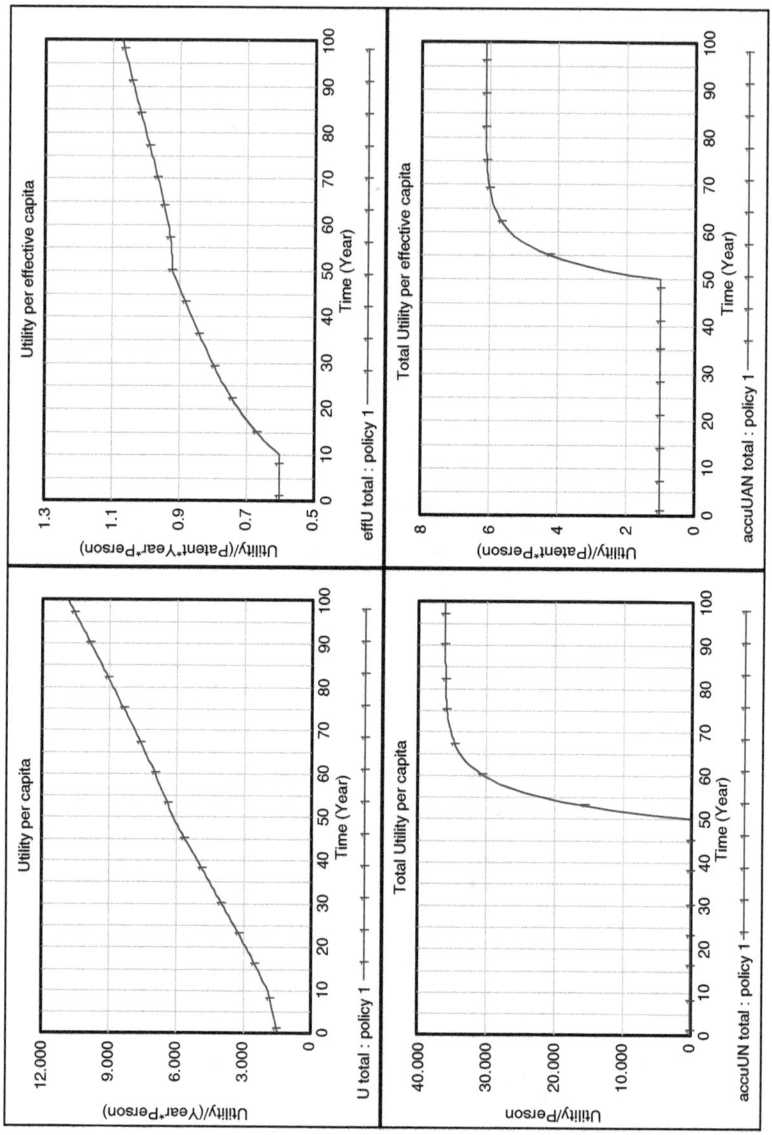

Fig. 5.23 Scenario 1: results utility sector
Source: own figure

increasing both, per capita and per effective capita values, reach the age groups at different points in time. Whereas the working population will have a positive effect within the simulation horizon, the oldest age group will not experience the positive effects of this policy.

The declining growth rate of the R&D sector cannot be stopped. The constant value of labor is not enough. Only an increase in high-skilled workers will lead to stable positive growth rates.

In general, the stabilization of the population is not enough, because the model does not show a new steady state. This is derived from the inherent model structure. Thus, one has to seek additional policies in order to achieve this effect.

5.3 Scenario 2 "Education Orientation"

5.3.1 Description

The previous scenario proved that stabilizing the population alone is not enough for an economy to reach a new steady state. Therefore, this scenario adds an education policy. At time t = 50 the education ratio changes for the 15-year old people, who are entering the workforce. Whereas the education ratio is 0.3 before t = 50, at t = 50 it rises to 0.5 until the simulation end. Hence, the percentage of high-skilled workers increases. However, the model does not consider additional governmental expenditures to finance this policy. The focus is more theoretical, and presents the question: Will family orientation with this education policy help overcome the disadvantages of an aging and shrinking economy?

5.3.2 Initialization

The initial values of the population sector follow the previous runs. But one can see in Fig. 5.24 that, in addition to the change in the total fertility rate, the education ratio shows a change.

The growth sector is identical to all previous runs. For the sake of completeness, Fig. 5.25 presents again the initial values.

For the utility sector it follows that the reference point is again t = 50. All other initial values are equal to previous runs. Figure 5.26 shows the summary of the initial utility values.

5.3.3 Results Population Sector

The population pyramid in the left-hand graph in Fig. 5.27 is already analyzed. The right-hand graph shows the simulation result at t = 100. One can recognize that

Model Part "Population"				
Description	**Variable**	**Unit**	**high**	**low**
initial value 0 to 14	init ac0014	Person	111.44	260.02
initial value 15 to 39	init ac1539	Person	106.36	248.17
initial value 40 to 64	init ac4064	Person	58.76	137.10
initial value 65 to 89	init ac6589	Person	23.45	54.72
migration 0 to 14	mig0014	Person/Year	0	0
migration 15 to 39	mig1539	Person/Year	0	0
migration 40 to 64	mig4064	Person/Year	0	0
migration 65 to 89	mig6589	Person/Year	0	0
capital per immigrant	mig capital	Euro/Person	0	0
Description	**Variable**	**Unit**	**Value**	
fractional death rate 0 to 14	fdr0014	Dmnl/Year	0.0050	
fractional death rate 15 to 39	fdr1539	Dmnl/Year	0.0348	
fractional death rate 40 to 64	fdr4064	Dmnl/Year	0.1000	
fractional death rate 65 to 89	fdr6589	Dmnl/Year	0.8000	
cohort size 0 to 14	size0014	Year	15	
cohort size 15 to 39	size1539	Year	25	
cohort size 40 to 64	size4064	Year	25	
cohort size 65 to 89	size6589	Year	25	
total fertility rate at t=50	*TFR*	*Person/Person*	*2.08*	
sex ratio female	female ratio	Dmnl	0.5	
education ratio at t=50	*education ratio*	*Dmnl*	*0.5*	

Fig. 5.24 Scenario 2: initialization of the population sector
Source: own figure

Model Part "Growth"				
Description	**Variable**	**Unit**	**Value**	
initial patent stock	*init A*	*Patent*	5.809	*calculated*
initial capital stock	*init K*	*Euro*	10.228.816	*calculated*
partial production elasticity of capital	alpha	Dmnl	0.3	
depletion rate	delta	Dmnl/Year	0	
degree of congestion	lambda	Dmnl	1	
return on stocks of ideas	phi	Dmnl	0	
accelerator	rho	Dmnl	1	
Description	**Variable**	**Unit**	**Value**	
wage age distribution	wage age [age0014]	Dmnl	0.00	
	wage age [age1539]	Dmnl	1.00	
	wage age [age4064]	Dmnl	1.50	
	wage age [age6589]	Dmnl	0.60	
Description	**Variable**	**Unit**	**high**	
wage level of high skilled worker	wage level	Dmnl	1.25	
Description	**Variable**	**Unit**	**high**	**low**
saving ratio	saving ratio [age0014]	Dmnl	0.00	0.00
	saving ratio [age1539]	Dmnl	0.20	0.10
	saving ratio [age4064]	Dmnl	0.25	0.15
	saving ratio [age6589]	Dmnl	0.10	0.05

Fig. 5.25 Scenario 2: initialization of the growth sector
Source: own figure

Model Part "Utility"

Description	Variable	Unit	high	low
initial accumulated utility stock	init U/N [age0014]	Utility/Person	1	1
per capita	init U/N [age1539]	Utility/Person	1	1
	init U/N [age4064]	Utility/Person	1	1
	init U/N [age6589]	Utility/Person	1	1
initial accumulated utility stock	init U/AN [age0014]	Utility/(Person*Patent)	1	1
per effective capita	init U/AN [age1539]	Utility/(Person*Patent)	1	1
	init U/AN [age4064]	Utility/(Person*Patent)	1	1
	init U/AN [age6589]	Utility/(Person*Patent)	1	1

Description	Variable	Unit	Value
elasticity of marginal utility	theta	Dmnl	0.10
time preference	sigma	Dmnl	0.20
reference time	*reference time*	*Year*	50

Fig. 5.26 Scenario 2: initialization of the utility sector
Source: own figure

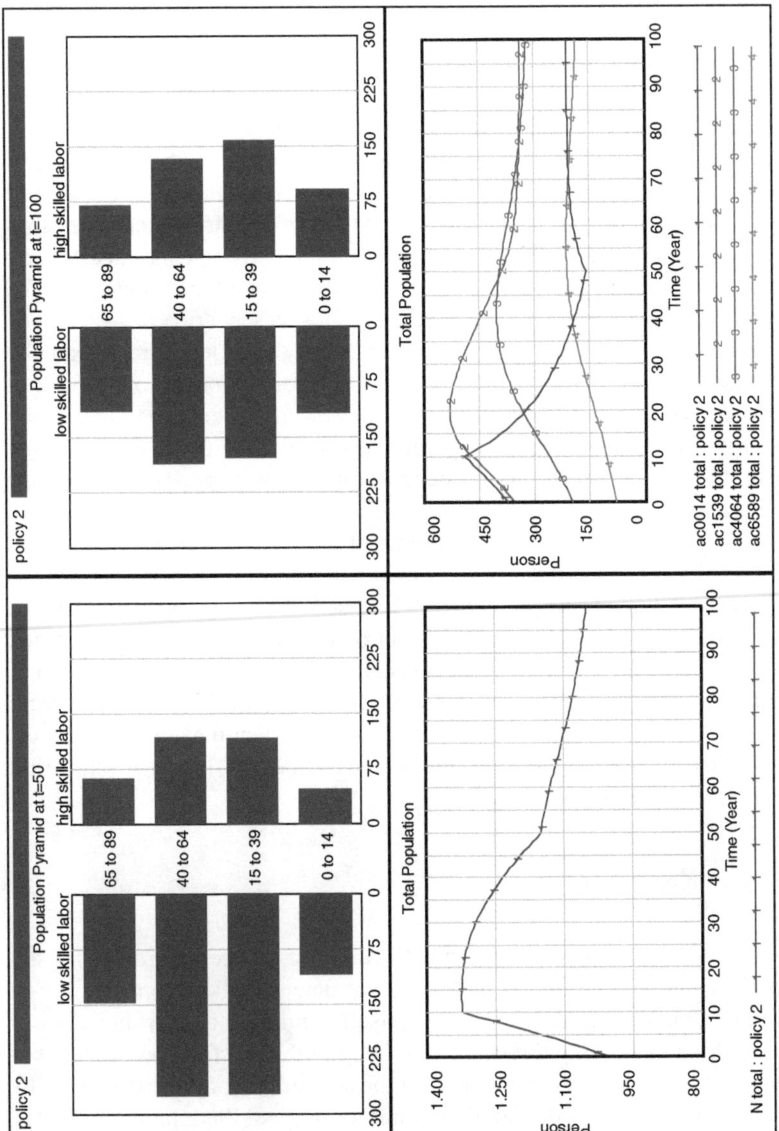

Fig. 5.27 Scenario 2: results total population
Source: own figure

both population streams of high- and low-skilled workers approach each other. Whereas the timeframe of 50 years is almost enough to equalize the number of high-skilled and low-skilled people in the age groups ac0014 and ac1539, the number of high- and low-skilled in the two last age cohorts is still unequally distributed. Eventually both streams will be equal; however it will take at least another generation to attain this.

The total number of people (lower left graph) does not differ to the previous run, because the total number of workers equals the scenario 1. This can only be different if the total fertility rate of high- and low-skilled labor is varied. Therefore, the disaggregation into separated age groups must be identical to the scenario 1.

Figure 5.28 concentrates on the in- and outflows. One can see the u-shaped change of the total fertility rate, as already known from scenario 1, and the step-change of the education ratio at $t = 50$. Only the total fertility rate has an effect on the number of births (see lower left graph). For the sake of completeness, the immigration is also shown, but does not take place in this scenario.

The key indicators for the population sector – the dependency ratio and the Billeter J – must be equal to scenario 1, because the population in total does not differ (see Fig. 5.29). The stabilization through the family orientation takes place since $t = 50$ and shifts both indicators upwards. Around $t = 70$ the youngest age cohort exceeds the number of the oldest people, but the process will continue for two more generations.

The Fig. 5.30 is new and will bridge the next section. It shows the total amount of high- and low-skilled workers and how they evolve over time. The top graph is the consolidated stock of the age cohorts ac1539 and ac4064. One can see that high-skilled labor increases due to the policy introduction and the low-skilled labor stock continuously declines. This adaption process is caused by the instant equalization of both flows of new entrants of the job market ("to work[skill]", lower left-hand graph). However, the adjustment process is not finished when the simulation ends, because the outflow of the two skill groups into retirement differs still ("to retire [skill]", lower right-hand graph).

5.3.4 Results R&D Sector

The number of high-skilled labor is the most important source of growth for the patent stock. It channels directly into the change of patent stock, as one can see in the top right-hand graph in Fig. 5.31. The stock itself continues to grow, but a closer look at the growth rate chart of gA reveals that the growth rate still slows down, but in smaller steps. This is due to the fact that after the adjustment of the different skills within the population sector, the total amount of high-skilled labor will stay constant over time. It is insufficient to let the patent stock grow with the current constant values of phi, rho and lambda. The phase plot turns right as the number of high-skilled labor increases, but it already slows down (shown by increasing space between the dots), similar to that of the scenario 1. Eventually the dotted line will move downwards, parallel to the y-axis.

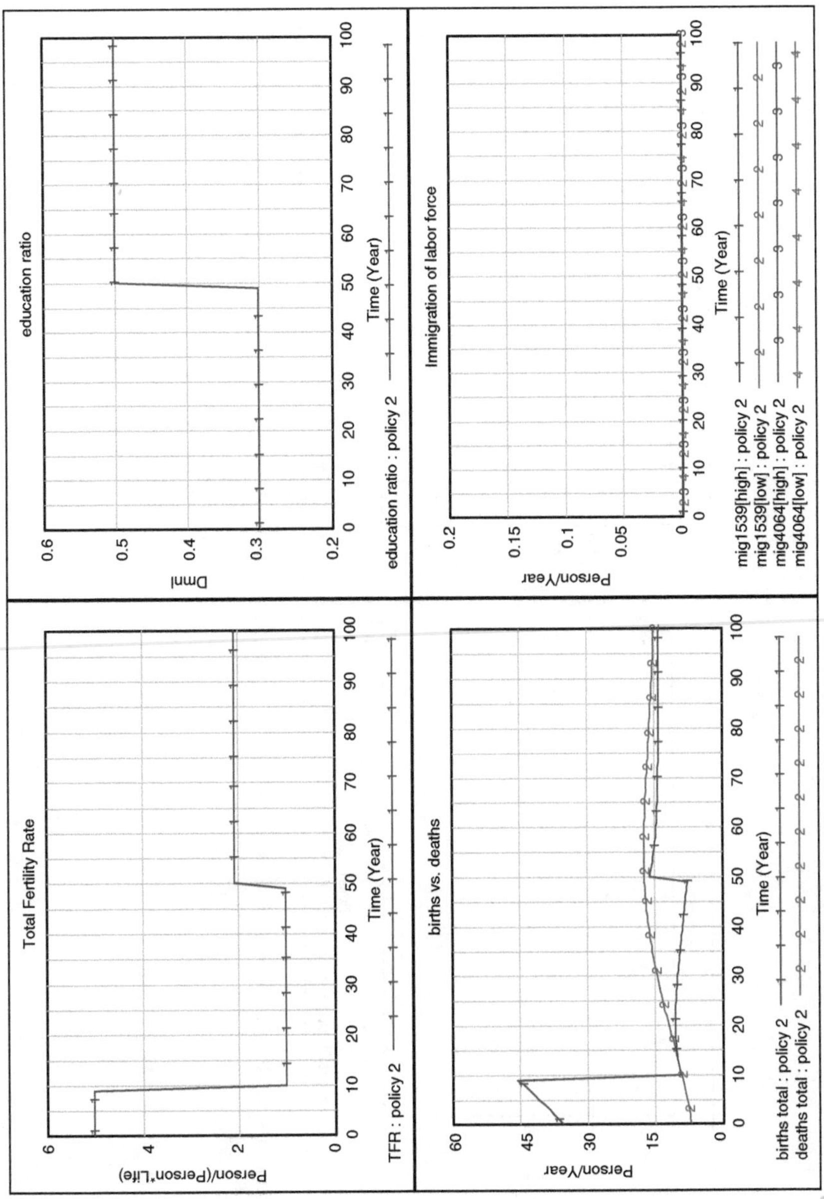

Fig. 5.28 Scenario 2: results changes in population sector
Source: own figure

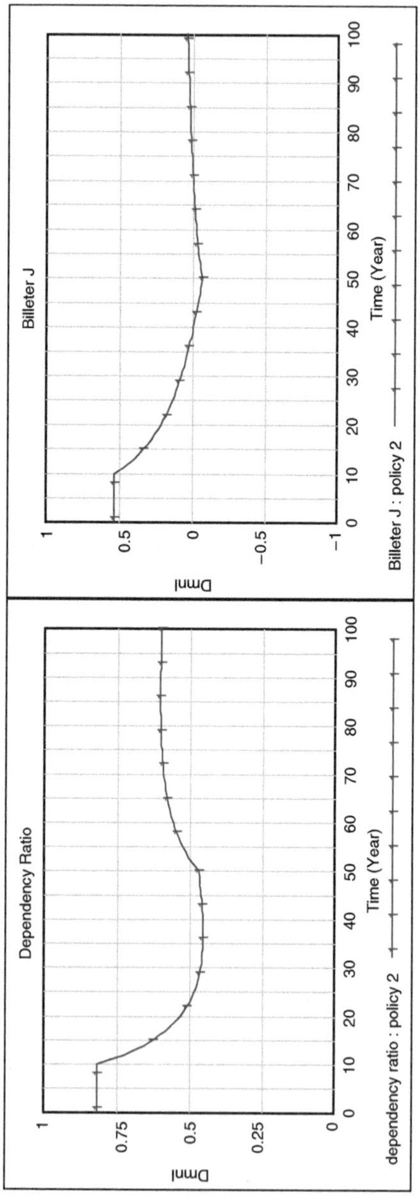

Fig. 5.29 Scenario 2: results population indicators
Source: own figure

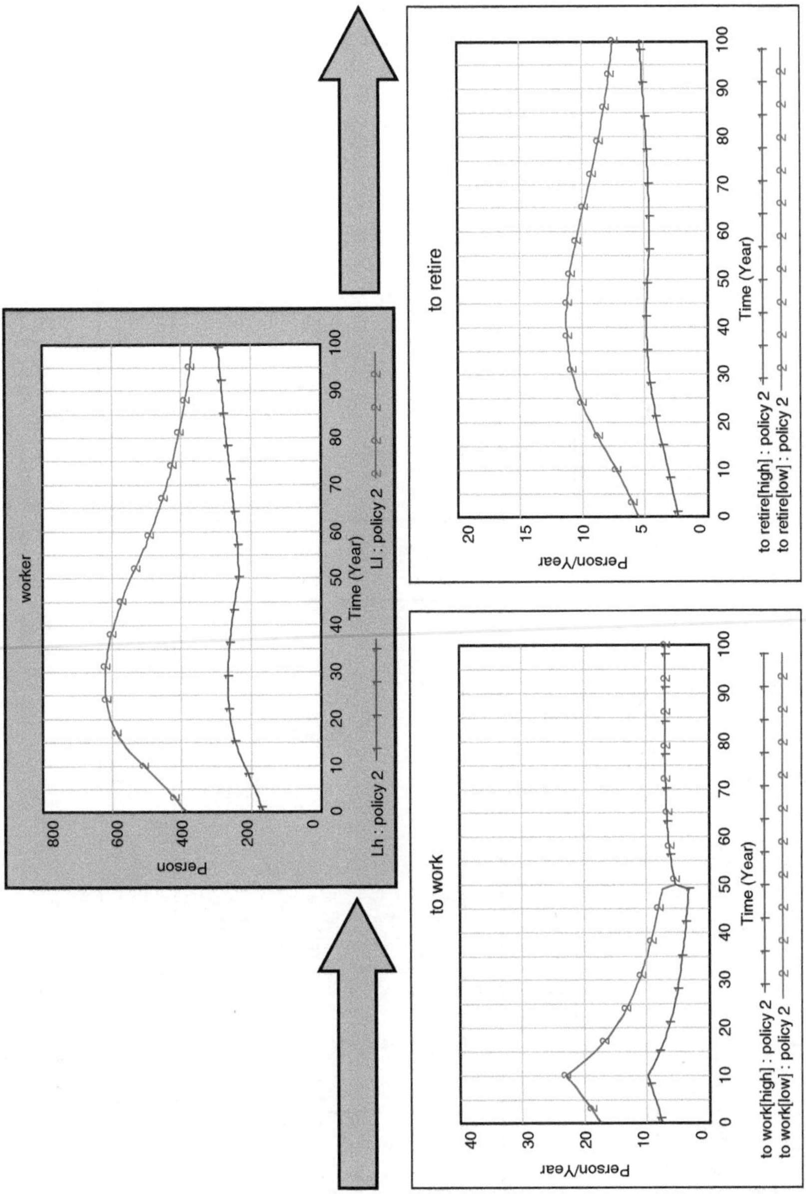

Fig. 5.30 Scenario 2: results high- and low-skilled workers
Source: own figure

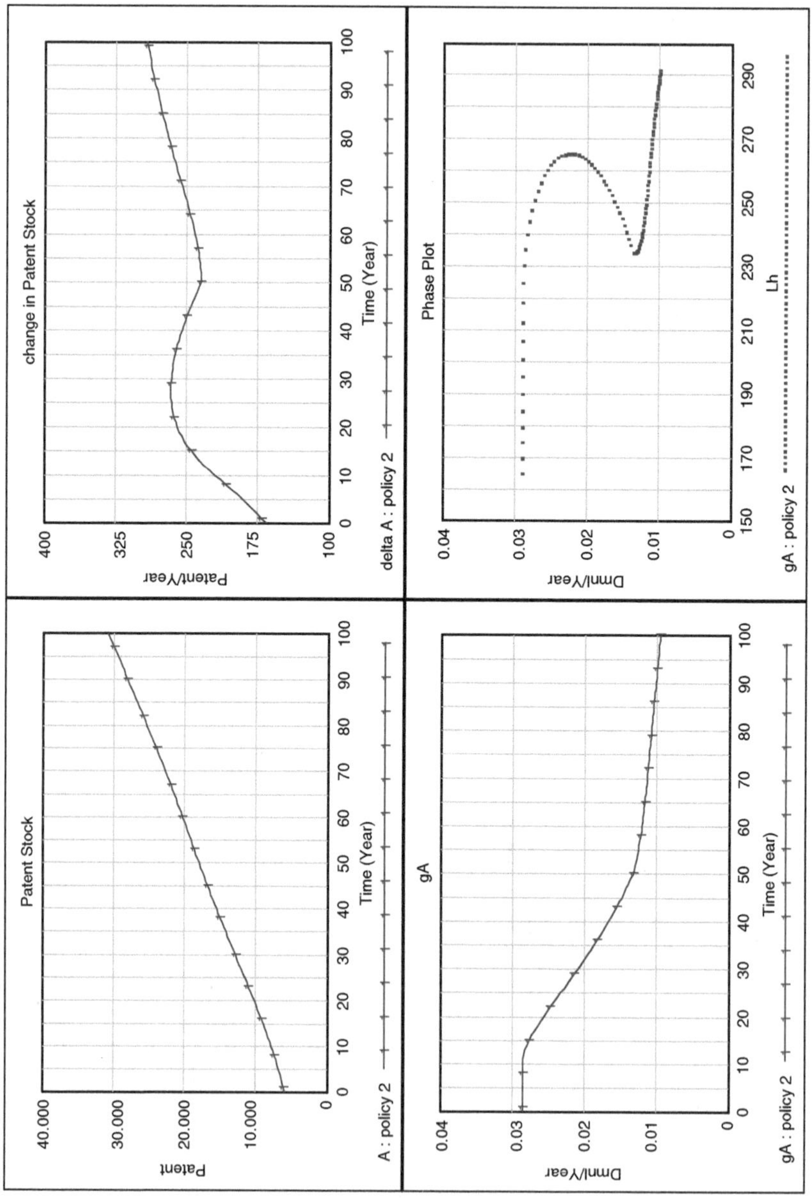

Fig. 5.31 Scenario 2: results R&D sector
Source: own figure

5.3.5 Results Growth Sector

The growth sector behavior differs from the base run and the scenario 1. In Fig. 5.32 one can see that the investment gap in the lower left graph declines, due to the decline in real investments per capita. This is mainly caused by the increase in the patent stock. Additionally, it forces the ratio S/AN to lower values. But the increase in the patent stock has another effect. The requirement line (I/AN) depends on the growth of population and on the growth of the patent stock. Because the population does not grow both the patent stock and the required investments shift upwards. Hence, the investment gap declines (technically it is a negative investment gap, because of the exceeding real investments). The capital investment per effective capita must also be lower than in scenario 1 because of the increased patent stock. Positive to note is that a stronger growth in the R&D sector increases the overall growth rate of the capital stock (see upper right graph in Fig. 5.32).

The influence of the additional patent growth on the major per effective capita variables is shown in Fig. 5.33. The saving rates are still the same, but the patent stock growth forces all per effective capita variables to shrink compared to scenario 1. Nevertheless, this negative outcome might have also positive effects: A lower value in these variables does not automatically imply a lower per capita value. Indeed, it is possible that the ratio of the per capita variables also increase. For this to occur, it would be necessary that the more intensified usage of high-skilled workers leads to the additional growth of the R&D sector. Based on Jones' recommendation, the patent sector's exogenFigous constants will not happen here; since the value of phi, for the accelerating growth is set to zero. But for values of $\varphi > 0$ the R&D loop reinforces growth in the patent stock. Additionally, high-skilled labor leads to higher growth rates.

In the case of $\varphi = 0$ one expects the disaggregated savings per effective capita in the different age cohorts to have negative outcomes. This is drastically visible in all of the graphs in. Fig. 5.34.

The increase of the savings in the cohorts ac1539 and ac4064 produces a strong counter reaction of the trend. After the introduction of the policy in $t = 50$ the upwards trend is broken. For the last cohort, it follows that the long delay in the population of the upwards trend has not yet begun.

5.3.6 Results Utility Sector

The previous comments illustrate the more or less negative effect of an increasing patent stock. This continues in the utility sector. Due to a lower per capita and per effective capita consumption the utility sector suffers also from these values. In the upper graphs in Fig. 5.35 one can observe the decline after the introduction of the policy.

Nevertheless, these graphs also show positive outcomes. Because of the strong discount of future utilities the accumulated utility values for both types (per capita

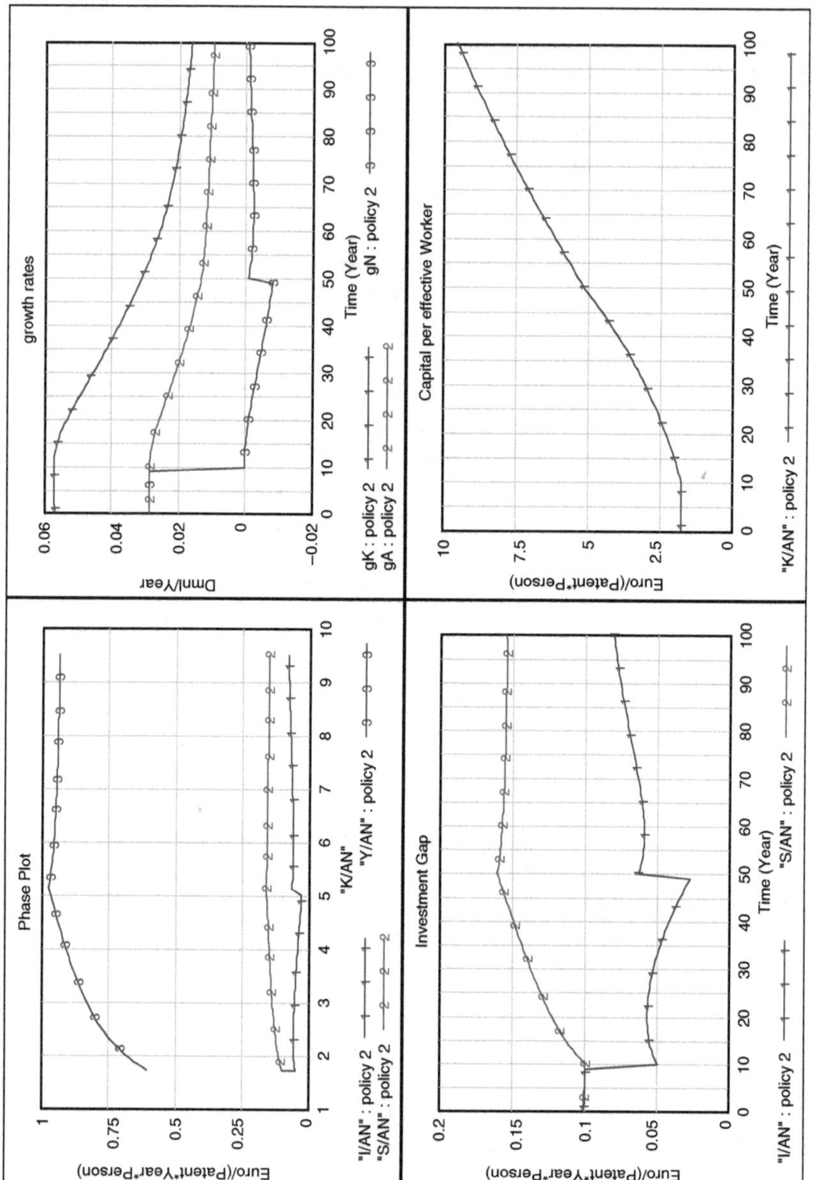

Fig. 5.32 Scenario 2: results growth sector
Source: own figure

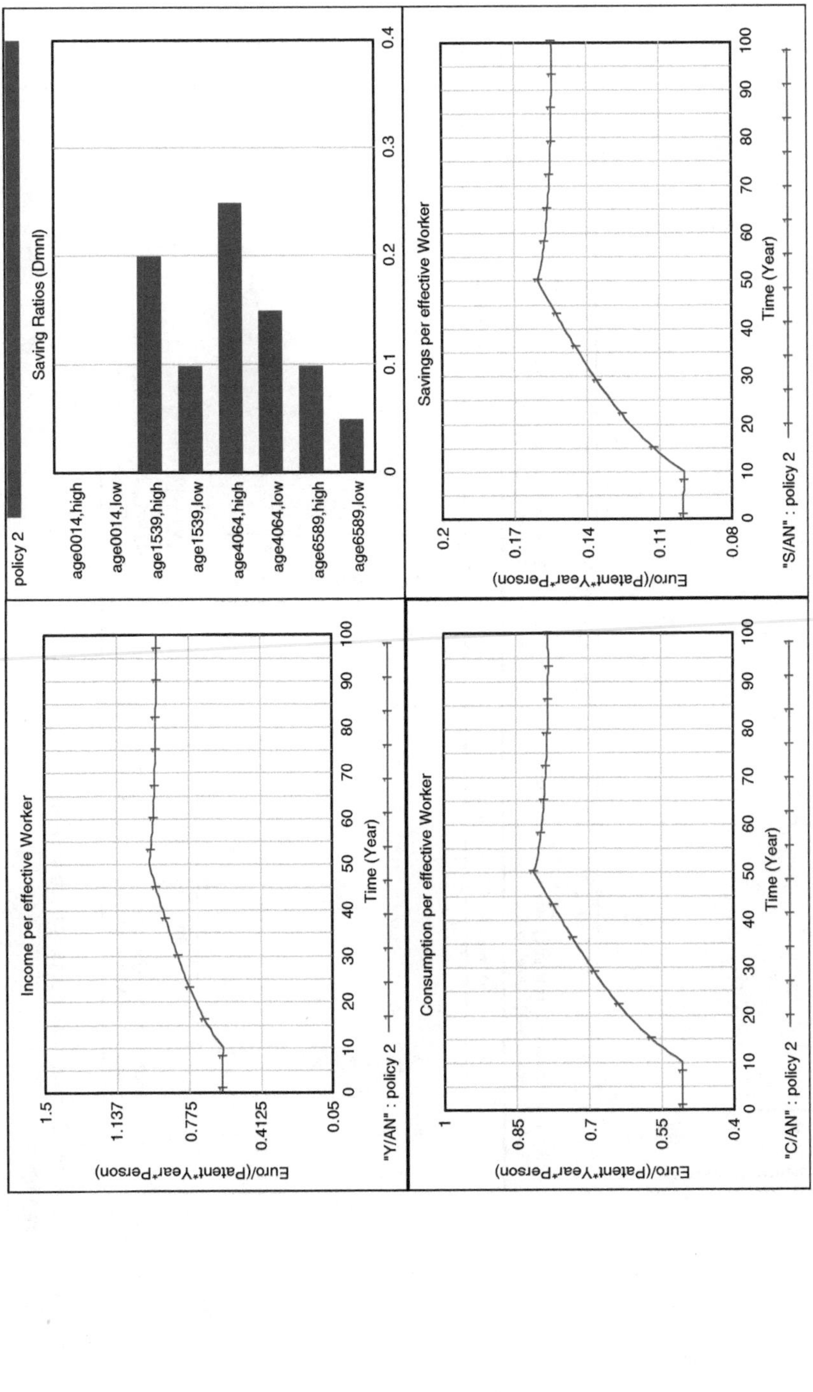

Fig. 5.33 Scenario 2: results per effective capita variables
Source: own figure

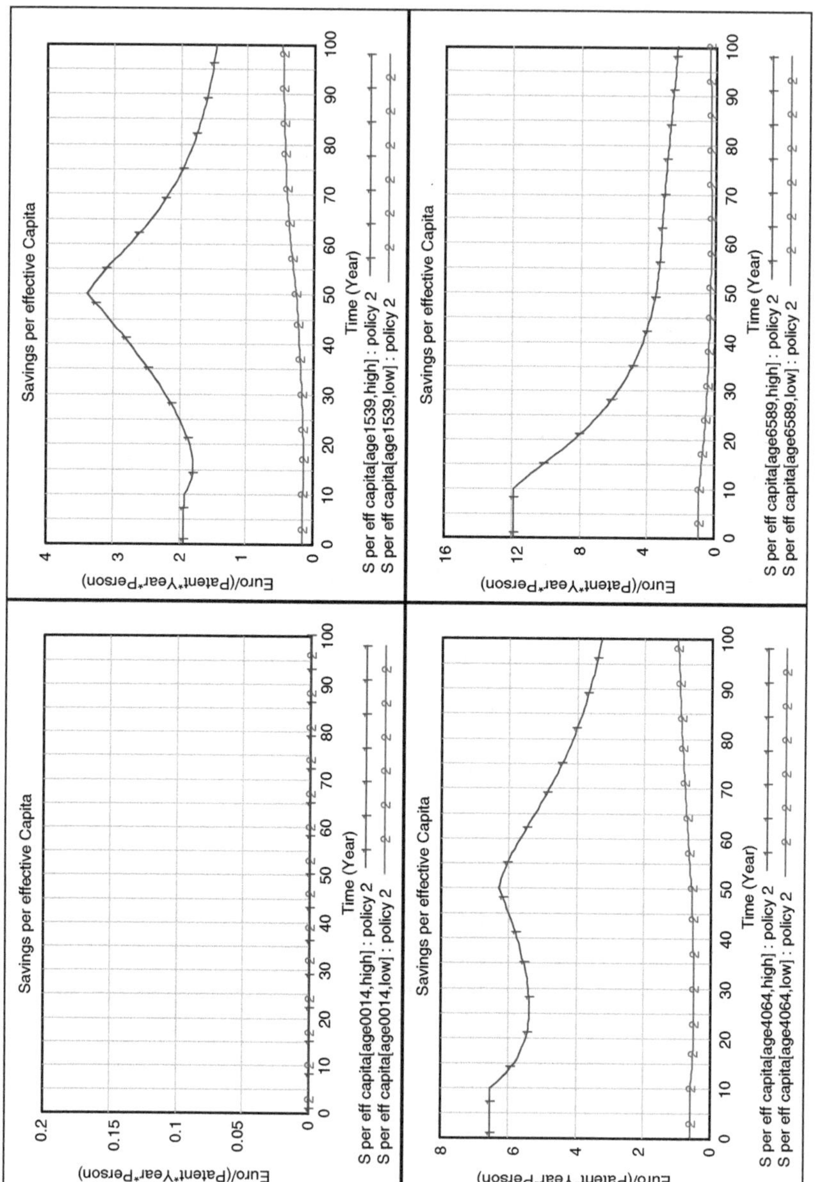

Fig. 5.34 Scenario 2: results savings per effective capita
Source: own figure

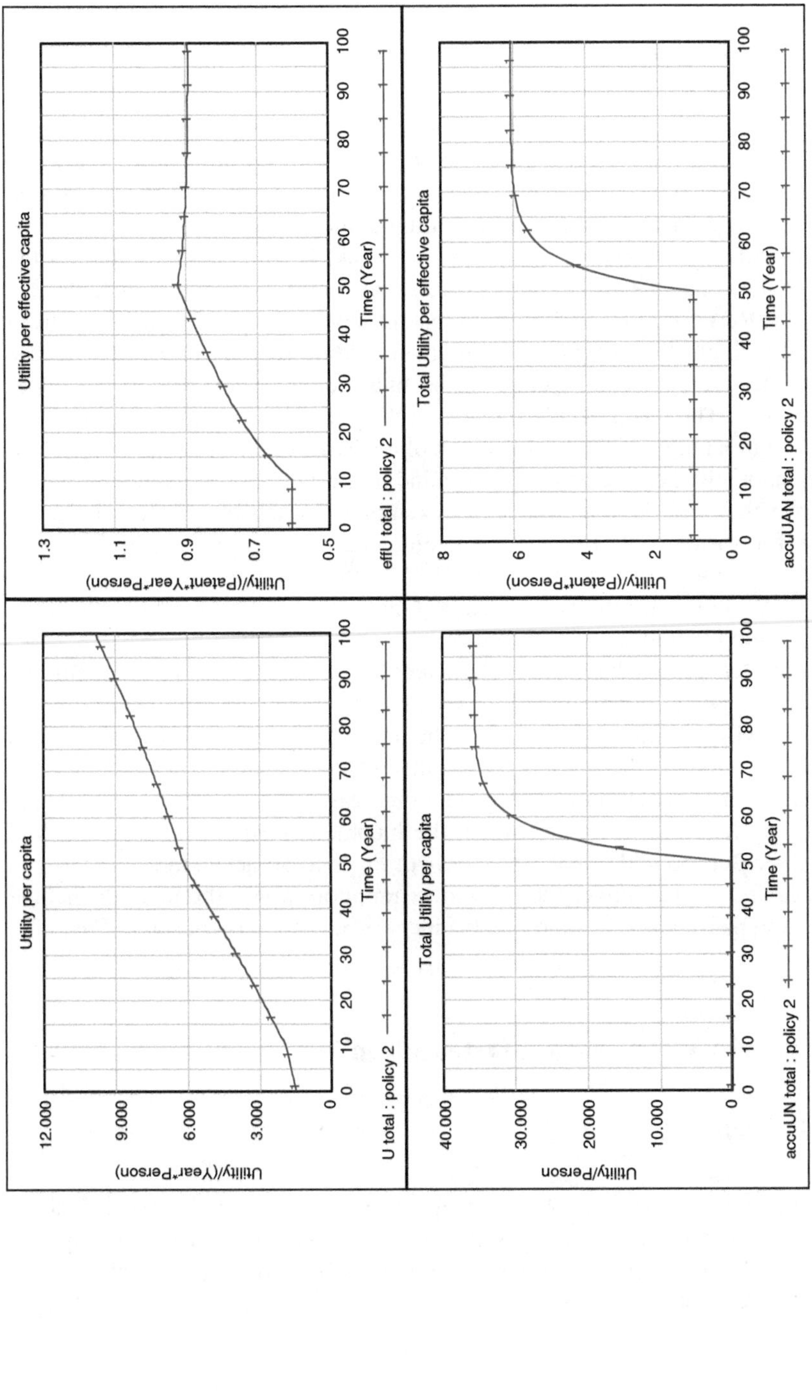

Fig. 5.35 Scenario 2: results utility sector
Source: own figure

and per effective capita) do not decline to a larger extent. Hence, policy-makers would favor scenario 2 if they find additional not-modeled promoting arguments.

5.3.7 Summary and Conclusion

This scenario reflects the impact of an additional education policy, in connection with a family policy. At first, one might think that this would show positive effects, because education is usually considered as important. However, these positive effects of $\varphi > 0$ are not explicitly reflected in the model.

Jones disabled the R&D loop in the patent stock. But this loop accelerates the creation of new patents, because engineers can build on existing patents. By enabling the R&D loop to reinforce the patent stock the transfer in labor, from low-skilled to high-skilled workers, can create additional growth effects. Such a growth would overcome the decline in the final goods sector, due to the lower number of labor The result of this shows that the per effective capita variables are lower than without the presented education policy. However, the per capita variables would dramatically increase as the "compound interest effect" evolved over time.

To prove this, Fig. 5.36 shows major exemplary variables and their behavior over time for various sets of φ. At the reference time $t = 50$ phi is set to six different values ranging from 0.00 to 0.25. All other settings are consistent with scenario 2. These sensitivity runs illustrate how an increase in education with an active R&D loop will affect the system.

The upper left graph shows how the patent stock benefits from this additional growth. Small changes in phi reinforce the patent stock dramatically. Therefore, the growth rates will also increase. But since the number of high-skilled workers does not grow continuously, the major disadvantage of the scenario 2 also applies: the growth effects are only temporary. Due to an increasing patent stock (A) all ratios depending on the stock as, for example, the income per effective capita (Y/AN) must decline. But the additional R&D growth leads to an acceleration of the per capita variables. Hence, under the relaxed assumption of $\varphi > 0$ one can conclude that education matters. As an example, the income per capita is chosen in Fig. 5.36.

5.4 Scenario 3 "Migration Orientation"

5.4.1 Description

The previous scenario showed, firstly, that higher education will project positive effects only if the patent sector enables accelerating growth. Second, the step-by-step entrance of additional high-skilled workers to the R&D sector creates a delay before the patent stock substantially grows.

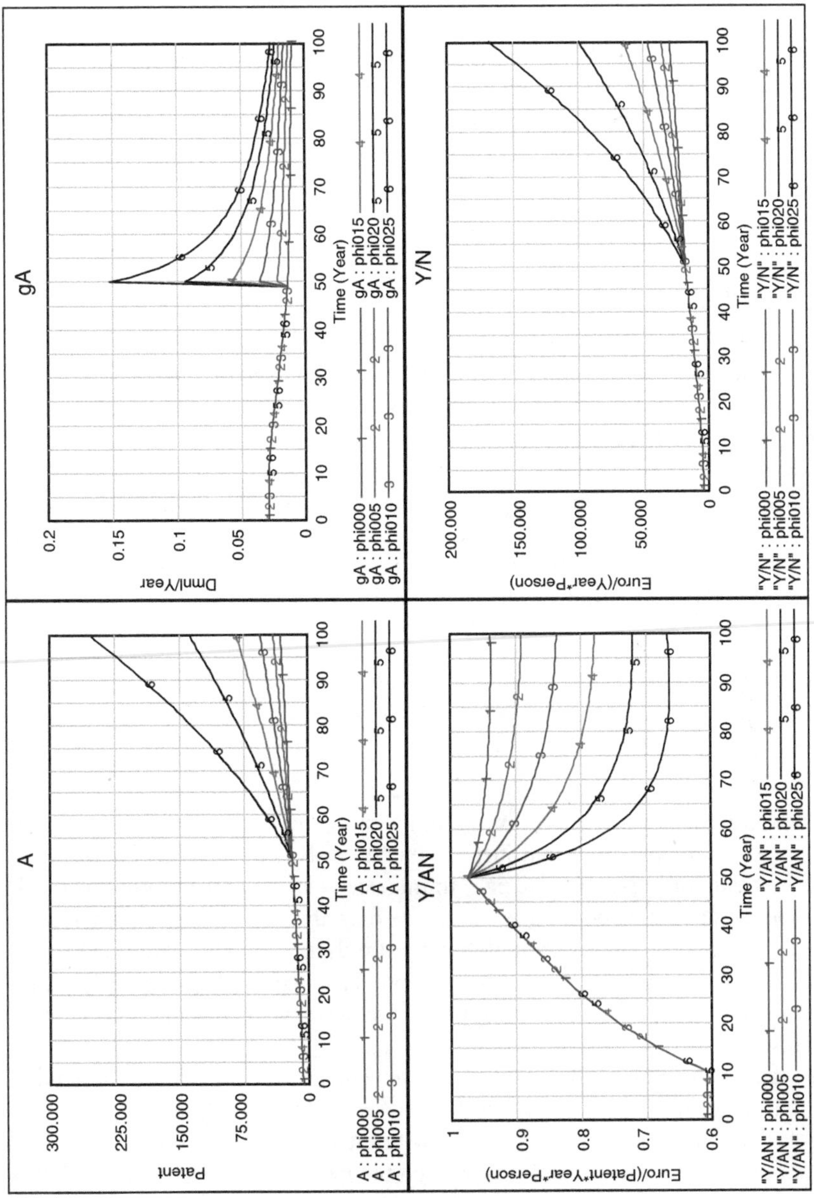

Fig. 5.36 Scenario 2: results sensitivity run R&D sector
Source: own figure

An intermediate solution, until the education policy reaches significant effects, could be immigration, which can easily overcome this delayed growth. Scenario 3 is dedicated to this idea and is founded on the scenario 1. At t = 50, the total fertility rate stabilizes again at the replacement level. New in this scenario is that 40 person per year immigrate to the considered economy. One assumes that every migrant brings capital with them. The migration flow is possible for all age groups, but for simplicity this model assumes that only the working age groups ac1539 and ac4064, subdivided into the two types of skills, move. This leads to an inflow of 10 persons per year per cohort type. It is also be possible for people to migrate with their children, but to keep this policy simple this is neglected here.

5.4.2 Initialization

Figure 5.37 presents the initial values in the population sector. One can see that migration is enabled, but only in the working age cohorts. Each immigrant brings the amount of 10,000 Euros with them. Additionally, the fertility rate increases to 2.08 at t = 50.

The growth sector does not change from the previous runs. Figure 5.38 shows phi as the variable for the return of ideas in the patent stock at 0, just as Jones did.

Finally, for the sake of completeness, the utility sector is presented with all exogenous constants and initial values in Fig. 5.39. Again, the reference time is set to 50.

5.4.3 Results Population Sector

From a demographer's perspective, migration is extremely powerful. In this model it is decoupled from any stocks and just set exogenously. From t = 50 forward, 40 people (4% of the initial population size) immigrate per year and already this small number changes the entire population structure over the course of one generation. Figure 5.40 reflects this. The two population pyramids are set to the same scale. One can see the dramatic increase in the population. The lower left graph shows that within one generation the population triples. The two working age cohorts dominate the population.

As the number of high- and low-skilled immigrants is symmetrical, the education ratio will temporarily change from 0.3 (caused by the initialization) to a more balancing ratio. But this effect will ease off with the declining ratio of migration to the total population. Finally, it will again reach the ratio of 0.3. One cannot see this whole effect in the simulation run as the time horizon is too short.

The next set of graphs in Fig. 5.41 shows the setting of exogenous values. The TFR increases, but the education ratio stays constant. Immigration, in the lower right-hand graph, shows the stacked values for the different migration flows.

Model Part "Population"				
Description	**Variable**	**Unit**	**high**	**low**
initial value 0 to 14	init ac0014	Person	111.44	260.02
initial value 15 to 39	init ac1539	Person	106.36	248.17
initial value 40 to 64	init ac4064	Person	58.76	137.10
initial value 65 to 89	init ac6589	Person	23.45	54.72
migration 0 to 14 at t=50	*mig0014*	*Person/Year*	0	0
migration 15 to 39 at t=50	*mig1539*	*Person/Year*	10	10
migration 40 to 64 at t=50	*mig4064*	*Person/Year*	10	10
migration 65 to 89 at t=50	*mig6589*	*Person/Year*	0	0
capital per immigrant at t=50	*mig capital*	*Euro/Person*	10.000	10.000
Description	**Variable**	**Unit**	**Value**	
fractional death rate 0 to 14	fdr0014	Dmnl/Year	0.0050	
fractional death rate 15 to 39	fdr1539	Dmnl/Year	0.0348	
fractional death rate 40 to 64	fdr4064	Dmnl/Year	0.1000	
fractional death rate 65 to 89	fdr6589	Dmnl/Year	0.8000	
cohort size 0 to 14	size0014	Year	15	
cohort size 15 to 39	size1539	Year	25	
cohort size 40 to 64	size4064	Year	25	
cohort size 65 to 89	size6589	Year	25	
total fertility rate at t=50	*TFR*	*Person/Person*	2.08	
sex ratio female	female ratio	Dmnl	0.5	
education ratio	education ratio	Dmnl	0.3	

Fig. 5.37 Scenario 3: initialization of the population sector
Source: own figure

Model Part "Growth"				
Description	**Variable**	**Unit**	**Value**	
initial patent stock	*init A*	*Patent*	5.809	*calculated*
initial capital stock	*init K*	*Euro*	10.228.816	*calculated*
partial production elasticity of capital	alpha	Dmnl	0.3	
depletion rate	delta	Dmnl/Year	0	
degree of congestion	lambda	Dmnl	1	
return on stocks of ideas	phi	Dmnl	0	
accelerator	rho	Dmnl	1	
Description	**Variable**	**Unit**	**Value**	
wage age distribution	wage age [age0014]	Dmnl	0.00	
	wage age [age1539]	Dmnl	1.00	
	wage age [age4064]	Dmnl	1.50	
	wage age [age6589]	Dmnl	0.60	
Description	**Variable**	**Unit**	**high**	
wage level of high skilled worker	wage level	Dmnl	1.25	
Description	**Variable**	**Unit**	**high**	**low**
saving ratio	saving ratio [age0014]	Dmnl	0.00	0.00
	saving ratio [age1539]	Dmnl	0.20	0.10
	saving ratio [age4064]	Dmnl	0.25	0.15
	saving ratio [age6589]	Dmnl	0.10	0.05

Fig. 5.38 Scenario 3: initialization of the growth sector
Source: own figure

Model Part "Utility"

Description	Variable	Unit	high	low
initial accumulated utility stock	init U/N [age0014]	Utility/Person	1	1
per capita	init U/N [age1539]	Utility/Person	1	1
	init U/N [age4064]	Utility/Person	1	1
	init U/N [age6589]	Utility/Person	1	1
initial accumulated utility stock	init U/AN [age0014]	Utility/(Person*Patent)	1	1
per effective capita	init U/AN [age1539]	Utility/(Person*Patent)	1	1
	init U/AN [age4064]	Utility/(Person*Patent)	1	1
	init U/AN [age6589]	Utility/(Person*Patent)	1	1
Description	**Variable**	**Unit**	**Value**	
elasticity of marginal utility	theta	Dmnl	0.10	
time preference	sigma	Dmnl	0.20	
reference time	*reference time*	*Year*	50	

Fig. 5.39 Scenario 3: initialization of the utility sector
Source: own figure

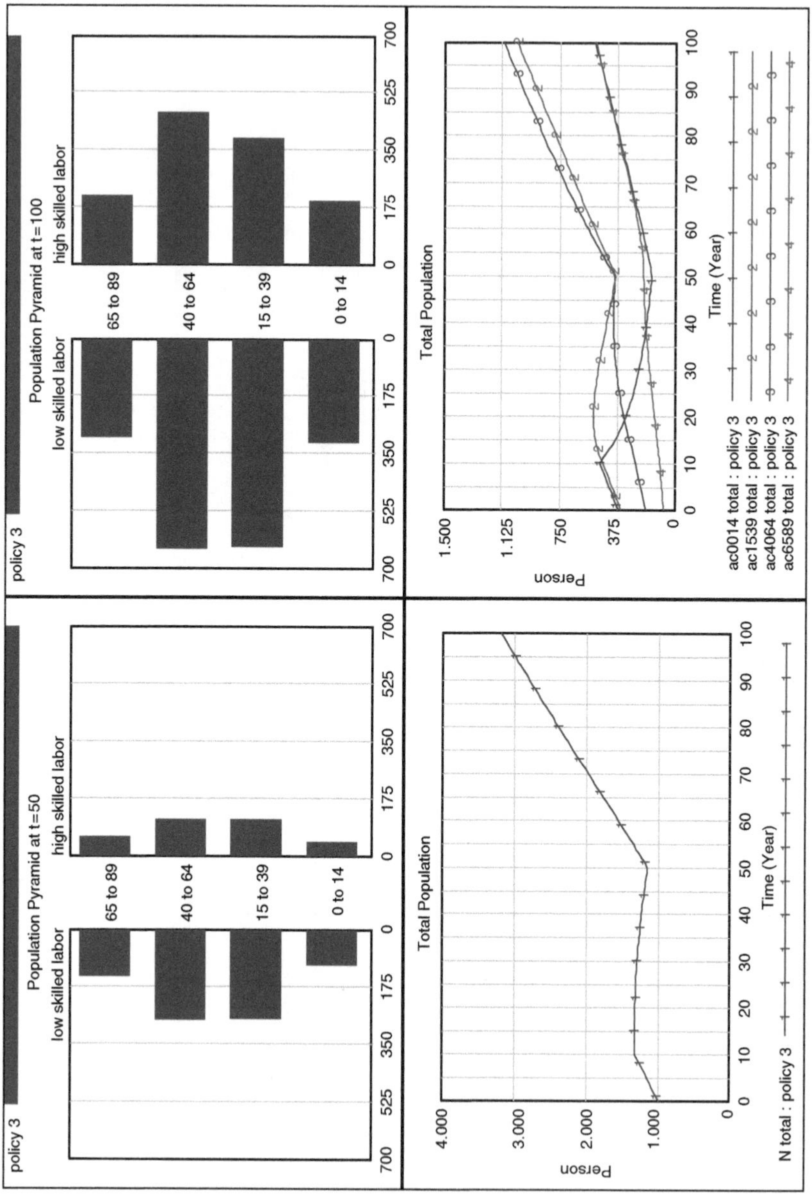

Fig. 5.40 Scenario 3: total population
Source: own figure

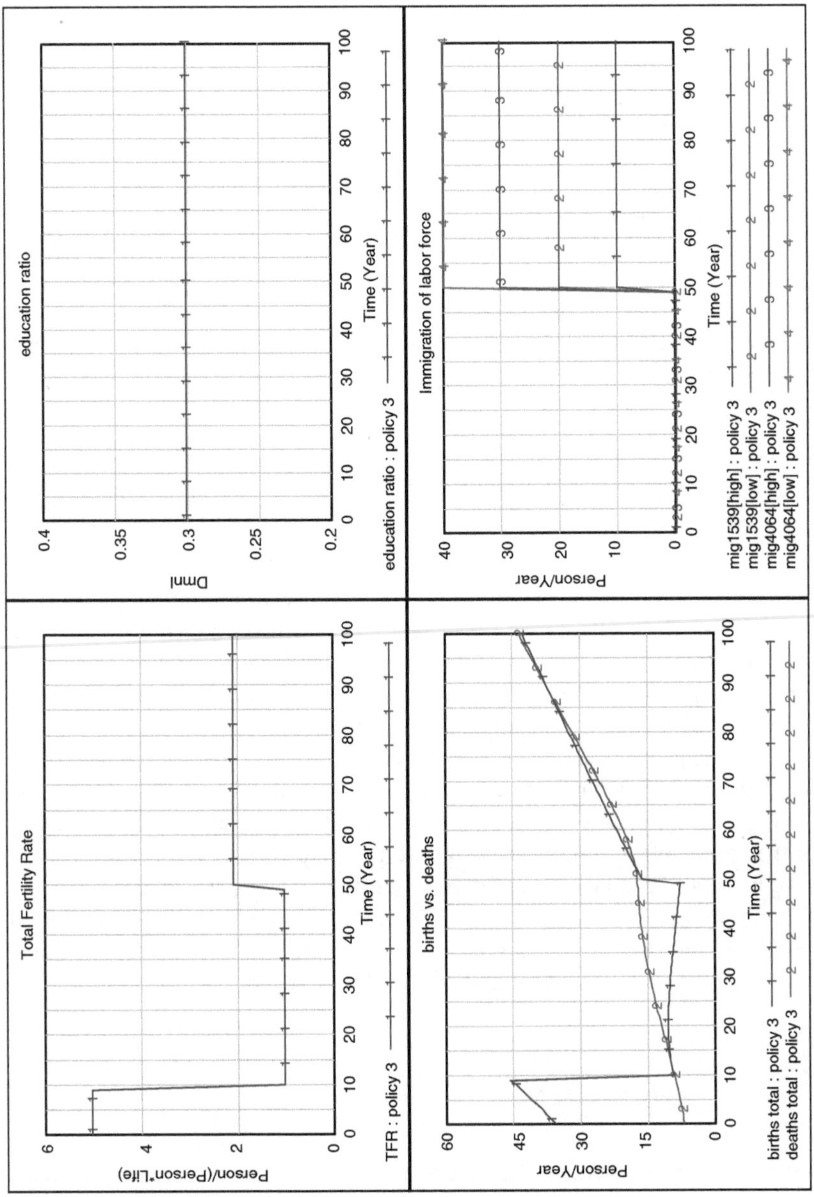

Fig. 5.41 Scenario 3: Results population sector
Source: own figure

The most important graph in this set is in the lower left, which illustrates the number of births and deaths. One can see that immigration leads to an increase of births, due to the rising number of potential mothers.

Similar to the increase in births is the increase in deaths. Deaths rise as the total number of people increases, thus the fractional death rates are constant. The births and deaths continue to grow over time. Without immigration the population would eventually stabilize and the net outflow would equal the net inflow. With migration the population will grow while the population structure stays constant.

Figure 5.42 shows the dependency ratio and the Billeter J. With the reference point t = 50 the number of workers will increase. This forces the dependency ratio to decline due to the increasing denominator. As outlined earlier, the effect will disappear so that the ratio of working to non-working population will re-adjust. Additionally, the Billeter J is zero when the total number of elderly people equals that of the youngest cohort. The migration accelerates the Billeter J to approach a value of zero. Although the total population is growing, the structure will not change much after the adjustment process. The Billeter J stays practically constant over time.

5.4.4 Results R&D Sector

The R&D sector reveals some interesting effects induced by the migration. Figure 5.43 shows, in the upper right, the change in patent stock. This is interlinked with the amount of labor. Because labor supply increases the change of patent stock (delta A) must change instantly as well. The growth rate of the change of patent stock is declining because of the shrinking migration effect.

Furthermore, the growth rate of the R&D sector depends on the ratio of the stock to its flow. The increasing flow leads to an increase in the stock. But due to the stabilization of inflow delta A, the growth rate gA will eventually decline. One can see this in the lower left graph, where migration has a positive effect. But one can also observe how quickly the migration growth effect depreciates over time.

The summarizing phase plot illustrates this as well. In this case, the high-skilled workers increase and therefore the graph moves to the right, whereas the space between the dots shrinks. This indicates the deceleration process.

5.4.5 Results Growth Sector

The openness of the model with higher movement of people leads to a new standard phase plot. In order to do this accurately, one should first take a closer look at the lower left graph in Fig. 5.44. The requirement line, with the needed investments to keep the capital intensity per effective capita constant, jumps above the real investments. This is due to the additional migration and, thus, the population

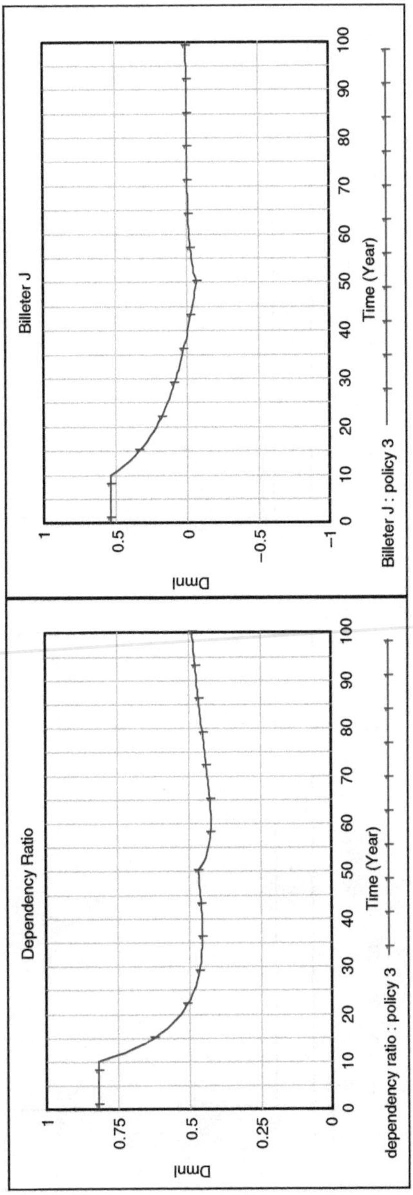

Fig. 5.42 Scenario 3: results population indicators
Source: own figure

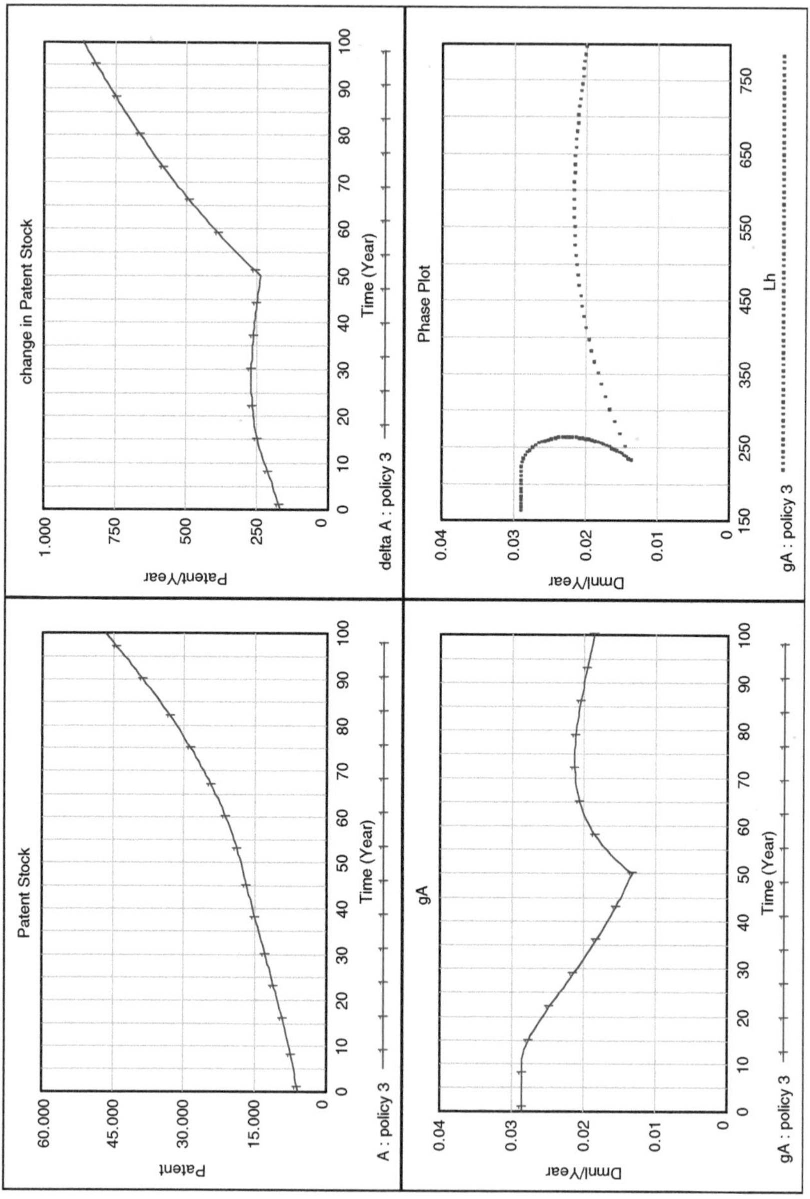

Fig. 5.43 Scenario 3: results R&D sector
Source: own figure

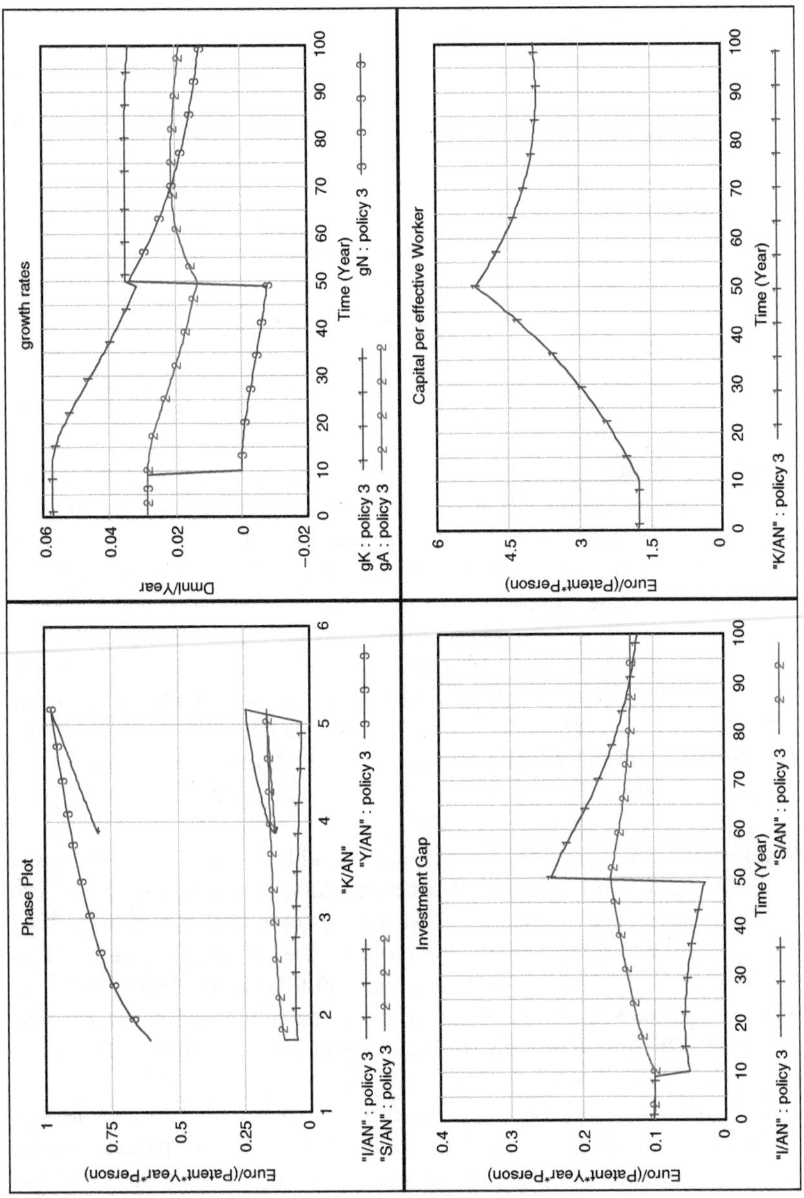

Fig. 5.44 Scenario 3: results growth sector
Source: own figure

growth. This growth rate must be fully adjusted by new investments to keep the capital intensity per effective capita constant. The migration policy reverses the relation of required investments to real investments. Now the situation occurs where the needed investments are higher than the real investments. In this case, the capital intensity will not grow, it will shrink (see lower right graph). This will continue as long as the real and the required investments are not equal. At t = 90 the minimum of the capital intensity is reached.

The required investments (I/AN) decline below the real investments at t = 90. Again the population growth causes this to occur. The additional migration effect levels out over time, thus, the population growth rate will decline to zero. The growth rate of the R&D sector will follow with a greater delay. Both growth rates contribute to the required investments, hence the needed investments will also fall. The shrinking process is so fast that within the simulation it falls below the real investments. Now the real investments exceed the required, so the capital intensity must consequently rise.

For verification, one can observe the decline of the growth rate in the upper right figure (no. 3). After a sudden increase in t = 50 it declines continuously. Also the growth rate of the patent stock lags.

Taking the standard phase plot as summary one can now understand the dynamic behavior. The shrinking capital intensity per effective capita leads to the left shifting graphs. Hardly visible is the increase at a per effective capita value close to 4.0 Euro/Patent*Person. The effect of immigration is therefore not permanent.

Figure 5.45 provides the development over time for important per effective capita variables. The saving ratio distribution is again similar to the previous runs. This ratio splits the income per effective worker into consumption and savings. The migration effect is strongly visible in all graphs. Due to the increase in population (N) the ratios Y/AN, C/AN and S/AN will fall. This creates the saw tooth shaped behavior. If the simulation were continued, one would observe the declining population effect. Finally all per effective capita variables would grow again.

The disaggregation of per effective capita variables can reveal additional insights. The savings per effective capita is exemplary shown in Fig. 5.46. The major fact is the difference between the working people and the non-working people. The age cohorts ac1539 and ac4064 increase due to the immigration. This leads to the shown decline. The last age cohort ac6589 follows a different behavior pattern. Here, no one moved in. But from the previous cohort ac4064 every year more people retire. The inflow into the stock ac6589 exceeds the outflow as long as the migration effect is persistent.

But this does not create a short upward trend, in fact, it will decrease it. The primarily reason for this can be found in the distribution of the patents among the age groups. As already outlined, the total amount of patents is split into the different age cohorts by the weighted arithmetic mean. The sudden increase in the working age cohorts leads to a decline of the amount of patent stock in the oldest cohort. Hence, the ratio S/AN will increase. During the simulation period this effect declines, because of retiring workers.

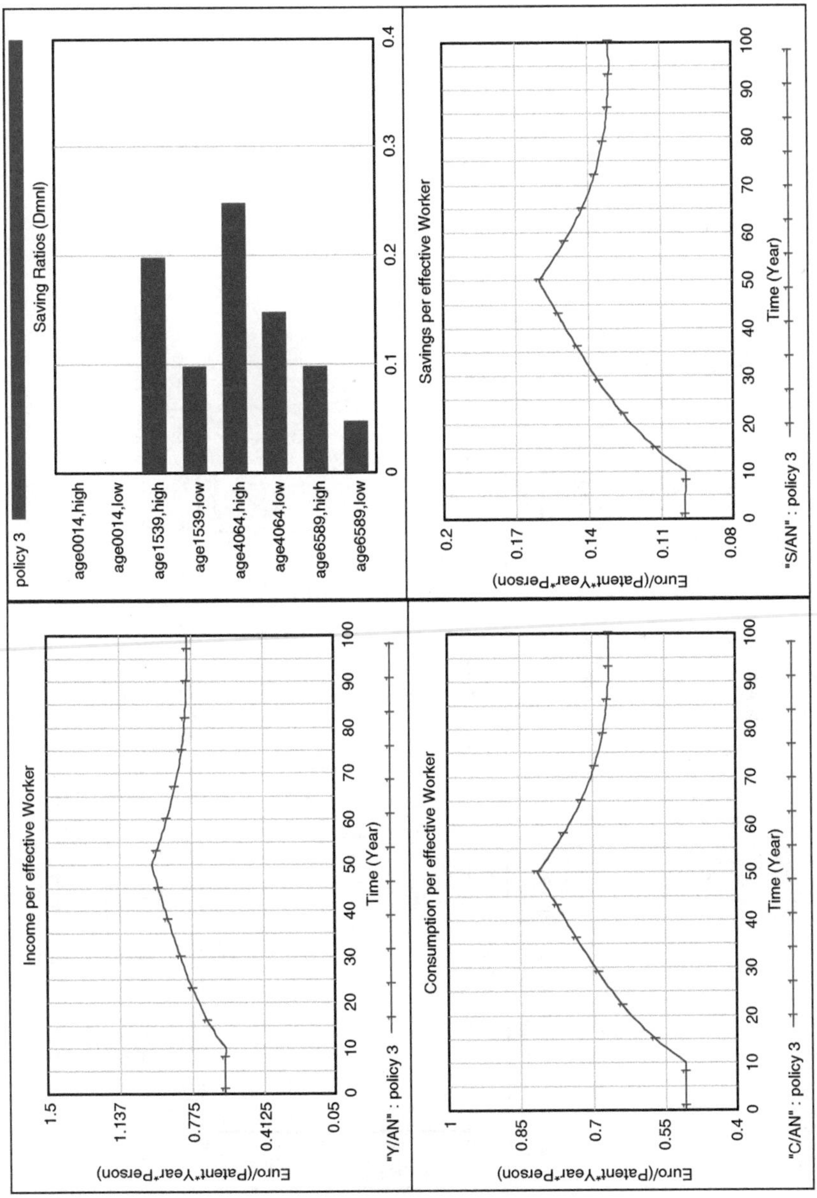

Fig. 5.45 Scenario 3: results per effective capita variables
Source: own figure

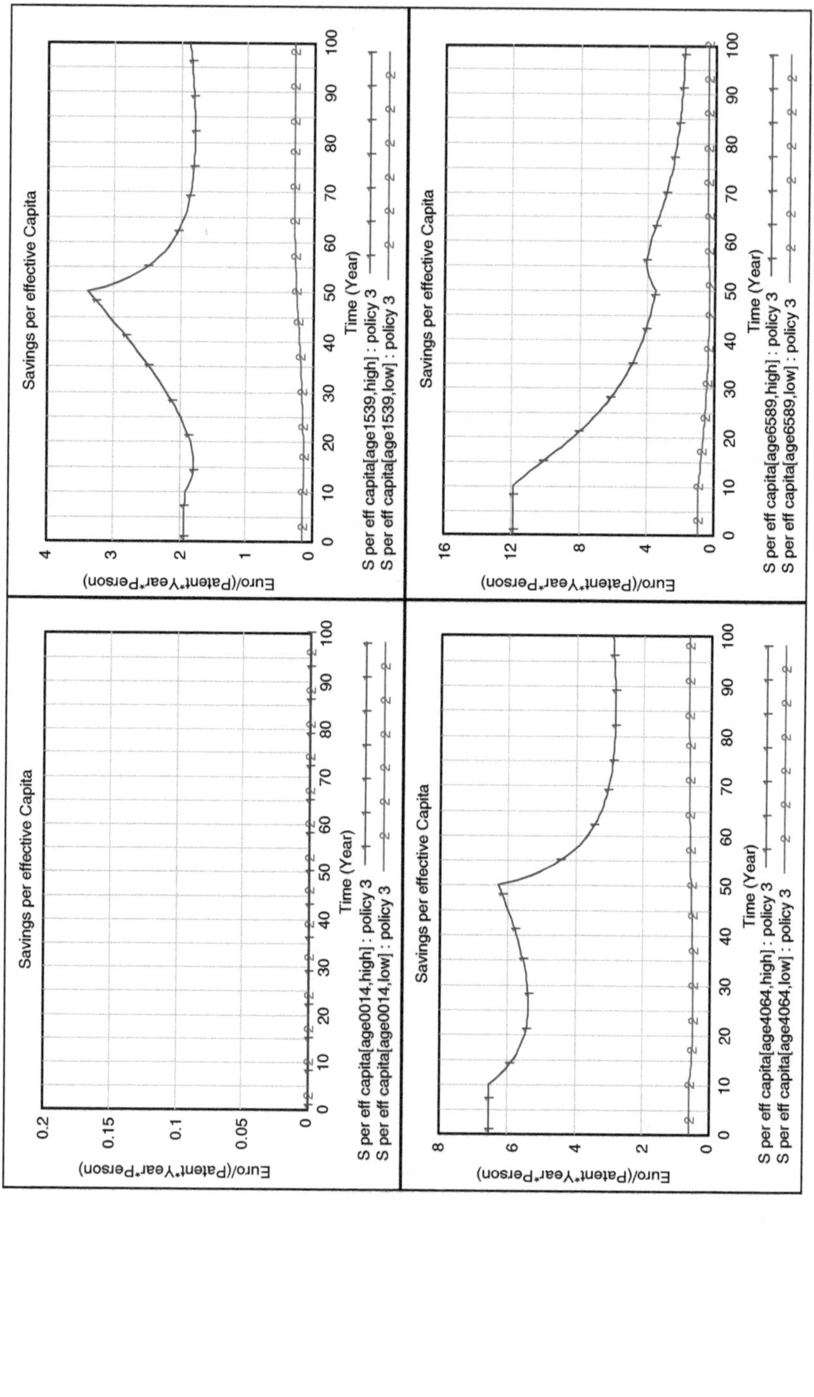

Fig. 5.46 Scenario 3: results savings per effective capita
Source: own figure

5.4.6 *Results Utility Sector*

The results of the utility sector are shown in Fig. 5.47. The population increase slows down the utility per capita growth, which leads to a smaller increase over time. More prominently one can observe the overall effect in the upper right graph. Population (N) forces the ratio U/AN to decline. Nevertheless, the accumulated negative effect is marginal as one can see in the two total utility charts.

5.4.7 *Summary and Conclusion*

This policy scenario helps stabilize the population's structure (ratio of age cohorts) faster and has various side effects. Because of the sudden increase in population growth all per effective capita variables show a declining effect. But the migration does not increase with the growing population, because it is only political set and not causally connected with the stock. This leads to a declining growth impulse so that a stabilizing process occurs during the simulation run. Various behaviors follow from that dynamic interaction. The most prominent effect is the shift of relation on real and required investments. At the beginning, the real investments are too low and this leads to a decline in the capital intensity per effective capita. At $t = 70$ the relation switches and the capital intensity starts to grow again. The impulse on the R&D sector is also not permanent. But the short growth impulse helps accelerate growth.

Summarizing these various outcomes, one can say that immigration is very powerful and can be used to achieve quick adjustments. However, sustaining this effect requires migration to increase as the population grows (relative constant ratio). Without doing so the effects are only temporarily.

5.5 Chapter Summary

This chapter analyzed the effect of an aging and shrinking society on economic growth. The model allows various, almost uncountable, tests for all exogenous constants and also for different changes over time. Thus, this work focused mainly on exemplary scenarios for special population determinants.

A population in general changes by its inflows and outflows. The number of births per year and mother, as one inflow, is controlled by the total fertility rate. Scenario 1 "family orientation" simulated a change in this TFR. The model indicated that a TFR at the replacement level of 2.08 leads to a constant population after more than one generation. This will happen beyond the simulation's end. The huge delay and persistence of the aging chain recommends this family policy mainly as a long-term strategy. Also the model showed that stabilization alone is not enough to maintain economic growth.

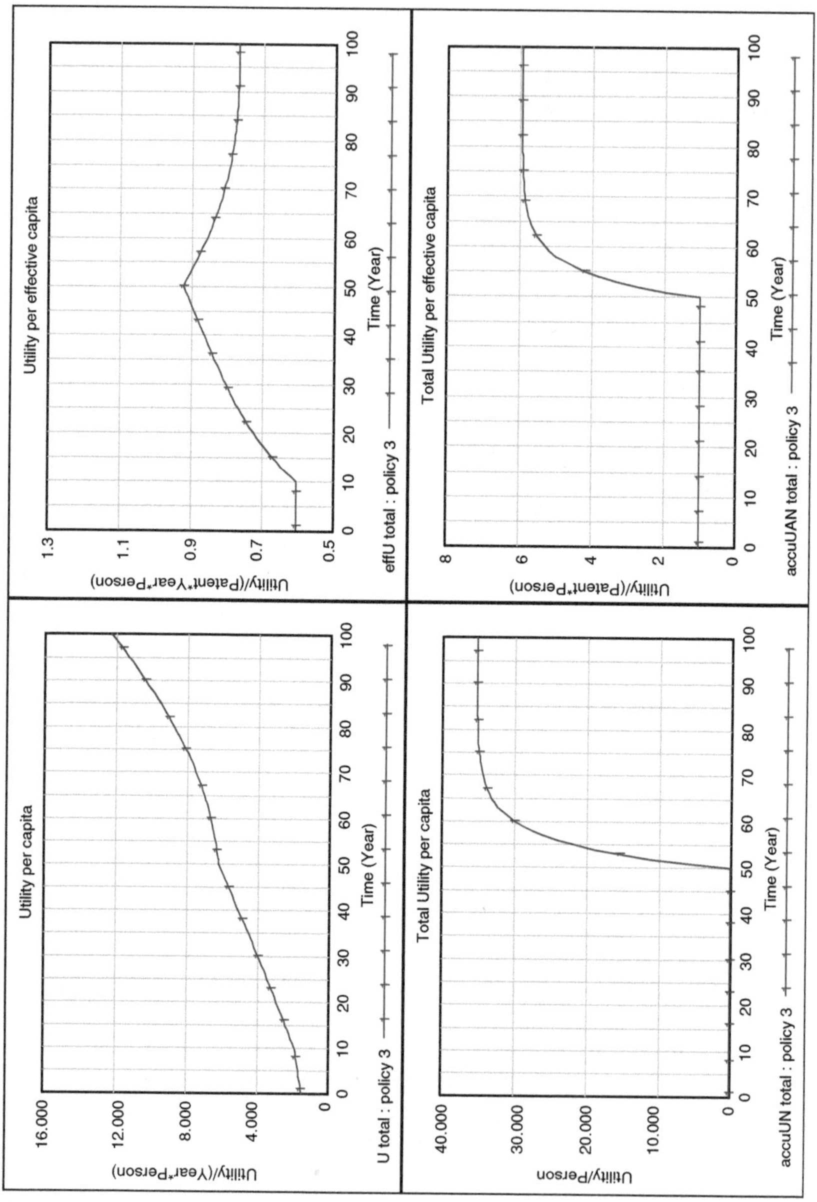

Fig. 5.47 Scenario 3: results utility sector
Source: own figure

The second scenario "education orientation" consequently built on the first scenario by adding a modified ratio between high- and low-skilled workers. The results revealed that Jones' assumptions for the patent stock in the R&D sector do not deploy its reinforcing power. Hence, a higher education and a detour of labor into the patent stocks do not matter. But the model showed that by enabling the exponential growth pattern in the R&D sector, the education evolves extra economic growth. The effects do not take as long as the results of the family policy to occur. Thus, the education policy is an appropriate strategy for mid-term focus.

The last scenario "migration orientation" analyzed the effects of immigration. The number of immigrants accounted 4% of the total initial population. One recognized that opening the model for foreign labor can dramatically change the economic situation in less than one generation. The effects are so strong that the seldom case of overinvestment happens, where the required investments are below the real investments. Due to the fact that the immigrants will also have children, according to the current total fertility rate, the net effect of in total 40 immigrants is greater. The migration strategy is therefore a designated policy for short-term adjustments.

The case of a declining death rate and therefore an increasing number of people in the oldest age cohort was not tested. One can argue that by neglecting this effect an important outflow determinant was not analyzed, but the effect was integrated indirectly in the previous scenarios. As the population net flow is the result of births minus deaths, a decline of the fractional death rates could be identically simulated by a smaller total fertility rate. The TFR was set from 5.0 to 1.0 in the base run. This very low level of the TFR, below the replacement setting of 2.08, indirectly showed the process of aging and lower death rates.

Other scenarios, which apply modified constants in other sectors as the population sector, are possible. One may think of modified saving ratios, wage distribution or technology changes. But these variables are not in the focus of this work. Nevertheless, further research can shed more light on these exogenous constants.

The following graphs provide a comparative summary for all four runs. Figure 5.48 shows the population pyramids in comparison to different points in time. The upper left-hand graph illustrates the starting population structure at $t = 10$ with a broad basis of young people. After the shrinking process, at $t = 50$ the policies were activated. The result is the right chart. Whereas in the base run the population continues to decline and provides the smallest number of people in the economy, scenario 2 and 3 differ only on the proportion of high- to low-skilled workers. Only the migration scenario leads to stronger population growth.

A closer look at the total population is provided in Fig. 5.49. All scenarios have a positive effect on the population, but only scenario 3 "migration orientation" can pursue higher growth rates. The dependency of a society on the working age population declines only in the case of migration. This is fairly obvious, because only labor migrates in this scenario. Finally, all considered policies have a positive effect on the population structure, because all increase the number of births (direct or indirect) and lead to a positive value of the Billeter J.

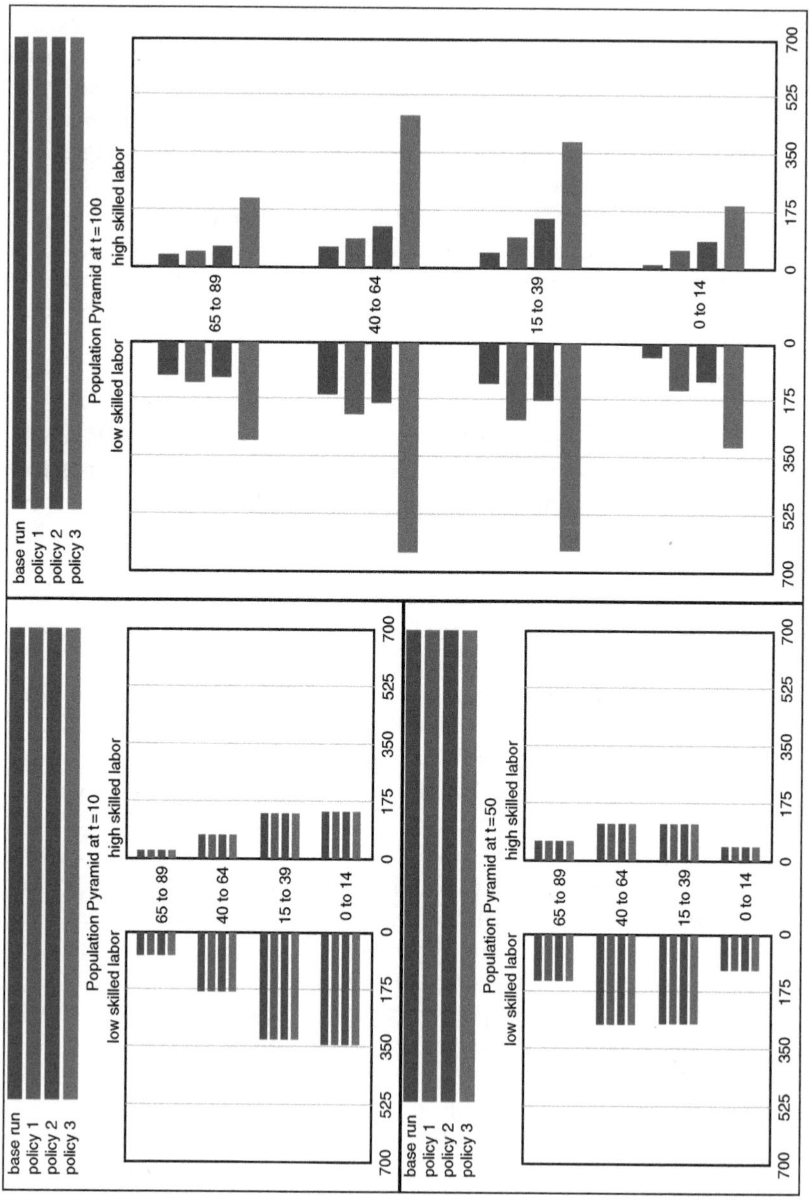

Fig. 5.48 Scenario comparison: population pyramids
Source: own figure

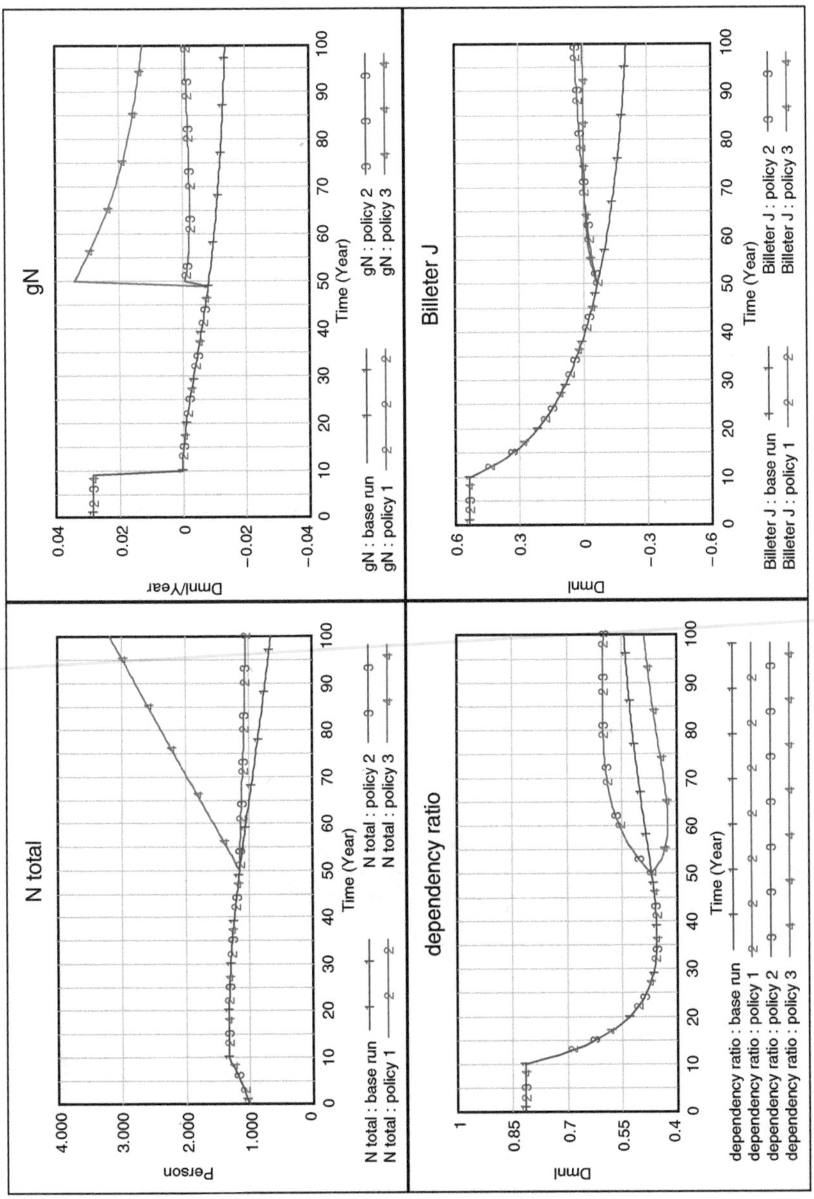

Fig. 5.49 Scenario comparison: total population
Source: own figure

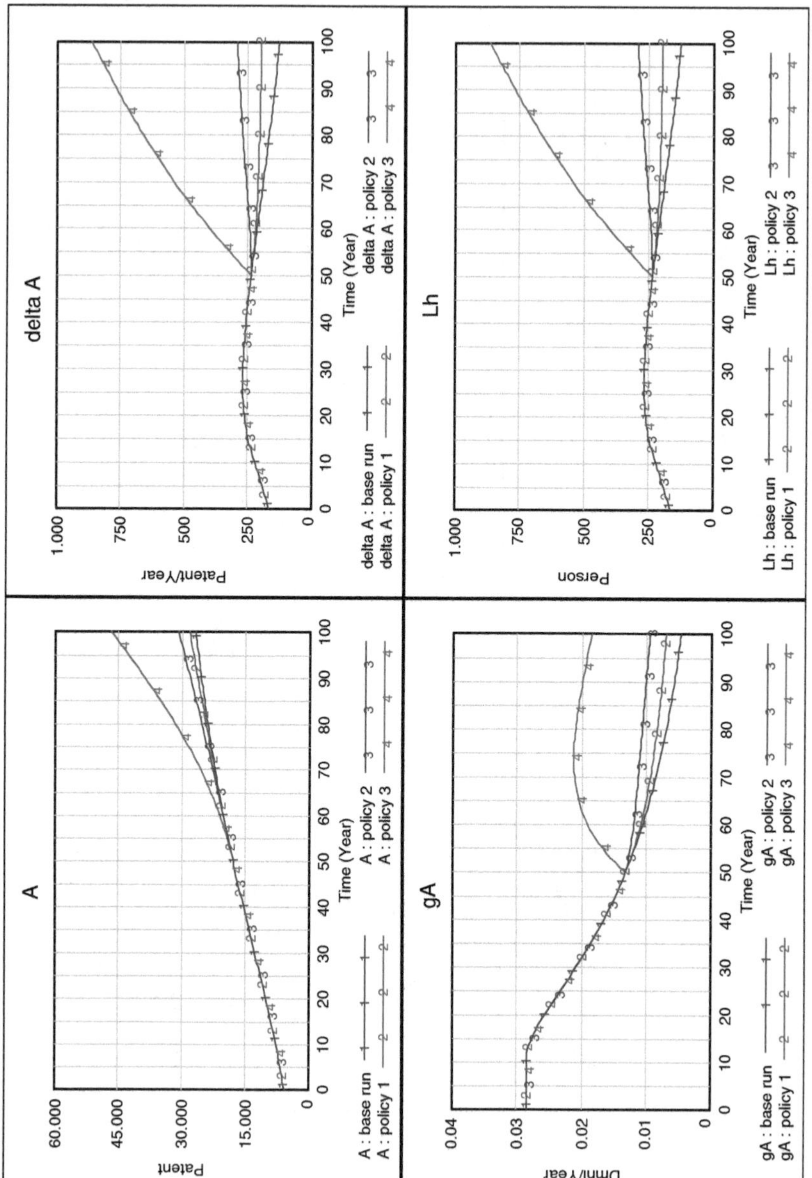

Fig. 5.50 Scenario comparison: R&D sector
Source: own figure

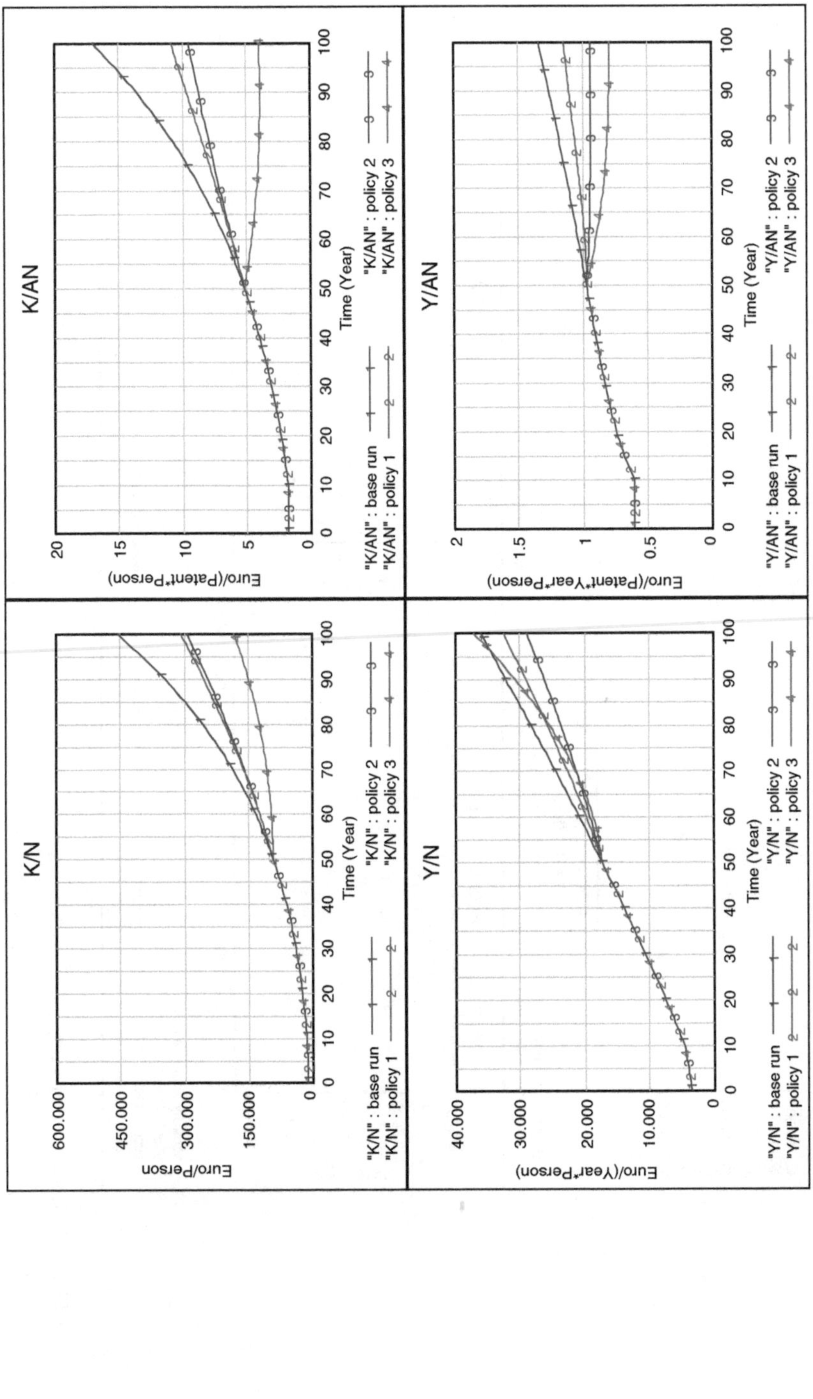

Fig. 5.51 Scenario comparison: growth sector
Source: own figure

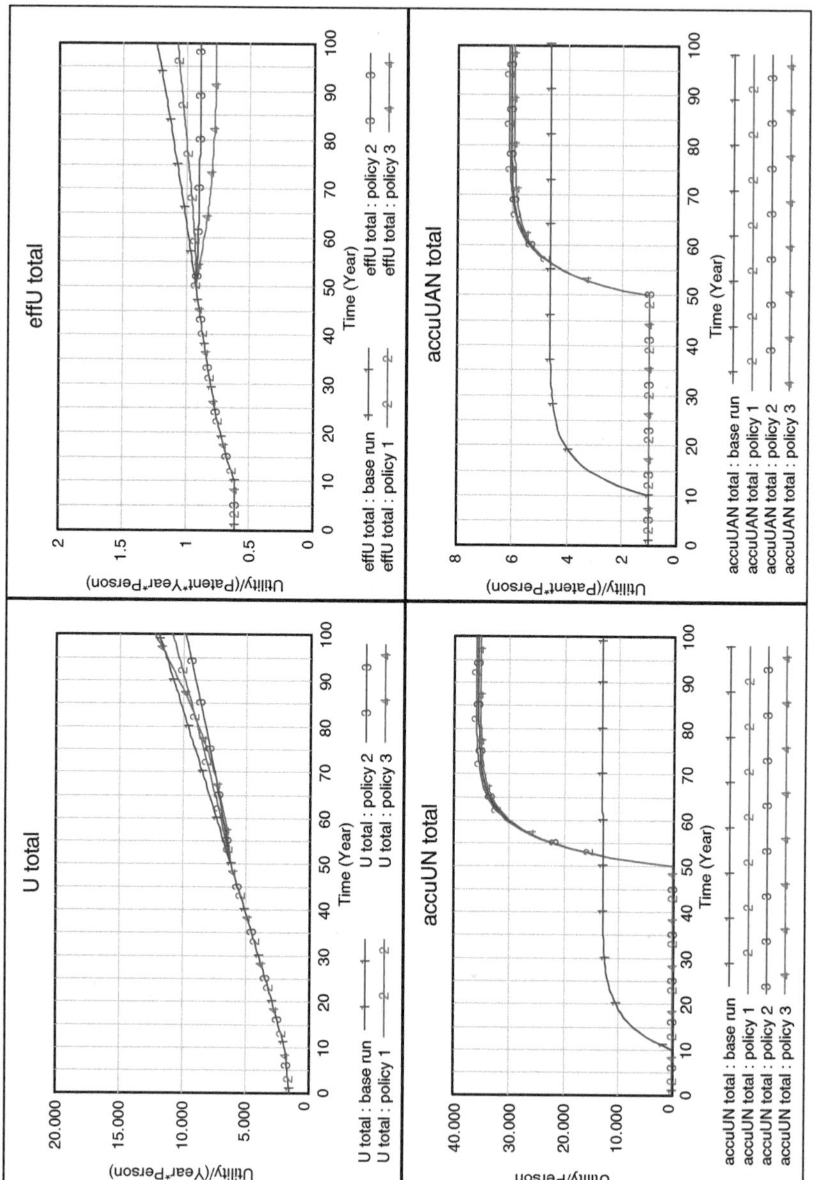

Fig. 5.52 Scenario comparison: utility sector
Source: own figure

Figure 5.50 compares the policy results in the R&D sector. The migration scenario is again the most powerful and leads to high growth rates in the patent stock. Nevertheless, it will eventually reach the same level as all other scenarios, because the population does not grow inherently with a high TFR. The zero value of phi leads to a change of the patent stock (delta A) which is identical to the amount of high-skilled labor. Policy 2 could easily dominate the model behavior by enabling the R&D loop to reinforce the patent stock. As long as this does not happen, scenario 2 is only the second best solution.

Rürup wrote that if capital and knowledge are the most important factors for economic growth, then the 20–30-years-old are the most prominent carrier of knowledge. New input in knowledge depends on the number of people in this cohort (Rürup, 2000, p. 97).

The growth sector reveals indicators such as per capita income or capital intensity. Figure 5.51 shows the comparison of all scenarios. The capital intensity directly depends, for all policies, on the total population. In the case of a shrinking society this indicator could mislead observers, as the capital intensity increases. However, the per capita income is very appropriate to measure economic outcome. It increases in those cases where extra growth is generated in the R&D sector. This happens mainly in scenario 3, but also in scenario 2 if φ would be unequal zero. Here (in the case of $\varphi = 0$) the results of the scenario 3 are below the results of the scenario "family orientation".

The last Fig. 5.52 of this chapter provides the comparative results in the utility sector. Similar to the growth sector, scenario 3 provokes the highest per capita value, but the lowest per effective capita value. Again, other R&D sector variables could show here also highest values.

More interesting are the accumulated utilities. One can recognize only small differences between the scenarios, but the highest value is achieved through a strong family orientation (scenario 1). Unfortunately, this takes the longest time to adjust. Thus, in the meantime other policies might be added. The base run is not comparable with the other scenarios, because it has the reference point $t = 10$ and not $t=50$. Furthermore it is important to note that policy-makers might not consider very long-term strategies, because a high discount rate would lead to almost negligible present effects. Especially with high additional short-term setup costs, long-term thinking might be impossible.

To sum it all up:

- Policy 1 "familiy orientation" is a long-term strategy
- Policy 2 "education orientation" reveals extra effects only for certain parameter settings and is mid-term orientated
- Policy 3 "migration orientation" provides the best short-term reactions to the demographic decline

There is a conflict of objectives. The best strategy (policy 1) has the slowest adoption rate. Therefore, mixed strategies are best suited to overcome the demographic decline with regards to the effect and adjustment time. However, without a stabilizing policy for the total population, all other strategies will lead to a dead end.

Chapter 6
Conclusion and Outlook

I have been impressed with the urgency of doing. Knowing is not enough; we must apply.
Being willing is not enough; we must do.
Leonardo da Vinci (Crookall & Thorngate, 2009)

This chapter summarizes the major outcomes of this work. The overall research question addressed the generated behavior of a semi-endogenous growth model with a detailed population sector, particularly in the case of an aging and shrinking society. To find an answer in today's time of mounting demographic challenges, this work conducted the research around the following set of goals (see Sect. 1.3):

1. The work provides an overview for theoretical aspects of demographic change.
2. The work provides an overview of neoclassical growth models and their behavior pertaining to demographic change.
3. The work presents a new semi-endogenous growth model with an explicit formulation of population.
4. The work shows the economic consequences of an aging and shrinking society on the basis of this new semi-endogenous growth model.
5. The work provides several policy scenarios to overcome the economic effects of demographic change.

This chapter also addresses further research questions, and is structured as follows: First, a general summary provides an overview of the previous chapters; the second part summarizes the demographic growth principles; and the third part presents further research challenges and unsolved questions.

6.1 General Summary

Chapter one outlined the general problem statement and connected the applied modeling method (system dynamics) to the scientific fields of economics and demographics. The characteristics of complex systems were discussed and the importance

L. Weber, *Demographic Change and Economic Growth*, Contributions to Economics, DOI 10.1007/978-3-7908-2590-9_6, © Springer-Verlag Berlin Heidelberg 2010 of a system dynamical approach to demographic and economic questions was emphasized. Furthermore, the chapter provided the framework for these questions and explained the use of conceptual tools. For doing so the concept of stock and flows, with their causal links and feedbacks to auxiliaries, was illustrated.

Chapter 2 focused first on demographic determinants: fertility, mortality, migration and the population structure itself. All of these population factors are influenced in turn by other economic and non-economic components. These are key factors in steering demographic systems. Without deeper understanding of interdependencies policy-makers cannot overcome the aging and shrinking process.

Fertility theories are numerous. In summary, they stress the importance of biographic parameters, opportunity costs, personal income and preferences, and also the socio-economic environment. Mortality, on the contrary, is a more non-economic determinant and is most influenced by medical health factors. Of course, the personal and social environment can change the medical factors significantly, but these were not the focus of this work. Furthermore important for any demographic projection is a valid assumption of migration. The literature is vast, but no theory can precisely explain or forecast the movements of people. Many different explanations stress economic motives as major push and pull factor for migration. But one should not neglect social motives. The population structure itself, as the last determinant, changes through in- and outflow determinants, and aging. This process can invert population structures with decisive economic consequences.

The second part of Chap. 2 intensely reflected the economic consequences of changing population determinants. Relevant sectors for the later simulation model were the financial sector, the labor market as well as the resource and development sector. Other important effects were outlined but only to a smaller extent.

The lifecycle hypothesis for consumption provided insight on how the saving ratios change over time. The economic interactions in the labor market were broadened to a demographic perspective. A shrinking population does not only have an effect on labor supply, but also on labor demand. Expectations and perceived changes influence future wages. This complex and dynamic problem was then extended to high- and low-skilled labor differentiation in the R&D sector. This section discussed the specification of innovation, skills and productivity. The analysis showed that personal characteristics and qualification as well as individual performance determine the productivity and the innovational outcome.

The second chapter highlighted the manifold interactions between economics and demography. The findings showed that demographic development will occur due to simultaneously effects, thus there will not be a single factor influencing the transition process.

Chapter 3 presented three major neoclassical growth theories:

- The Solow-model with exogenous technology
- The endogenous Romer-model and
- The model with semi-endogenous growth according to Jones

The models were outlined in chronological order. Every analysis included major assumptions, structures and dynamics. Additionally, policy experiments were conducted.

The model created by Robert Solow is the foundation for various augmentations. Important ones which focus on demographic problems were outlined as well. The original Solow-model does not reflect demographic challenges, because the population is not explicitly modeled. Augmentations of this model typically grasp specific demographic parameters, but not all components. This lack of a holistic approach was one of the founding ideas of this work. The second subchapter endogenizes the technology (Romer-model). As precursors of this model serves the Ak-model, the Uzawa–Lucas-model and Schumpeter's theory of "Creative Destruction". Paul Romer took his idea a step further than Solow to explain economic growth. The technology (patent stock) depends in his understanding on a fixed number of high-skilled workers. They create patents which help to produce intermediate goods. An increase in patents leads to more specialization of the intermediate goods sector. The Romer-model was criticized by Charles Jones. He argued that despite the marvelous idea of endogenizing technology, the model does not hold with the empirics. Jones used Romer's model as a starting point and developed a so-called semi-endogenous model. The model reflected characteristics from both the Romer-model and the Solow-model. Population growth was now possible again and the model fitted to empirical observations. However, like Solow and Romer, Jones did not consider demographic specifications.

Because no previous neoclassical growth model is able to replicate aging and shrinking societies, a new, self-developed demographic growth model was introduced. Chapter four focused on and evaluated this model. The chapter introduction justified the modeling technique system dynamics in comparison to econometrics. Both approaches would work complementary. System dynamics is used in general to model the systemic structure of a population and to address feedbacks and delays. The last two aspects lead to system dynamics as applied method, because it can deal with these two types easily. The demographic growth model consists of four sectors:

1. The population sector with four age groups and a subscript for skills
2. The R&D sector with a patent stock
3. The growth sector with the capital growth trough investments
4. The utility sector with accumulated utilities

The R&D sector and the growth sector are connected with the population sector via the labor force. The utility sector depends on the consumption from the growth sector. The new population sector with the aging structure was shown in greater detail, because all other model parts depend on this sector. The total system dynamics model is characterized by:

1. A stock-flow-consistent system dynamic representation of neoclassical economic growth
2. A dynamic population sector with only few exogenous parameters
3. Partial openness for migration with capital import
4. Model endogenous interdependencies with other model parts
5. Distinguishing of high- and low-skilled labor
6. Specific saving ratios with respect to age and skills

7. The personal income distribution of the age groups
8. Considering net foreign assets if domestic savings will not be able to support capital growth
9. Implemented total accumulated utility as welfare indicator
10. Enabling of policy scenarios for decision support

Chapter five dealt with the model-based simulation of an aging and shrinking society. The base run showed how an economy would evolve over time. Three policy scenarios to overcome the negative outcome of the base run were conducted. The first scenario "family orientation" assumed a stabilization of the birth rate. The second scenario "education orientation" added to the stabilization policy and assumed an increase on high-skilled workers. By doing so the patent stock grows stronger than in scenario 1. Scenario 3 "migration orientation" opened the model for immigration. In conjunction with a total fertility rate on the replacement level the population started to grow again. The various interactions in the demographic growth model recommend having a holistic view on economic growth, otherwise overlapping effects will be neglected by mistake. In turn, this would lead to misleading results.

In addition, this work provides several theories in a causal-loop structure or a stock-flow structure. All of these visualized structures are new except the theory of Malthus and the population sector of the World3-model. Figure 6.1 presents the applied theories. Although it was not the major goal, the collection of demographic and neoclassic growth theories can serve as a starting point for further structural discussions.

6.2 Principles of Demographic Growth

This section summarizes important findings of the simulation model and its behavior as general principals. Principles that could only be derived from the theoretical findings are not explicitly listed here because the major outcome of this work was the demographic growth model.

Demographic Theories (Chapter 2)

- Easterlin Hypothesis
- Low fertility trap
- Dodd's gravity model
- Malthus theory of population growth
- Population sector World3-Model (Limits to Growth)
- Lifecycle hypothesis on consumption
- Labor supply and labor demand
- Skill biased technological change

Economic Theories (Chapter 3)

- Solow's exogenous growth model
- Gruescu's model of silver growth
- Barro/ Sali-i-Martin model with migration
- Model with variable population growth according to Solow
- AK-model according to Rebelo
- Uzawa-Lucas model of human capital
- Schumpeter's theory of "Creative Destruction"
- Jones semi-endogenous growth model

Fig. 6.1 Self-constructed causal-loop and stock-flow diagrams
Source: own figure

Principle 1: Economic systems are complex systems and, therefore, special techniques which can deal with complexity should be applied to economic research.

Complex systems are dynamic, non-linear, governed by feedback processes, path-depended and often counterintuitive through delays. Thus, static analyses of complex systems are insufficient and are unable to predict future consequences. Especially in the case of demographic problems for long-term behavior, the systemic approach is indispensable.

Principle 2: Capital intensity is not a sufficient indicator for economic growth, because the growth rate increases in the case of aging societies.

Often it is assumed that a greater capital intense society can overcome negative demographic processes more easily. This is true so far, but capital intensity is an output indicator and not an input variable. Thus, if one analyzes shrinking societies, the capital intensity must ceteris paribus grow faster. This effect differs to usual argumentations, where the capital intensity is often a starting point for developing strategies. Here it was shown that behavior of the capital intensity is the effect and not the cause.

Principle 3: Population decline can mislead interpretations of per-capita-variables as they may increase.

An analogy as for the capital intensity applies here. A declining population will cause aggregated per capita values to increase. The income per capita might increase, but this can only take as long as there is no shortage of labor supply for the provided capital stock. Neoclassical models assume full employment because the wage is flexible. The per capita variables will continue to increase without reflecting the employment situation. The missing counter effects from the labor market avoid adjustments of the increasing per-capita-variables. The use of per-capita definitions without employment considerations is only feasible for growing populations. In these cases new capital can be provided through investments. But if the population declines the capital stock is not disinvested.

Principle 4: The behavior persistence for populations creates in the case of declining economy a better-before-worse behavior.

Models with an aggregated population in only one stock cannot show the delay between births and availability on the labor market. But this delay of fifteen years or more has a tremendous importance for the system's behavior. The persistence in the previous condition leads to misleading interpretations and discourages policy-makers to act in advance. The system dynamics standard archetype which applies for such patterns is called "fixes that fail" and explains the short-term versus long-term interactions (Senge, 1994, pp. 388–389).

Principle 5: Fertility stabilizing policies create strong delays, which take more than a generation to adjust.

A population cannot stabilize within one generation, because potential mothers must be born first. This should be considered if one proclaims family orientation as the gold standard for an economy. Of course, the final population will be stable, but the transition process is than neglected as well as the time frame.

Principle 6: Only a total fertility rate above the replacement level can lead to sustain growth of a population.

Although it is fairly obvious, the country specific replacement level is the achievable benchmark. This principle is frequently forgotten in practice. Below the replacement level a population will continue to decline. An increase of the total fertility rate below this level leads, therefore, only to a slower shrinking process.

Principle 7: Family orientation is a long-term strategy.
Principle 8: Education orientation is a mid-term strategy.
Principle 9: Migration orientation is a short-term strategy.

These three principles are the direct outcomes of the policy scenarios. It can be shown that each demographic determinant needs a certain timeframe to take action. For comparison, a mid-term strategy takes about one generation to provide strong effects.

Principle 10: Only mixed strategies of long-, mid- and short-term focus can overcome cyclical behavior and long adjustment processes of populations.

A consequence of the above outlined three principles 7–9 is that only mixed strategies can shorten cyclical behavior of population adjustment. The longest strategy with the greatest persistence should continuously be provided, whereas the short-term strategy can work as a buffer and dampen unintended negative fluctuations in the total population.

Principle 11: The importance of education depends on economic parameters of the technological sector.

Scenario 2 "education orientation" showed ambiguous results. Standard parameters of semi-endogenous growth models education leads to lower total output per capita for an economy. This is due to the fact that an increase in higher skilled labor will not produce scale effects in the R&D sector. Transferred into practical terms one would say, that each economy has its own certain amount of required high-skilled labor. Any additional high-skilled labor will not provide additional output. But by changing the exogenous parameters of the R&D sector, an extra growth from the patent stock would be revealed, so that more education matters.

Principle 12: The discount rate and the time preference of the society determine how policy-makers consider long-term strategies.

Policy-makers will have to consider future effects in addition to current effects. Discounting future utilities to the reference time delivers their present value. Positive outcomes that payback only far into the future do not have any significant present value. The present value depends on the discount rate. Adjustments to the time scope of policy-makers will create indicators for valuable policy decisions. One can see the accumulated discounted utility as such an indicator.

Principle 13: The dependency ratio is only a weak indicator to evaluate changing populations.

The relation of working to non-working population cannot capture the difference of few or much young non-workers in the group of the non-working people. Growing and shrinking economies can have the same amount of non-workers, but they differ in the ratio of young to old people. The dependency ratio will be the same in both cases. Whereas the dependency ratio increases for a growing population it will shrink in the opposite case. Usually, a low dependency ratio is assumed as better. However, it could also be misinterpreted in these cases.

Principle 14: Because national per capita values do not capture age cohort specific behavior, disaggregated variables should be favored.

This principle is very important. Age cohorts can show very different behavior throughout an overall population change. Aggregation of age groups can eradicate opposed effects. Policies that are deduced from aggregated variables could miss the specific requirements of the age groups.

Principle 15: Because population change causes technological change in reality, demographic growth models should provide explicitly depreciation of capital.

Technological change also means a change of capital equipment. Growth models with net investments neglect the case of scrapping. It is usually assumed that investments are positive, and that disinvestments are excluded. Hence, the capital stock can only increase over time and not decline. In the case of aging and shrinking societies this is not sufficient because the simulation model than does not have the mechanism to adjust the capital stock.

The main research question was answered in Chap. 6 regarding scenario and policy analysis. In this chapter, the major system behavior was outlined. Each scenario served as an extreme case to provide the whole range of possible behavior. Empirical foundation will enable the model to switch from behavior modeling to prediction modeling. Then the demographic growth model can provide a country specific long-term forecast.

The five goals of this work were fulfilled step by step with every chapter. Nevertheless, the development of a new demographic growth model and its successful scenario testing were the most important outcomes of this work.

6.3 Implications for Further Research

After outlining the model and its results in such detail, a few remarks must be added regarding the research outlook. There are three groups of implications: economics, system dynamics modeling and policy design.

The first group of implication for future research focuses on economics. According to Jay Forrester's objections to standard economics the following aspects must be fulfilled to successfully approach new economic insights (Forrester, 1979, p. 83):

1. Permitting a full range of economic behavior and not focusing on the limitation of equilibrium theory
2. Broad and careful observations from real world economic
3. Representation of decision making and realistic constraints that impose uncertainty
4. Approaching validation as multi-dimensional process in which a variety of testable assertions can be compared
5. Creating a approach that implements nonlinear relationships
6. The understanding that no sharp boundaries separates structure from parameters
7. Necessary complexity rather than simplicity
8. Organized groups, large enough to unify many aspects of economics

This leads to a few general challenges for the presented demographic growth model. The most important one is the missing employment sector. The neoclassical assumption of fully flexible wages and no unemployment may work fine for growing populations; however, it will fail in the case of an aging and shrinking population. The decline will certainly effect professions in different manner. Thus, a shortage of labor supply may be expected. The in Sect. 2.3.3 outlined problem of a skill biased technology change is currently not implemented in the model.

A possible labor shortage also causes firms to adjust their production technology (represented as partial production elasticity of capital) to overcome the increase in wages.

Also important and still neglected: capital investments are only considered as net investments. Negative investments are not possible in this model. However, for long run simulations the replacement of capital should be implemented. Capital depreciation enables one opportunity to do so. In this case, the saving ratio turns into a gross-saving ratio. Current scientific discussions, however, stress importance to specific problems with the system of national accounting (Cezanne, Titze, & Weber, 2006; Lorenz & Pasche, 2007). This would hamper the interpretation of the outcome.

Neoclassical assumptions focus on the supply side of an economy. But demographic change will also have demand effects. The model indirectly reflects this by disaggregating into age groups. The consumption amount of the older people (ac6589) compared to younger age cohorts can then be interpreted by assuming a different basket of goods. Much better would be a more detailed demand sector instead of assuming $Y^s=Y^d$.

Since the demographic growth model consists of short-term foci, it might be useful to introduce business cyclical behavior. The feasibility of combining long- and short-term behavior was already proven by Werner Rothengatter and Axel Schaffer for the case of a simple growth model with a multiplier-accelerator-model (Rothengatter & Schaffer, 2006, pp. 192–202). Besides this, numerous models of long-term economic behavior exists already in system dynamics (Forrester, Mass, & Charles J., 1976; Forrester, 1973; Sterman, 1983).

The second group of implications for future research focuses on system dynamics modeling, and is highly correlated with the founding economic assumptions. One can easily add new causal links to the demographic growth model, but the challenge of modeling is to find the most important connections to describe the reality appropriately (Birg, 2004, p. 70). Likewise, John Sterman verbalized the famous proverb of "challenging the clouds" (Sterman, 2004, p. 222), concerning the most adequate model boundary.

The demographic growth model consists, especially in the population sector, of important exogenous constants, such as the total fertility rate, education ration, fractional death rate or migration. A future demographic growth model could try to endogenize these decisive parameters. This was not addressed in this work, because there was no specific empirical justification. Thus, the causal links could have been modeled only qualitatively. But this would weaken the entire model and would make it arbitrary in its evaluation of outcomes. Based on the current theories one might think of connecting:

1. The utility sector with the total fertility rate
2. The partial production elasticity of capital with the population sector
3. The consumption of goods with the fractional death rate
4. The individual income with the education ratio

By doing so new feedback loops are created. This, in turn, leads to a non-linear model behavior. Further research with these interconnections could provide valid data and present new theories, which could augment the presented model.

And finally, the third group of implications for future research focuses on policy design. The most important and very first next step would be the test of the demographic model's practicability. Until now, the presented work is solely theoretical. Empirical, country specific data would quickly reveal whether or not the theoretical implications are sufficient. Comparative studies between countries would add important information about the speed of demographic change.

The current model provides ample space to test various policy scenarios. The growth sector, with specific saving ratios and wage distribution, could be tested. In addition one could also look at varying total fertility rates for higher- and lower-skilled workers.

The overall aim of this work was to furnish an interdisciplinary, systemic and theoretical view on economic growth for aging and shrinking societies. The current growth literature does not reflect this. Therefore, the focus was on disclosing, visualizing and linking interdependencies in order to simulate consequences of political activities.

The result is a powerful model with an emergent structure to simulate the future system's development. To close with a modification of the chapter's introducing proverb, from Da Vinci:

> This work proves the urgency of doing. While we knew that we must apply, now we know how to apply. We only must do.

Zusammenfassung

Große Teile der ökonomischen Forschung haben sich mit der Frage der Optimierung beschäftigt, aber diese setzt eine stabile Welt voraus, in der es keine Überraschungen gibt und alle Unsicherheiten quantifiziert werden können.
(Gigerenzer, 2009)

Westeuropa und insbesondere auch Deutschland ist zunehmend von den Auswirkungen des demografischen Wandels betroffen. Infolge der sinkenden Geburtenraten unter das Bestandserhaltungsniveau altert und schrumpft die Bevölkerung. Verstärkt wird die Alterung durch sinkende Mortalitätsraten und eine immer längere Lebenszeit. Obwohl schon seit den 1970igern von Demografen darauf hingewiesen wurde, fand dieser demografische Wandel bis vor kurzem kaum wissenschaftliche Bedeutung. Erst mit der zunehmenden Veränderungsdynamik rückte er in den Fokus der Betrachtungen. Meist werden die Auswirkungen deskriptiv beschrieben und nur teilweise gibt es ökonomische Betrachtungen zu den Folgen, die jedoch häufig aus einfachen Modellen oder Angebots-Nachfrage-Kurven abgeleitet werden. Dem stehen Überlappende-Generationen-Modelle gegenüber, die auf einem hohen mathematischen Niveau Veränderungswerte für eine Vielzahl von ökonomischen Kennziffern ableiten. In der öffentlichen Wahrnehmung wird meist nur ein möglicher Zustand für 2025 oder später beschrieben. Kaum wird diskutiert, wie die Dynamik dieses Prozesses aussieht.

Das Gebiet der neoklassischen Wachstumstheorie wurde vor allem durch die grundlegende Arbeit von Robert Solow begründet. Problematisch war dabei, dass das Erklärungsmuster für Wachstum – der technische Fortschritt – nur exogen beschrieben werden konnte. In den 1980igern erlebte die Wachstumsforschung eine Renaissance, als Paul Romer ein Modell mit endogenem Wachstum vorstellte. Hier wurde der technische Fortschritt integriert. Des Weiteren fanden die Gedanken Alois Schumpeters und sein "kreativer Zerstörungsprozess" Eingang in Romers Modell. Empirisch war jedoch Romers Modell schwer zu bestätigen, da zwar die Anzahl der Beschäftigten im F&E Sektor nach dem 2. Weltkrieg anstieg, nicht jedoch die Wachstumsraten der totalen Faktorproduktivität (Jones Kritik). Semi-endogene Wachstumsmodelle zeigen endogenes Wachstum, jedoch nur bei ansteigender Bevölkerung. Üblicherweise wird der Bevölkerungssektor als eine expotentiell wachsende Bestandsgröße modelliert.

Demografische Komponenten wurden vereinzelt in Wachstumsmodellen berücksichtigt, bspw. durch die Implementierung von Migration oder die Endogenisierung der totalen Fertilitätsrate. Betrachtungen zu sinkenden Bevölkerungen sind kaum vorhanden (meist eher im Zusammenhang mit "weniger wachsend"). Hier setzt die Dissertation an. Wenn der Bevölkerung eine zentrale Rolle in den semi-endogenen Wachstumsmodellen zukommt, dann ist der nächste logische Schritt die explizite Formulierung eines Bevölkerungssektors.

Die zentrale Forschungsfrage der Arbeit ist:

Welches Modellverhalten generiert ein semi-endogenes Wachstumsmodell mit explizit formuliertem Bevölkerungssektor für den Fall einer alternden und schrumpfenden Bevölkerung?

Ziel der Arbeit ist es daher:

1. einen Überblick über die theoretischen Aspekte des demographischen Wandels zu geben.
2. einen Überblick über neoklassische Wachstumsmodelle und deren Verhalten bei demographischen Veränderungen zu geben.
3. ein semi-endogenes Wachstumsmodell mit einem expliziten Bevölkerungssektor zu entwickeln.
4. die Auswirkungen des demographischen Wandels in einem semi-endogenen Wachstumsmodell zu analysieren.
5. die Konsequenzen ausgewählter Politikmaßnahmen in einem demographischen Wachstumsmodell zu evaluieren.

Als Modellierungsansatz wird dabei auf System Dynamics zurückgegriffen. Es geht auf Jay Forrester, Professor Emeritus des MIT, zurück und kann als Weiterentwicklung des Systemdenkens durch Computerunterstützung verstanden werden. System Dynamics berücksichtigt explizit Bestands- und Flussgrößen, Zeitverzögerungen, Feedback-Prozesse und nichtlineare Zusammenhänge. System Dynamics liegt die Annahme zugrunde, dass die Struktur das Verhalten bestimmt. Modelle werden deshalb in Bestands- und Flussgrößen Diagrammen oder in Kausalschleifen dargestellt. Dies ermöglicht es, grundlegende logische Sachverhalte grafisch anschaulich zu visualisieren. Ein Nebenziel der Arbeit ist es daher, möglichst alle verwendeten Modelle und erklärten Zusammenhänge in eine einheitliche systemgerechte Darstellung zu überführen und dem Leser damit einen tieferen Einblick in die Grundstrukturen der Modelle zu gewähren.

Die Arbeit gliedert sich neben der Einleitung und dem Schluss in vier Hauptkapitel (zur Struktur der Theoriekapitel siehe Abbildung 1). Im Kapitel "Demographic Determinants and Economic Impact" werden zwei Ziele verfolgt: zum einen die Darstellung der ökonomischen Konsequenzen des demografischen Wandels und zum anderen die Herleitung der Einflussfaktoren der demografischen Determinanten. Der Schwerpunkt liegt dabei nicht auf einer Wiedergabe prognostizierter Veränderungen einzelner Länder, sondern in einer sehr stark theoriegeleiteten umfassenden

Demographic Determinants and Economic Impact

EFFECTS ON POPULATION
- Fertility (Economic Theory of Fertility Choice, Easterlin Hypothesis, Biographic Theory of Fertility, Other Fertility Theories)
- Mortality (Determinants of Mortality, Trend and Effects on Mortality)
- Migration (Macroeconomic Push-Pull and Gravity-Models, Micro-economic Behavioral Models, Social Network and Social Capital Models)
- Structure (Population Pyramids, Malthusian Growth)

ECONOMIC EFFECTS
- Financial Sector (Lifecycle Hypothesis of Consumption, Ricardian Equivalence and Saving Patterns, Rate of Return and Asset Meltdown Hypothesis)
- Labor Market (Labor Supply, Labor Demand)
- R&D Sector (Skills, Labor Productivity, Innovation)
- Other Effects (Consumption Pattern, Health and Long Term Care, Pension Systems, Fiscal Policy, Transport Infrastructure, Election and Governance, Housing Demand)

Neoclassical Growth Theories

EXOGENOUS GROWTH MODEL (SOLOW 1956)
- Assumptions, Structure, Dynamics, Policy Experiments
- Augmentation (Model of "Silver Growth"(Gruescu2006), Model with Migration (Barro/Sala-i-Martin 2004), Model with variable Population Growth (Solow 1956)

ENDOGENOUS GROWTH MODEL (ROMER 1990)
- Precursor (AK-Model, Uzawa-Lucas-Model, Theory of "Creative Destruction" (Schumpeter)),
- Assumptions, Structure, Dynamics, Policy Experiments

SEMI-ENDOGENOUS GROWTH MODEL (JONES 1995)
- Assumptions, Structure, Dynamics, Policy Experimentssdfdsf

Abbildung 1 Struktur der Kapitel 2 und 3.
Quelle: eigene Darstellung

Darstellung. Dabei werden zunächst die Fertilität, die Mortalität, die Migration und die Bevölkerungsstruktur auf ihre Einflussfaktoren untersucht. Anschließend werden die ökonomischen Konsequenzen einer veränderten Fertilität, Mortalität, Migration und Bevölkerungsstruktur auf das Wirtschaftswachstum aufgezeigt.

Im Kapitel "Neoclassical Growth Theories" werden zur Herleitung des semi-endogenen Wachstumsmodells von Jones das Modell von Solow und das endogene Modell von Romer erläutert. Alle Modelle werden mit wichtigen Modellerweiterungen oder bedeutenden Vorläufer-Modellen dargestellt. Es wird untersucht, inwiefern bereits demografische Komponenten Berücksichtigung finden und welche Auswirkungen eine alternde und schrumpfende Bevölkerung in den Modellen hat.

Das Kapitel "Demographic Growth Model" erläutert dezidiert das neue und erweiterte, eigens entwickelte semi-endogene Wachstumsmodell (zur Modellstruktur siehe Abbildung 2 und Abbildung 3). Die einzelnen Teilabschnitte werden initialisiert und verschiedenen Testverfahren zur Validierung und Plausibilisierung unterzogen.

Der Bevölkerungssektor wird dabei besonders erläutert. Er setzt sich aus vier Altersgruppen zusammen: Kinder, junge Arbeitnehmer, ältere Arbeitnehmer und Rentner. Alle vier Altersgruppen werden zusätzlich in hoch- und niedrigqualifizierte Arbeitskräfte unterschieden. Im Teilmodul Wachstum ist es damit möglich, in einer 2×4 Matrix die abgesetzten Produkte auf die Alters- und Qualifikationsstrukturen entsprechend einer Einkommensstruktur zu verteilen. Welcher Anteil gespart oder konsumiert wird ist für jede Gruppe der 2×4 Matrix individuell bestimmbar, da die Sparquote für jede Gruppe unterschiedlich sein kann. Damit können beispielsweise die Grundgedanken des Lebens-Zyklus-Konzeptes berücksichtigt werden.

Im Kapitel "Policy Scenarios" werden neben einem Basislauf drei Politikmaßnahmen getestet. Der Basislauf ergibt sich aus typischen Parametern schrumpfender Gesellschaften, beispielsweise einer sehr geringen Fertilität. Außerdem werden die individuellen Sparquoten, Ausbildungs- und Lohnniveaus berücksichtigt. Die erste Politikmaßnahme (Familienpolitik) stabilisiert die schrumpfende Bevölkerung auf niedrigerem Niveau. Es zeigt sich, dass durch die große Trägheit des Systems (nur Frauen im gebärfähigen Alter können Kinder bekommen) die Bevölkerung zunächst weiter schrumpft bevor sie sich stabilisiert. Als gesamtvolkswirtschaftliche Bewertungskennziffern werden u.a. der Pro-Kopf-Konsum und der Nutzen pro Person herangezogen. Insgesamt reicht dies nicht aus, um dauerhaftes Wachstum zu erreichen. Die zweite Politikmaßnahme (Bildungspolitik) testet deshalb zusätzlich eine Erhöhung der Qualifikation der Bevölkerung. Ob dies einen positiven Effekt hat, hängt sehr stark von der genauen Modellierung des Forschungssektors ab. Die Effekte sind marginal. Da die Fertilitätsraten von hoch und niedrig Qualifizierten gleich sind, ergeben sich bevölkerungsseitig keine Unterschiede zur Politikmaßnahme 1. Bei unterschiedlichen Fertilitätsraten ergäbe sich jedoch ein anders Verlaufsmuster. Die dritte Politikmaßnahme (Migrationspolitik) überprüft, ob eine Zuwanderung von Arbeitskräften zusätzlich zur Maßnahme 1 eine positive Auswirkung hat. Jeder Immigrant kann dabei Kapital mitbringen.

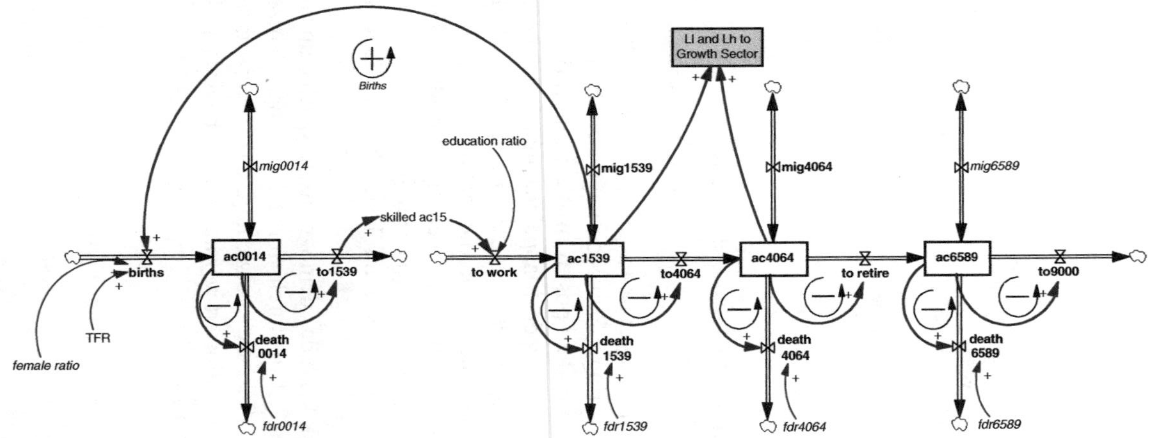

Abbildung 2 vereinfachte Struktur des Teilmodells “Population”.
Quelle: eigene Darstellung

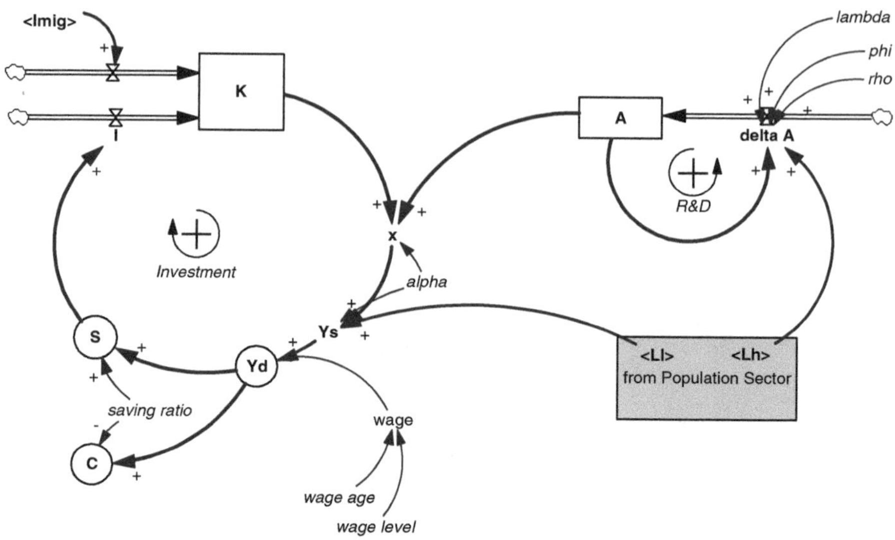

Abbildung 3 vereinfachte Struktur des Teilmodells "Growth".
Quelle: eigene Darstellung

Das Modell ist damit nicht länger eine geschlossene Volkswirtschaft, sondern teilweise offen. Bereits geringe Zuwanderungsraten können die Bevölkerung dauerhaft anwachsen lassen und zu positiven Wachstumseffekten führen.

Die Ergebnisse zeigen, dass jede Maßnahme ihre Wirkung über einen spezifischen Zeitraum entfaltet. Die größte Trägheit besitzt die Stabilisierung der Bevölkerung durch Politikmaßnahme 1 (Familienpolitik). Sie eignet sich deshalb vor allem als langfristige Strategie. Eine Verbesserung der Bildung (Politikmaßnahme 2) wirkt dagegen eher mittelfristig. Für eine zügige und daher kurzfristige Veränderung der Bevölkerungsstruktur kommt letztlich nur die Politikmaßnahme 3 (Migrationspolitik) in Frage.

Als Forschungsausblick kann das demografische Wachstumsmodell weiter ausdifferenziert werden und ist dadurch für Länder oder einzelne Agglomerationsräume anwendbar. Dafür ist es notwendig, dass die exogenen Größen durch empirische Untersuchungen kalibriert werden. Dadurch wird aus dem theoretischen Ansatz ein Prognoseinstrument.

Annex

A.1 Model Initialization

A.1.1 Test 1: Stable Population

See Figs. A.1–A.3

A.1.2 Test 2: Growing Population

See Figs. A.4–A.6

A.1.3 Base Run

See Figs. A.7–A.9

1. Initialization Population Stock						
Description	**Variable**	**Unit**	**Value high**	**low**	**Remark**	
initial total population	init N	Person	1000,0		sum of inital age cohorts	sum of init ac [age,skill]
initial births	init births	Person/Year	6,9	6,9	births from ac1539 with respect to female ratio and TFR	ac1539[skill]/size1539*female ratio*TFR
initial deaths	init deaths	Person/Year	3,5	3,5	sum of all deaths in each cohort	sum of (init ac [age,skill]*fractional death rate[age])
initial migration	init migration	Person/Year	0,0	0,0	sum of initial migration	sum of migration [age,skill]
initial ageing	init ageing to 90	Person/Year	3,3	3,3	ageing out of the model	ac6489[skill]/size6489
initial change in population	init delta N	Person/Year	0,0	0,0	inital total population with respect to all changes	init N [skill]+birth[skill]-deaths[skill]+migration[skill]-ageing[skill]
growth rate population stock	gN	Dmnl	0,0000		population change to total population	sum of (delta N [skill]) / N
initial labor force	init L	Person	314,5	314,5	sum of cohort 1539 and 4064	sum of ac 1539[skill] and ac 4064 [skill]
labor force ratio	sR	Dmnl	0,3145	0,3145	ratio labor force to total population	L [skill] / N

Fig. A.1 Test 1 calculation of initial values: population stock
Source: own calculation

2. Initialization Patent Stock					
Description	**Variable**	**Unit**	**Value**	**Remark**	
inital growth rate patent stock	gA	Dmnl	0,0000	derived ouf of the high skilled labor force and influencing parameters	lambda * gN / (1-phi) = 0
inital patent stock	***init A***	***Patent***	***9682***	***change of patent stock / growth rate***	***(gA / L^lambda*rho)^(1/(1–phi)) = 1***

Fig. A.2 Test 1 calculation of initial values: patent stock
Source: own calculation

3. Initialization Capital Stock					
Description	**Variable**	**Unit**	**Value**	**Remark**	
inital wage distribuation	wage [age0014] wage [age1539] wage [age4064] wage [age6589]	Dmnl Dmnl Dmnl Dmnl	0,15 0,15 0,22 0,07	0,09 derived out of wage 0,12 distribution 0,18 [age,skill] 0,06	(wage level [skill] / sum wage level [skill]) * (wage level [age] / sum wage
inital saving ratio	saving ratio wage	Dmnl	0,01 0,03 0,07 0,03	0,01 derived out of saving 0,03 ratios and wage 0,06 distribution 0,03	saving ratio [age,skill]*wage [age,skill]
total saving ratio	saving ratio total	Dmnl	0,27	ratio of income that is saved	sum of saving ratios
steady state K/AN	steady K/AN	Euro/(Person*Patent)	infinity	derived from exogenous parameter - saving ratio, population growth rate, depletion rate, patent stock growth rate, marginal capital productivity, and low-skilled labor force ratio	(saving ratio total / (gN + gA + delta))^(1/(1–alpha))*sR[low] = infinity
inital capital stock	***init K***	***Euro***	***92.934.205***	***initial stocks leads to steady K/AN***	***steady K/AN*init A * init N = selectable***

Fig. A.3 Test 1 calculation of initial values: capital stock
Source: own calculation

1. Initialization Population Stock						
Description	**Variable**	**Unit**	**Value high**	**low**	**Remark**	
initial total population	init N	Person	1000,0		sum of inital age cohorts	sum of init ac [age,skill]
initial births	init births	Person/Year	17,7	17,7	births from ac1539 with respect to female ratio and TFR	ac1539[skill]/size1539*female ratio*TFR
initial deaths	init deaths	Person/Year	2,0	2,0	sum of all deaths in each cohort	sum of (init ac [age,skill]*fractional death rate[age])
initial migration	init migration	Person/Year	0,0	0,0	sum of initial migration	sum of migration [age,skill]
initial ageing	init ageing to 90	Person/Year	1,6	1,6	ageing out of the model	ac6489[skill]/size6489
initial change in population	init delta N	Person/Year	14,2	14,2	inital total population with respect to all changes	init N [skill]+birth[skill]-deaths[skill]+migration[skill]-ageing[skill]
growth rate population stock	gN	Dmnl	0,0284		population change to total population	sum of (delta N [skill]) / N
initial labor force	init L	Person	275,2	275,19	sum of cohort 1539 and 4064	sum of ac 1539[skill] and ac 4064 [skill]
labor force ratio	sR	Dmnl	0,2752	0,2752	ratio labor force to total population	L [skill] / N

Fig. A.4 Test 2 calculation of initial values: population stock
Source: own calculation

2. Initialization Patent Stock					
Description	**Variable**	**Unit**	**Value**	**Remark**	
inital growth rate patent stock	gA	Dmnl	0,0284	derived ouf of the high skilled labor force and influencing parameters	lambda * gN / (1–phi)
inital patent stock	***init A***	***Patent***	***9682***	***change of patent stock / growth rate***	***(gA / L^lambda*rho)^(1/(1-phi))***

Fig. A.5 Test 2 calculation of initial values: patent stock
Source: own calculation

3. Initialization Capital Stock

Description	Variable	Unit	Value		Remark	
inital wage distribuation	wage [age0014] wage [age1539] wage [age4064] wage [age6589]	Dmnl Dmnl Dmnl Dmnl	0,15 0,15 0,22 0,07	0,09 0,12 0,18 0,06	derived out of wage distribution [age,skill]	(wage level [skill] / sum wage level [skill]) * (wage level [age] / sum wage
inital saving ratio	saving ratio wage	Dmnl	0,01 0,03 0,07 0,03	0,01 0,03 0,06 0,03	derived out of saving ratios and wage distribution	saving ratio [age,skill]*wage [age,skill]
total saving ratio	saving ratio total	Dmnl	0,27		ratio of income that is saved	sum of saving ratios
steady state K/AN	steady K/AN	Euro/(Person*Patent)	6,3276		derived from exogenous parameter - saving ratio, population growth rate, depletion rate, patent stock growth rate, marginal capital productivity, and low-skilled labor force ratio	(saving ratio total / (gN + gA + delta))^(1/(1–alpha))*sR[low]
inital capital stock	***init K***	***Euro***	***61.262.625***		***initial stocks leads to steady K/AN***	***steady K/AN*init A * init N***

Fig. A.6 Test 2 calculation of initial values: capital stock
Source: own calculation

1. Initialization Population Stock

Description	Variable	Unit	Value high	low	Remark	
initial total population	init N	Person	1000,0		sum of inital age cohorts	sum of init ac [age,skill]
initial births	init births	Person/Year	10,6	24,8	births from ac1539 with respect to female ratio and TFR	ac1539[skill]/size1539*female ratio*TFR
initial deaths	init deaths	Person/Year	1,2	2,7	sum of all deaths in each cohort	sum of (init ac [age,skill]*fractional death rate[age])
initial migration	init migration	Person/Year	0,0	0,0	sum of initial migration	sum of migration [age,skill]
initial ageing	init ageing to 90	Person/Year	0,9	2,2	ageing out of the model	ac6489[skill]/size6489
initial change in population	init delta N	Person/Year	8,5	19,9	inital total population with respect to all changes	init N [skill]+birth[skill]-deaths[skill]+migration[skill]-ageing[skill]
growh rate population stock	gN	Dmnl	0,0284		population change to total population	sum of (delta N [skill]) / N
initial labor force	init L	Person	165,1	385,266	sum of cohort 1539 and 4064	sum of ac 1539[skill] and ac 4064 [skill]
labor force ratio	sR	Dmnl	0,1651	0,3853	ratio labor force to total population	L [skill] / N

Fig. A.7 Base run calculation of initial values: population stock
Source: own calculation

2. *Initialization Patent Stock*					
Description	**Variable**	**Unit**	**Value**	**Remark**	
inital growth rate patent stock	gA	Dmnl	0,0284	derived ouf of the high skilled labor force and influencing parameters	lambda * gN / (1–phi)
inital patent stock	***init A***	***Patent***	***5809***	***change of patent stock / growth rate***	***(gA / L^lambda*rho)^(1/(1–phi))***

Fig. A.8 Base run calculation of initial values: patent stock
Source: own calculation

3. Initialization Capital Stock					
Description	**Variable**	**Unit**	**Value**	**Remark**	
inital wage distribuation	wage [age0014] wage [age1539] wage [age4064] wage [age6589]	Dmnl Dmnl Dmnl Dmnl	0,18 0,18 0,27 0,11	0,00 derived out of wage 0,14 distribution 0,22 [age,skill] 0,09	(wage level [skill] / sum wage level [skill]) * (wage level [age] / sum wage
inital saving ratio	saving ratio wage	Dmnl	0,00 0,04 0,07 0,01	0,00 derived out of saving 0,01 ratios and wage 0,03 distribution 0,00	saving ratio [age,skill]*wage [age,skill]
total saving ratio	saving ratio total	Dmnl	0,16	ratio of income that is saved	sum of saving ratios
steady state K/AN	steady K/AN	Euro/(Person*Patent)	1,7608	derived from exogenous parameter - saving ratio, population growth rate, depletion rate, patent stock growth rate, marginal capital productivity, and low-skilled labor force ratio	(saving ratio total / (gN + gA + delta))^(1/(1–alpha))*sR[low]
inital capital stock	***init K***	***Euro***	***10.228.816***	***initial stocks leads to steady K/AN***	***steady K/AN*init A * init N***

Fig. A.9 Base run calculation of initial values: capital stock
Source: own calculation

A.2 Model Equations

A.2.1 Model Part "Population"

ac0014[skill] = INTEG(births[skill] + mig0014[skill] − death0014[skill] − to1539[skill], init ac0014[skill])
ac1539[skill] = INTEG(to work[skill] + mig1539[skill] − death1539[skill] − to4064[skill], init ac1539[skill])
ac4064[skill] = INTEG(mig4064[skill] + to4064[skill] − death4064[skill] − to retire[skill], init ac4064[skill])
ac6589[skill] = INTEG(mig6589[skill] + to retire[skill] − death6589[skill] − to9000[skill], init ac6590[skill])
Unit: Person [0,?]
Comment: age cohort
*births[skill] = ac1539[skill]/size1539 * female ratio * TFR*
Unit: Person/Year [0,?]
Comment: births per year
*death0014[skill] = fdr0014/size0014 * ac0014[skill]*
*death1539[skill] = fdr1539/size1539 * ac1539[skill]*
*death4064[skill] = fdr4064/size4064 * ac4064[skill]*
*death6589[skill] = fdr6589/size6589 * ac6589[skill]*
Unit: Person/Year [0,?]
Comment: dead persons in cohort 65 to 89
*education ratio = (education ratio input + policy2 * STEP (0.2, 50))*
Unit: Dmnl [0,1,0.02]
Comment: percentage of high skilled worker
*mig1539[skill] = IF THEN ELSE (Time >= 50, mig1539 input[skill] * policy3, 0)*
*mig4064[skill] = IF THEN ELSE (Time >= 50, mig4064 input[skill] * policy3, 0)*
Unit: Person/Year [0,?,10]
Comment: migration cohort 15 to 39 and 40 to 64 with respect to skills
skilled ac15 = SUM (to1539[skill!])
Unit: Person/Year [0,?]
Comment: sum of skilled young population
*TFR = TFR input − (base run * STEP (4, 10)) + (policy1 * STEP (1.08, 50))*
Unit: Person/Person [1,5,0.02]
Comment: TFR with policies
to retire[skill] = ac4064[skill]/size4064
Person/Year [0,?,10]
aging from 64 to 65 (retirement)
*to work[high] = education ratio * skilled ac15*
*to work[low] = (1 − education ratio) * skilled ac15*
Unit: Person/Year [0,?]
Comment: enter in working age with respect to education (high and low skilled)
to1539[skill] = ac0014[skill]/size0014

to4064[skill] = ac1539[skill]/size1539
to9000[skill] = ac6589[skill]/size6589
Unit: Person/Year [0,?,10]
Comment: aging from XX to XX

A.2.2 Model Part "Population": Calculation

Biletter J = (SUM (ac0014[skill!]) − SUM (ac6589[skill!]))/(SUM (ac1539[skill!]) + SUM (ac4064[skill!]))
Unit: Dmnl
Comment: Biletter J differs from dependency ratio as the non-working age cohort 65 to 89 gets negative in
births total = SUM (births[skill!])
Unit: Person/Year [0,?]
Comment: total births
deaths total = SUM (death0014[skill!] + death1539[skill!] + death4064[skill!] + death6589[skill!] + to9000[skill!])
Unit: Person/Year [0,?]
Comment: total deaths
delta N = SUM (delta N skill[skill!])
Unit: Person/Year
Comment: change in total population
delta N skill[skill] = births[skill] + mig0014[skill] + mig1539[skill] + mig4064[skill] + mig6589[skill] − death0014[skill] − death1539[skill] − death4064[skill] − death6589[skill] − to9000[skill]
Unit: Person/Year
Comment: net change of total population with respect to skills
dependency ratio = (SUM (ac0014[skill!]) + SUM (ac6589[skill!]))/(SUM (ac1539[skill!]) + SUM (ac4064[skill!]))
Unit: Dmnl [0,?]
Comment: age dependency ratio non-working population to working population
gN = delta N/N total
Unit: Dmnl/Year
Comment: growth rate of the population
Imig = SUM (Imig skill[skill!])
Unit: Euro/Year [0,?]
Comment: total capital brought by immigrants
*Imig skill[skill] = (mig0014[skill] + mig1539[skill] + mig4064[skill] + mig6589[skill]) * mig capital[skill]*
Unit: Euro/Year [0,?]
Comment: capital that brought by immigrants with respect to skills
init pop total = SUM (init ac0014[skill!]) + SUM (init ac1539[skill!]) + SUM (init ac4064[skill!]) + SUM (init ac6590[skill!]

Unit: Person [0,?]
Comment: initial total population

Lh = ac1539[high] + ac4064[high]
Unit: Person [0,?]
Comment: total number of high skilled workers

Ll = ac1539[low] + ac4064[low]
Unit: Person [0,?]
Comment: total number of low skilled workers

momentum = N total/init pop total
Unit: Dmnl [0,?]
Comment: population momentum

N total = SUM (N total skill[skill!])
Unit: Person [0,?]
Comment: total population

N total skill[skill] = ac0014[skill] + ac1539[skill] + ac4064[skill] + ac6589 [skill]
Unit: Person [0,?]
Comment: total skilled and total unskilled population

A.2.3 Model Part "Growth"

A = INTEG(delta A , init A)
Unit: Patent [0,?]
Comment: current stock of patents

*C[age,skill] = (1 − saving ratio[age,skill]) * Yd[age,skill]*
Unit: Euro/Year [0,?]
Comment: current consumption

*delta A = ((Lh/unit Person) ^ lambda) * ((A/unit Patent) ^ (phi)) * rho*
Unit: Patent/Year [0,?]
Comment: change in R&D sector

*depletion = delta * K*
Unit: Euro/Year [0,?]
Comment: amount of scrapped capital

deltaNFAd = IF THEN ELSE (SUM (S[age!,skill!]) < 0, − SUM (S[age!,skill!]) , 0)
Unit: Euro/Year [0,?]
Comment: amount of foreign direct investments (capital import) to set investments to zero.

I = SUM (S[age!,skill!]) + deltaNFAd
Unit: Euro/Year [0,?]
Comment: Investments equals Spending and capital imports

K = INTEG(I + Imig − depletion , init K)
Unit: Euro [0,?]
Comment: capital stock

*S[age,skill] = saving ratio[age,skill] * Yd[age,skill]*

Unit: Euro/Year [0,?]
Comment: saved income
*wage[age0014,high] = (wage level/(1 + wage level)) * (wage age[age0014]/SUM (wage age[age!]))*
*wage[age1539,high] = (wage level/(1 + wage level)) * (wage age[age1539]/SUM (wage age[age!]))*
*wage[age4064,high] = (wage level/(1 + wage level)) * (wage age[age4064]/SUM (wage age[age!]))*
*wage[age6589,high] = (wage level/(1 + wage level)) * (wage age[age6589]/SUM (wage age[age!]))*
*wage[age0014,low] = (1/(1 + wage level)) * (wage age[age0014]/SUM (wage age [age!]))*
*wage[age1539,low] = (1/(1 + wage level)) * (wage age[age1539]/SUM (wage age [age!]))*
*wage[age4064,low] = (1/1 + wage level)) * (wage age[age4064]/SUM (wage age [age!]))*
*wage[age6589,low] = (1/(1 + wage level)) * (wage age[age6589]/SUM (wage age [age!]))*
Unit: Dmnl [0,2,0.1]
Comment: low skilled wage always 100%, high skilled wage in % of low skilled wage wage age distribution as external provided – Standard (0;1;1.5;0.6)
*x = (K/unit Euro) ^ (alpha) * (A/unit Patent) ^ (1 – alpha) * unit Euro per Year*
Unit: Euro/Year [0,?]
Comment: Intermediate goods sector
*Yd[age,skill] = wage[age,skill] * Ys*
Unit: Euro/Year [0,?]
Comment: income (demand final goods sector)
*Ys = (x) * ((Ll/unit Person) ^ (1 – alpha))*
Unit: Euro/Year [0,?]
Comment: production (supply final goods sector)

A.2.4 Model Part "Growth": Calculation

*A0014[skill] = A/N total * ac0014[skill]*
*A1539[skill] = A/N total * ac1539[skill]*
*A4064[skill] = A/N total * ac1539[skill]*
*A6589[skill] = A/N total * ac6589[skill]*
Unit: Patent [0,?]
Comment: R&D expenditures per age group
C total = SUM (C[age!,skill!])
Unit: Euro/Year [0,?]
Comment: sum of all consumption
C total age[age] = SUM (C[age,skill!])

Unit: Euro/Year [0,?]
Comment: sum of all consumption with respect to age
C total skill[skill] = SUM (C[age!,skill])
Unit: Euro/Year [0,?]
Comment: sum of all consumption with respect to skills
*C/AN = C total/(A * N total)*
*Unit: Euro/(Year*Person*Patent) [0,?]*
Comment: current C/AN
C/N = C total/N total
*Unit: Euro/(Year*Person) [0,?]*
Comment: current C/N
gA = delta A/A
Unit: Dmnl/Year [0,?]
Comment: growth rate of R&D sector
gK = (I + Imig − depletion)/K
Unit: Dmnl/Year
Comment: growth rate capital stock
*I/AN = (gN + gA + delta) * K/AN*
*Unit: Euro/(Year*Person*Patent) [0,?]*
Comment: required investments
*K/AN = K/(A * N total)*
*Unit: Euro/(Person*Patent) [0,?]*
Comment: current K/AN
K/N = K/N total
Unit: Euro/Person [0,?]
Comment: current K/N
Lh/A = Lh/A
Unit: Person/Patent [0,?]
Comment: labor per Research
logA = LN (A/unit Patent)
Unit: Dmnl
Comment: log of current R&D stock
S per capita[age0014,skill] = S[age0014,skill]/ac0014[skill]
S per capita[age1539,skill] = S[age1539,skill]/ac1539[skill]
S per capita[age4064,skill] = S[age4064,skill]/ac4064[skill]
S per capita[age6589,skill] = S[age6589,skill]/ac6589[skill]
*Unit: Euro/(Person*Year) [0,?]*
Comment: savings per capita
S per eff capita[age0014,skill] = S per capita[age0014,skill]/A0014[skill]
S per eff capita[age1539,skill] = S per capita[age1539,skill]/A1539[skill]
S per eff capita[age4064,skill] = S per capita[age4064,skill]/A4064[skill]
S per eff capita[age6589,skill] = S per capita[age6589,skill]/A6589[skill]
*Unit: Euro/(Person*Year*Patent) [0,?]*
Comment: savings per effective capita
S total = SUM (S[age!,skill!])

Unit: Euro/Year [0,?]
Comment: sum of all savings
S total age[age] = SUM (S[age,skill!])
Unit: Euro/Year [0,?]
Comment: sum of savings with respect to age
S total skill[skill] = SUM (S[age!,skill])
Unit: Euro/Year [0,?]
sum of savings with respect to skills
*S/AN = S total/(A * N total)*
Unit: Euro/Year/Person/Patent [0,?]
Comment: current S/AN
S/N = S total/N total
Unit: Euro/Year/Person [0,?]
Comment: current S/N
saving ratio total = SUM (saving ratio wage[age!,skill!])
Unit: Dmnl [0,1]
Comment: total saving ratio
saving ratio total age[age] = SUM (saving ratio wage[age,skill!])
Unit: Dmnl [0,1]
Comment: saving ratio with respect to age
saving ratio total skill[skill] = SUM (saving ratio wage[age!,skill])
Unit: Dmnl [0,1]
Comment: saving ratio with respect to skills
*saving ratio wage[age,skill] = saving ratio[age,skill] * wage[age,skill]*
Unit: Dmnl [0,1]
Comment: saving ratio with respect to wage differentiation
*velocity gA = (1 + gA * unit Time) ^ (1 − phi) * (1 + gN * unit Time) ^ lambda*
Unit: Dmnl/Year
Comment: change of growth rate R&D
*Y/AN = Ys/(A * N total)*
*Unit: Euro/(Year*Person*Patent) [0,?]*
Comment: current Y/AN
Y/N = Ys/N total
*Unit: Euro/(Year*Person) [0,?]*
Comment: current Y/N

A.2.5 Model Part "Utility"

accU/AN[age,skill] = INTEG(discounted effU[age,skill] , init U/AN[age,skill])
*Unit: Utility/(Person*Patent) [0,?]*
Comment: accumulated discounted utiltiy per effective capita
accU/N[age,skill] = INTEG(discounted u[age,skill] , init U/N[age,skill])

Unit: Utility/Person [0,?]
Comment: accumulated discounted utility per capita
C per capita[age0014,skill] = C[age0014,skill]/ac0014[skill]
C per capita[age1539,skill] = C[age1539,skill]/ac1539[skill]
C per capita[age4064,skill] = C[age4064,skill]/ac4064[skill]
C per capita[age6589,skill] = C[age6589,skill]/ac6589[skill]
Unit: Euro/(Person*Year) [0,?]
Comment: consumption per capita with respect to age and skills
C per eff capita[age0014,skill] = C per capita[age0014,skill]/A0014[skill]
C per eff capita[age1539,skill] = C per capita[age1539,skill]/A1539[skill]
C per eff capita[age4064,skill] = C per capita[age4064,skill]/A4064[skill]
C per eff capita[age6589,skill] = C per capita[age6589,skill]/A6589[skill]
Unit: Euro/(Person*Year*Patent) [0,?]
Comment: consumption per effective capita
discounted effU[age,skill] = IF THEN ELSE (Time < reference time , 0, effU[age, skill] * EXP (− sigma * (Time − reference time)/unit Time))
Unit: Utility/(Person*Patent*Year) [0,?]
Comment: discounted effectice utility
discounted u[age,skill] = IF THEN ELSE (Time < reference time , 0, U[age,skill] * EXP (− sigma * (Time − reference time)/unit Time))
Unit: Utility/(Person*Year) [0,?]
Comment: discounted utility at point t in time
effU[age,skill] = IF THEN ELSE (theta <> 1, ((C per eff capita[age,skill] * (unit Time * unit Person * unit Patent/unit Euro)) ^ (1 − theta))/(1 − theta) , LN (C per eff capita[age,skill] * unit Time * unit Person * unit Patent/unit Euro)) * (unit Utility/(unit Time * unit Person * unit Patent))
Unit: Utility/(Person*Year*Patent) [0,?]
Comment: utility per effective capita
U[age,skill] = IF THEN ELSE (theta <> 1, ((C per capita[age,skill] * (unit Time * unit Person/unit Euro)) ^ (1 − theta))/(1 − theta), LN (C per capita[age,skill] * (unit Person * unit Time/unit Euro))) * (unit Utility/(unit Person * unit Time))
Unit: Utility/(Person*Year) [0,?]
Comment: utility at current time

A.2.6 Model Part "Utility": Calculation

accuU/AN total = INTEG(discounted effU total , init U/AN total)
Unit: Utility/(Person*Patent)
Comment: accumulated utility per effective capita in total
accuU/N total = INTEG(discounted u total , init U/N total)
Unit: Utility/Person [1,?]
Comment: accumulated total utility per person

discounted effU total = IF THEN ELSE (Time < reference time , 0, effU total * EXP (− sigma * (Time − reference time)/unit Time))
Unit: Utility/(Person*Year*Patent) [0,?]
Comment: discounted utility per effective capital in total
discounted u total = IF THEN ELSE (Time < reference time , 0, U total * EXP (− sigma * (Time − reference time)/unit Time))
Unit: Utility/(Year*Person) [0,?]
Comment: discounted utility per person in total
effU total = IF THEN ELSE (theta <> 1, ((C/AN * (unit Time * unit Person * unit Patent/unit Euro)) ^(1 − theta))/(1 − theta), LN ("C/AN" * unit Time * unit Person * unit Patent/unit Euro)) * (unit Utility/(unit Time * unit Person * unit Patent))
Unit: Utility/(Person*Year*Patent) [0,?]
Comment: utility per effective capita in total
init U/AN total = SUM (init U/AN[age!,skill!])
Unit: Utility/(Patent*Person) [1,?]
Comment: inital accumulated utility per effective capita
init U/N total = SUM (init U/N[age!,skill!])
Unit: Utility/Person [1,?]
Comment: inital accumulated utility per person
U total = IF THEN ELSE (theta <> 1, ((C/N * (unit Time * unit Person/unit Euro)) ^(1 − theta))/(1 − theta) , LN ("C/N" * (unit Person * unit Time/unit Euro))) * (unit Utility/(unit Person * unit Time))
Unit: Utility/(Year*Person) [0,?]
Comment: utility per person in total

A.2.7 Input Variables from External Spreadsheet

alpha = GET XLS CONSTANTS('modelinput.xls', 'input', 'D8')
Unit: Dmnl [0,1,0.01]
Comment: capital elasticity
delta = GET XLS CONSTANTS('modelinput.xls', 'input', 'D9')
Unit: Dmnl/Year [0,1,0.05]
Comment: rate of depletion
education ratio input = GET XLS CONSTANTS('modelinput.xls', 'input', 'D56')
Unit: Dmnl [0,1,0.02]
Comment: percentage of high skilled worker
fdr0014 = GET XLS CONSTANTS('modelinput.xls', 'input', 'D44')
fdr1539 = GET XLS CONSTANTS('modelinput.xls', 'input', 'D45')
fdr4064 = GET XLS CONSTANTS('modelinput.xls', 'input', 'D46')
fdr6589 = GET XLS CONSTANTS('modelinput.xls', 'input', 'D47')
Unit: Dmnl [0,1,0.02]
Comment: fractional death rate cohorts
female ratio = GET XLS CONSTANTS('modelinput.xls', 'input', 'D55')

Unit: Dmnl [0,1,0.005]
Comment: sex ratio female
init A = GET XLS CONSTANTS('modelinput.xls', 'input', 'D5')
Unit: Patent [0,?,1]
Comment: initial stock of patents
init ac0014[skill] = GET XLS CONSTANTS('modelinput.xls', 'input', 'D33')
init ac1539[skill] = GET XLS CONSTANTS('modelinput.xls', 'input', 'D34')
init ac4064[skill] = GET XLS CONSTANTS('modelinput.xls', 'input', 'D35')
init ac6590[skill] = GET XLS CONSTANTS('modelinput.xls', 'input', 'D36')
Unit: Person [0,?,10]
Comment: initial value age cohort 65 to 90
init K = GET XLS CONSTANTS('modelinput.xls', 'input', 'D6')
Unit: Euro [1000,?,100]
Comment: init capital stock
init U/AN[age,skill] = GET XLS CONSTANTS('modelinput.xls', 'input', 'D68')
*Unit: Utility/(Person*Patent) [0,?]*
Comment: initial accumulated utility per effective capita
init U/N[age,skill] = GET XLS CONSTANTS('modelinput.xls', 'input', 'D64')
Unit: Utility/Person [0,?]
Comment: initial accumulated utility per capita
lambda = GET XLS CONSTANTS('modelinput.xls', 'input', 'D11')
Unit: Dmnl [0,2,0.1]
Comment: degree of congestion in current research; lambda<1 stepping on toes; lambda>1 network externality
mig capital[skill] = GET XLS CONSTANTS('modelinput.xls", 'input", 'D42")
Unit: Euro/Person [0,?,1000]
Comment: capital per immigrated person with respect to skills
mig0014[skill] = GET XLS CONSTANTS('modelinput.xls', 'input', 'D38')
mig1539 input[skill] = GET XLS CONSTANTS('modelinput.xls', 'input', 'D39')
mig4064 input[skill] = GET XLS CONSTANTS('modelinput.xls', 'input', 'D40')
mig6589[skill] = GET XLS CONSTANTS('modelinput.xls', 'input', 'D41')
Unit: Person/Year [0,?,10]
Comment: migration cohort 65 to 89
phi = GET XLS CONSTANTS('modelinput.xls', 'input', 'D12')
Unit: Dmnl [0,2,0.1]
Comment: return on stocks of idea; phi >1 standing on shoulders; phi <1 fishing-out phi = 1 Romer Model
reference time = GET XLS CONSTANTS('modelinput.xls', 'input', 'D76')
Unit: Year [0,100,10]
Comment: relevant point ot time reference for discounting utility
rho = GET XLS CONSTANTS('modelinput.xls', 'input', 'D13')
Unit: Patent/Year [0,2,0.1]
Comment: accelarator
saving ratio[age,skill] = GET XLS CONSTANTS('modelinput.xls', 'input', 'D22')

Unit: Dmnl [0,1,0.01]
Comment: saving ratio – percentage that is saved from the income
sigma = GET XLS CONSTANTS('modelinput.xls', 'input', 'D75')
Unit: Dmnl [0,2,0.05]
Comment: time preference
size0014 == GET XLS CONSTANTS('modelinput.xls', 'input', 'D49')
size1539 == GET XLS CONSTANTS('modelinput.xls', 'input', 'D50')
size4064 == GET XLS CONSTANTS('modelinput.xls', 'input', 'D51')
size6589 == GET XLS CONSTANTS('modelinput.xls', 'input', 'D52')
Unit: Year [25,25,25]
Comment: cohort size age group
TFR input = GET XLS CONSTANTS('modelinput.xls', 'input', 'D54')
Unit: Person/Person [1,5,0.02]
Comment: total fertility rate – births per women per life – input from table
theta = GET XLS CONSTANTS('modelinput.xls', 'input', 'D74')
Unit: Dmnl [0,2,0.05]
Comment: marginal utility
wage age[age] = GET XLS CONSTANTS('modelinput.xls', 'input', 'D16')
Unit: Dmnl [0,?]
Comment: wage age distribution for all cohorts
wage level = GET XLS CONSTANTS('modelinput.xls', 'input', 'D19')
Unit: Dmnl [1,2,0.1]
Comment: wage level of high skilled worker to low skilled worker

A.2.8 Policy Switches

base run = 0
Unit: Dmnl [0,1,1]
Comment: if 1 than base run is on – change in TFR from growing to declining at t=20
policy1 = 0
Unit: Dmnl [0,1,1]
Comment: if 1 than policy 1 is on – population decline from t = 20 to t = 50 and than stabilization TFR=2.08
policy2 = 0
Unit: Dmnl [0,1,1]
Comment: if 1 than policy2 is on – raise of education level from 0.3 to 0.5 at time t=50
policy3 = 0
Unit: Dmnl [0,1,1]
Comment: if 1 than policy3 is on – immigration of 50 workers per working age cohort and skill (ac1539 and ac4064)

A.2.9 Subscripts and Unit Dummies

age: age0014, age1539, age4064, age6589
Comment age cohorts
skill: high, low
Comment: high skilled labor to work in R&D; low skilled labor to work in final goods sector
unit Euro == 1
Unit: Euro [1,1,1]
Comment: to correct units of the production function
unit Euro per Year == 1
Unit: Euro/Year [1,1,1]
Comment: to correct units of the production function
unit Patent == 1
Unit: Patent [1,1,1]
Comment: to correct units of the patent stock
unit Person == 1
Unit: Person [1,1,1]
Comment to correct units of the production function
unit Time == 1
Unit: Year [1,1,1]
Comment: to correct time
unit Utility == 1
Unit: Utility [1,1,1]
Comment: to correct utility function

References

Abel, A. B., Bernanke, B. S., & McNabb, R. (1998). *Macroeconomics*. Harlow: Pearson Education.

Aghion, P., Howitt, P., & García-Peúnalosa, C. (1999). *Endogenous growth theory*. Cambridge, MA: MIT.

Ando, A., & Modigliani, F. (1963). The "life cycle" hypothesis of saving: Aggregate implications and tests. *The American Economic Review, 53*(1), 55–84.

Arnds, P., & Bonin, H. (2003). Arbeitsmarkteffekte und finanzpolitische Folgen der demographischen Alterung in Deutschland. In M. Herfurth, M. Kohli, & K. F. Zimmermann (Eds.), *Arbeit in einer alternden Gesellschaft. Problembereiche und Entwicklungstendenzen der Erwerbssituation Älterer* (pp. 131–177). Opladen: Leske + Budrich.

Arnold, L. G. (1997). *Wachstumstheorie*. München: Vahlen.

Arnold, L. G. (2006). The dynamics of the Jones R&D growth model. *Review of Economic Dynamics, 9*(1), 143–152. Retrieved January 25, 2009, from doi:10.1016/j.red.2005.09.001.

Auerbach, A. J., & Herrmann, H. (Eds.). (2002). *Ageing, financial markets and monetary policy*. Berlin: Springer.

Auerbach, A. J., & Kotlikoff, L. J. (1999). *Macroeconomics: An integrated approach* (2nd ed.). Cambridge, MA: MIT.

Bähr, J. (2004). *Bevölkerungsgeographie* (4th ed., Vol. 1249). Stuttgart: Eugen Ulmer.

Barnett, W. A., & Rose, M. (2001). Joseph Schumpeter and modern nonlinear dynamics. In V. Orati, S. B. Dahiya, & J. A. Schumpeter (Eds.), *Economic theory in the light of Schumpeter's scientific heritage. Essays in memory of Schumpeter on his 50th death anniversary* (pp. 187–196). Rohtak: Spellbound.

Barro, R. J. (1974). Are government bonds net wealth? *The Journal of Political Economy, 82*(6), 1095–1117.

Barro, R. J. (1991). Economic growth in a cross section of countries. *The Quarterly Journal of Economics, 106*(2), 407–443.

Barro, R. J., & Becker, G. S. (1989). Fertility choice in a model of economic growth. *Econometrica, 57*(2), 481–501.

Barro, R. J., & Sala-i-Martin, X. (2004). *Economic growth*. Cambridge, MA: MIT.

Bass, F. M. (2004). A new product growth for model consumer durables: Reprint form 1969. *Management Science, 50*(12), 1825–1832.

Becker, G. S., & Barro, R. J. (1988). A reformulation of the economic theory of fertility. *The Quarterly Journal of Economics, 103*(1), 1–25.

Becker, G. S., Murphy, K. M., & Tamura, R. (1990). Human capital, fertility, and economic growth. *The Journal of Political Economy, 98*(5), S12–S37.

Billeter, E. P. (1954). Eine Maßzahl zur Beurteilung der Altersverteilung einer Bevölkerung. *Schweizerische Zeitschrift für Volkswirtschaft und Statistik, 90*, 496–505.

Birg, H. (Ed.). (2000). *Prosperität in einer alternden Gesellschaft*. Bad Homburg: Frankfurter Inst. – Stiftung Marktwirtschaft und Politik.

Birg, H. (2004). *Die Weltbevölkerung: Dynamik und Gefahren* (2nd ed., Vol. 2050). München: Beck Wissen.

Birg, H., Flöthmann, E.-J., & Reiter, I. (1991). *Biographische Theorie der demographischen Reproduktion*. Frankfurt/Main: Campus.

Blackburn, K., & Cipriani, G. P. (1998). Endogenous fertility, mortality and growth. *Journal of Population Economics, 11*(4), 517–534.

Blum, U. (1994). *Volkswirtschaftslehre: Studienhandbuch* (2nd ed.). München: Oldenbourg.

Boockmann, B., & Steinter, V. (2000). Gesellschaftliche Alterung, Humankapital und Produktivität. In H. Birg (Ed.), *Prosperität in einer alternden Gesellschaft* (pp. 107–136). Bad Homburg: Frankfurter Inst. – Stiftung Marktwirtschaft und Politik.

Börsch-Supan, A. H. (2004). *Global aging: Issues, answers, more questions* (Research Paper No. 2004-084). Retrieved May 08, 2009. Available at http://www.sfb504.uni-mannheim.de/.

Börsch-Supan, A. H., Coppola, M., Essig, L., Eymann, A., & Schunk, D. (2008). *The German Save study: Design and results*. Retrieved May 08, 2009, from Mannheimer Research Institute for the Economics of Ageing, http://madoc.bib.uni-mannheim.de/madoc/volltexte/2008/1935/.

Börsch-Supan, A. H., Düzgün, I., & Weiss, M. (2005). *Altern und Produktivität: Zum Stand der Forschung* (No. 075-05). Mannheim. Retrieved June 09, 2009. Available at http://www.mea.uni-mannheim.de/.

Börsch-Supan, A. H., & Essig, L. (2002). *Sparen in Deutschland: Ergebnisse der ersten SAVE-Studie*. Köln: Deutsches Institut für Altersvorsorge.

Börsch-Supan, A. H., Ludwig, A., & Winter, S. (2002). Ageing and international capital flows. In A. J. Auerbach & H. Herrmann (Eds.), *Ageing, financial markets and monetary policy* (pp. 55–83). Berlin: Springer.

Bossel, H. (1994). *Modeling and simulation*. Wellesley: A K Peters.

Bound, J., & Johnson, G. (1992). Changes in the structure of wages in the 1980's: An evaluation of alternative explanations. *The American Economic Review, 82*(3), 371–392.

Braun, J. (1993). *Essays on economic growth and migration*. Cambridge, MA: Harvard University.

Braun, N. (2000). Ökonomische Theorien in der Bevölkerungswissenschaft. In U. Mueller, B. Nauck, & A. Diekmann (Eds.), *Handbuch der Demographie 2. Anwendungen* (pp. 298–398). Berlin: Springer.

Bräuninger, D., Gräf, B., Gruber, K., Neuhaus, M., & Schneider, J. F. (2002). *The demographic challenge*. Retrieved April 21, 2008, from Deutsche Bank Research. Available at http://www.dbresearch.com/.

Brentano, L. (1910). The doctrine of malthus and the increase of population during the last decades. *The Economic Journal, 20*(79), 371–393.

Bretschger, L. (1999). *Growth theory and sustainable development* (1st ed.). Cheltenham: Edward Elgar.

Brown, L. A., & Sanders, R. L. (1981). Toward a development paradigm of migration, with particular reference to third world setting. In G. F. DeJong & R. W. Gardner (Eds.), *Pergamon policy studies on international development. Migration decision making. Multidisciplinary approaches to microlevel studies in developed and developing countries* (pp. 149–185). New York: Pergamon.

Brügelmann, R. (2004). Öffentliche Finanzen. In Institut der deutschen Wirtschaft (Ed.), *Perspektive 2050. Ökonomik des demographischen Wandels* (pp. 220–238). Köln: Deutscher Instituts-Verlag.

Brugiavini, A. (2002). Aging and saving in Europe. In A. J. Auerbach & H. Herrmann (Eds.), *Ageing, financial markets and monetary policy* (pp. 9–48). Berlin: Springer.

Cass, D. (1966). Optimum growth in an aggregative model of capital accumulation: A Turnpike theorem. *Econometrica, 34*(4), 833–850.

Cezanne, W. (2005). *Allgemeine Volkswirtschaftslehre* (Wolls Lehr- und Handbücher der Wirtschafts- und Sozialwissenschaften 6th ed.). München: Oldenbourg.

Cezanne, W., Titze, M., & Weber, L. (2006). Revision des neoklassischen Wachstumsmodells: Sind alle Lehrbücher falsch? *Wirtschaftswissenschaftliches Studium, 35*(9), 482–489.

Chamberlain, J., & Smallwood, S. (2004). Estimates of true birth order for Scotland, 1945–1999. *Population Trends, 117*, 27–42. Retrieved April 02, 2009. Available at http://www.statistics.gov.uk/.

Christiaans, T. (2004). *Neoklassische Wachstumstheorie: Darstellung, Kritik und Erweiterung*. Norderstedt: Books on Demand.

Cobb, C. W., & Douglas, P. H. (1928). A theory of production. *The American Economic Review, 18*(1), 139–165.

Crookall, D., & Thorngate, W. (2009). Acting, knowing, learning, simulating, gaming. *Simulation Gaming, 40*(1), 8–26. Retrieved June 11, 2009, from http://dx.doi.org/10.1177/1046878108330364.

Cutler, D., Deaton, A., & Lleras-Muney, A. (2006). The determinants of mortality. *The Journal of Economic Perspectives, 20*(3), 97–120.

DeJong, G. F., & Fawcett, J. T. (1981). Motivations for migration: An assessment and a value-expectancy research model. In G. F. DeJong & R. W. Gardner (Eds.), *Pergamon policy studies on international development. Migration decision making. Multidisciplinary approaches to microlevel studies in developed and developing countries* (pp. 13–58). New York: Pergamon.

DeJong, G. F., & Gardner, R. W. (Eds.). (1981). *Pergamon policy studies on international development. Migration decision making: Multidisciplinary approaches to microlevel studies in developed and developing countries*. New York: Pergamon.

Delbrück, C., & Raffelhüschen, B. (1993). The theory of migration. *Journal of Economics and Statistics, 212*(3), 341–356. Retrieved March 02, 2009, from http://www.digizeitschriften.de/index.php?id=166&ID=219081.

Desbarats, J. M. (1983). Constrained choice and migration. *Geografiska Annaler, 65*(1), 11–22.

Dickmann, N., & Seyda, S. (2004). Gründe für den Geburtenrückgang. In Institut der deutschen Wirtschaft (Ed.), *Perspektive 2050. Ökonomik des demographischen Wandels* (pp. 35–66). Köln: Deutscher Instituts-Verlag.

Dinopoulos, E., & Thompson, P. (1998). Schumpeterian growth without scale effects. *Journal of Economic Growth, 3*(4), 313–335. Retrieved February 05, 2009, from http://dx.doi.org/10.1023/A:1009711822294.

Dixit, A. K., & Stiglitz, J. E. (1977). Monopolistic competition and optimum product diversity. *The American Economic Review, 67*(3), 297–308.

Dodd, S. C. (1950). The interactance hypothesis: A gravity model fitting physical masses and human groups. *American Sociological Review, 15*(2), 245–256.

Domar, E. D. (1946). Capital expansion, rate of growth, and employment. *Econometrica, 14*(2), 137–147.

Easterlin, R. A. (1961). The American baby boom in historical perspective. *The American Economic Review, 51*(5), 869–911.

Easterlin, R. A. (1965). Long swings in U.S. demographic and economic growth: Some findings on the historical pattern. *Demography, 2*, 490–507.

Easterlin, R. A. (1966). Economic-demographic interactions and long swings in economic growth. *The American Economic Review, 56*(5), 1063–1104.

Easterlin, R. A. (1990). *Birth and fortune: The impact of numbers on personal welfare* (2nd ed.). Chicago: The University of Chicago Press.

Federal Statistical Office. (2008). *Statistical yearbook 2008 for the Ferderal Republic of Germany. Statistisches Jahrbuch für die Bundesrepublik Deutschland: Vol. 2008*. Wiesbaden: Federal Statistical Office.

Feldstein, M., & Horioka, C. (1980). Domestic saving and international capital flows. *The Economic Journal, 90*(358), 314–329.

Fisher, D. M. (2001). *Lessons in mathematics a dynamic approach: With applications across the sciences*. Lebanon, OH: iseesystems.

Fisher, D. M. (2005). *Modeling dynamic systems: Lessons for a first course. Teacher's and trainer's guide*. Lebanon: iseesystems. Teacher's and Trainer's Guide.

Forrester, J. W. (1968). *Principles of systems*. Waltham, MA: Pegasus Communications.

Forrester, J. W. (1971). *World dynamics* (2nd ed.). Waltham, MA: Pegasus Communications.

Forrester, N. B. (1973). *The life cycle of economic development*. Cambridge, MA.: MIT.

Forrester, J. W. (1979). An alternative approach to economic policy: Macrobehavior from microstructure. In N. M. Kamrany & R. H. Day (Eds.), *Economic issues of the eighties* (pp. 80–108). Baltimore: Johns Hopkins University Press.

Forrester, J. W. (1999). *Industrial dynamics*. Waltham, MA: Pegasus Communications.

Forrester, J. W., Low, G. W., & Mass, N. J. (1974). The debate on World dynamics: A response to Nordhaus. *Policy Sciences, 5*(2), 169–190. Retrieved August 17, 2009, from Doi:10.1007/BF00148039.

Forrester, J. W., Mass, N. J., & Charles J. (1976). The System Dynamics National Model: Understanding Socio-Economic Behavior and Policy Alternatives. *Technological Forecasting and Social Change, 9*(1–2), 51–68.

Forrester, J. W., & Senge, P. M. (1980). Tests for building confidence in system dynamics models. In A. A. Legasto, J. W. Forrester, & J. M. Lyneis (Eds.), *System dynamics* (pp. 209–228). Amsterdam: North-Holland.

Frenkel, M. R., & Hemmer, H.-R. (1999). *Grundlagen der Wachstumstheorie* (Vahlens Handbücher der Wirtschafts- und Sozialwissenschaften 1st ed.). München: Vahlen.

Frerichs, W., & Kübler, K. (1980). *Gesamtwirtschaftliche Prognoseverfahren. WiSo Kurzlehrbücher*. München: Vahlen.

Fricke, T. (2009, February 06). Zeit für eine Bad-Ideas Bank. *Financial Times Deutschland*, 05.02.2009. Retrieved February 06, 2009, from http://www.ftd.de/wirtschaftswunder.

Fürnkranz-Prskawetz, A. (2002). Technological innovation, productivity, and economicgrowth in ageing societies: Comments on Koichi Futagami, Tatsuro Iwaisako, Tesuya Nakajima. In H. Siebert (Ed.), *Economic policy for aging societies* (pp. 174–179). Berlin: Springer.

Gaertner, M. (2003). *Macroeconomics* (1st ed.). Harlow: Pearson Education.

Gigerenzer, G. (2009, June 11). Wir solltem dem Bauch vertrauen. *Handelsblatt*, 11.06.2009. Retrieved June 12, 2009, from http://www.handelsblatt.com/politik/nachrichten/wir-sollten-dem-bauch-vertrauen;2338246.

Grossman, G. M., & Helpman, E. (1995). *Innovation and growth in the global economy* (5th ed.). Cambridge, MA: MIT.

Gruescu, S. (2006). *Population ageing and economic growth: Education policy and family policy in a model of endogenous growth. Contributions to economics*. Heidelberg Neckar: Physica-Verlag.

Guilford, J. P. (1967). *Nature of human intelligence*. New York NY: McGraw-Hill.

Gylfason, T. (2003). *Principles of economic growth* (1st ed.). Oxford: Oxford University Press.

Hamm, I., Seitz, H., & Werding, M. (Eds.). (2008). *Demographic change in Germany: The economic and fiscal consequences*. Berlin: Springer.

Harbision, S. F. (1981). Family structure and family strategy in migration decision making. In G. F. DeJong & R. W. Gardner (Eds.), *Pergamon policy studies on international development. Migration decision making. Multidisciplinary approaches to microlevel studies in developed and developing countries* (pp. 225–251). New York: Pergamon.

Harrod, R. F. (1966). *Towards a dynamic economics: Some recent developments of economic theory and their application to policy*. London: Macmillan.

Haug, S. (2000). *Klassische und neuere Theorien der Migration* (No. 30). Mannheim: Mannheimer Zentrum für Europäische Sozialforschung. Retrieved March 02, 2009. Available at http://www.mzes.uni.mannheim.de/.

Heertje, A., & Wenzel, H.-D. (1997). *Grundlagen der Volkswirtschaftslehre* (5th ed.). Berlin: Springer.

Hicks, J. R. (1932). *The theory of wages*. London: Macmillan.

Higgins, B. H. (1968). *Economic development: Principles, problems, and policies* (1st ed.). New York: W.W. Norton.

Hirschhäuser, K.-F. (1981). *Konjunkturanalyse mit Hilfe von System Dynamics-Simulationsmodellen.* Göttingen: Vandenhoeck and Ruprecht.

Hobbes, T., & Gaskin, J Ch. (1998). *Leviathan.* Oxford: Oxford University Press.

Hoffman, L. W., & Hoffman, M. L. (1973). The value of children to the parents. In J. T. Fawcett (Ed.), *Psychological perspectives on population* (pp. 19–76). New York: Basic Books.

Hoffman, L. W., & Manis, J. D. (1979). The value of children in the United States: A new approach to the study of fertility. *Journal of Marriage and the Family, 41*(3), 583–596.

Howitt, P. (1999). Steady endogenous growth with population and R & D inputs growing. *The Journal of Political Economy, 107*(4), 715–730.

Huinink, J. (2000). Soziologische Ansätze zur Bevölkerungsentwicklung. In U. Mueller, B. Nauck, & A. Diekmann (Eds.), *Handbuch der Demographie 1. Modelle und Methoden* (pp. 339–386). Berlin: Springer.

Imboden, D. M., & Koch, S. (2005). *Systemanalyse: Einführung in die mathematische Modellierung natürlicher Systeme* (2nd ed.). Berlin: Springer.

Inada, K.-I. (1963). On a two-sector model of economic growth: Comments and a generalization. *The Review of Economic Studies, 30*(2), 119–127.

Jones, C. I. (1995a). R & D-based models of economic growth. *The Journal of Political Economy, 103*(4), 759–784.

Jones, C. I. (1995b). Time series tests of endogenous growth models. *The Quarterly Journal of Economics, 110*(2), 495–525.

Jones, C. I. (2001). *Introduction to economic growth* (2nd ed.). New York: W.W.Norton.

Just, T. (2004). *Demographic developments will not spare the public infrastructure.* Retrieved November 01, 2006.from Deutsche Bank Research. Available at http://www.dbresearch.com/.

Just, T. (2007). Wie viel Infrastruktur benötigt die alternde und schrumpfende Bevölkerung in Deutschland? *List Forum für Wirtschafts- und Finanzpolitik, 33*(1), 37–55.

Kaldor, N. (1961). *Capital accumulation and economic growth.* London: Macmillan.

Kalter, F. (2000). Theorien der migration. In U. Mueller, B. Nauck, & A. Diekmann (Eds.), *Handbuch der Demographie 1. Modelle und Methoden* (pp. 438–475). Berlin: Springer.

Kaufmann, F.-X. (2005). *Schrumpfende Gesellschaft: Vom Bevölkerungsrückgang und seinen Folgen. Edition Suhrkamp: Vol. 2406.* Frankfurt am Main: Suhrkamp Verlag.

Keyfitz, N. (1971). On the momentum of population growth. *Demography, 8*(1), 71–80.

Keyfitz, N., & Caswell, H. (2005). *Applied mathematical demography. Statistics for biology and health.* New York: Springer.

Keynes, J. M. (1936). *The general theory of employment, interest, and money: Reprint 1997.* Amherst: Prometheus Books.

Kleinewefers, H., & Jans, A. (1983). *Einführung in die volkswirtschaftliche und wirtschaftspolitische Modellbildung. Vahlens Handbücher der Wirtschafts- und Sozialwissenschaften.* München: Vahlen.

Koopmans, T. C. (1963). *On the concept of optimal economic growth* (Cowles Foundation Discussion Papers No. 163). Cowles Foundation. Retrieved August 16, 2009. Available at http://cowles.econ.yale.edu/.

Kortum, S. (1993). Equilibrium R&D and the patent–R&D ratio: U.S. evidence. *The American Economic Review, 83*(2), 450–457.

Kremer, M. (1993). Population growth and technological change: One Million B.C. to 1990. *The Quarterly Journal of Economics, 108*(3), 681–716.

Krey, K., & Meier, B. (2004). Innovationsfähigkeit. In Institut der deutschen Wirtschaft (Ed.), *Perspektive 2050. Ökonomik des demographischen Wandels* (pp. 146–172). Köln: Deutscher Instituts-Verlag.

Lee, E. S. (1966). A theory of migration. *Demography, 3*(1), 47–57.

Leibfritz, W., & Roeger, W. (2008). The effects of aging on labor markets and economic growth. In I. Hamm, H. Seitz, & M. Werding (Eds.), *Demographic change in Germany. The economic and fiscal consequences* (pp. 35–63). Berlin: Springer.

Leim, I. (2008). *Die Modellierung der Fertilitätsentwicklung als Folge individueller Entscheidungsprozesse mit Hilfe der Mikrosimulation* (Social science simulations, Vol. 5). Metropolis: Marburg.

Li, C.-W. (2000). Endogenous vs semi-endogenous growth in a two-R&D-sector model. *The Economic Journal, 110*(462), 109–122. Retrieved January 15, 2009, from http://dx.doi.org/10.1111/1468-0297.00524.

Lorenz, H.-W., & Pasche, M. (2007). *Bemerkungen zum Solow-Swan-Modell.* Jena: University of Jena. Retrieved August 30, 2009. Available at http://www.wiwi.uni-jena.de/.

Lucas, R. E. (1988). On the mechanics of economic development. *Journal of Monetary Economics, 22*(1), 3–42. Retrieved February 11, 2009. Available at http://www.sciencedirect.com/.

Lucas, R. E. (1990). Why doesn't capital flow from rich to poor countries? *The American Economic Review, 80*(2), 92–96.

Lührmann, M. (2006). *Essays on the Impact of demographic Change on Capital, Goods and Labor Markets.* Dissertation, Universität Mannheim, Mannheim. Retrieved December 13, 2006, from http://bibserv7.bib.uni-mannheim.de/madoc/volltexte/2006/1271/.

Lutz, C., Meyer, B., Schnur, P., & Zika, G. (2002). Projektion des Arbeitskräftebedarfs bis 2015: Modellrechnungen auf Basis des IAB/INFORGE-Modells. *Mitteilungen aus der Arbeitsmarkt- und Berufsforschung, 35*(3), 305–326. Retrieved June 06, 2009. Available at http://doku.iab.de/.

Lutz, W., Skirbekk, V., & Testa, M. R. (2005). *The Low Fertility Trap Hypothesis: Forces that may lead to further postponement and fewer births in Europe.* Retrieved April 07, 2009, from http://www.oeaw.ac.at/vid/download/edrp_4_05.pdf.

Luy, M., & Caselli, G. (2008). *The impact of a migration-caused selection effect on regional mortality differences in Italy and Germany.* Retrieved April 13, 2009, from http://econpapers.repec.org/RePEc:dem:wpaper:wp-2008-027.

Macunovich, D. J. (1998). Fertility and the Easterlin hypothesis: An assessment of the literature. *Journal of Population Economics, 11*(1), 53–111.

Malik, F. (2009, January 24). Mit herkömmlichen Methoden nicht zu lösen. *Frankfurter Allgemeine Zeitung,* 23.01.2009. Retrieved January 24, 2009, from http://www.faz.net.

Malthus, T. R. (1826). *An essay of the principle of population: A view of its pas and present effects on human happiness* (6th ed.). Cambridge: University of Cambridge.

Mankiw, N. G. (2007). *Macroeconomics* (6th ed.). New York: Worth Publishers.

Mankiw, N. G., Romer, D., & Weil, D. N. (1992). A contribution to the empirics of economic growth. *The Quarterly Journal of Economics, 107*(2), 407–437.

Mass, N. J. (1980). Stock and flow variables and the dynamics of supply and demand. In J. Randers (Ed.), *Elements of the system dynamics method* (1st ed., pp. 95–114). Waltham, MA: Pegasus Communications.

Massey, D. S. (1990). The social and economic origins of immigration. *Annals of the American Academy of Political and Social Science, 510,* 60–72.

Massey, D. S., Arango, J., Hugo, G., Kouaouci, A., Pellegrino, A., & Taylor, J. E. (1993). Theories of international migration: A review and appraisal. *Population and Development Review, 19*(3), 431–466.

Matthes, J., & Römer, C. (2004). Kapitalmärkte. In Institut der deutschen Wirtschaft (Ed.), *Perspektive 2050. Ökonomik des demographischen Wandels* (pp. 293–319). Deutscher Instituts-Verlag: Köln.

Mayer, A. (2008). Demografischer Wandel: Auswirkungen auf den Wohnungsmarkt. In L. Weber, C. Lubk, & Annette Mayer (Eds.), *Gesellschaft im Wandel. Aktuelle ökonomische Herausforderungen* (pp. 435–460). Wiesbaden: Gabler.

Mc Morrow, K., & Roeger, W. (2004). *The economic and financial market consequences of global ageing.* Berlin: Springer.

Meadows, D. H. (1972). *The limits to growth: A report for the Club of Rome's project on the predicament of mankind*. New York: Universe Books.

Meadows, D. H., Randers, J., & Meadows, D. L. (2004). *Limits to growth: The 30-years update* (1st ed.). Vermont: Chelsea Green Publishing.

Meadows, D. H., & Robinson, J. M. (2007). *The electronic Oracle: Computer models and social decisions*. Albany, NY: Wiley.

Milan, A., & Martel, L. (2008). Current demographic situation in Canada, 2005 and 2006. Population growth and age structure. In Minister of Industry (Ed.), *Report on the demographic situation in Canada* (Vol. 91-209-X, pp. 10–27). Ottawa: Minister of Industry.

Milling, P. (2008). Verzögerungsstrukturen in System-Dynamics Modellen. In J. Strohhecke & J. Sehnert (Eds.), *System Dynamics für die Finanzindustrie. Simulieren und analysieren dynamisch-komplexer Probleme* (1st ed., pp. 210–229). Frankfurt am Main: Frankfurt-School-Verlag.

Modigliani, F., & Brumberg, R. E. (1954). Utility analysis and the consumption function: An interpretation of cross-section data. In K. K. Kurihara (Ed.), *Keynesian & post-Keynesian economics. Post Keynesian Economics* (pp. 388–436). New Brunswick: Rutgers University Press.

Moffat, I. (1992). *Causal and simulation modelling using system dynamics. Concepts and techniques in modern geography*. Norwich: Environmental Publications.

Moll, P. G. (1991). *From scarcity to sustainability: Futures studies and the environment; the role of the Club of Rome*. Frankfurt am Main: Lang.

Mueller, U. (2000). Die Maßzahlen der Bevölkerungsstatistik. In U. Mueller, B. Nauck, & A. Diekmann (Eds.), *Handbuch der Demographie 1. Modelle und Methoden* (pp. 1–91). Berlin: Springer.

Myrdal, G. (1957). *Rich lands and poor: The road to prosperity*. New York: Harper and Row.

Myrtveit, M. (2005). *The World model controversy* (Working Papers in System Dynamics No. WPSD 1/05). Bergen: The system dynamics group department of geography. Retrieved August 17, 2009. Available at www.ifi.uib.no/.

Nickell, S., & Bell, B. (1995). The collapse in demand for the unskilled and unemployment across the OECD. *Oxford Review of Economic Policy, 11*(1), 40–62.

Nordhaus, W. D. (1973). World dynamics: Measurement without data. *The Economic Journal, 83*(332), 1156–1183.

Nyce, S. A., & Schieber, S. J. (2005). *The economic implications of aging societies: The costs of living happily ever after*. Cambrigde: Cambrigde University Press.

Office for Official Publications of the European Communities. (2007). *Europe's demographic future: Facts and figures on challenges and opportunities*. Luxembourg: Office for Official Publications of the European Communities.

Olshansky, S. J., & Carnes, B. A. (1997). Ever since Gompertz. *Demography, 34*(1), 1–15.

Omran, A. R. (1971). The epidemiologic transition: A theory of the epidemiology of population change. *The Milbank Memorial Fund Quarterly, 49*(4), 509–538.

Ossimitz, G. (2000). *Entwicklung systemischen Denkens: theoretische Konzepte und empirische Untersuchungen* (Klagenfurter Beiträge zur Didaktik der Mathematik, Vol. 1). München: Profil-Verl.

Phelps, E. (1961). The golden rule of accumulation: A fable for growthmen. *The American Economic Review, 51*(4), 638–643.

Plünnecke, A., & Seyda, S. (2004). Bildung. In Institut der deutschen Wirtschaft (Ed.), *Perspektive 2050. Ökonomik des demographischen Wandels* (pp. 122–143). Köln: Deutscher Instituts-Verlag.

Poterba, J. M. (2001). Demographic structure and asset returns. *Review of Economics and Statistics, 83*(4), 565–584.

Radzicki, M. J. (1994). Evolutionary economics and system dynamics. In R. W. England (Ed.), *Evolutionary concepts in contemporary economics* (pp. 61–89). Michigan: The University of Michigan Press.

Radzicki, M. J. (2003). Mr. Hamilton, Mr. Forrester, and a foundation for evolutionary economics. *Journal of Economic Issues, 37*(1), 133–173. Retrieved August 17, 2009. Available at http://michaeljosephradzicki.com/.

Ramsey, F. P. (1928). A mathematical theory of saving. *The Economic Journal, 38*(152), 543–559.
Ravenstein, E. G. (1885). The laws of migration. *Journal of the Statistical Society of London, 48*(2), 167–235.
Ravenstein, E. G. (1889). The laws of migration. *Journal of the Royal Statistical Society, 52*(2), 241–305.
Rebelo, S. (1991). Long-run policy analysis and long-run growth. *The Journal of Political Economy, 99*(3), 500–521.
Reinhardt, U. (2002). Health care for the ageing baby boomers: How serious a problem? In H. Siebert (Ed.), *Economic policy for aging societies* (pp. 235–262). Berlin: Springer.
Richardson, G. P. (1999). *Feedback thought: In social science and system theory*. Waltham, MA: Pegasus Communications.
Richmond, B. (1994). *Systems thinking: Let's get on with it. Delivered at the 1994 International systems dynamics conference in sterling*. Retrieved August 05, 2009. Available at http://www.iseesystems.com/.
Robinson, J. V. (1971). Solow on the rate of return. In G. C. Harcourt & N. F. Laing (Eds.), *Penguin education. Capital and growth. Selected readings*. Harmondsworth: Penguin.
Rodepeter, R. (2000). *Konsum- und Sparentscheidungen im Lebenszyklus: Theorie, Evidenz ud Simulation unter klassischen und alternativen Ansätzen*. Mannheim: Mateo.
Romer, P. M. (1987). Growth based on increasing returns due to specialization. *The American Economic Review, 77*(2), 56–62.
Romer, P. M. (1989). Capital accumulation in the theory of long run growth. In R. J. Barro (Ed.), *Modern business cycle theory*. Oxford: Blackwell.
Romer, P. M. (1990). Endogenous technological change. *The Journal of Political Economy, 98*(5), 71–102.
Romer, P. M. (1994). The origins of endogenous growth. *The Journal of Economic Perspectives, 8*(1), 3–22.
Romer, D. (2006). *Advanced macroeconomics* (3rd ed.). New York: McGraw-Hill.
Rothengatter, W., & Schaffer, A. (2006). *Makro kompakt: Grundzüge der Makroökonomik. Physica-Lehrbuch*. Heidelberg: Physica-Verlag.
Rowland, D. T. (2003). *Demographic methods and concepts*. Oxford: Oxford University Press.
Rürup, B. (2000). Bevölkerungsalterung und Wirtschaftswachstum: Hypothesen und empirische Befunde. In H. Birg (Ed.), *Prosperität in einer alternden Gesellschaft* (pp. 83–106). Bad Homburg: Frankfurter Inst. - Stiftung Marktwirtschaft und Politik.
Ruschinski, M. (1996). *Neuere Entwicklungen in der Wachstumstheorie* (1st ed.). Wiesbaden: DUV. Gabler Edition Wissenschaft.
Saeed, K. (2008). *Limits to growth concepts in classical economics* (WP). WPI. Retrieved February 10, 2009. Available at http://cms-dev.wpi.edu/.
Saint-Paul, G. (2002). The impact of ageing: The supply of labour and human capital: Comment on Paul Johnson. In H. Siebert (Ed.), *Economic policy for aging societies* (pp. 126–129). Berlin: Springer.
Samuelson, P. A. (1954). The pure theory of public expenditure. *The Review of Economic Studies, 36*(4), 387–389.
Sanderson, W. C., & Scherbov, S. (2005). Average remaining lifetimes can increase as human populations age. *Nature, 435*(7043), 811–813. Retrieved June 10, 2009, from http://dx.doi.org/10.1038/nature03593.
Schäfer, H., & Seyda, S. (2004). Arbeitsmärkte. In Institut der deutschen Wirtschaft (Ed.), *Perspektive 2050. Ökonomik des demographischen Wandels* (pp. 97–120). Köln: Deutscher Instituts-Verlag.
Schaffnit-Chatterjee, C. (2007). *How will senior Germans spend their money?* Retrieved April 21, 2008, from Deutsche Bank Research. Available at http://www.dbresearch.de/.
Scheidges, R. (2009, January 09). Die Blindheit der Profis. *Handelsblatt*, 6, 9. Retrieved January 10, 2009, from http://www.handelsblatt.com.
Schmidt, G. W. (2003). *Dynamics of endogenous economic growth: A case study of the 'romer model'* (Contributions to Economic Analysis 1st ed., Vol. 257). Amsterdam: Elsevier.

Schnaars, S. P. (1989). *Megamistakes: Forecasting and the myth of rapid technological change.* New York: Free Press.

Schulz, V. (2008). Politische Durchsetzbarkeit von Reformen des deutschen Rentensystems vor dem Hintergrund demografischer Veränderungen. In L. Weber, C. Lubk, & Annette Mayer (Eds.), *Gesellschaft im Wandel. Aktuelle ökonomische Herausforderungen* (pp. 393–408). Wiesbaden: Gabler.

Schumpeter, J. A. (1996a). How the economic system generates evolution: Business cycles. A theoretical, historical, and statistical analysis of the capitalist process (1939). In J. A. Schumpeter & K. R. Leube (Eds.), *Manz Wirtschaft: Vol. 3. The essence of J. A. Schumpeter. Die wesentlichen Texte* (pp. 215–276). Wien: Manz.

Schumpeter, J. A. (1996b). Unternehmer: Handwörterbuch Staatswissenschaften (1928). In J. A. Schumpeter & K. R. Leube (Eds.), *Manz Wirtschaft: Vol. 3. The essence of J. A. Schumpeter. Die wesentlichen Texte* (pp. 155–173). Wien: Manz.

Schumpeter, J. A. (1996c). The fundamental phenomenon of economic development: The theory of economic development (1934). In J. A. Schumpeter & K. R. Leube (Eds.), *Manz Wirtschaft: Vol. 3. The essence of J.A.Schumpeter. Die wesentlichen Texte* (pp. 182–214). Wien: Manz.

Schumpeter, J. A., & Seifert, E. K. (1993). *Kapitalismus, Sozialismus und Demokratie* (UTB für Wissenschaft Uni-Taschenbücher 7th ed., Vol. 172). Tübingen: Francke.

Segerstrom, P. S. (1998). Endogenous growth without scale effects. *The American Economic Review, 88*(5), 1290–1310.

Seitz, H. (2008). The impact of demographic change on fiscal policy in Germany. In I. Hamm, H. Seitz, & M. Werding (Eds.), *Demographic change in Germany. The economic and fiscal consequences* (pp. 129–163). Berlin: Springer.

Sen, A. (1998). Mortality as an indicator of economic success and failure. *The Economic Journal, 108*(446), 1–25.

Senge, P. M. (1994). *The fifth discipline: The art & practice of the learning organization.* New York: Currency Doubleday.

Siebert, H. (2002). Economic perspectives for ageing societies: The issues. In H. Siebert (Ed.), *Economic policy for aging societies* (pp. 1–6). Berlin: Springer.

Sinn, H.-W. (2003). The demographic deficit – the facts, the consequences, the causes and their politics implications. *ifo-Schnelldienst, 5*, 20–36.

Sinn, H.-W. (2005). Das demographische Defizit: Die Fakten, die Folgen, die Ursachen und die Politikimplikationen. In H. Birg (Ed.), *Auswirkungen der demographischen Alterung und der Bevölkerungsschrumpfung auf Wirtschaft, Staat und Gesellschaft. Plenarvorträge der Jahrestagung der Deutschen Gesellschaft für Demographie an der Universität Bielefeld, 4. März 2004* (pp. 53–90). Münster: LIT.

Sinn, H.-W., & Uebelmesser, S. (2001). *When will the Germans get trapped in their pension system?* (Working Paper No. 561). München: CES-ifo. Retrieved August 31, 2006. Available at http://www.cesifo-group.de/.

Sjaastad, L. A. (1962). The costs and returns of human migration. *The Journal of Political Economy, 70*(5), 80–93.

Smith, P. C., & Ackere, A. V. (2002). A note on the integration of system dynamics and economic models. *Journal of Economic Dynamics and Control, 26*(1), 1–10. Retrieved August 17, 2009, from doi:10.1016/S0165-1889(00)00025-7.

Snowdon, B., & Vane, H. R. (1999). *Conversation with leading economists: Interpreting modern macroeconomics.* Cheltenham: Edward Elgar.

Snowdon, B., & Vane, H. R. (2006). *Modern macroeconomics: Its origins, development and current state* (1st ed.). Cheltenham: Edward Elgar.

Solow, R. M. (1956). A Contribution to the Theory of Economic Growth. *The Quarterly Journal of Economics, 70*(1), 65–94.

Sommer, M. (1981). *System Dynamics und Makroökonometrie: Dynamische makroökonomische Modellierung in multimethodologischer Sicht* (Sozioökonomische Forschungen, Vol. 17). Bern: Paul Haupt.

Sommer, M. (1984). The econometric challenge to system dynamics and vice versa: Some future perspectives. *Technological Forecasting and Social Change, 25*(3), 263–280. Retrieved August 17, 2009, from doi:10.1016/0040-1625(84)90005-2.

Spiegelman, M. (1958). Mortality trends and prospects and their implications. *Annals of the American Academy of Political and Social Science, 316*, 25–33.

Sterman, J. D. (1983). A simple model of the economic long wave. Retrieved May 01, 2009, from http://dspace.mit.edu/bitstream/handle/1721.1/2042/SWP-1422-09869245.pdf.

Sterman, J. D. (1986). The economic long wave: Theory and evidence. *System Dynamics Review, 22*(2), 87–125. Retrieved August 17, 2009, from doi:10.1002/sdr.4260020202.

Sterman, J. D. (1989). Deterministic chaos in an experimental economic system. *Journal of Economic Behavior and Organization, 12*(1), 1–28.

Sterman, J. D. (1994). Learning in and about complex systems. *System Dynamics Review, 10*(2–3), 291–330.

Sterman, J. D. (2004). *Business dynamics: Systems thinking and modeling for a complex World*. Boston, MA: McGraw-Hill.

Stiglitz, J. E. (1993). Comments: Some retrospective views on growth theory. In P. A. Diamond & R. M. Solow (Eds.), *Growth, productivity, unemployment. Essays to celebrate Bob Solow's birthday* (2nd ed., pp. 50–70). Cambridge, MA: MIT.

Stokey, N. L. (1995). R&D and economic growth. *The Review of Economic Studies, 62*(3), 469–489.

Strohhecker, J., & Fischer, M. M. (2008). Feedback-Diagramme. In J. Strohhecker & J. Sehnert (Eds.), *System Dynamics für die Finanzindustrie. Simulieren und analysieren dynamisch-komplexer Probleme* (1st ed., pp. 71–104). Frankfurt am Main: Frankfurt-School-Verlag.

Swan, T. W. (1956). Economic growth and capital accumulation. *The Economic Record, 32*(2), 334–361. Retrieved from http://dx.doi.org/10.1111/j.1475-4932.1956.tb00434.x.

The German Council of Economic Experts. (2007). *Das Erreichte nicht verspielen: Jahresgutachten 2007/08*. Wiesbaden: Federal Statistical Office.

Todaro, M. P., & Smith, S. C. (2006). *Economic development*. Harlow: Pearson Education.

Uzawa, H. (1965). Optimum technical change in an aggregative model of economic growth. *International Economic Review, 1*, 18–31.

van de Kaa, D. (2002). *The idea of a second demographic transition in industrialized countries*. Paper presented at the Sixth Welfare Policy Seminar. Tokyo.

Verspagen, B. (2007). Innovation and economic growth. In J. Fagerberg, D. C. Mowery, & R. R. Nelson (Eds.), *The Oxford handbook of innovation* (pp. 487–513). Oxford: Oxford University Press.

Verworn, B., & Hipp, C. (2008). Demografischer Wandel und Innovation in Deutschland. In L. Weber, C. Lubk, Annette Mayer, & Annette Mayer (Eds.), *Gesellschaft im Wandel. Aktuelle ökonomische Herausforderungen* (p. 377). Wiesbaden: Gabler.

Wohltmann, H.-W. (1994). *Grundzüge der makroökonomischen Theorie: Totalanalyse geschlossener und offener Volkswirtschaften*. München: Oldenbourg.

Wolstenholme, E. (1985). A methodology for qualitative system dynamics. In System Dynamics Society (Ed.), *Proceedings of the 1985 International conference of the system dynamics society*, Keystone, USA (pp. 1049–1057), Albany, NY.

Young, A. (1998). Growth without scale effects. *The Journal of Political Economy, 106*(1), 41–63.

Zelinsky, W. (1971). The hypothesis of the mobility transition. *Geographical Review, 61*(2), 219–249.

Zimmermann, K. F., Bauer, T. K., Bonin, H., Fahr, R., & Hinte, H. (2002). *Arbeitskräftebedarf bei hoher Arbeitslosigkeit: Ein ökonomisches Zuwanderungskonzept für Deutschland*. Berlin: Springer.

Zipf, G. K. (1946). The P1 P2/D hypothesis: On the intercity movement of persons. *American Sociological Review, 11*(6), 677–686.

Zweifel, P., Felder, S., & Meiers, M. (1999). Ageing of population and health care expenditure: A red herring? *Health Economics, 8*(6), 485–496. Retrieved June 10, 2009, from http://dx.doi.org/10.1002/(SICI)1099-1050(199909)8:6<485::AID-HEC461>3.0.CO;2-4.

FSC
www.fsc.org
MIX
Papier | Fördert gute Waldnutzung
FSC® C083411

Kolibri 360 GmbH
Ferdinand-Jühlke-Straße 7
99095 Erfurt, Deutschland
produktsicherheit@kolibri360.de